W9-AFN-852

AMERICAN MEDICAL
ASSOCIATION

MANUAL
OF STYLE

Eighth Edition

AMERICAN MEDICAL ASSOCIATION

MANUAL

OF STYLE

Eighth Edition

Cheryl Iverson (*Chair*)
Bruce B. Dan, MD
Paula Glitman
Lester S. King, MD
Elizabeth Knoll, PhD
Harriet S. Meyer, MD
Kathryn Simmons Raithel
Don Riesenberg, MD
Roxanne K. Young

Williams & Wilkins

BALTIMORE • PHILADELPHIA • HONG KONG
LONDON • MUNICH • SYDNEY • TOKYO

A WAVERLY COMPANY

Editor: William Hensyl
Associate Editor: Harriet Felscher
Copy Editor: Miriam Kleiger
Design: Norman W. Och
Illustration Planning: Lorraine Wrzosek
Production: Raymond E. Reter
Cover Design: Norman W. Och
Index: Ann Cassar

Copyright © 1989
American Medical Association
515 N Dearborn Street
Chicago, IL 60610

Printed in the United States of America

Library of Congress Cataloging-in-Publication Data

The American Medical Association manual of style.—8th ed. / Cheryl Iverson, chair . . . [et al.]
   p. cm.
   Rev. ed. of: Manual for authors & editors. 7th ed. / compiled for the American Medical Association by William R. Barclay. 1981.
   Includes bibliographies and index.
   ISBN 0-683-04351-X
   1. Medical writing—Handbooks, manuals, etc. 2. Medicine—Authorship—Handbooks, manuals, etc. 3. Authorship—Style manuals. I. Iverson, Cheryl. II. Barclay, William R. (William Robert), 1919– Manual for authors & editors. III. American Medical Association.
   [DNLM: 1. Writing.   WZ 345 A511]
R119.A533 1988
808′.06661021—dc19
DNLM/DLC
for Library of Congress
               88-5504
               CIP

ISBN 0-683-04351-X

90000

96 97
9 10

9 780683 043518

FOREWORD

The word *style* has many different meanings, two of which hold special interest here. One concerns the usage of language. What is considered correct? What is considered wrong? If more than one usage is acceptable, which is preferable?

Language involves a complex aggregate of rules. Who makes them? In part they derive from past conventions, enshrined by grammarians, lexicographers, and scholars. However, these authorities always encounter an opposing tide of popular speech that tends to disregard rules and create new words, forms, constructions, and usages. Language merges these two trends. It is an organic whole whose vital essence is change.

In this flux, rules are useful in promoting clarity. Dictionaries and other scholarly documents that provide standards will slowly take account of linguistic change, although often grudgingly.

Oral language is subject to buffetings and distortions, but written language has much greater stability. Organizations that control the printed word—publishers of newspapers, journals, and books, for example—adopt rules and usages that they consider both correct and desirable. These constitute the editorial style of the publications in question and, when formally compiled, become a style manual.

Publishing organizations differ enormously in what they consider desirable. Lurid and sensational newspapers contrast with scholarly publications, with intermediate gradations for all tastes. What one considers vulgar, clumsy, awkward, ambiguous, and even grammatically wrong another will accept without a qualm as fresh and vigorous. When publishers offer a style manual they serve two functions: they indicate the particular rules that apply to their publications and they offer a set of conventions, recommended but not in any way binding. For the public a codified style manual can be a lexicographic "Guide for the Perplexed."

The manual of style presented here relates primarily to medical communications, where clarity is of the utmost importance. Yet clarity must also take account of literary tradition; we must not give up our literary heritage under the illusion that writing thereby becomes more "scientific."

The second meaning of style is concerned with the manner of writing—the so-called authorial style. For this we offer the following pragmatic definition. Authorial style consists of those verbal qualities that permit us to distinguish the writing of one author from that of another, not by what is said but by the manner in which it is said. We have no trouble in distinguishing among Samuel Johnson, Thomas Carlyle, and Ernest Hemingway, regardless of subject matter, just as we can tell Bach from Mendelssohn or the Beatles. We may not be able to identify specific authors but we may at least recognize their general eras and cultural environments, as we may not be able to name composers but can tell baroque music from rock and roll.

The mode of writing will vary with the historical period, the subject matter, and the occasion, as well as the personality of the author. Today we are often amused by the long-winded and flamboyant oratory popular in the last century. It is often associated with political speeches, but it appears in medical writing as well. Here, for example, is how the president of the American Medical Association expressed his appreciation for the honor bestowed on him, in his inaugural speech of 1885: "Exalted as may be the position, by the grand object of the organization, and by the long years through which it has exercised its improving and perfecting influence over the minds, and hearts, and destinies of the medical profession, the honor is still further emphasized by the long line of noble and illustrious men who have recently and in the past guided the deliberations of this national representative body" (*JAMA*. 1885;4:477).

Clearly, the style of writing has changed; the leisurely pace has quickened, and the precision has increased. Yet if we look beyond the modes of expression and the authorial style, we find great similarities between the medical journals of a century or more ago and those of today. This is especially true in regard to the *kinds* of communication published. Present-day journals, despite their increased number and progressive specialization, have a composition not unlike that of their earlier days.

The communications in medical journals fall into two major groups. These we may call the subjective and the objective, depending on the degree to which the personality of the author is involved. Although the distinction is not always sharp, it does provide a working schema.

In the subjective mode the writer is expressing his opinions, reactions, and evaluations. The most obvious example is the editorial, in which the writer is expressing a personal view, usually bolstered by evidence. Evidence is at least partly objective, but the attitude toward such data, their very selection, and the references and conclusions derived therefrom bear a clear personal imprint. In varying degrees, letters to the editor, book reviews, and reviews of the literature exhibit the same subjectivity; they draw on evidence but reflect the experience and opinions of the author.

There is a popular contrast between opinion, which is frankly subjective, and fact, which purports to be objective. Objective presentations supposedly deal with facts considered as independent of the observer. The facts are *there*, available to all, with the implication that anyone who examines them under the same circumstances will make the same observations.

Objective studies fall readily into three groups. The simplest we may call the *reportial*. It tells what happened at some particular event—a convention, a meeting, a conference. As in any reporting, no two observers will come up with the same details, for the personality of the reporter determines what seems important. Such a limitation is inescapable—Francis Bacon had already recognized it in the 17th century. However, the selection of facts differs sharply from the deliberate interjection of personal opinion. The latter constitutes editorializing, which is out of place in objective reporting.

The second type of objective writing we call *descriptive*. This goes back to earlier days when an observer, often called a naturalist, described and recorded natural phenomena, without changing them or their appearance. The descriptive writer says, in essence, "This is what I saw, and I found it interesting."

Description provided most of the earlier medical literature. For example, anatomists and pathologists described what seemed new in their gross dissections and later in the microscopic examination. They furnished progressively more exact details and also recorded the rare and anomalous. Clinicians too described their unusual cases, indicating the observed lesions, symptoms, treatment, and outcome. These are the "case reports" that still comprise a substantial part of the medical literature.

A description records observations for their own intrinsic interest. In an *experiment*, however, the goal is not the reporting of phenomena for their own sake but rather the solution of a problem. The problem may have stemmed from various sources—perhaps a casual observation, or some detailed description, or even some purely theoretical consideration. But in any case the problem is the starting point and the experiment is one mode of problem solving.

In experiments, nature is manipulated. Circumstances are altered, limited within specific boundaries so that the answer to the problem may emerge. In the descriptive mode the important consideration is the accuracy of the description. The value of experiments depends on the care and precision with which the circumstances and variables are manipulated so that the resulting inferences will be cogent and unambiguous.

Since the contributions to the medical literature fall into many different categories, do they call for different modes of writing? A common attitude holds that all medical writing should conform to certain vague canons that supposedly characterize science. Chief among these is the canon of objectivity: science is objective, medicine is a science, and therefore medical writing should be objective. As a corollary, medical writers should therefore suppress all personal and subjective elements in their work. The more objective and impersonal, it would follow, the more scientific. This, we maintain, is a fallacy.

Any exhortation that writing should be objective—or subjective—is likely to be useless, self-defeating, or simply wrong-headed. For example, the studied avoidance of personal pronouns in an attempt to be objective is likely to yield drab, stereotyped, ponderous writing that is generally dull and often repulsive. The description of an experiment, the report of a case, an editorial expression of opinion will all differ in presentation, and uniformity would be absurd. But they should all have the characteristics of good expository writing: clarity and precision.

These primary values do not exclude grace and eloquence; however, cultivation of a graceful style is a procedure outside the scope of this book. The editors of this manual will rest content if they can lead prospective authors to clarity and precision, whatever the category of medical writing.

Lester S. King, MD

PREFACE

With this edition of the AMA style manual, we perpetuate a 25-year tradition. Our style manual, like most, began as an in-house guide and, although never losing that function, ranged far beyond it to serve as a resource for other publishers and for authors and their assistants. The AMA stylebook was first published in October 1962, although it had existed as an informal in-house document for many years before. The 1981 edition, like the first manual, was divided into two parts: one, "Editorial Manual," addressed questions of copyright, preparation of abstracts, and definitions of printing terms. The other, "Style Book," gave specific advice on abbreviations, punctuation, correct usage, and references.

In preparing this revision, we kept in mind the distinct but interrelated audiences of the book—authors and editors—and chose to address them simultaneously, rather than separately. This revision contains all the information that was useful in the former edition. Additionally, new sections abound, such as those on types of articles, fraud and plagiarism, grammar, the publication process, and on-line resources. Nomenclature, statistics, mathematical composition, and correct and preferred usage sections have been expanded. Certain guidelines are now more clearly delineated, such as those on sexist language and duplicate publication.

The style manual committee—staff editors from *JAMA* and the AMA specialty journals—began work on the revision of the 1981 manual in May 1984. Most of the material for the revision was prepared by committee members and reviewed in draft form at biweekly meetings until consensus was reached. Sections were then sent to expert reviewers. The completed manual was finally offered for review to in-house staff, *JAMA* editorial board members, and a group of physician and managing editors at other leading publications.

The style manual committee is indebted not only to those named in Acknowledgments but to the many persons on staff and outside the AMA who reviewed individual sections or the book in its entirety. Their contributions have strengthened and enriched this edition. Any omissions or errors are the responsibility of the committee alone. We welcome correspondence about the manual and will consider each comment received before preparation of the next edition. Address comments to Cheryl Iverson, American Medical Association, 515 N Dearborn St, Chicago, IL 60610.

ACKNOWLEDGMENTS

Many individuals have provided invaluable help during this revision, and to them we extend our gratitude and appreciation. We single out below those who gave extensive review, expertise, comment, and advice for particular sections.

Chapter 2. MANUSCRIPT PREPARATION
- *References*
  Norman Frankel, MA, AMA Department of Automation and Technical Services; Robert S. Tannehill, Jr, MSIS, Chemical Abstracts Service, Columbus, Ohio; and Jean A. Hellman, JD, Roosevelt University, Chicago, Ill.
- *Illustrations*
  JoAnne Weiskopf and Thomas Handrigan, AMA Department of Permissions and Graphic Design.

Chapter 3. LEGAL AND ETHICAL CONSIDERATIONS
- *Duplicate Publication and Repetitive Publication*
  Michael Springer, AMA Department of Specialty Journals.
- *Fraud and Plagiarism*
  M. Therese Southgate, MD, AMA Division of Scientific Information; Veda Britt, JD, AMA Corporate Law Section of the Office of the General Counsel.
- *Copyright*
  Veda Britt, JD, AMA Corporate Law Section of the Office of the General Counsel.

Chapter 9. CORRECT USAGE
  Charlene Breedlove, AMA Department of Editorial Affairs.

Chapter 12. NOMENCLATURE
  The Departments of Reference Services and Automation and Technical Services, AMA Division of Library and Information Management.
- *Diabetes*
  Richard Landau, MD, University of Chicago, Chicago, Ill; Donald O. Schiffman, PhD, and Ruta Freimanis, RPh, AMA Department of Medical Terminology.
- *Drugs*
  Lori Barba and Edward Jyväskylä, AMA Department of Editorial Processing; Donald O. Schiffman, PhD, Ruta Freimanis, RPh, and the late Joseph B. Jerome, PhD, AMA Department of Medical Terminology; Veda Britt, JD, AMA Corporate Law Section of the Office of the General Counsel.

Acknowledgments

- *Endocrinology*
  Richard Landau, MD, University of Chicago, Chicago, Ill; and Donald O. Schiffman, PhD, and Ruta Freimanis, RPh, AMA Department of Medical Terminology.
- *Immunology*
  Lymphocytes and Monoclonal Antibodies
  Edward Jyväskylä, AMA Department of Editorial Processing; Dennis K. Ledford, MD, University of South Florida, College of Medicine, Tampa, Fla.
- *Isotopes*
  Vickey Golden, AMA Department of Editorial Processing; Ruta Freimanis, RPh, AMA Department of Medical Terminology.
- *Organisms*
  Helene Cole, MD, AMA Department of Editorial Affairs; Norbert Rapoza, PhD, AMA Department of Drugs.

Chapter 15. MEASUREMENT AND QUANTITATION
- *Units of Measure*
  M. J. McQueen, MB, ChB, FRCPC, Hamilton General Hospital, Hamilton, Ontario, Canada.
- *Statistics*
  Naomi Vaisrub, PhD, AMA Department of Scientific Affairs; Arthur Hafner, PhD, AMA Division of Library and Information Management; Daniel Seigel, ScD, National Institutes of Health, Bethesda, Md; and George W. Brown, MD, Los Lunas Hospital and Training School, Los Lunas, NM.

Chapter 19. PRINTING TERMS: DEFINITIONS
Marlene Hinsch, AMA Division of Publication Production and Printing.

Chapter 20. COPY EDITING AND PROOFREADING MARKS
Elizabeth Petrikenas, AMA Department of Permissions and Graphic Design.

Chapter 21. RESOURCE BIBLIOGRAPHY
- *On-line Resources*
  Jane Larkin, Information Services Division, Continental Illinois, Chicago, Ill.

A special thanks to Nicole Netter, Lake Bluff, Ill, for copy editing the stylebook.

CONTENTS

Foreword / v
Preface / ix
Acknowledgments / xi

1. Preparing an Article for Publication

1.0	**Types of Articles**	1
1.1	Experimental	1
1.2	Descriptive	1
1.3	Review/Essay/Critique	2
1.4	Editorial	2
1.5	Correspondence	2
1.6	Book Reviews	2
1.7	Miscellaneous	2
2.0	**Manuscript Preparation**	5
2.1	Titles and Subtitles	5
2.2	Bylines	6
2.3	Footnotes	8
2.4	Running Feet	10
2.5	Synopsis-Abstract	11
2.6	Headings, Subheadings, and Side Headings	11
2.7	Addenda	13
2.8	Acknowledgments	13
2.9	Key Words	15
2.10	References	15
2.10.13-25	References to Journals	20
2.10.26-31	References to Books	23
2.10.32-42	Special Materials	25
2.11	Legends	33
2.12	Illustrations	39
2.13	Tables	44
2.14	Appendixes	68
2.15	National Auxiliary Publications Service (NAPS)	68
3.0	**Legal and Ethical Considerations**	71
3.1	Duplicate Publication	71
3.2	Fraud and Plagiarism	72
3.3	Copyright	73

Contents

3.4   Informed Consent 79

4.0   Editorial Assessment and Processing 81
4.1   Assignment to Category 81
4.2   Peer Review 82
4.3   Copy Editing 83
4.4   Layout 83
4.5   Typesetting/Proofreading 83
4.6   Advertising 84
4.7   Makeup 84
4.8   Reprints 84
4.9   Corrections 84
4.10   Index 84

2. Style

5.0   Grammar 85
5.1   The Sentence 85
5.2   The Paragraph 85
5.3   Punctuation 86
5.4   Modifiers 86
5.5   Parallel Construction 87
5.6   Nouns 88
5.7   Pronouns 88
5.8   Verbs 90
5.9   Subject-Verb Agreement 92

6.0   Punctuation 97
6.1   Comma 97
6.2   Semicolon 101
6.3   Colon 102
6.4   Question Mark, Exclamation Point, Period 103
6.5   Dashes 105
6.6   Quotation Marks 106
6.7   Ellipses 109
6.8   Parentheses 112
6.9   Brackets 115
6.10   Virgule (Solidus) 116
6.11   Apostrophe 118
6.12   Hyphen 120

7.0 **Plurals** 127
7.1 Abbreviations 127
7.2 Collective Nouns 127
7.3 Compound Nouns 127
7.4 Latin and Greek vs English 128
7.5 Microorganisms 128
7.6 Other Plurals 129

8.0 **Capitalization** 131
8.1 Proper Nouns 131
8.2 Titles and Degrees of Persons 135
8.3 Official Names 135
8.4 Titles and Headings 137
8.5 First Word of Statements, Quotations, or Subtitles .. 138
8.6 Acronyms 139
8.7 Designators 139

9.0 **Correct and Preferred Usage** 141
9.1 Commonly Misused Words and Phrases 141
9.2 Redundant, Expendable, and Incomparable Words 154
9.3 Back-formations 155
9.4 Medicalese and Jargon 155
9.5 Age and Sex Referents 157
9.6 Body Parts 157
9.7 Clock Referents 157
9.8 Laboratory Values 158
9.9 Articles 158
9.10 Sexist Language 158

10.0 **Foreign-Language Words and Phrases and**
     Accents (Diacritics) 161
10.1 Foreign-Language Words and Phrases 161
10.2 Accents (Diacritics) 161

3. Terminology

11.0 **Abbreviations** 165
11.1 Academic Degrees and Honors 166
11.2 Military Services and Titles 168
11.3 Days of the Week, Months, Eras 169
11.4 Local Addresses 170

Contents

11.5	States, Territories, and Possessions	171
11.6	Names and Titles of Persons	173
11.7	Business Firms	175
11.8	Agencies and Organizations	176
11.9	Names of Journals	178
11.10	Clinical and Technical Terms	185
11.11	Units of Measure	189
11.12	Elements and Chemicals	194
12.0	**Nomenclature**	197
12.1	Blood Groups	198
12.2	Cancer Staging	199
12.3	Cardiology	202
12.3.1	Electrocardiographic Terms	202
12.3.2	Heart Sounds and Murmurs	203
12.4	Clotting Factors	204
12.5	Diabetes Mellitus	206
12.6	Drugs	207
12.7	Endocrinology	214
12.8	Equipment and Reagents	215
12.9	Genetics	216
12.9.1	DNA, RNA, and Amino Acids	216
12.9.2	Restriction Enzymes	218
12.9.3	Human Gene Nomenclature	219
12.9.4	Oncogenes	221
12.9.5	Human Chromosomes	222
12.9.6	Animal Genetic Terms	225
12.10	Globulins	227
12.11	Hepatitis	227
12.12	Immunology	228
12.12.1	Complement	228
12.12.2	Human Leukocyte (HLA) and Other Histocompatibility Antigens	229
12.12.3	Immunoglobulins	232
12.12.4	Lymphocytes and Monoclonal Antibodies	233
12.13	Isotopes	235
12.14	Neurology	239
12.14.1	Cranial Nerves	239
12.14.2	Electroencephalographic (EEG) Terms	239
12.15	Obstetric Terms	241
12.16	Organisms	242
12.16.1	Genus and Species	242

12.16.2	Viruses	244
12.17	Pulmonary and Respiratory Terminology	247
12.18	Vertebrae, Dermatomes, and Spinal Nerves	249
13.0	**Eponyms**	251
13.1	Possessive Form	251
13.2	Eponymous vs Noneponymous Terms	251
14.0	**Greek Letters**	253
14.1	Greek Letter vs Word	253
14.2	Capitalization After a Greek Letter	254

4. Measurement and Quantitation

15.0	**Units of Measure**	255
15.1	SI Units	255
15.2	Quantities	259
15.3	Abbreviations	259
15.4	Punctuation	260
15.5	Subject-Verb Agreement	260
15.6	Dosage	260
15.7	Solution	260
15.8	Volume	261
15.9	Fractions vs Decimals	261
15.10	Conversion Tables	261
16.0	**Numbers and Percentages**	297
16.1	Usage	297
16.2	Forms of Numbers	299
16.3	Numerals	302
17.0	**Statistics**	305
17.1	Study Design	305
17.2	Reporting of Results	305
17.3	Significant Digits	306
17.4	Rounding Off	307
17.5	Commonly Used Statistical Symbols and Tests	307
18.0	**Mathematical Composition**	311
18.1	Copy Preparation	311
18.2	Copy Marking	311
18.3	Simplifying	312

5. Technical Information and Bibliography

19.0   **Printing and Production Terms** 315

20.0   **Copy Editing and Proofreading Marks** 323
20.1   Copy Editing Marks 323
20.2   Copy Editing Sample 325
20.3   Proofreading Marks 326
20.4   Proofreading Sample 328

21.0   **Resource Bibliography** 331
21.1   References 331
21.2   Additional Readings 342
21.3   On-line Resources 345

6. Appendix

Virus Names 351

Index

1

PREPARING
AN ARTICLE
FOR PUBLICATION

Chapter 1

1.0   Types of Articles

General medical journals publish a wide variety of articles, reflecting the diversity of clinical medicine. Submissions to the AMA journals far exceed the space available. For example, only 12% of unsolicited manuscripts received by *JAMA* in 1986 were accepted.

As Huth (1982) pointed out, all articles are similar in one important respect: they open by stating a question, consider the evidence and counterevidence, and conclude with an answer. Within that framework, the focus shifts depending on the type of article. Here we offer some guidelines to help authors decide what form of article best suits their material and purpose. Clarity on these points can only increase the chance of a manuscript's attracting the attention of a busy editor.

1.1   **Experimental.**—Original investigations are the backbone of medical publications. In fact, certain other types of articles, eg, editorials, exist as responses to—or perspectives on—original work. When organized to contain the elements described in 2.0, Manuscript Preparation, experimental articles state the research objective, explain the methods used, and conclude with an exposition of results accompanied by elucidating comments.

1.2   **Descriptive.**—Case reports are examples of articles that document observations of diseases, symptoms, autopsy results, etc. They comprise new combinations of diseases, previously unreported adverse effects of treat-

1

ment, and—in the extreme—novel observations that can change a medical model.

These articles lack experimental intervention; nonetheless, descriptive works are indispensable to medical journals. Often an unusual observation sparks interest that leads to original research. That is not to say that all ''interesting cases'' merit publication. The complex case, though of undeniable teaching value, rarely possesses the unique or provocative features essential for acceptance for publication.

1.3   **Review/Essay/Critique.**—Summaries of the current state of knowledge serve an important function, especially in journals with a general-medical readership. Such articles provide an update in areas that may be removed from the reader's expertise, include references for further reading, and highlight the experience of an authority. These papers range from comprehensive reviews, such as State of the Art/Review articles in *JAMA*, to more speculative pieces, such as Sounding Board in *The New England Journal of Medicine* or Commentaries in *JAMA*.

1.4   **Editorial.**—Traditionally, editorials express the views of the editor or the policies of the journal. They are short essays that comment on original work appearing in the same issue or on other timely subjects. These articles may be written by the editor or may speak for the editor through a member of the staff or an invited, outside author. Editorials should provide logical exposition—question, evidence/counterevidence, and answer—in much the same way as other articles.

1.5   **Correspondence.**—The rapid publication of correspondence is essential to the vitality of a medical journal. Confirmation and rebuttal of observations are the lifeblood of scientific discourse. Other useful letters are those that are descriptive but do not contain enough data to warrant inclusion as full-length articles. Most journals receive a large volume of correspondence. For example, about 150 letters arrive at *JAMA*'s editorial offices each month; such numbers necessitate considerable selectivity. Often one or two letters are chosen as representative of the response to a particular subject. Correspondents should note whether their letters to the editor are to be considered for publication.

1.6   **Book Reviews.**—No less thoroughness is required for book reviews than for other scientific writing. The reader seeks not only a brief overview of the book but an assessment of its quality relative to similar works. Although style variations are acceptable (even welcome) in this category, supporting evidence for the reviewer's praise or criticism is essential.

1.7   **Miscellaneous.**—Journals also publish other articles that do not fall into the above categories. These pieces may illustrate diagnostic methods using, for example, photographs, as in the Off-Center Fold of *Archives of Der-*

matology, report on conferences, such as in the Symposium section of *Annals of Internal Medicine*, or provide the personal reflections characterized by A Piece of My Mind in *JAMA*.

2.0 Manuscript Preparation

A scholarly manuscript should be composed by thoughtful consideration of the subject itself and anticipation of the reader's needs and questions, not by means of an outline; however, certain elements either are standard parts of all manuscripts or are used so frequently as to merit special instruction. These parts will be discussed in this section in the order in which they appear, and are paginated, in the manuscript. (*Note:* For AMA journals, the title, subtitle, byline, footnotes, and running foot appear on a topsheet prepared by the copy editor. This topsheet becomes page 1 of the manuscript.)

Of course, the preparation of any manuscript for publication should take the requirements of the publisher into account; this will help expedite publication. For the author, this requires familiarity with the journal to which the article is submitted. Most journals publish instructions for authors that are useful guides; some also publish style manuals, which provide in-depth instruction. For those journals that subscribe to the *Uniform Requirements for Manuscripts Submitted to Biomedical Journals* (see *Ann Intern Med.* 1982;96:766-771 or *Br Med J.* 1982;284:1766-1770), as the journals published by the AMA do, adherence to the guidelines described therein will be acceptable, although the journal in question may make alterations to suit its house style.

2.1   **Titles and Subtitles.**—Titles should be concise, specific, informative, and clear and should emphasize the main point of the article. This will facilitate the direction of interested readers, scanning the Table of Contents, to the article and will also aid in information retrieval by computer search and from published bibliographies, many of which list only titles, not subtitles. Phrases such as "The Effects of," "The Treatment of," and "Report of a Case of" can usually be omitted. Subtitles may be used to amplify the title; however, they should be able to stand alone (ie, they should not be a continuation of the title or a substitute for a succinct title). If possible, the title should be no more than two lines of no more than 42 characters and spaces per line.

> *Avoid:* Extramammary Paget's Disease: Arising in Knee Region With Sweat Gland Carcinoma
> *Better:* Extramammary Paget's Disease in the Knee, With Associated Sweat Gland Carcinoma

> *Or:*   Extramammary Paget's Disease and Sweat Gland Carcinoma: An Unusual Association Occurring in the Knee Region
>
> *Avoid:*   Psychiatric Disorders: A Rural-Urban Comparison
> *Better:*   Rural-Urban Differences in the Prevalence of Psychiatric Disorders
>
> *Avoid:*   Immunology of Kidney Disease
> *Better:*   Cyclosporine's Effectiveness in Treating Kidney Transplant Rejection

2.1.1 *Quotation Marks.*—If quotation marks are required in the title or subtitle, they should be *single*, not *double*.

2.1.2 *Numbers.*—Follow standard style for numbers (see 16.0, Numbers and Percentages). If numbers appear at the beginning of a title or subtitle, however, they—and any unit of measure associated with them—should be spelled out.

> *Example:*   The Health of *JAMA* in 1984: One Hundred Years of Publication

2.1.3 *Drugs.*—If drug names appear in the title or subtitle, (1) use the approved generic name, (2) omit the salt or ester, unless it is required (see 12.6, Nomenclature, Drugs), and (3) avoid the use of trademarks unless (*a*) several products are being compared, (*b*) the article is commenting on only one brand of the product in question, or (*c*) the ingredients are so many that the resulting title would be clumsy and a crude generic, such as "multivitamin tablet," would not do.

2.1.4 *Genus and Species.*—Genus and species names appearing in the title or subtitle should be italicized, and an initial capital letter should be used on the genus name but not the species, just as in the text. (See also 12.16.1, Nomenclature, Genus and Species.)

2.1.5 *Abbreviations.*—Avoid the use of abbreviations in the title and subtitle, unless space considerations require an exception. (See also 11.0, Abbreviations.)

2.1.6 *Capitalization.*—Capitalize the first letter of each major word in titles and subtitles. Do not capitalize articles, prepositions of three or fewer letters, coordinate conjunctions (*and, or, for, nor, but*), or the *to* in infinitives. *Do* capitalize a two-letter verb. Exceptions are made for some expressions:

> Ethical Questions Surrounding In Vitro Fertilization

For capitalization of hyphenated compounds, see 8.4, Capitalization, Titles and Headings.

2.2 **Bylines.**—In major contributions, authorship is indicated by a byline, which appears immediately below the title or subtitle. The byline should contain each author's full name (unless initials are preferred to given names), including, for example, Jr, Sr, II, III, and middle initials, and highest academic degree(s). Authors are encouraged to be consistent in the presentation of their names for ease of use by indexers, catalogers, and data searchers.

The persons listed as authors should be those who contributed to the study and manuscript preparation. All coauthors should be thoroughly familiar with the substance of the final manuscript and be able to defend its conclusions. Persons who made subsidiary contributions may be listed in the "Acknowledgments" section (see 2.8.3, Acknowledgments, Other Assistance). Generally, the byline should be limited to six persons.

2.2.1   *Degrees.*—If an author holds two doctoral degrees (eg, MD and PhD, or MD and DDS), either or both may be used, as the author prefers. In this case, use the order preferred by the author. If the author has a doctorate, degrees at the master's level are not usually included, although exceptions may be made when the master's degree represents a different or specialized field.

Academic degrees below the master's level are usually omitted, although specialized professional certifications other than the master's may be used if pertinent (eg, RN, RD, COT, PA).

Honorary designations earned in the United States (eg, FACP or FACS) are omitted. Honorary degrees earned in foreign countries (eg, FRCP or FRCS) are included.

If an author is on active duty in the armed services, only the service designation should be used. (See also 11.2, Abbreviations, Military Services and Titles.)

When the byline contains three or more names, use semicolons to separate the authors' names. If the byline contains only two names, use a comma.

> CPT James B. Dane, MC, USA, LTC Carl Seller, Jr, MC, USA
>
> Melvin H. Freedman, MD, FRCPC; E. Fred Saunders, MD, FRCP; Louise Jones, MD, PhD; Kurt Grant, RN

2.2.2   *Signatures.*—In copy such as letters to the editor and editorials, the authors' names appear as signatures at the end of the text, rather than as a byline on the first page. In this case, the authors' names and academic degrees are used, as in the byline, but they may be set in capital and small capital letters (eg, CPT JAMES B. DANE, MC, USA). Further information given in the signature varies with the journal and with the department therein; some list, in addition to the authors, the names and locations of their affiliated institutions; some list only the city in which the authors are located; some list the complete mailing address.

2.3   Footnotes.—Footnotes within the text should be avoided. Such explanatory material can usually be incorporated parenthetically into the text. The footnotes discussed below are those that appear at the bottom of the first page of major articles.

2.3.1   *Order of Footnotes.*—The preferred order of the footnotes at the bottom of the first page of an article is as follows: acceptance date, affiliations, death of author (death dagger [†]), "read before," disclaimer, and reprint address.

2.3.2   *Acceptance Date.*—Not all journals include the date of acceptance; others include not only the date of acceptance but also the date of submission. Most AMA journals use the following form:

> Accepted for publication November 1, 1986.

2.3.3   *Affiliations.*—The institutions with which an author is professionally affiliated are given in a footnote. Title and rank are *not* included in this footnote. The affiliation listed, including departmental affiliation if appropriate, should reflect the author's affiliation at the time the study was done. If the author has since moved, the current affiliation may be given in addition. The locations of the institutions should also be given. If there are several authors affiliated with different institutions or different departments at the same institution, this should be indicated parenthetically. (*Note:* If the byline includes Chinese, Japanese, Indian, or Vietnamese names, or other names in which the family name is traditionally given *first*, ask the author to verify the surname when it is used parenthetically in the affiliation footnote.) List the affiliations in the order of the authors as given in the byline, but combine the listings of authors affiliated with the same institution (eg, if the byline includes authors A, B, and C and if authors A and C are at the same institution, list the institution that authors A and C are with first and then the institution that author B is with).

> From the Department of Health Policy and Management, The Johns Hopkins University School of Hygiene and Public Health, Baltimore, Md. Dr Lloyd is now with the Emergency Department, St Luke's Hospital, Milwaukee, Wis.
>
> From the Department of Pathology, Stanford (Calif) University Medical Center.
>
> From the Departments of Pediatrics (Dr Nelson), Pathology (Dr Ellenberg), and Radiology (Dr Chan), Emory University School of Medicine, Atlanta, Ga.
>
> From the Hematology Laboratory Service, Duke University Medical Center, Durham, NC (Dr Ioachim), and the Hematology Department, Ball Memorial Hospital, Muncie, Ind (Dr Hanson).

> From the Departments of Pediatrics, Northwestern University School of Medicine (Dr Wright) and Stritch School of Medicine, Loyola University (Dr Anderson), Maywood, Ill.

> Dr Dodson is in private practice in Madison, Wis.

> From the Department of Pediatrics (Drs Doberczak and Kandall) and Biomathematics (Dr Thornton and Ms Bernstein), Beth Israel Medical Center, Mt Sinai School of Medicine, New York, NY.

If an author is a fellow doing research sponsored by an organization, this may be included in the affiliation footnote.

> From the Argonne Cancer Research Hospital, Chicago, Ill. Dr Blank is a fellow of the American Cancer Society.

If the authors of a manuscript are a large group of persons, the name of the group may be given in the byline and the affiliation footnote could refer the reader to the end of the article for a complete listing of the participants. (See also 2.8.5, Acknowledgments, List of Participants in a Group Study.)

> A complete list of the participants in this research study appears at the end of this article.

2.3.4   *Death.*—If an author of an article has died, a death dagger (†) should follow the author's name in the byline, and one of the following footnotes should be inserted after the affiliation footnote:

> †Dr Jones died October 29, 1985.

> †Deceased.

2.3.5   *"Read Before."*—The following forms are used for material that has been read or exhibited at a professional meeting. Retain the original spelling and capitalization of the meeting name.

> Presented in part as the Tenth Annual Shelley Lecture at the annual meeting of the North and South Carolina Societies of Pathologists, Charlotte, NC, February 4, 1984.

> Read before the annual joint meeting of the American Society for Head and Neck Surgery and the Society of Head and Neck Surgeons, Cerromar Beach, Puerto Rico, May 7, 1985.

> Presented as a poster exhibit at the 126th annual convention of the American Medical Association, San Francisco, Calif, June 18-22, 1977.

2.3.6   *Disclaimer.*—A footnote of disclaimer is used only when provided by the author. This notation precedes the reprint address. Editors should retain the author's phrasing.

> The views expressed herein are those of the authors and do not necessarily reflect the views of the US Army or the Department of Defense.

2.3 Footnotes

2.3.7 *Reprint Address.*—A complete mailing address is given in a footnote for readers who want reprints or additional information. This should include a street address, if possible, and ZIP or postal code. Even if there is only one author, the name of the person to contact should be included at the end of the address, in parentheses.

> Reprint requests to Office of Health Policy Development, American Medical Association, 515 N Dearborn St, Chicago, IL 60610 (Dr Block).

> Reprint requests to Department of Pathology, Hospital for Sick Children, 555 University Ave, Toronto, Ontario, Canada M56 1X8 (Dr Edwards).

> Reprint requests to Medical Research Council, Brain Metabolism Unit, Royal Edinburgh Hospital, Morningside Place, Edinburgh, Scotland EH10 5HF (Dr Goodwin).

> Reprint requests to PO Box 30.001, 9700 RB Groningen, the Netherlands (Dr Mahiea).

To distinguish between authors with the same last name, use the first initial or, if necessary, the full name.

For the case in which reprint requests are to be directed to someone whose name is not included in the byline, use the following form:

> Reprint requests to Bridge Defense Foundation, 111 N First St, French Lick, IN 47432 (Daniel M. Barry, MD).

If the author does not intend to offer reprints, use "Reprints not available."

2.4 **Running Feet.**—Printed pages customarily carry identification of the publication (ie, journal name or abbreviation, volume number, date of issue), the article (by truncated title and authors), and the page number. When this information appears at the top of the page, it is called a *running head.* When the information appears at the bottom of the page, as it does in AMA publications, it is called a *running foot.*

2.4.1 *Identification of the Publication.*—Use the accepted *Index Medicus* abbreviations of the journal names (see 11.9, Abbreviations, Names of Journals) and the following forms, as applicable to the journal involved:

> JAMA: JAMA, November 1, 1985—Vol 254, No. 17
> Specialty journals: Arch Pathol Lab Med—Vol 109, July 1985

2.4.2 *Identification of the Article.*—This truncated version of the title should be kept short (approximately 45 characters and spaces in AMA journals). It should identify the article beginning on that page and give the author's surname. If there are two authors, their surnames should be joined by an ampersand. If there are three or more authors, the surname of the first is used, followed by "et al." Separate the truncated title of the article and

10

the name(s) of the author(s) by an em dash. No punctuation follows the running foot.

Lymphoma in Pregnancy—Ioachim

Hepatic Granulomas—Nishimura et al

Antecedents of Cerebral Palsy—Nelson & Ellenberg

In some instances the article will be identified by its department rather than by its title and author, eg, "Editorials," "Resident's Page," "Radiological Case of the Month."

2.5   **Synopsis-Abstract.**—In this age of electronic data retrieval, a well-written synopsis-abstract has become increasingly important in directing readers to articles of potential clinical and research value. The synopsis-abstract summarizes the main points of an article: (1) the purpose of the study, (2) the basic procedures followed, (3) the main findings, and (4) the *principal* conclusions. Expressions such as "X is described," "Y is discussed," "Z is also reviewed" should be avoided in favor of a *concise* (limited to 135 or 150 words in AMA's journals) statement. A few specific guidelines to consider in preparing a synopsis-abstract follow:

- Do not begin the abstract with repetition of the title.
- Omit *P* values.
- Cite no references.
- Avoid abbreviations (see 11.0, Abbreviations).
- Use the salt or ester of a drug at first mention (see 12.6, Nomenclature, Drugs).
- If an isotope is mentioned, when first used spell out the name of the element and then, on line, give the isotope number (see 12.13, Nomenclature, Isotopes).
- Avoid the use of trademarks or manufacturers' names unless they are essential to the study (see 12.8, Nomenclature, Equipment and Reagents).
- Include major terms in the abstract, since the abstract can be text searched in many data retrieval systems. This will enable the article to be retrieved when relevant.

2.6   **Headings, Subheadings, and Side Headings.**—Although not all articles will conform to one pattern, there is a fairly standard pattern of organization in current scientific journal articles.

Introduction:	Purpose of the study (*Note:* The introduction is usually *not* given a heading.)
Subjects and Methods, *Report of Cases:*	Basic procedures (*Note:* These sections are set in reduced type in some AMA journals.)

11

Results:	Main findings
Comment:	Principal conclusions (*Note:* AMA journals avoid the use of the heading "Discussion" here, as that heading is reserved for articles that are part of symposium proceedings, in which discussion followed the presentation of the paper.)

2.6.1   *Levels of Headings.*—Regardless of the headings used, it is important that a consistent style be used for each level throughout a manuscript so that the reader may graphically see what is primary and what is subsidiary; for example, a first-level heading should appear in the same style throughout the manuscript.

The styles used for the various levels of headings will vary from one publisher to the next and, within publishing houses, from one category of article to another; the hierarchy of center and side heading styles for AMA journals is shown below:

FIRST-LEVEL CENTER HEADING

Second-Level Center Heading

¶**First-Level Side Heading.—**

¶*Second-Level Side Heading.—*

¶**Third-Level Side Heading.—**

¶Fourth-Level Side Heading.—

¶Fifth-Level Side Heading.—

Note that in AMA publications, a period and an em dash follow the side headings, and these headings have a paragraph indent. The text runs in following the side heading.

Mention should be made of AMA's special handling of the "Report of Cases" section. In letters to the editor, in which this side heading is used, followed by individual case reports, adopt the following format:

¶*Report of Cases.*—Case 1.—

In articles, if subheadings are used after individual case report side headings, adopt the following format:

¶Case 1.—**Laboratory Findings.**—

Note: When one side heading is immediately followed by another side heading, they are separated by a period and an em dash.

2.6.2   *Number of Headings.*—There is no requisite number of headings. However, because headings below the first level are meant to divide a primary part into secondary parts, and so on, there must be a minimum of two.

Besides reflecting the skeleton of an article and thereby guiding the reader, headings also help break up the copy, making the article more attractive and easier to read. Hence headings may be used even in material such as editorials, which may not follow the "standard" organization described above. (Other typographic and design elements, such as bullets [●], enumerations, tabulations, figures, and tables, may be used for these purposes too.)

2.7   **Addenda.**—The use of addenda per se is discouraged in AMA publications. If material is added after a manuscript has been accepted for publication (eg, an additional case report, longer follow-up, recent legislation, or the publication of new studies that bear on the present article), this is best handled by adding a final paragraph to the existing manuscript: "Since this manuscript was submitted for publication. . . ." If desired, this paragraph may be set off by extra space and/or a half-column-wide centered hairline rule. Any references cited for the first time in this final paragraph or addendum should follow the numbering of the existing reference list.

If an article is one part of a several-part article, a sentence to that effect may be added as the last paragraph of the article. This is usually set in reduced type and italicized.

> *This article is the first of a three-part series. The second part will appear next month.*

2.8   **Acknowledgments.**—Acknowledgments are unnumbered end notes that follow the body of the article and precede the references. Examples of various types of acknowledgment are given below.

2.8.1   *Financial Support.*—Financial support or provision of supplies used in the study should be acknowledged first. Grant or contract numbers should be included whenever possible. The complete name of the funding institution or agency should be given, along with the city and state in which it is located.

> This study was supported in part by a grant from Alcon Laboratories Inc, Fort Worth, Tex.

> This study was supported by research grants EY-03812 and EY-03454 from the National Eye Institute, Bethesda, Md.

> The fluorouracil used in this study was provided by Hoffmann-La Roche Inc, Nutley, NJ.

If individual authors were the recipients of funds, their names should be listed parenthetically.

2.8 Acknowledgments

This study was supported in part by grant CA34988 from the National Institutes of Health, Bethesda, Md, and by a teaching and research scholarship from the American College of Physicians, Philadelphia, Pa (Dr Fischl).

2.8.2 Proprietary Statement.—Most AMA journals now require authors to submit to the journal editor a footnote specifying whether they have any commercial or proprietary interest in any device, equipment, instrument, or drug that is the subject of the article in question. Authors must also reveal whether they have any financial interest (as a consultant, reviewer, or evaluator) in a drug or device described in the article. The editor then decides whether this information will be published.

The authors have no commercial or proprietary interest in fluorouracil, nor do they have any financial interest (as consultant, reviewer, or evaluator) in fluorouracil.

2.8.3 Other Assistance.—Acknowledgment of other forms of assistance (eg, statistical review, preparation of the report, performance of special tests or research, editorial assistance, or clerical assistance) may also be included, as the author desires. Note that when specific individuals are named, the given name and the highest academic degrees (see 2.2.1, Bylines, Degrees) should be included.

Appreciation is expressed to Marlene Heneghan and LaWanda Tucker for secretarial assistance; Diane Frohlichstein, COT, for technical assistance; Maxine Gere for editorial services; Nancy Snyder for the artwork; and Norm Jednock and his staff for photographic services.

The Branch Retinal Vein Occlusion Study Group is grateful for the contributions of the many referring ophthalmologists, without whom this study could not have been carried out, and to the study patients, whose faithfulness to the study led to conclusions that promise hope for others with branch vein occlusion.

2.8.4 Reproduction of Figures and Tables.—If credit for reproduction of a figure or a table is not easily incorporated in the figure legend (see 2.11.7, Legends, Figures Reproduced From Other Sources) or a footnote to the table (see 2.13.6, Tables, Setup), it should be placed in the acknowledgments. *Note:* If the copyright holder requests that the copyright symbol and year appear in the credit line, this must be complied with. Other wording suggested by the copyright holder may be modified to suit house style. (See also 3.3.5, Copyright, Copying and Reproducing.)

Figure 1 was reproduced from the *American Journal of Nursing* (1980;80:62), ©1980, American Journal of Nursing Co.

2.8.5 List of Participants in a Group Study.—If the study was done by a large group of persons, the names of the participants may be given in the ''Ac-

14

knowledgments'' section (see also 2.3.3, Footnotes, Affiliations). An alternative would be to place the list of participants in a box wherever it best fits in the layout.

2.8.6   *National Auxiliary Publications Service (NAPS) or Other Supplementary Information.*—If portions of a manuscript are stored in NAPS or some similar service (see 2.15, National Auxiliary Publications Service [NAPS]), or if more extensive data are available from the author on request, information on how to obtain this material is given in the acknowledgments.

> See National Auxiliary Publications Service document 04275 for 12 pages of supplementary material. Order from NAPS c/o Microfiche Publications, PO Box 3513, Grand Central Station, New York, NY 10163-3513. Remit in advance, in US funds only, $7.75 for photocopies or $4 for microfiche. Outside the United States or Canada, add postage of $4.50 for the first 20 pages and $1 for each 10 pages of material thereafter. The postage charge for any microfiche order is $1.50.

> A complete list of documents surveyed is available on request from the author.

2.9   **Key Words.**—Some medical journals publish a short list (three to five terms) of key words at the end of the abstract. These descriptors are provided by the author and are the terms the author believes represent the key concepts of the article. AMA journals do not use key words. Articles in AMA journals are indexed by professional indexers using subject headings such as Medical Subject Headings (MeSH) for indexes such as *Index Medicus* databases like MEDLINE.

2.10   **References.**—To effect greater uniformity in reference style among publications, the AMA has adopted a modified version of the format described in American National Standards Institute (ANSI) document Z39.29.1977. Each reference is divided by periods into the following *bibliographic groups* (listed in order): author(s), title, edition, imprint (place and name of publisher, date of publication, volume number, issue number, inclusive page numbers), physical description (physical construction or form), series statement, and supplementary notes (identifiers of the uniqueness of the reference or material necessary for added clarity). The period serves as a field delimiter, making each bibliographic group distinct and helping establish a sequence of bibliographic elements in a reference. The items within a bibliographic group are referred to as *bibliographic elements.* They may be separated by a semicolon (if the elements are different or if there are multiple occurrences of logically related elements within a group; also, before volume identification data), a comma (if the items are subelements of a bibliographic element or a set of closely related elements), or a colon (before the publisher's name, between the title and the subtitle, and after a connective phrase [for example, "In," "Taken from," "Located at," "Accompanied by," "Available from"]).

The *Uniform Requirements for Manuscripts Submitted to Biomedical Journals* is also based on the ANSI document but, in some cases, has made modifications different from the ones described herein. Articles adhering exactly to the *Uniform Requirements* will be acceptable without challenge if accepted for publication in the AMA journals and any necessary changes will be made by the AMA copy editors.

Because the reference style presented herein differs substantially from the previous AMA reference style, examples, where possible, will use the "old" example changed to the new style.

2.10.1   *Listed References.*—References to articles or books published or accepted for publication or to papers presented at professional meetings are listed in numerical order at the end of the communication (except as specified in 2.10.2, References, References Given in Text, and 2.10.6, References, Numbering). Each reference is a separate entry. References to mass circulation magazines or newspapers, material not yet accepted for publication, and personal communications (both oral and written) are not acceptable as listed references, except in unusual circumstances, and should be given parenthetically in the text (see 2.10.2, References, References Given in Text, and 2.10.39, References, Unpublished Material).

2.10.2   *References Given in Text.*—In some circumstances, references may be included parenthetically in the text. Examples of forms are given here. Note that in the text (1) author(s) may or may not be named, (2) the title is not given, (3) the name of the journal is abbreviated only when enclosed in parentheses, and (4) inclusive page numbers are given.

> The results were reported recently by West (*Br Med J*. 1981;282:355-357).

> The results were reported recently in the *British Medical Journal* (1981;282:355-377).

References to publications not acceptable as listed references (see 2.10.1, References, Listed References) may be included parenthetically in the text. Use a concise form: name of periodical, date, initial page number.

> The explanation is given in one recent account (*Newsweek*. March 17, 1980:102).

> The *Archives of Surgery* article on surgeon glut was picked up by a local newspaper (*Chicago Tribune*. October 2, 1986:6).

2.10.3   *Author's Responsibility for Accuracy.*—Authors are responsible for the accuracy and completeness of the references in their communications. Any reference that appears to be inaccurate should be queried by the copy editor. Consult the bibliographic resources in the library or ask the author to verify and complete the reference.

2.10.4   *Minimum Acceptable Data.*—To be acceptable, a reference must include certain minimum data, as follows:

> *Journals:*   Author(s), article title, journal, year, volume, inclusive page numbers
> *Books:*   Author(s), title, place of publication, publisher, year

Enough information to identify and retrieve the material should be provided. More complete data (see 2.10.13, References to Journals, Complete Data, and 2.10.26, References to Books, Complete Data) should be used when available.

2.10.5   *Number Permitted.*—A good indication of the reliability of an author's work is the type and number of references selected. Too many references may indicate a lack of critical thinking; too few references may suggest the possibility of unwarranted speculation. References have two major purposes: documentation and acknowledgment. Acknowledgment references should be limited to reports that have contributed substantially to the author's own current work. Some journals suggest a limit for the number of references for a particular type of article. This will usually be described in the journal's instructions for authors. Exceptions to such limits may be permitted for special cases.

2.10.6   *Numbering.*—References should be numbered consecutively, using arabic numerals, in the order in which they are cited in the text. Unnumbered references are only occasionally used in AMA journals. In these exceptional cases, they usually appear alphabetically as a list of selected readings.

2.10.7   *Citation.*—Each reference should be cited *in the text.* Citation may *also* be made in tables, figures, and legends. Use arabic superscript numerals. These numerals appear *outside* periods and commas, *inside* colons and semicolons. When *more than two* references are cited at a given place in the copy, use hyphens to join the first and last numbers of a closed series; use commas without space to separate other parts of a multiple citation.

> As reported previously,[1,3-8,19]
>
> The derived data were as follows[3,4]:
>
> As reported previously,*

When a multiple citation involves more than 23 characters, use an asterisk in the text and give the citation in a footnote at the bottom of the page. Note that reference numerals in such a footnote are set full size, on line

17

rather than as superscripts. Also note that the spacing is different from that in superscript reference citations.

---

    *References 3, 5, 7, 9, 11, 13, 21, 24,29, 31.

If the author wishes to cite different page numbers from a single reference source at different places in the text, the page numbers are included in the superscript citation and the source appears only once in the list of references. Note that (1) the superscript may include more than one page number, citation of more than one reference, or both, and (2) all spaces are closed up. In listed references, do not use *ibid* or *op cit*.

These patients showed no sign of protective sphincteric adduction.[3(p21),9]

Westman [5(pp3.5),9] has reported eight cases in which vomiting occurred.

2.10.8 *Authors.*—Use the author's surname followed by initials without punctuation. In listed references, the names of all authors should be given unless there are more than six, in which case the names of *the first three authors* are used, followed by "et al." Note spacing and punctuation. Do not use *and* between names. (Abbreviations for Junior and Senior and Roman numerals *follow* author's initials.)

One author:	Doe JF.
Two authors:	Doe JF, Roe JP III.
Six authors:	Doe JF, Roe JP III, Coe RT Jr, Loe JT Sr, Poe EA, van Voe AE.
More than six authors:	Doe JF, Roe JP III, Coe RT Jr, et al.

When mentioned in the text, only surnames of authors are used. For a two-author reference, give both surnames. For references with more than two authors, give the first author's surname followed by "et al," "and associates," "and coworkers," or "and colleagues."

Doe[7] reported on the survey.

Doe and Roe[8] reported on the survey.

Doe et al[9] reported on the survey.

Note: Never use the possessive form *et al's*; rephrase the sentence.

The data of Doe et al[9] were reported.

2.10.9 *Prefixes and Particles.*—Surnames containing prefixes or particles should be spelled and capitalized according to the preference of the persons concerned.

    1. van Gylswyk NO, Roche CI.

2. Van Rosevelt RF, Bakker JC, Sinclair DM, Damen J, Van Mourik JA.

2.10.10 *Titles.*—In titles of articles, books, parts of books, and other material, retain the spelling, abbreviations, and style for numbers used in the original. Note, however, that *all* numbers are spelled out at the beginning of a title.

Articles and parts of books: In English-language titles, capitalize only the first letter of the first word, proper names, and abbreviations that are ordinarily capitalized (eg, DNA, EEG, VDRL). Do *not* enclose parts of books in quotation marks.

Books, journals, government bulletins, documents, and pamphlets: In English-language titles, capitalize the first and last words and each word that is not an article, preposition, or conjunction of less than four letters. In every language, italicize the title.

Genus and species: In all titles, follow AMA style for capitalization of genus and species and use of italics (see 8.1.7, Capitalization, Organisms, and 12.16.1, Nomenclature, Genus and Species). Use roman type for genus and species names in book titles.

2.10.11 *Foreign-Language Titles.*—Foreign-language titles are usually not translated; if they have been, bracketed indication of the original language should follow the title.

1. Kojima M. Studies on the pathomechanism of solar urticaria [in Japanese]. *Areugi*. 1984;33:224-230.
2. Abernathy JD. De la nécessité de traiter l'hypertension modérée; une mauvaise interprétation des données de l'étude australienne. *JAMA Suisse*. 1987;7:237-241. Originally published, in English, in: *JAMA*. 1986;256:3134-3137.

Reference to a foreign-language translation of an article should be permitted only when the original article is not readily available.

Foreign-language titles should be verified from the original when possible. Consult foreign-language dictionaries for accents, spelling, and other particulars.

Capitalization: For journal articles, follow the capitalization in *Index Medicus*. For books, pamphlets, and parts of books, retain the capitalization used in the original or consult the author or publisher. *Note:* In foreign-language titles, capitalization does not necessarily follow the rules given in 2.10.10, References, Titles. For example, in German titles (both articles and books), all nouns *and only nouns* are capitalized; in French, Spanish, and Italian book titles, capitalize only the first word, proper names, and abbreviations that are capitalized in English.

2.10   References

Foreign words of reference: Such words as *tome* (volume), *fascicolo* (part), *Seite* (page), *Teil* (part), *Auflage* (edition), *Abteilung* (section or part), *Band* (volume), *Heft* (number), *Beiheft* (supplement), and *Lieferung* (part or number) should be translated into English.

2.10.12 Subtitles.—Style for subtitles follows that for titles (see 2.10.10, References, Titles) in regard to spelling, abbreviations, numbers, capitalization, and use of italics, except that for *journal articles* the subtitle begins with a *lowercase* letter. A colon separates title and subtitle. If the subtitle is numbered, use a roman numeral followed by a colon.

> 1. Milunsky A. Prenatal detection of neural tube defects, VI: experience with 20,000 pregnancies. *JAMA.* 1980;244:2731-2735.

References to Journals

2.10.13 Complete Data.—A complete journal reference includes (1) authors' names and initials; (2) title of article and subtitle, if any; (3) abbreviated name of journal; (4) year; (5) volume number; (6) part or supplement number, when pertinent, and issue month or number when pagination is not consecutive throughout a volume; and (7) inclusive page numbers.

2.10.14 Names of Journals.—Abbreviate and italicize names of journals. Use initial capital letters. Abbreviate according to the listing in the current *Index Medicus* (see 11.9, Abbreviations, Names of Journals). Include parenthetical designation of a city if it is included in the abbreviations given in *List of Journals Indexed in Index Medicus;* for example, *Acta Anat (Basel), J Physiol (Lond).* In journal titles listed in *Index Medicus,* information enclosed in brackets should be retained *without* brackets, eg, *J Bone Joint Surg Br.*

2.10.15 Page Numbers and Dates.—Do not omit digits from inclusive page numbers. The year, the semicolon following it, the volume number, the colon following it, and the page numbers are set with the spaces closed up.

> 1. Jones J. Necrotizing *Candida* esophagitis. *JAMA.* 1980;244:2190-2191.

2.10.16 Serialized Article.—For a serialized article, the cited parts of which appear in the same volume, follow this example:

> 1. Lerner PI, Weinstein L. Infective endocarditis in the antibiotic era. *N Engl J Med.* 1966;274:199-206, 388-393.

2.10.17 Journals Without Volume Numbers.—In reference to journals that have no volume numbers or that have volume numbers but paginate each issue beginning with page 1, use one of the following styles:

> 1. Amar L. Cataracte et implant de Binkhorst. *Bull Soc Ophtalmol Fr.* 1976:351-356.

20

2. Shands KN, Fraser WA. Legionnaires' disease. *Dis Mon.* December 1980;27:1-59.

3. Abraham EP. The beta-lactam antibiotics. *Sci Am.* June 1981:76-97.

2.10.18 *Parts of an Issue.*—If an issue has two or more parts, the part cited should be indicated in accordance with the following example:

1. Border WA, Cohen AH. Renal biopsy diagnosis of clinically silent multiple myeloma. *Ann Intern Med.* 1980;93(pt 1):43-46.

2.10.19 *Issue Number.*—Do not include the issue number or month except in the case of a special issue (see 2.10.20, References, Special Issue) or when pagination is not consecutive throughout the volume (ie, when each issue begins with page 1). In the latter case, the month or the date of the issue is preferable to the issue number.

Psychiatr Opinion. October 1973;10:34-38.

2.10.20 *Special Issue.*—References to all or part of a special issue of a journal should be given as follows:

1. Standards and guidelines for cardiopulmonary resuscitation (CPR) and emergency cardiac care (ECC). *JAMA.* 1986;255:2905-2984.

2. McDonald WI. Attitudes to the treatment of multiple sclerosis. *Arch Neurol.* October 21, 1983;40(special issue):667-670.

(Note that the issue date may be needed for identification.)

The following example shows the pagination in a supplementary special issue:

3. Hebert GA. Improved salt fractionation of animal serums for immunofluorescence studies. *J Dent Res.* 1976;55:A33-A38.

2.10.21 *Supplements.*—The following forms are used:

1. Gordon AS, chairman. Standards for cardiopulmonary resuscitation (CPR) and emergency cardiac care (ECC). *JAMA.* 1974;277(suppl):833-868.

(Use this form whether or not pagination is consecutive with volume pagination and whether this is the only supplement to the volume or there are others.)

2. Blendon RJ. The prospects for state and local governments playing a broader role in health care in the 1980s. *Am J Public Health.* January 1981;71(suppl):9-15.

(Pagination is not consecutive with that of the volume; there may be several supplements to a volume, referred to by month.)

3. Keys A. Coronary heart disease in seven countries. *Circulation.* 1970;41(suppl 1):I-1-I-211.

2.10   References

(Supplements are published independently of volumes and are numbered; pagination in each is independent of that in others.)

> 4. Flodmark S. Clinical detection of blood-brain barrier alteration by means of EEG: part 1. *Acta Neurol Scand*. 1965;41(suppl 13, pt 1):163-177.

(Volume 41 has multiple supplements; this supplement has two parts, each with independent pagination.)

> 5. Centers for Disease Control. Health information for international travel: including United States designated yellow fever vaccination centers. *MMWR*. September 1974;23(suppl):1S-76S.

(This refers to a supplement published in September, although there is an annual supplement [now called a summary] to the volume as well, which has an issue number.)

> 6. Centers for Disease Control. Vaccination certificate requirements for international travel. *MMWR*. 1973;22(suppl to No. 17):1S-54S.

(This is a supplement to No. 17, although there are both monthly and annual supplements as well.)

2.10.22 Abstracts.—Reference to an abstract of an article should be permitted only when the original article is not readily available (eg, foreign-language articles or papers presented at meetings but not yet published). If possible, references for both the original article and the abstract should be given. If the abstract is in the society proceedings section of a journal, the name of the society before which the paper was read need not be included unless the subject of the paper, the aims of the society, and the usual content of the journal are widely divergent.

> 1. Kremer H, Kellner E, Schierl W, Zöllner N. Ultrasonic diagnosis in infiltrative gastrointestinal diseases [in German]. *Dtsch Med Wochenschr*. 1978;103:965-967. Taken from: *JAMA*. 1978;240:2784. English abstract.
> 2. Paillard M, Resnick N. Natural history of nosocomial urinary incontinence. *Gerontologist*. 1981;24:212. Abstract.

2.10.23 Special Department of a Journal.—When reference is made to material from a special department in a journal, the department should be identified only if the cited material has no byline or signature, or no page number. This is preferable to citing Anonymous.

> 1. How far to lower blood pressure. *Lancet*. 1987;2:251-252. Editorial.
> 2. Services for the mentally handicapped. *Br Med J*. 1981;282:489. News and Notes.
> 3. Interferon production by genetic engineering. *Br Med J*. 1981;282:674-675. Leading Article.

4. The development of scientific research in UK. *Lancet.* 1987;2:288. Notes and News.
5. Case records of the Massachusetts General Hospital: weekly clinicopathological exercises. *N Engl J Med.* 1981;304:831-836. Case 14-1981.
6. Parsons GH, reviewer. *West J Med.* 1981;134:92-93. Review of: Grodin FS. *Respiratory Function of the Lung and Its Control.*

2.10.24 *Other Material Without Author(s).*—Reference may be made to material that has no author or is prepared by a committee or other group. The following forms are used:

1. Centers for Disease Control. Influenza—worldwide. *MMWR.* 1979;28:51-52.
2. Immunization Practices Advisory Committee. Influenza vaccine—recommendations of the ACIP. *MMWR.* 1979;28:231-238.
3. Council on Scientific Affairs. Scientific issues in drug testing. *JAMA.* 1987;257:3110-3114.
4. Oxford Cataract Treatment and Evaluation Team (OCTET). Long-term corneal endothelial cell loss after cataract surgery: results of a randomized controlled trial. *Arch Ophthalmol.* 1986;104:1170-1175.

2.10.25 *Discussants.*—If reference citation in the text names a discussant specifically rather than the author(s), eg, "as noted by Sachs,[5]" the following form is used (see also 2.10.40, References, Secondary Citations and Quotations).

1. Sachs W. In discussion: Baer RL, Andrade R, Seimanowitz VJ. Pemphigus erythematosus. *Arch Dermatol.* 1966;93:374-375.

References to Books

2.10.26 *Complete Data.*—A complete reference to a book includes (1) authors' surnames and initials; (2) surname and initials of editor or translator, or both, if any; (3) title of book and subtitle, if any; (4) number of editions after the first; (5) place of publication; (6) name of publisher; (7) year of publication; (8) volume number, if there is more than one volume; and (9) page numbers, if specific pages are cited.

1. Stryer L. *Biochemistry.* 2nd ed. San Francisco, Calif: WH Freeman Co; 1981:559-596.
2. Kavet J. Trends in the utilization of influenza vaccine: an examination of the implementation of public policy in the United States. In: Selby P, ed. *Influenza: Virus, Vaccines, and Strategy.* Orlando, Fla: Academic Press Inc; 1976:297-308.

2.10.27 *Publishers.*—The full name of the publisher should be given, abbreviated in accordance with AMA style, but *without* punctuation. If the name of a publishing firm has changed, use the name that was given on the work.

To verify names of publishers, consult *Books in Print,* the current issue of *Cumulative Book Index,* or *Publisher's Trade List Annual.*

2.10   References

2.10.28 Place of Publication.—Use the name of the city in which the main office of the publishing firm is located. Follow AMA style in the use of state names (see 11.5, Abbreviations, States, Territories, and Possessions). A colon separates the place of publication and the name of the publisher.

> 1. Barrows HS. *Simulated Patients (Programmed Patients): The Development and Use of a New Technique in Medical Education.* Springfield, Ill: Charles C Thomas Publisher; 1971.

In the case of overseas publishers with major US offices, use the US locations.

> 2. Fischer DH. *Growing Old in America.* New York, NY: Oxford University Press Inc; 1977:210-216.

2.10.29 Page, Volume, and Edition Numbers.—Use arabic numerals. Give specific page or pages if indicated by the author. The volume should be given if the work cited includes more than one volume. Do not indicate a first edition; if a subsequent edition is cited, the number should be given. (See also 2.10.41, References, Classical References.)

> 1. Spencer H. *Pathology of the Lung.* 3rd ed. Elmsford, NY: Pergamon Press Inc; 1976;2:980.
> 2. Fishbein M. *Medical Writing: The Technic and the Art.* 4th ed. Springfield, Ill: Charles C Thomas Publisher; 1978:46-51.

2.10.30 Editors and Translators.—Names of editors, translators, translator-editors, or executive and section editors are given in accordance with the following forms:

> 1. Gray H; Goss CM, ed. *Gray's Anatomy of the Human Body.* 29th ed. Philadelphia, Pa: Lea & Febiger; 1973:1206.

(Gray is the author, Goss is the editor.)

> 2. Kuschinsky G, Lüllmann H; Hoffmann PC, trans. *Textbook of Pharmacology.* Orlando, Fla: Academic Press Inc; 1973.

(Kuschinsky and Lüllmann are the authors, Hoffmann is the translator.)

> 3. Plato; Taylor EA, trans-ed. *The Laws.* London, England: JM Dent & Sons Ltd; 1934:104-105.

(Plato is the author, Taylor is the translator-editor.)

> 4. Gaunt R. History of the adrenal cortex. In: Geiger SR, exec ed. *Handbook of Physiology: A Critical Comprehensive Presentation of Physiologic Knowledge and Concepts.* Baltimore, Md: Williams & Wilkins; 1975;6:1-12.
> 5. Buege JA, Aust SD. Microsomal lipid peroxidation. In: Fleischer S, Packer L, eds. *Methods in Enzymology.* Orlando, Fla: Academic Press Inc; 1978;52:302.

6. MacLeod GK. Marketplace and regulatory trade-offs. In: MacLeod GK, Perlman M, eds. *Health Care Capital: Competition and Control.* Cambridge, Mass: Ballinger Publishing Co; 1978:1-6.

(MacLeod is the author of a chapter in a book of which he is also one of the editors.)

If a book has an editor but no author(s), the following form is used:

1. Boyer PD, ed. *The Enzymes.* 3rd ed. Orlando, Fla: Academic Press Inc; 1976;13:346.

When a book title includes a volume number, follow this example:

1. Walton WH, ed. *Inhaled Particles, IV.* Elmsford, NY: Pergamon Press Inc; 1975.

2.10.31 *Parts of Books.*—In some instances, reference is made to a part of a book that has a number of contributors as well as major authors or editors. In the title of the part (chapter or section), capitalize as for a journal title (see 2.10.10, References, Titles); do *not* enclose in quotation marks. Either inclusive page numbers or numerical designation of the part should be given, but not both.

1. Schulman JL. Immunology of influenza. In: Kilbourne ED, ed. *The Influenza Viruses and Influenza.* Orlando, Fla: Academic Press Inc; 1975:373-393.
2. Sencer DJ, Rubin RJ. Risk as the basis for immunization policy in the United States. In: *International Symposium on Influenza Vaccines for Men and Horses, London 1972.* New York, NY: S Karger AG; 1973;20:244-251.
3. Pinnell SR. Disorders of collagen. In: Stansbury JB, Wyngaarden JB, Fredrickson DS, eds. *The Metabolic Basis of Inherited Disease.* 4th ed. New York, NY: McGraw-Hill International Book Co; 1978: chap 57.

Special Materials

2.10.32 *Government Bulletins.*—References to bulletins published by departments or agencies of the US government should include the following information, in the order indicated: (1) name of author (if given); (2) title of bulletin; (3) place of publication; (4) name of issuing bureau, agency, department, or other governmental division; (5) date of publication; (6) page numbers, if specified; (7) publication number, if any; and (8) series number, if given.

1. Butler R. *Alternatives to Retirement, Testimony Before the Subcommittee on Retirement Income and Employment.* Washington, DC: House Select Committee on Aging; 1978. US Dept of Health, Education, and Welfare publication NIH 780-243.

2. Melvin DM, Brooke MM. *Laboratory Procedures for the Diagnosis of Intestinal Parasites.* Atlanta, Ga: Centers for Disease Control; 1974. US Dept of Health, Education, and Welfare publication 75-8282.
3. *Accommodating the Spectrum of Individual Abilities.* Washington, DC: US Commission on Civil Rights; 1981:108-114.
4. *Peanuts and Tea: A Selected Glossary of Terms Used by Drug Addicts.* Lexington, Ky: National Institute of Mental Health Clinical Research Center; 1972.

2.10.33 *Serial Publications.*—If a monograph or report is one of a series, include the name of the series and the number of the publication.

1. McNulty JG. *Radiology of the Liver.* Philadelphia, Pa: WB Saunders Co; 1977:13. Saunders Monographs in Clinical Radiology.
2. Abbott MH, Folstein SE, Jensen BA, Pyeritz RE. Cognitive and psychiatric features of 68 persons with homocystinuria. In: Program and abstracts of the 34th annual meeting of the American Society of Human Genetics; October 30-November 2, 1983; Norfolk, Va. Abstract 217.

2.10.34 *Theses and Dissertations.*—Titles are given in italics. References to these should include the location of the university (or other institution), its name, and year of completion. If it has been published, the publisher's name and location should also be given.

1. Raymond CA. *Uncovering Ideology: Occupational Health in the Mainstream and Advocacy Press, 1970-1982.* Ithaca, NY: Cornell University; 1983. Thesis.
2. Van Praag HM. *Monoamine Oxidase Inhibition as a Therapeutic Principle in the Treatment of Depression.* Utrecht, the Netherlands: University of Utrecht; 1962. Thesis.

2.10.35 *Special Collections.*—References to material available only in special collections of a library take this form:

1. Hunter J. An account of the dissection of morbid bodies: a monograph or lecture. 1757;(No. 32):30-32. Available in: Library of Royal College of Surgeons, London, England.

2.10.36 *Congressional Record and Federal Register.*—References to the *Congressional Record* and *Federal Register* take these forms:

1. Bregan PR. The return of lobotomy and psychosurgery. *Congressional Record.* February 24, 1972;118:E1602-E1612.
2. Federal Motor Vehicle Standard 213: child seating systems. *Federal Register.* March 26, 1970;35:5120; amended September 23, 1970;35:14778; April 10, 1971;36:6895-6896; June 29, 1971;36:12224-12226; March 23, 1973;38:7562.
3. Inceptive grant criteria for state safety belt use laws (23 CFR 1213). *Federal Register.* April 11, 1974;39:13154.
4. Notice of proposed rule-making on Federal Vehicle Safety Standard 213: child seating systems. *Federal Register.* March 1, 1974;39:7959-7960.

2.10.37 *Statutory Publications.*—Occasionally, the need arises to cite a Congressional Act. The form for citation is as follows:

> 1. The Allied Health Profession Personnel Training Act of 1966. 42 USC §295h.

2.10.38 *Audiotapes, Videotapes.*—Occasionally, references may include citation of audiotapes or videotapes. The form for such references is as follows:

> 1. Blaustein AU, Gostein F, Demopoulos R. *Pathology of the Cervix* [tape/filmstrip]. Philadelphia, Pa: WB Saunders Co; 1974.
> 2. Platt WR. *Color Atlas and Textbook of Hematology* [slide presentation]. Philadelphia, Pa: JB Lippincott; 1975.
> 3. Ikeda S. *Techniques of Flexible Bronchofiberscopy* [videotape or 16-mm film]. Baltimore, Md: University Park Press; 1974.

2.10.39 *Unpublished Material.*—References to unpublished material may include (1) articles that have been read before a society but not published and (2) material accepted for publication but not published. Date of publication and additional data should be added when they become known.

> 1. Reinarz JA. Percutaneous lung aspiration: a useful diagnostic adjunct in pneumonia. Presented at the Ninth Interscience Conference on Antimicrobial Agents and Chemotherapy; October 19, 1974; Atlantic City, NJ.
> 2. Siegler M. The nature and limits of clinical medicine. In: Cassell EJ, Siegler M, eds. *Changing Values in Medicine.* Chicago, Ill: University of Chicago Press. In press.

In the list of references, do not include material that has been submitted for publication but has not yet been accepted. This material, with its date, should be noted in the text as "unpublished data," as follows:

> These findings have recently been corroborated (H. E. Marman, MD, unpublished data, January 1975).

> Similar findings have been noted by Roberts[6] and H. E. Marman, MD (unpublished data, 1974).

If the unpublished data referred to are those of the author, list as follows:

> Other data (H.E.M., unpublished data, 1987). . . .

Do not include "personal communications" in the list of references. The following forms may be used:

> In a conversation with H. E. Marman, MD (August 1966). . . .

> According to a letter from H. E. Marman, MD, in August 1966. . . :

> Similar findings have been noted by Roberts[6] and by H. E. Marman, MD (written communication, August 1966).

(Note that the author should give the date of the communication and indicate whether it was in conversation or in writing. Highest academic degrees should also be given.)

2.10.40 *Secondary Citations and Quotations.*—Reference may be made to one author's citation of, or quotation from, another's work. Distinguish between citation and quotation, ie, between work mentioned and words actually quoted. In the text, the name of the original author should be mentioned rather than the secondary source. (See also 2.10.25, References, Discussants.) The forms for listed references are as follows:

> 1. Hooper PJ. Cited by: Wilson CB, Cronic F. Traumatic arteriovenous fistulas involving middle meningeal vessels. *JAMA.* 1964;188:953-957.
> 2. Mitchell J. Quoted by: Goodfield GJ. *Growth of Scientific Physiology.* Mineola, NY: Dover Publications Inc; 1960:89.

2.10.41 *Classical References.*—These may deviate from the usual forms in some details. In many instances, the facts of publication are irrelevant and may be omitted. Date of publication should be given when available and pertinent.

> 1. Shakespeare W. *Midsummer Night's Dream.* Act II; scene 3; line 24.
> 2. Donne J. *Second Anniversary.* Verse 243.

For some classical references, *The Chicago Manual of Style* may be used as a guide, but use a period after an author's name.

> 3. Aristotle. *Metaphysics.* 3. 2.966^b 5-8.

In biblical references, do not abbreviate the names of books. The version may be included parenthetically if the information is provided. References to the Bible are usually included in the text, but they may occasionally appear as listed references at the end of the article.

> The story begins in Genesis 3:28.

> Paul admonished against temptation (I Corinthians 10:6-13).

> 4. I Corinthians 10:6-13 (RSV).

2.10.42 *Legal References.*—A specific style variation is used for references to legal citations. Because the system of citation used is quite complex, with numerous variations for different types of sources and among various jurisdictions, only a brief outline can be presented here. For more details, consult *A Uniform System of Citation* (1986), frequently referred to as the Harvard "blue book" because of its cover.

Method of citation: A legal reference may be included in full in the text or in a footnote, or partially in the text and partially in a footnote.

In a leading decision on informed consent (*Cobbs v Grant*, 502 P2d 1 [Cal 1972]), the California Supreme Court stated. . . .

In a leading decision on informed consent,[1] the California Supreme Court stated. . . .

In the case of *Cobbs v Grant* (502 P2d 1 [Cal 1972]). . . .

In the case of *Cobbs v Grant*[1]. . . .

Citation of cases: The citation of a case (ie, a court opinion) generally includes, in the following order, (1) the name of the case in italics (only the names of the first party on each side are used, never with "et al," and only the last names of individuals); (2) the volume number, name, and series number (if any) of the case reporter in which it is published; (3) the page in the volume on which the case begins and, if applicable, the specific page or pages on which is discussed the point for which the case is being cited; and (4) in parentheses, the name of the court that rendered the opinion (unless the court is identified by the name of the reporter) and the year of the decision. If the opinion is published in more than one reporter, the citations to each reporter (known as parallel citations) are separated by commas. Note that *v*, 2d, and 3d are standard usage in legal citations.

Canterbury v Spence, 464 F2d 772, 775 (DC Cir 1972).

(This case is published in volume 464 of the *Federal Reporter*, second series. The case begins on page 772, and the specific point for which it was cited is on page 775. The case was decided by the US Court of Appeals, District of Columbia Circuit, in 1972.)

The proper reporter to cite depends on the court that wrote the opinion. Part H of *A Uniform System of Citation* contains a complete set of tables for all current and former state and federal jurisdictions.

US Supreme Court: Cite to *US Reports* (abbreviated as US). If the case is too recent to be published there, cite to *Supreme Court Reporter* (SCt) or *US Law Week* (USLW). If an author gives a citation to *US Reports, Lawyer's Edition* (LEd), ask for the citation to *US Reports* or *Supreme Court Reporter*. Do *not* include parallel citation.

US Court of Appeals (formerly known as Circuit Courts of Appeals): Cite to *Federal Reporter*, original or second series (F or F2d). These intermediate appellate-level courts hear appeals from US district courts, federal administrative agencies, and other federal trial-level courts. There are currently 13 US Courts of Appeals, known as circuits and referred to by number (1st Cir, 2d Cir, etc) except for the District of Columbia Circuit (DC Cir) and the new Federal Circuit (Fed Cir), which hears appeals from the US Claims Court and various customs and patent cases. Citations to the *Federal Reporter* must include the circuit designation in parentheses with the year of the decision.

> *Wilcox v United States,* 387 F2d 60 (5th Cir 1967).

US District Court and Claims Courts: Cite to *Federal Supplement* (F Supp). (There is only the original series so far.) These trial-level courts are not as prolific as the appellate courts; their function is to hear the original cases rather than review them. There are over 100 of these courts, which are referred to by geographical designations that must be included in the citation (eg, the Northern District of Illinois [ND Ill], the Central District of California [CD Cal], *but* District of New Jersey [D NJ], as New Jersey has only one federal district).

> *Sierra Club v Froehlke,* 359 F Supp 1289 (SD Tex 1973).

State Courts: Cite to the appropriate official (ie, state-sanctioned and state-financed) reporter (if any) *and* the appropriate regional reporter. Most states have separate official reporters for their highest and intermediate appellate courts (eg, *Illinois Reports* and *Illinois Appellate Reports),* but the regional reporters include cases from both levels. (State trial court opinions are generally not published.) Official reporters are always listed first, although an increasing number of states are no longer publishing them. The regional reporters are the *Atlantic Reporter* (A or A2d), *Northeastern Reporter* (NE or NE2d), *Southeastern Reporter* (SE2d), *Southern Reporter* (So or So2d), *Northwestern Reporter* (NW or NW2d), *Southwestern Reporter* (SW or SW2d), and *Pacific Reporter* (P or P2d). If only the regional reporter citation is given, the name of the court must appear in parentheses with the year of the decision. If the opinion is from the highest court of a state (usually but not always known as the supreme court), the abbreviated state name is sufficient (except for Ohio St); otherwise the full name of the court is abbreviated (eg, Ill App, NJ Super Ct App Div, NY App Div). A third, also unofficial, reporter is published for a few states; citation solely to these reporters must include the court name (eg, *California Reporter* [Cal Rptr], *Illinois Decisions* [Ill Dec], *New York Supplement* [NYS]).

> *People v Carpenter,* 28 Ill2d 116, 190 NE2d 738 (1963).
>
> *Webb v Stone,* 445 SW2d 842 (Ky 1969).

When a case has been reviewed or otherwise dealt with by a higher court, the subsequent history of the case should be given in the citation. If the year is the same for both opinions, include it only at the end of the citation. The phrases indicating the subsequent history are set off by commas, italicized, and abbreviated (eg, *aff'd* [affirmed by the higher court], *rev'd* [reversed], *vacated, appeal dismissed, cert denied* [application for a writ of certiorari, ie, a request that a court hear an appeal, has been denied]).

> *Glazer v Glazer*, 374 F2d 390 (5th Cir), *cert denied*, 389 US 831 (1967).

(This opinion was written by the US Court of Appeals for the Fifth Circuit in 1967. In the same year, the US Supreme Court was asked to review the case in an application for a writ of certiorari, but denied the request. This particular subsequent history is important because it indicates that the case has been taken to the highest court available and thus strengthens the case's value as precedent for future legal decisions.)

Citation of statutes: Once a bill is enacted into law by the US Congress, it is integrated into the US Code (USC). Citations of statutes include the title number (similar to a chapter number) and the section number.

> 33 USC §407.

(Section 407 of title 33 of the US Code)

> Environmental Quality Improvement Act of 1970, 42 USC §4371.
>
> *But:* IRC §501(c)(3).

(While it is part of the US Code, the Internal Revenue Code is commonly referred to by its own nomenclature. The section numbers in any act are not necessarily retained in the US Code.)

If a federal statute has not yet been codified, cite to Statutes at Large (abbreviated Stat, preceded by a volume number, and followed by a page number), if available, and the Public Law number of the statute.

> Pub L No. 93-627, 88 Stat 2126.

Citation forms for state statutes vary considerably. The tables in part H of *A Uniform System of Citation* list examples for each state.

> Ill Rev Stat ch 38, §2.

(Section 2 of chapter 38 of Illinois Revised Statutes)

> Fla Stat §202.

(Section 202 of Florida Statutes)

> Mich Comp Laws §145.

(Section 145 of Michigan Compiled Laws)

> Wash Rev Code §45.

(Section 45 of Revised Code of Washington)

2.10   References

Cal Corp Code §300.

(Section 300 of California Corporations Code)

Citation of federal administrative regulations: Federal regulations are published in the *Federal Register* and then codified in the Code of Federal Regulations.

41 *Federal Register* 16950.

40 CFR §247.

(Section 247 of title 40 of the Code of Federal Regulations; title and section numbers for CFR do not necessarily correspond to those for USC.)

But: Treas Reg §1.52.

(Regulations promulgated by the Internal Revenue Service retain their unique format.)

Citation forms for state administrative regulations are especially diverse. Again, part H in *A Uniform System of Citation* lists the appropriate form for each state.

Citation of congressional hearings: Include the full title of the hearing, the subcommittee (if any) and committee name, the number and session of the Congress, the date, and a short description if desired.

Hearings Before the Consumer Subcommittee of the Senate Committee on Commerce, 90th Cong, 1st Sess (1965) (testimony of William Stewart, MD, surgeon general).

Citations to services: Many legal materials, including some cases and administrative materials, are published by commercial "services," often in looseleaf format. These services attempt to provide a comprehensive overview of rapidly changing areas of the law (eg, tax law, labor law, securities regulation) and are updated frequently, sometimes weekly. The citation should include the volume number of the service, its abbreviated title, the publisher's name (also abbreviated), the paragraph or section or page number, and the date.

7 Sec Reg Guide (P-H) ¶2333 (1984).

(Volume 7, paragraph 2333 of the *Securities Regulation Guide*, published by Prentice-Hall)

54 Ins L Rep (CCH) 137 (1979).

(Volume 54, page 137 of *Insurance Law Reports*, published by Commerce Clearing House)

32

4 OSH Rep (BNA) 750 (1980).

(Volume 4, page 750 of the *Occupational Safety and Health Reporter*, published by the Bureau of National Affairs)

2.11   **Legends.**—Legends are brief captions that should identify and describe the illustrations without including the obvious. (*Avoid:* "Photograph of . . . .) AMA publications attempt to limit each legend to approximately 40 words, although multiple-part figures may require more explanation. Reference to the text or to other figure legends may be used to shorten legends.

Fig 4.—The course of hepatitis delta virus infection in a carrier of hepatitis B surface antigen with chronic active hepatitis (CAH). His disease evolved to chronic persistent hepatitis (CPH). Symbols are explained in the legend for Fig 3.

Fig 7.—Separate category of cutaneous adnexal carcinomas (see the text for discussion), which are composed of basaloid cells that form large numbers of tubular (ductal) structures and cribriform or solid nests (hematoxylin-eosin, ×25).

In bar graphs or charts, keys may also be used to shorten the legends.

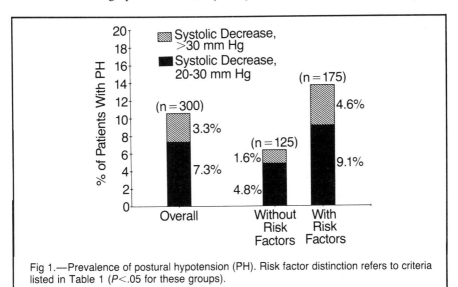

Fig 1.—Prevalence of postural hypotension (PH). Risk factor distinction refers to criteria listed in Table 1 ($P<.05$ for these groups).

Brief keys, however, may be included in the legend easily.

Age-specific incidence in men (shaded bars) and women (unshaded bars).

But, attempt to be consistent throughout a manuscript in the descriptions of the symbols in the illustrations; for example, if *shaded* and *unshaded* are used in one figure, do not switch to *tinted* and *untinted* or *closed* and *open* in another. Do, however, use the words that best describe what is shown; *stippled*, *hatched*, and *crosshatched*, for example, each have a distinct meaning.

2.11.1   *Figure Designations.*—Most figure legends are set flush left and begin with the figure designation (eg, Fig 1, Fig 2), followed by a period and an em dash. Legends consist of complete sentences or noun phrases and necessary modifiers and conclude with a period. If there is only one figure, the legend begins flush left *without* a figure designation.

> The proposed pathogenesis of, factors involved in, and potential therapies for bronchopulmonary dysplasia (BPD).

Certain journal features, such as quizzes, use no legend with the figure other than the figure designation. In these cases, the full word ''Figure'' is written out: Figure 2. (Note that these, too, conclude with a period.) In these cases, the legend is centered, not flush left.

In other special circumstances, such as a news item that includes a figure, the name of the person pictured is usually used as the legend. The legend is centered but does *not* take a final period.

2.11.2   *Parts of Figures.*—Some figures may consist of several parts, or a primary part and an inset that shows an enlargement of a section of the illustration. If the parts all share much of the same explanation, parenthetical mention of the parts is most appropriate.

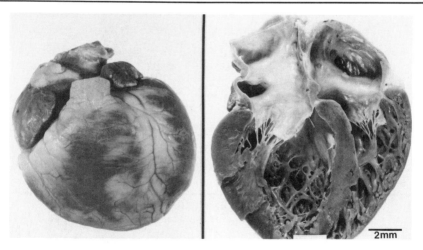

Fig 2.—Globular myopathic heart (left) with four-chamber enlargement on section in four-chamber echocardiographic plane (right).

Usually, however, the parts of the figure are described in separate sentences, beginning with the part designation, followed by a comma. The initial letter of the description also takes a capital letter.

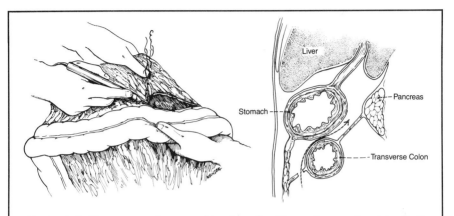

Fig 3.—Left, The pancreas is exposed by dissecting the greater omentum from its attachment to the transverse colon. The stomach and the omentum are then reflected upward to give access to the lesser omental sac. Right, Sagittal section shows the approach to the pancreas (arrow).

In other cases, the parts of a figure may be treated in run-on fashion, like a series.

Cyst types. I is an extrahepatic bile duct cyst; II, diverticulum of the common bile duct; III, choledochocele; IV, combined intrahepatic and extrahepatic bile duct cysts; and V, cysts demonstrating both isolated and diffuse cystic dilatation of intrahepatic bile ducts.

2.11   Legends

When a figure has many parts, it becomes cumbersome to call the parts "top left," etc. In these cases, capital letters or roman numerals are often used to refer to the parts of the figure.

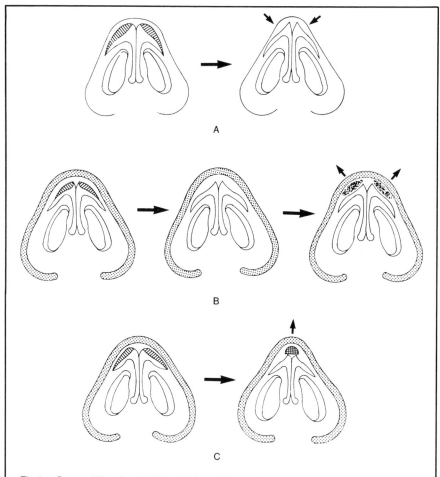

Fig 4.—Supramid implant in thick-skin flap. A shows thin-skin tip undergoing alar cartilage resection; B, thick-skin tip undergoing alar cartilage resection; and C, Supramid implant in thick-skin tip.

The figure should be referred to in the text by its general and specific designation, eg, Fig 2, left, or Fig 3, A, or Fig 5, I, unless, of course, the entire figure is cited. Then Fig 3, for example, is correct.

In some cases, even though an illustration has only one part, the layout may necessitate a designation as to location.

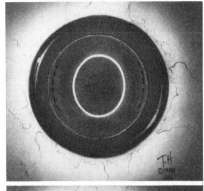

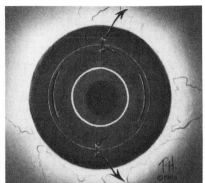

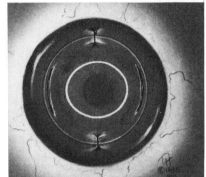

Fig 5.—Top left, Unguarded diamond knife is used to incise donor cornea tissue in steep meridian (180°) 0.5 mm central to the graft/host wound (broken lines). Steep meridian is indicated by oval keratoscopic light reflex.

Fig 6.—Top right, Deepened incisions are extended until circular keratoscopic light reflex is obtained. Compression sutures are placed through the graft/host wound (90% depth) perpendicular to relaxing incisions.

Fig 7.—Bottom, Compression sutures are tied with a slip knot to achieve 100% overcorrection. Keratoscopic light reflex indicates that new steep axis is at 90°.

When these figures are cited in the text, they should *not* include a position designation; for example, Fig 5 would simply be cited as Fig 5, not Fig 5, top left.

2.11.3 *Symbols, Arrows, Arrowheads, and Abbreviations.*—Such markers as arrows, arrowheads, letters, or other symbols draw readers' attention to items illustrated. Any symbol, arrow, arrowhead, or abbreviation in a figure should be explained in the legend.

Fig 1.—Distribution of aminopyrine breath test and antithrombin III values in controls (C) and in patients with liver disease. S indicates steatosis; SF, steatofibrosis; LC, liver cirrhosis; AH, acute hepatitis; and CH, chronic hepatitis.

Fig 2.—Representative patient who received an estimated uniform total-body gamma exposure of 3.3 Gy. Broken line indicates prediction of neutrophil profile based on early cytogenetic studies; solid line, actual neutrophil profile as measured in days following the accident.

2.11   Legends

Abbreviations may be expanded collectively, at the end of the legend, as noted above; however, expansion is most eloquently done as a part of the legend itself, if possible.

> Fig 2.—Correlations between changes ($\Delta\%$) in renal blood flow (RBF), cardiac output (CO), and mean arterial pressure (MAP) during nitrendipine therapy.

As noted earlier in this section, if several illustrations share many of the same abbreviations and symbols, full explanation in the first figure legend is adequate, and subsequent legends may refer back to it.

2.11.4   *Photomicrographs.*—Photomicrographs should include stain and magnification. If the original illustration has been modified (enlarged or reduced), the original magnification should also be noted.

> Fig 1.—Left hilar lymph node with typical targetoid follicles separated by a capillary-rich interfollicular area (hematoxylin-eosin, $\times 100$).

> Fig 2.—Small peripheral nerve in subcutaneous fat shows a small vascular channel filled with pleomorphic cells and surrounded by lymphoplasmacytic reaction (hematoxylin-eosin, original magnification $\times 400$).

In figures with several parts, the stains and/or magnifications may be noted at the end rather than after the description of each part.

> Fig 5.—Proliferating undifferentiated cells fill and distend tortuous thin-walled blood vessels in subcutaneous fat of an excision specimen from the lateral aspect of the right knee (hematoxylin-eosin, original magnification $\times 100$ [left], $\times 250$ [right]).

Note: Electron micrographs may specify only magnification, often without a stain.

> Fig 3.—Transmission electron micrograph showing remnants of a capillary. Leukocytes, cellular debris, and platelets are present. Endothelial cells are not seen. Tapetum is at bottom right (original magnification $\times 8900$).

2.11.5   *Patient Identification.*—If an illustration refers to a specific case report in the text, the patient or case may be referred to as follows:

> Color Fig 3.—Patient 2. Saddle-nose deformity. Note small ulcerations at the nasal vestibule and on the collapsed bridge.

> Fig 1.—Clinical appearance of tumor in patient 1. Note the subtle surface changes.

> Fig 4.—Deeply infiltrating ducts, cords, and strands of neoplasm within desmoplastic stroma (case 2) (hematoxylin-eosin, original magnification $\times 50$).

38

Illustrations   2.12

2.11.6   *Armed Forces Institute of Pathology (AFIP) Negative Number.*—If an AFIP negative number is included in the legend, give it as follows:

> Fig 1.—Case 2. Fragmented needle biopsy specimen reveals cirrhosis and carcinoma (arrow) (AFIP Neg 80-3248; hematoxylin-eosin, original magnification ×60).

2.11.7   *Figures Reproduced From Other Sources.*—If an illustration has been published previously, even by the same author, written permission for its use must be obtained from the copyright holder (usually the publisher). The original source should be acknowledged. This may be done by citing in the legend a reference that is included in the reference list.

> Fig 1.—Effect of chronic hepatic venous congestion (from Ayers[10]).

> Fig 1.—Basic design of osteofasciocutaneous flap containing skin and bone supplied by branches of the radial artery that run in fascial septa between muscles of the forearm (adapted from Timmons[1]).

Otherwise, acknowledgment is made in a footnote at the end of the article (See 2.8.4, Acknowledgments, Reproduction of Figures and Tables).

2.12   Illustrations.—Illustrations include any graphic material used to increase or enhance the understanding of the text. These may be halftones (tone patterns of shapes from white through black of a continuous tone image made by photographing or scanning through a finely ruled screen with crossing opaque lines; the screening reduces the tones to a dot formation for reproduction by printing), or line art (graphs, algorithms, tracings, schematic drawings, charts), or combinations of these two. Occasionally color illustrations are used. Each illustration should be cited, in consecutive numerical order, in the text and accompanied by a legend (see 2.11, Legends), except in those rare instances (such as a Photo/Essay in *JAMA*) in which the illustrations may not be referred to directly.

2.12.1   *Technical Specifications.*—Each journal has its own technical requirements for illustrations submitted. This section will illustrate those for the 10 AMA journals.

Black-and-white illustrations: These should be submitted as unmounted, high-contrast, glossy photographic prints. The preferred size is 13 × 17 cm (5 × 7 in). Line drawings, graphs, and charts should be professionally drawn, photographed, and sent as prints. Do not send original artwork. If it is essential to use computer-generated graphics, submit a high-contrast, glossy print of a clean printout. Avoid using a dot matrix printer for preparation of line art as the quality is inadequate for good reproduction. Do not submit original roentgenograms; rather, send high-contrast, right-reading glossy prints. Be aware that illustrations that already have a horizontal or vertical linear pattern when submitted (eg, photographs from

39

printed materials, scans) will result in an undesirable wavelike or checkered effect (moiré pattern) when the halftone is photographed or scanned through a screen.

Submit three sets of illustrations. On one set, suggested cropping may be marked on the top and right margins. On the reverse, attach a gummed label, with the figure number, name of the author, journal name, and an arrow indicating the top. (*Note:* Prepare the label *before* affixing it to the figure.)

Four-color illustrations: These illustrations—made up a full range of color values from the basic primary colors, red, yellow, and blue, and black—should be submitted as positive four-color transparencies, preferably 35-mm slides. Color prints (commercial type C or standard Kodacolor prints) or 4 × 5-in transparencies will also be accepted if no 35-mm transparencies are available. Send one set of transparencies and two sets of unmounted glossy prints. Provide the figure number, journal name, manuscript number, and an arrow indicating the top on the cardboard frame of the transparency. The glossy film side of the transparency should always be up and the emulsion side of the transparency down for the correct image position, unless otherwise indicated. Do not submit color negatives.

Transparencies should never be mounted in glass for shipment. Enclose transparencies and prints in an envelope packed between two pieces of pressboard and marked "Do not bend."

There is no charge for reproducing four-color illustrations in *JAMA.* In the nine AMA specialty journals, the author's share of the reproduction expenses is $400 per page for as many as six illustrations. For each illustration over six the author will be charged $48. Special effects on each illustration (addition of lettering and arrows, opaquing out of background, adding inserts, etc) require an additional fee. A letter of intent to pay the color fee must accompany submission.

2.12.2   *Lettering and Symbols on Figures.*—If letters or symbols (such as arrows) would aid the understanding of an illustration, either (1) put them on the glossy figure using press-on art type or, (2) using a duplicate set of illustrations, indicate where you would like the graphics department to place these symbols. Never mark on a four-color transparency.

Lettering and symbols should be matched in size and weight to the illustration so that when the illustration is appropriately reduced or enlarged for publication, these letters or symbols will not be disproportionately large or small.

2.12.3   *Scales.*—If it is important to indicate scale on an illustration, rather than including a ruler in the photograph it is preferable to use a bar, with the size of the bar shown on the figure directly below the bar or given in the legend.

2.12.4 *Grouping of Photographs.*—If several photographs are conceived of as a group (for example, "before" and "after" photographs of a patient who has undergone plastic surgery or a halftone and a schematic drawing of an operative procedure), it is preferable to group these so that they are parts of a single figure rather than two sequential figures. This ensures their grouping in the layout. (*Note:* Indicate grouping by placement designation, eg, top left, top right, bottom left, bottom right, *not* by mounting.)

2.12.5 *Insets.*—An enlargement of a section of a photograph may easily be shown by circumscribing the area to be enlarged on the full photograph and showing that enlargement in an inset, placed in the corner of the full illustration and set off with a white rule.

2.12.6 *Axis Captions.*—On line art graphs, each axis should be clearly labeled with the quantity measured and the units of measure used. Although customary abbreviations for units of measure (see 11.11, Abbreviations, Units of Measure) and other symbols should be used, if the *only* axis caption is an abbreviation it should be spelled out so that it is easily visible (eg, instead of s use Seconds; instead of $, Dollars; instead of °, Degrees).

2.12.7 *Numbering of Black-and-White and Four-Color Illustrations in a Single Manuscript.*—If both black-and-white and four-color illustrations appear in a manuscript, they are numbered—as are black-and-white-only or four-color-only—sequentially (Fig 1, Fig 2, etc) *unless* the four-color illustrations are interspersed with the black-and-white illustrations. In this case, sequential numbering would raise the cost of the four-color reproduction as the four-color illustrations could not all be placed on one page. To avoid this expense, in this situation number the black-and-white illustrations and the four-color illustrations separately: Fig 1, Fig 2, etc for the black-and-white illustrations and Color Fig 1, Color Fig 2, etc for the four-color. If in doubt as to the fit of the six color illustrations on one page, check with the graphics department.

2.12.8 *Photographic Consent.*—Signed consent forms must be submitted by authors for photographs in which patients can be identified. In some instances the subject may be identifiable even when facial features are not visible. Masking the eyes does not obviate the need for obtaining permission, although it may be a condition for granting permission. It is advisable to obtain appropriate consents when the photographs are taken or before, since it is often difficult to locate patients or other subjects at a later time. Figure 8 is a sample form for obtaining consent for taking and publishing clinical photographs of patients in connection with the rendering of professional services. This form would allow for publication of photographs at a later time if the treating physician thought publication would benefit medical research, education, or science. This form may not be appropriate in all circumstances.

For pictures of minors (persons younger than 18 years) or wards, written permission must be obtained from *both* parents or from the legal guardian. (This is required by the AMA even though some states' laws may not require the signature of both parents.) If the parents of a minor are divorced, permission must be obtained from both for the use of the photograph. If a parent is deceased, the permission of the surviving parent is sufficient.

Consent for Taking and Publication of Photographs

Patient _____ Place _____ Date _____
    (Print name)

In connection with the medical services that I am receiving from my physician, Dr _____, I consent that photographs may be taken of me or parts of my body and published under the following conditions:

1. The photographs may be taken only with the consent of my physician and under such conditions and at such times as may be approved by my physician.

2. The photographs shall be taken by my physician or by a photographer approved by my physician.

3. The photographs shall be used for medical records and if in the judgment of my physician, medical research, education, or science will be benefited by their use, such photographs and information relating to my case may be published and republished, either separately or in connection with each other, in professional journals or medical books, or used for any other purpose that my physician may deem proper in the interest of medical education, knowledge, or research; provided, however, that it is specifically understood that in any such publication or use I shall not be identified by name.

4. The aforementioned photographs may be modified or retouched in any way that my physician, at his or her discretion, may consider desirable.

Signed _____
    (Patient)

Witness _____

Figure 8.

If a minor is married, consult state law. Figure 9 is a sample form for obtaining permission from both parents of a minor child to take and publish photographs in connection with medical services. This form should be modified appropriately when one parent is deceased, when the minor has a legal guardian, or in other circumstances as appropriate.

For pictures of persons who are legally incompetent, written permission must be obtained from the legal guardian or conservator.

Publication of a composite photograph of various family members requires written authorization from each adult in the picture and from both parents (or legal guardian) of each child in the picture. The permission of the senior member of the family in such cases is not sufficient.

Consent for Taking and Publication of Photographs of Minors

Patient _____ Place _____ Date _____
    (Print name)

In connection with the medical services that are being rendered by Dr _____ to the above-named patient, we consent that photographs may be taken of the said patient or of parts of his or her body and published under the following conditions:

1. The photographs may be taken only with the consent of the above-named physician and under such conditions and at such times as may be approved by him or her.

2. The photographs shall be taken by the above-named physician or by a photographer approved by him or her.

3. The photographs shall be used for medical records and if, in the judgment of the above-named physician, medical research, education, or science will be benefited by their use, such photographs and information relating to this case regarding the above-named patient may be published and republished, either separately or in connection with each other, in professional journals or medical books, or used for any other purpose that the above-named physician may deem proper in the interest of medical education, knowledge, or research; provided, however, that it is specifically understood that in any such publication or use the patient shall not be identified by name.

4. The aforementioned photographs may be modified or retouched in any way that the above-named physician, at his or her discretion, may consider desirable.

We warrant by our signatures below that we are the parents of the above-named patient, and that he or she is _____ years of age.

                              Signed _____
                                        (Father)

_____

Date   (Print name)

                              Signed _____
                                        (Mother)

_____

Date   (Print name)

Witness _____

Figure 9.

2.13   Tables

2.13   Tables.—Tables should be self-explanatory and should supplement, not duplicate, the text. They should provide a more vivid and concise presentation of data than is possible in the text. Each table should be typed double-spaced on a separate sheet of paper. Tables should not be submitted in reduced type. Oversized paper should not be used, nor should several pieces of paper be taped together. Do not submit tables as photographs. There are various "right" ways to construct tables. What follows is based on AMA journals' style.

2.13.1   *Tables vs Graphs and Figures*.—If the intent is to highlight specific numbers, tables are preferable. If, instead, the intent is to present a pattern or trend, a major change or difference, an illustration would be more suitable.

2.13.2   *Tables Containing Supplementary Information*.—Tables containing supplementary information too extensive to be published in the journal may be deposited (by the copy editor) with the National Auxiliary Publications Service (see 2.15, National Auxiliary Publications Service [NAPS]) or made available by the author (see 2.8, Acknowledgments). In either event, an appropriate statement should be added to the text.

2.13.3   *Tables vs Tabulations*.—In some cases it is desirable to set material off from the text, even though this material comprises only two columns or two rows of data or is a listing. In these cases, a tabulation serves the purpose. Tabulations have boldface column headings and no rules. There should be a 4-point space above and below the tabulation. The tabulation, which is *not* numbered, should fit in a single column. It should be set centered in the column and may be set in reduced type.

Assume that two memories are stored in the system. Each memory corresponds to a specification of the state (either "on" or "off") of all five neurons:

	n_1	n_2	n_3	n_4	n_5
Memory 1	+	−	+	+	−
Memory 2	+	+	+	−	−

44

The causes of the complications follow.

Cause	No.
Drugs	
Antihypertensives	8
Physiologic modulators	7
Cancer therapy	6
Diabetes therapy	5
Anticonvulsants	4
Cardiac medications	2
Antibiotics	2
Miscellaneous	1
Total	**35**
Procedures	
Dialysis	2
Inpatient surgery	4
Outpatient surgery	1
Diagnostic procedures	2
Total	**9**
Blood transfusion	1
Infection (hospital acquired)	1
Radiotherapy	1
Total	**47**

2.13.4 *Numbering.*—Tables should be numbered consecutively according to their first citation in the text. If there is only one table in the article, it is referred to in the text simply as "the Table." The layout artist will attempt to place each table as close as possible to its first citation in the text.

2.13.5 *Titles.*—Each table should have a brief title. Further explanation, if needed, may be included in a footnote (see 2.13.6, Tables, Setup). The table number is part of the table title. If there is only one table in an article, the caption should contain only the title.

Table 1.—Correlation of Primary Tumor Site With DNA Content

Table 2.—Correlation of Primary Tumor Site With Stage

Immunoassay Results in Mice Irradiated via Head vs Pelvic Portal

(Single table in article)

As can be seen in these examples, in AMA journals the table number is followed by a period and an em dash (see 6.5.1, Punctuation, Em Dash). Note that there is *no* punctuation following the title.

2.13   Tables

Tables that are continued from one page to the next (this does *not* refer to tables set in a double-page spread) repeat the title as indicated below, as well as repeating the column headings.

Table 3.—Clinical Characteristics of Patients (cont)

2.13.6   Setup.—In setting up a table, consider which comparisons are primary. Since readers usually make comparisons first *across* the table and then *down*, the primary comparisons should be shown horizontally, if space considerations allow. In the diagram below, the major elements in a table are indicated. Each will be discussed separately.

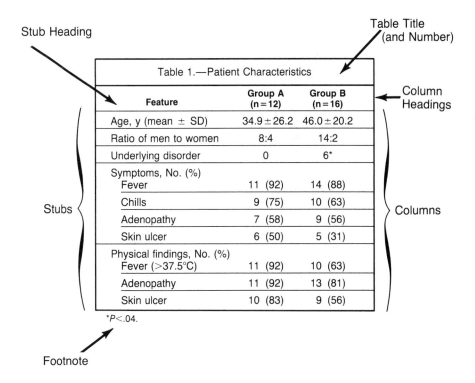

Table 1.—Patient Characteristics

Feature	Group A (n = 12)	Group B (n = 16)
Age, y (mean ± SD)	34.9 ± 26.2	46.0 ± 20.2
Ratio of men to women	8:4	14:2
Underlying disorder	0	6*
Symptoms, No. (%)		
Fever	11 (92)	14 (88)
Chills	9 (75)	10 (63)
Adenopathy	7 (58)	9 (56)
Skin ulcer	6 (50)	5 (31)
Physical findings, No. (%)		
Fever (>37.5°C)	11 (92)	10 (63)
Adenopathy	11 (92)	13 (81)
Skin ulcer	10 (83)	9 (56)

*P<.04.

46

Column headings: Each column should have a heading and these headings are set in boldface type. Column headings should be brief and should indicate what is shown in the column below. If appropriate, the unit of measure should be indicated in the column heading (unless it is given in the stub), following a comma. For more complex headings, use braces or give additional information in the footnotes (see Table 2).

Table 2.—Total Survival After Diagnosis of Lymphoma and Chemotherapeutic Response of Treated Patients, by Working Formulation Grade

Grade (No. of Cases)	Therapeutic Response, %*			Median Survival, mo†	Range, mo†
	Complete	Partial	None		
Intermediate (13)	38	38	24	6	1-37
High (8)	13	62	25	3	1-18
Total (21)	28	48	24	4	1-37

*Percentage of treated patients with indicated response.
†All cases, treated and untreated.

2.13 Tables

Usually a column head should serve for the entire column, but occasionally a style variation is necessary to group data (see Table 3).

Table 3.—Non-Hodgkin's Lymphoma in Farmers in Relation to Use of Herbicides and Insecticides

Annual Days of Use	Never Used Insecticides			Ever Used Insecticides			Adjusted for Insecticide Use		
	No. of Cases	No. of Controls	Odds Ratio* (95% Confidence Interval)	No. of Cases	No. of Controls	Odds Ratio (95% Confidence Interval)	No. of Cases	No. of Controls	Odds Ratio (95% Confidence Interval)
Herbicides									
0	90	474	1.0	4	21	1.1 (0.3, 3.5)	94	495	1.0
1-5	11	57	1.1 (0.5, 2.3)	8	43	1.2 (0.5, 2.9)	19	100	1.1 (0.6, 2.1)
≥6	6	18	2.1 (0.7, 5.9)	12	35	2.3 (1.0, 4.9)	18	53	2.1 (0.9, 4.9)
Insecticide use, adjusted for herbicide use						1.1 (0.6, 2.2)			

Annual Days of Use	Never Used Herbicides			Ever Used Herbicides			Adjusted for Herbicide Use		
	No. of Cases	No. of Controls	Odds Ratio* (95% Confidence Interval)	No. of Cases	No. of Controls	Odds Ratio* (95% Confidence Interval)	No. of Cases	No. of Controls	Odds Ratio* (95% Confidence Interval)
Insecticides									
0	90	474	1.0	17	75	1.3 (0.7, 2.4)	107	549	1.0
1-2	9	12	0.9 (0.1, 4.2)	8	30	1.7 (0.7, 4.1)	10	42	1.2 (0.5, 2.8)
≥3	2	9	1.5 (0.2, 8.1)	12	48	1.7 (0.8, 3.5)	14	57	1.4 (0.6, 3.1)
Herbicide use, adjusted for insecticide use						1.4 (0.8, 2.4)			

*Odds ratio relative to farmers, no herbicide or insecticide use.

If all elements in a column are identical (eg, if all patients were male and there was a column indicating the patients' sex), it might be preferable to give this information in a footnote to the table and delete the column (eg, use a footnote saying that all patients were male, *or* include mention of this in the table title [eg, Table 2.—Summary of Results of Photosensitivity Phase in 100 Male Patients]).

In column headings, standard rules regarding numbers and abbreviations may be relaxed to save space, with abbreviations being expanded in a footnote (see Tables 4 and 5). However, when spacing easily allows spelling out headings, use the expansions in preference to the abbreviations. Use the capitalization style used in titles (see 2.1.6, Titles and Subtitles, Capitalization, and 8.4, Capitalization, Titles and Headings).

Table 4.—Results of Laboratory Investigation			
Date of Testing			
10/25/84	2/14/85	4/18/85	5/23/85
Bilirubin, mg/dL (μmol/L)	0.5 (8.6)	0.6 (10.3)	16.7 (285.6)	7.9 (135.1)
Albumin, g/dL (g/L)	4.5 (45)	4.1 (41)	3.0 (30)	1.7 (17)
Globulin, g/dL (g/L)	3.3 (33)	3.8 (38)	5.9 (59)	5.3 (53)
Aspartate aminotransferase, IU/L (U/L)	39	225	1050	199
Alanine aminotransferase, IU/L (U/L)	31	235	560	133
Alkaline phosphatase, IU/L (U/L)	...	...	...	107
Prothrombin activity, %	...	...	23	21
Hepatitis B surface antigen*	+	+	+	+
Hepatitis B e antigen*	+	+	+	...
Antibody to hepatitis B core antigen IgM*	+ (1:500)†	+ (1:1500)	+ (1:1500)	+ (1:1500)

*Plus sign indicates positive result.
†A value of 1:1500 is indicative of acute hepatitis B virus infection in our laboratory.

2.13   Tables

Table 5.—Relationship of Recent Life Events and RDC* Major Depressive Disorder to Percentage of Addicts Remaining Abstinent (n = 261)

Characteristic		No. (%) of Addicts		
Recent Life Events	RDC* Major Depression	>8 Recent Life Events	Exits	Arguments
No	No	125 (58)	62 (64)	107 (60)
No	Yes	36 (39)	21 (62)	26 (42)
Yes	No	67 (33)	130 (42)	85 (37)
Yes	Yes	33 (39)	48 (29)	43 (37)
χ^2†	. . .	38.3	39.3	31.1

*RDC indicates Research Diagnostic Criteria.
†χ^2 is for linear trend and has 1 df; any value above 3.86 is significant at $P<.05$. Higher values have substantially higher significance levels.

Note that the table stubs do not always need a column heading (see Table 4), and that not all tables have stubs (see Tables 2, 3, and 5).

Table stubs: As with column headings, table stubs should be brief and should indicate what is shown in the row across. If a unit of measure is appropriate and it is not indicated in the column heading, it should be indicated in the table stub. Just as braces may be useful to clarify and organize complex column headings, indentions may be used for a similar purpose in table stubs. In the example below (Table 6), note how indention is used to list the subentries under "Adverse effects."

Table 6.—Duration of Antimicrobial Therapy and Adverse Experience Attributable to Antimicrobial Therapy in Patients Randomized to the Two Study Regimens

	Cefoxitin Plus Tobramycin Sulfate (N=51)	Clindamycin Phosphate Plus Tobramycin (N=45)
Duration of study drug therapy, d (mean ± SD)	8.5 ± 3.5*	7.6 ± 3.7*
Duration of tobramycin therapy, d (mean ± SD)	4.1 ± 1.8†	7.0 ± 3.2†
Adverse effects, No. (%)		
Rash	2 (2)	0
Diarrhea	2 (5)	3 (7.9)‡
Increase in aspartate aminotransferase level	9 (22.5)§	1 (2.6)§
Renal impairment	2 (5)	5 (13)

*$P>.05$, unpaired t test.   ‡One each with documented pseudomembranous colitis.
†$P<.001$, unpaired t test.   §$P<.05$, χ^2 with Yates' correction.

The first indention is a 1-em indention. Runovers, or secondary indentions, would take a 2-em indention, and so on as needed.

Reformatting tables: Depending on which comparisons in a table the author wishes to highlight, and on the space available, a table may require reformatting (ie, making the column headings into table stubs, and vice versa). In the two versions of Table 7, the first version shows a setup in which the primary comparison would be that between the "no wound sepsis" and "wound sepsis" groups. In the second version, which has been reformatted from the first, the primary comparison would be between "aerobes," "anaerobes," and "aerobes and anaerobes."

Cut-in heads: Where space considerations do not allow the option of reformatting, or where a large table is readily divided into parts, or two small, closely related tables would be better combined, cut-in heads are useful. In Table 8, the cut-in heads "Men" and "Women" achieve what a complex brace construction in the table headings would have achieved had space permitted and yet allow all the information to be given neatly in a single table. Note that cut-in heads are set boldface and centered and, although they have no rule below them, have a 1-point rule *above* (see next section, page 56).

Table 7.—Bacterial Densities During Operation

	No Wound Sepsis			Wound Sepsis		
	Peritoneal Exudate, CFUs·mL^{-1}	Appendix, CFUs·cm^{-2}	Wound, CFUs·cm^{-2}	Peritoneal Exudate, CFUs·mL^{-1}	Appendix, CFUs·cm^{-2}	Wound, CFUs·cm^{-2}
Aerobes						
Range	$0\text{-}5.0\times10^8$	$0\text{-}3.7\times10^6$	$0\text{-}3.2\times10^6$	$2.0\times10^4\text{-}2.0\times10^{10}$	$3.3\text{-}1.1\times10^9$	$0\text{-}2.3\times10^9$
Median	1.1×10^5*†‡	1.1×10^3†	7.1×10^1†	2.2×10^6‡	2.8×10^5	4.4×10^3
Anaerobes						
Range	$0\text{-}3.0\times10^{10}$	$0\text{-}1.1\times10^6$	$0\text{-}2.6\times10^5$	$1.6\times10^5\text{-}1.4\times10^{10}$	$1.0\times10^2\text{-}1.1\times10^7$	$0\text{-}1.1\times10^7$
Median	2.3×10^5*	3.3×10^3	7.0×10^1	1.9×10^6	1.9×10^5	7.7×10^3
Aerobes and anaerobes						
Range	$0\text{-}3.0\times10^{10}$	$0\text{-}3.7\times10^6$	$0\text{-}3.2\times10^6$	$3.0\times10^1\text{-}3.4\times10^{10}$	$0\text{-}2.3\times10^9$	$1.1\times10^2\text{-}1.1\times10^9$
Median	6.2×10^5	1.0×10^4	3.1×10^2	6.3×10^6	1.1×10^5	4.6×10^5§

*Comparisons between aerobes and anaerobes within the sampling sites: $P>.01$ (all columns).
†Comparisons between sampling sites within the aerobes and anaerobes: $P<.01$ (all rows).
‡Comparisons between no wound sepsis and wound sepsis for each sampling site, for aerobes, anaerobes, and both together: $P<.01$.
§Infective dose.

Version 2:

Table 7.—Bacterial Densities During Operation

	Aerobes		Anaerobes		Aerobes and Anaerobes	
	Range	Median	Range	Median	Range	Median
No wound sepsis						
Peritoneal exudate, CFUs·mL^{-1}	0-5.0×10^8	1.1×10^{5}*†‡	0-3.0×10^{10}	2.3×10^{5}*	0-3.0×10^{10}	6.2×10^5
Appendix, CFUs·cm^{-2}	0-3.7×10^6	1.1×10^{3}†	0-1.1×10^6	3.3×10^3	0-3.7×10^6	1.0×10^4
Wound, CFUs·cm^{-2}	0-3.2×10^6	7.1×10^{1}†	0-2.6×10^5	7.0×10^1	0-3.2×10^6	3.1×10^2
Wound sepsis						
Peritoneal exudate, CFUs·mL^{-1}	2.0×10^4-2.0×10^{10}	2.2×10^{6}‡	1.6×10^5-1.4×10^{10}	1.9×10^6	3.0×10^1-3.4×10^{10}	6.3×10^6
Appendix, CFUs·cm^{-2}	3.3-1.1×10^9	2.8×10^5	1.0×10^2-1.1×10^7	1.9×10^5	0-2.3×10^9	1.1×10^5
Wound, CFUs·cm^{-2}	0-2.3×10^9	4.4×10^3	0-1.1×10^7	7.7×10^3	1.1×10^2-1.1×10^9	4.6×10^{5}§

*Comparisons between aerobes and anaerobes within the sampling sites: $P>.01$ (all rows).
†Comparisons between sampling sites within the aerobes and anaerobes: $P<.01$ (all columns).
‡Comparisons between no wound sepsis and wound sepsis for each sampling site, for aerobes, anaerobes, and both together: $P<.01$.
§Infective dose.

Table 8.—Drug Use in Adolescence and Young Adulthood as Predictors of Drug Use in Adulthood*

Drugs Used	Cigarettes		Alcohol		Marijuana		Illicit Drugs		3 Prescription Drugs	
	r	β	r	β	r	β	r	β	r	β
Men										
Time 1: ever used										
Cigarettes	.32†	.02‡	.15§	.02	.17†	−.03	.17†	.01	.04	.07
Alcohol	.14§	.04	.18†	.03	.21†	.01	.14§	−.04	−.03	−.09
Marijuana	.10‖	−.03	.13§	.02	.29†	−.01‡	.30†	.08‡	.05	.05
Other illicit drugs	.07	.02	.09	.02	.21†	.03	.23†	.08	.02	.00
Used between time 1 and 12 mo before Adult Survey										
Model 1										
Cigarettes	.80†	.82†	.19†	.11‖	.22†	.09‖	.23†	.14§	.02	.02
Alcohol	.17†	.00	.59†	.52†	.26†	−.06¶	.23†	.01	−.04	−.06
Marijuana	.20†	.06	.33†	.12‖	.78†	.77†	.51†	.40†	.06	.07
Illicit drugs (10 classes)										
Total R^2	.67		.42		.63		.35		.05	
Model 2										
Cigarettes	.80†	.81†	.19†	.11‖	.22†	.08¶	.23†	.07¶	.02	.01
Alcohol	.17†	.00	.59†	.54†	.26†	−.01	.23†	.00	−.04	−.06
Marijuana	.18†	.00	.28†	.06	.72†	.61‖	.55†	.09¶	.05	−.02
Illicit drugs (9 classes)	.24†	.08¶	.23†	.01	.57†	.12‖	.74†	.64†	.12‖	.16‖
Total R^2	.68		.41		.57		.58		.06	

54

Table 8.—Drug Use in Adolescence and Young Adulthood as Predictors of Drug Use in Adulthood* (cont)

	Frequency Used in Past Year in Adulthood									
	Cigarettes		Alcohol		Marijuana		Illicit Drugs		3 Prescription Drugs	
Drugs Used	r	β	r	β	r	β	r	β	r	β
Women										
Time 1: ever used										
Cigarettes	.34†	.00‡	.17†	.08†	.21†	.06‡	.08	−.04	.08	.06
Alcohol	.19†	.01	.21†	.08†	.16†	.01	.06	.00	.03	.00
Marijuana	.30†	.01‡	.13§	−.05	.26†	−.01‡	.20†	−.01#	.01	−.17‡‖
Other illicit drugs	.27†	−.02	.08	−.05	.13§	−.06	.16†	.09	.16†	.22†‡
Used between time 1 and 12 mo before Adult Survey										
Model 1										
Cigarettes	.83†	.81†	.14†	.04	.21†	−.02	.16†	.07	.06	.03
Alcohol	.12§	.01	.56†	.44†	.22†	−.04	.17†	.04	.03	−.01
Illicit drugs (10 classes)	.28†	.02	.34†	.09¶	.72†	.75†	.42†	.39†	.00	−.02
Total R²	.69		.41		.56		.21		.07	
Model 2										
Cigarettes	.83†	.82†	.14†	.05	.21†	.02	.16§	.04	.06	.02
Alcohol	.12§	.02	.56†	.46†	.22†	.05	.17†	.04	.03	−.02
Marijuana	.22†	−.02	.18†	.00	.65†	.58†	.52†	.23†	.02	.00
Illicit drugs (9 classes)	.18†	.02	.15†	.01	.35†	.01	.68†	.58†	.08	.06
Total R²	.69		.40		.46		.52		.08	

*All variables listed in Table 4 were included in the regressions, but coefficients are not given. For model 1 and model 2, values are for change between time 1 (initial interview) and 12 months before time 3 (interview at 24 or 25 years of age), with months used adjusted by frequency of use in period of highest use.

†P<.001.

‡Coefficient significant when all intervening time 1 to time 3 variables are excluded from equation.

§P<.01.

‖P<.05.

¶P<.10.

#Coefficient significant at P<.10 when all intervening time 1 to time 3 drug use variables are excluded from equation.

2.13   Tables

Rules: No vertical rules should appear in tables. Horizontal rules should be clearly indicated by the copy editor if either rules or tints will be used to assist the reader in following the rows across. No rules are used in two-column or two-row tables, or in 13-pica tables. In these cases, the size makes the table "accessible" without rules. No hairline rule is set at the bottom of a table. The table may eventually be boxed, or set off at top and bottom by heavy rules, hence obviating the need for a final hairline rule.

Hairline Rules: Most of the horizontal rules that appear in AMA journal tables are hairline rules. These rules should be clearly marked for the typesetter on each table in a blanket instruction; for example, "Set hairline rules as indicated." These rules may be full (ie, from one side of the table to the other) or partial (when they separate subentries under a stub [see Table 6 for an example of a table with stubs that include subentries]).

One-Point Rules: In tables with cut-in heads, a 1-point rule, rather than a hairline rule, is used *above* the cut-in head. These rules should be marked clearly for the typesetter wherever they appear.

Alignment: Explicit instructions should be given to the typesetter regarding alignment, either on each individual table or as a "blanket" instruction. Both horizontal alignment (across rows) and vertical alignment (up and down columns) must be considered.

Horizontal Alignment: For the AMA journals, a blanket instruction for horizontal alignment is used to instruct the typesetter how to proceed. If the table stubs contain runover lines and the remaining table entries do not, the remaining table entries are set aligned across on the last runover line (see fourth and fifth stubs in the example below [Table 9]).

Table 9.—Histologic Patterns of Small Congenital Nevi		
	Characteristic	
Pattern	Present Study, % (n = 29)	Study of Stenn et al,[3] % (n = 38)
Junctional nevi	17	0
Upper patchy	59	46
Upper diffuse	3	18
Upper and lower patchy	6	18
Upper and lower diffuse	15	18

If other table entries contain runovers, however, all the table entries are set aligned across on the *first* or top line (see stubs "Carbohydrates" and "Fat" in the example below [Table 10]).

Table 10.—Diet Composition		
	Needle-Catheter-Jejunostomy Group*	**Total-Parenteral-Nutrition Group***
Amino acids	15.2	14.5
Branched chain	33.1 of total	23.3 of total
Essential	52.3 of total	47.8 of total
Nonessential	47.7 of total	52.2 of total
Carbohydrates (source)	82.4 (maltodextrin)	85.5 (dextrose)
Fat (source)	2.5 (safflower oil)	10 (intravenous fat emulsion)[†]

*Values given in percentages.
†Intralipid 10%, KabiVitrum Inc, Berkeley, Calif.

Vertical Alignment: Although it is tempting to make a similar blanket style for vertical alignment in tables, here a consideration of each individual table—and, moreover, each column within a table—is advised for the best overall visual presentation of data. A few guidelines are listed below:

- Align columns on common elements (see Tables 11 and 12) such as decimal points, plus and minus signs, hyphens (used in ranges), virgules, and parentheses whenever possible.
- Center ellipses.
- If table entries consist of lengthy text, use flush left format, with 1-em indent for runovers (see Table 13).
- If entries in a column are mixed (ie, if no common element exists), give primary consideration to the visual aspect of the entire table and the type of material presented. (See Tables 14 through 17.)

2.13 Tables

Note that in Table 11 columns are aligned on a common element, in this case plus and minus signs.

Table 11.—Plasma Amino Acid Levels*

Amino Acid	Time After CLP or Sham Operation, h					
	4		8		16	
	Control (N=8)	CLP (N=8)	Control (N=9)	CLP (N=9)	Control (N=9)	CLP (N=6)
Asp	19±1	23±2	20±2	32±5	16±1	55±7†
Hpr	38±3	34±2	28±2‡	19±1†	39±3	16±4†
Thr	148±15	104±10†	131±5	145±8	246±13‡§	153±9†
Ser	198±11	161±12	218±6	183±15	293±13‡§	190±12§
Asn	39±2	30±1	35±3	35±1	58±2†§	25±9†
Glu	84±4	77±3	61±6	101±16	49±5	257±71†
Gln	518±19	465±25	495±28	435±11	622±21	514±83
Pro	129±8	81±3†	102±7‡	93±4	159±5†§	92±9†
Gly	373±22	371±22	370±11	411±12	534±36‡§	386±25
Ala	417±26	267±22†	280±10†	279±27	368±22‡	409±49
Cit	114±11	111±10	94±5	128±6†	111±6	71±7†
Val	103±5	80±4	106±6	187±17†	226±13‡§	172±17†
Met	36±2	25±2	37±1	28±1	55±2	44±3
Ile	61±4	44±3	58±4	97±10†	113±5†§	79±5†
Leu	91±7	72±4	91±7	168±16†	186±10‡§	145±12†
Tyrosine	42±2	33±2†	40±1	58±4†	62±3†§	58±5
Phenylalanine	51±3	45±2	60±3	84±4†	63±3‡	93±5†
Try	43±3	39±2	39±3	53±2†	40±2	31±2†
Ornithine	45±4	34±2	43±2	88±11†	59±7	143±13†
Lys	338±15	302±16	222±15‡	241±13	455±18‡§	325±21†
Histadine	65±2	60±3	61±3	89±4†	63±3	85±5†
Arginine	75±6	62±3	85±4	65±10†	133±10	33±4†
Total	3026±109	2484±125†	2678±79	2999±122	3947±133‡§	3341±97†

*CLP indicates cecal ligation and perfusion. All values are in micromoles per liter (mean±SEM). ‡Significant difference vs control at 4 hours.
†Significant difference vs control at the same time point. §Significant difference vs control at 8 hours.

Note that in Table 12 columns are aligned on a common element, in this case parentheses. Also, the ellipses (which don't have this common element) are centered. (Another common element, the decimal point, is superseded by the choice of parentheses as the common element.)

Table 12.—Mean (SEM) Values for Cognitive Measures Before and/or After Naloxone or Placebo*

	Placebo		Naloxone Hydrochloride, 0.1 mg/kg		Naloxone Hydrochloride, 2.0 mg/kg	
	Before	After‡	Before	After	Before	After
Attention						
Digit span†	4.8 (0.50)	5.3 (0.35)	5.1 (0.33)	4.8 (0.30)	4.7 (0.51)	5.0 (0.44)
Vigilance attention (n = 9)	..§	2.4 (0.68)	...	3.0 (0.52)	...	2.7 (0.66)
Motor performance						
Speed: finger tapping†						
Dominant hand	41.2 (1.7)	42.5 (2.0)	41.9 (3.1)	39.9 (3.4)	41.5 (2.8)	43.1 (2.9)
Nondominant hand	36.1 (2.3)	35.9 (1.9)	37.7 (2.5)	35.8 (2.6)	36.7 (2.4)	35.8 (2.8)
Effort: dynamometry, s (n = 10)						
Dominant hand	...	13.1 (5.9)	...	8.8 (3.3)	...	15.7 (6.6)
Nondominant hand	...	7.4 (2.9)	...	16.8 (7.3)	...	10.7 (4.4)
Episodic learning and memory						
Serial reminding task						
Free recall trials 1-2	...	2.0 (0.34)	...	2.1 (0.46)	...	1.9 (0.40)
Free recall trials 3-5	...	2.8 (0.41)	...	2.3 (0.52)	...	2.7 (0.46)
Consistency trials 1-2	...	0.24 (0.10)	...	0.19 (0.08)	...	0.40 (0.11)
Consistency trials 3-5	...	0.31 (0.08)	...	0.20 (0.09)	...	0.27 (0.07)
Vigilance task (n = 9)						
Free recall	...	2.8 (0.47)	...	2.2 (0.50)	...	2.9 (0.51)
Intrusions	...	1.3 (0.30)	...	0.7 (0.30)	...	0.8 (0.47)
Knowledge memory						
Category retrieval†						
Appropriate responses	4.1 (0.90)	3.3 (0.70)	5.1 (1.1)	2.7 (0.72)‖	3.8 (0.93)	3.0 (0.65)
Inappropriate responses	0.9 (0.51)	1.3 (0.51)	0.2 (0.2)	3.3 (1.1)¶	0.1 (0.11)	1.8 (0.74)
Identification of degraded figures, s (n = 11)	...	32.4 (7.6)	...	28.2 (7.9)	...	34.7 (8.2)

*N = 12 unless indicated otherwise. Measures after test dose and in afternoon were unchanged from baseline.
†Measures obtained four times each day. All other measures were obtained once each day.
‡Forty-five to 90 minutes after second infusion. Same sequence of tests for all subjects.
§Ellipses indicate measures were obtained once each day.
‖$P < .05$ compared with baseline using Tukey's Honestly Significant Difference (HSD).
¶$P < .01$ compared with baseline using Tukey's HSD.

2.13   Tables

Note use of flush left format, with indents for runovers, for tables with entries that are primarily lengthy text. No periods are used after entries.

Table 13.—Criteria for Assignment to Risk Groups	
Risk Group	**Criteria**
Known coagulopathy	Discharge diagnosis code indicating coagulation disorder,* or determination (chart audit for evaluation of hemorrhage, excessive transfusion requirement, or preoperative procoagulant administration) that patient was taking an anticoagulant before surgery
Potential factor deficiency	Any discharge diagnosis code indicative of liver disease, malabsorption, or malnutrition
Trauma/ hemorrhage	Diagnosis code indicative of acute injury or hemorrhage at any site, or principal procedure code indicative of repair of laceration, surgical control of epistaxis, or suturing of gastric or duodenal ulcer site
Low risk	All others

*Each case was confirmed at chart review to have been diagnosed before the screening test was ordered and not as a result of that test.

Table 14 uses the centered format for all columns. Column entries are short enough to fit on one line. Centering column entries provides a balanced look and leaves less white space than would a flush left format.

Table 14.—Rabies Antibody Titers* in Persons Given Primary Preexposure Immunization and Booster Immunization at 1 or 2 Years With Human Diploid Cell Rabies Vaccine

	\[All Subjects After Immunization\]			\[Subjects Who Received Booster at — Day 365\]		\[Day 730\]	
Group and Primary Regimen†	**49**	**90**	**365**	**386**	**730**	**730**	**751**
1: 1.0 mL IM							
N	18	18	17	8	9	9	4
Titer, IU/mL Mean	12.9	5.1	3.3	60.3	15.7	1.3	5.1
Range	2.8–55.0	1.8–12.3	1.1–10.0	50.0–224.9	2.2–54.9	0.05–11.0	2.4–12.2
2: 0.1 mL ID (syringe)							
N	26	25	24	11	11	11	8
Titer, IU/mL Mean	7.4	2.8	1.5	42.5	4.4	1.7	7.7
Range	1.5–25.7	0.5–13.0	0.3–10.0	3.6–794.1	0.3–16.5	0.4–5.5	2.4–25.3
3: 0.1 mL ID (jet injector)							
N	28	27	23	10	10	10	6
Titer, IU/mL Mean	3.1	1.4	0.6	32.8	3.6	0.4	10.8
Range	0.4–26.9	0.2–11.3	<0.04–10.0	10.0–50.0	0.4–11.0	0.1–1.2	2.6–27.4
4: 0.1 mL SC							
N	24	22	22	10	9	13	5
Titer, IU/L Mean	3.2	1.4	0.6	48.4	4.1	0.4	10.5
Range	0.2–25.7	0.4–3.8	<0.04–10.0	10.0–200.0	1.2–11.0	<0.04–4.8	5.9–21.0
5: 0.25 mL SC							
N	28	27	26	9	11	12	5
Titer, IU/mL Mean	6.5	1.6	1.6	26.7	3.4	0.7	8.4
Range	1.5–27.5	0.4–13.0	1.1–10.0	10.0–50.0	0.4–32.9	0.1–5.3	4.2–13.1

(Day of Testing)

*Neutralizing antibodies measured by the rapid fluorescent focus inhibition test and expressed as geometric mean titers.
†Three doses of human diploid cell rabies vaccine were given, one each on days 0, 7, and 28. IM indicates intramuscular; ID, intradermal; and SC, subcutaneous.

2.13   Tables

Note that in Table 15 the entries in columns 2 and 3 are centered in row 1 and aligned on the common element (the plus and minus signs in column 2 and the hyphens in column 3) in the remaining rows. This mixing of formats *within* columns allows the parenthetical Système International (SI) values in the first row to be set on the same line as the conventional values, rather than indented on the line below, as might have been necessary had *all* entries been aligned on the common element.

Table 15.—Complete Blood Cell Count in 153 Children With *Shigella*-Associated Convulsions		
Value	**Mean ± SD**	**Range**
Hemoglobin, g/dL (g/L)	11.7 ± 1.4 (117 ± 14)	7.6-15.0 (76-150)
Leukocytes × 10³/mm³ (× 10⁹/L)	9.3 ± 4.0	3.7-33.2
Absolute band cells × 10³/mm³ (× 10⁹/L)	1.9 ± 1.4	0.0-4.7
Thrombocytes × 10³/mm³ (× 10⁹/L)	181.6 ± 58.1	72.0-310.0

Note that in Table 16 the flush left format was used for all entries. Since the primary comparisons in this case are down the columns (usually the case when there are no table stubs), the flush left format produces a clean, easily readable column. (*But:* See Table 17 for an equally good alternative.)

Table 16.—Chronology of Test Procedures*

Year	Investigators	Procedure
1895	Magnus-Levy	Initial studies of basal metabolism rate (BMR) in thyroid disease
1922	Roth and Benedict	Development of instrumentation for BMR
1951	Barker et al	First practical protein-bound iodine (PBI) test
1951	Man et al	Introduction of butanol extractable iodine
1952	Recant and Riggs	First complete statement of free thyroxine hypothesis
1955	Adams and Purves	Early assay for thyrotropic hormone (TSH)
1955	Freinkel et al	Concept of thyroxine binding by serum protein
1956	Roitt and Doniach	Early studies of autoantibodies in thyroid disease
1956	Rose and Witebsky	Early studies of autoantibodies in thyroid disease
1956	Adams and Purves	Studies of long-acting thyroid stimulator (LATS)
1958	McKenzie	Studies of LATS
1959	Berson and Yalow	Development of radioimmunoassay (RIA)
1959	Shibusawa	Proposed existence of thyroid-releasing hormore (TRH)
1961	Pileggi	First T_4 column method
1961	Elzinga et al	Methods for study of thyroxine-binding globulin (TBG)
1962	Sterling and Hegedus	Determination of free T_4 in serum
1964	Murphy and Pattee	Determination of T_4 by competitive protein binding
1964	Lee et al	Studies of free T_4
1967	Odell et al	Developed method for TSH by RIA
1968	Hollander	Determination of T_3 by gas chromatography
1969	Bøler et al	Identification of TRH as a tripeptide
1970	Burgus et al	Identification of TRH as a tripeptide
1971	Gharib et al	Developed T_3 RIA
1972	Chopra and Mitsuma	Developed T_4 RIA
1972–1978	. . .	Screening for neonatal congenital hypothyroidism
1974	Chopra	Developed reverse T_3 (rT_3) RIA

*References for data included in this table and in Tables 2 and 3 are included within the text.

63

2.13 Tables

Table 17 demonstrates that it is possible to use the flush left format for some columns and the centered format for others within the same table. Here there were some long entries (columns 2 and 3) and some very short entries (columns 4 and 5). The last two columns were set centered for a more pleasing balance that does not detract from readability.

Table 17.—Lectin Binding to Normal Human Peripheral Nerves

Lectin*	Source	Inhibiting Sugar	Binding†	
			Nerve Fibers	Perineurium
Suc ConA	Canavalia ensiformis	Methyl-α-mannopyranoside	++	++
LCA	Lens culinaris	Methyl-α-mannopyranoside	++	++
WGA	Triticum vulgare (wheat germ)	D-N-acetylglucosamine	++	++
STA	Solanum tuberosum	D-N-acetylglucosamine	−	−
GSA-II	Griffonia simplicifolia	D-N-acetylglucosamine	−	−
DBA	Dolichos biflorus	D-N-acetylgalactosamine	−	−
SBA	Glycine max (soybean)	D-N-acetylgalactosamine	−	−
VVA	Vicia villosa	D-N-acetylgalactosamine	−	−
PWM	Pokeweed	D-N-acetylgalactosamine	−	−
HPA	Helix pomatia	D-N-acetylgalactosamine	−	+
WFA	Wistaria floribunda	D-N-acetylgalactosamine	+	+
MPA	Maclura pomifera	D-N-acetylgalactosamine	−	+
PHA-E	Phaseolus vulgaris (E$_4$)	D-N-acetylgalactosamine	+	+
PHA-L	P vulgaris (L$_4$)	D-N-acetylgalactosamine	+	+
PNA	Arachis hypogaea (peanut)	D-galactose	−	−
GSA-I	G simplicifolia	D-galactose	−	−
RCA-I	Ricinus communis	D-galactose	+	+
RCA-II	R communis	D-galactose	+/−	+
UEA-I	Ulex europaeus	α-L-fucose	−	−
BPA	Bauchinia purpurea	D-N-acetylgalactosamine	−	−

*Suc ConA indicates succinyl concanavalin A. All other abbreviations for lectins are given according to common usage.[24]
†Binding was scored as negative (−), weakly positive (+), or strongly positive (++).

Footnotes: Explanatory footnotes are indicated by the following symbols, used in the order shown: * (asterisk), † (dagger), ‡ (double dagger), § (section mark), ‖ (parallels), ¶ (paragraph symbol), and # (number sign). These symbols are repeated, doubled, if more are needed. They are set as superscripts and appear *before* colons and semicolons and *after* commas and periods. The order of the footnotes in the table may be determined by reading left to right or top to bottom, but it must be consistent throughout the table. A footnote that applies to the entire table (eg, explaining all abbreviations used throughout the table, or crediting previous publication of the table) should be placed after the table title. If a footnote applies to one or two columns or stubs, the appropriate placement of the footnote symbol is after the column or stub heading(s). If a footnote applies only to a single entry in the table, or to several individual entries, the footnote symbol should be placed next to (and following) those entries.

Footnotes appear at the bottom of the table, with a paragraph indent. They should be complete sentences and should always end with a period. (*Note:* The less than or greater than or equal to signs, or any operational signs, are abbreviations for inflected verbs and hence imply a verb even though one may not be used. Hence, $P<.01$ would be considered a complete sentence *as a table footnote.*) If several tables share a long footnote explaining abbreviations or methods, this footnote may be retained in the first table only, with a footnote in the succeeding tables that refers to the footnote in the first table: "Symbols are explained in the footnote to Table 1." Also, the reader may be referred to a relevant discussion in the text by a footnote: "See text for a description of this method."

A few of the most common uses of footnotes are listed below:

- To expand abbreviations. *Note:* In tables, no expansion of M and F listed under "Sex," of W and B listed under "Race," or of L and R (for *left* and *right*) is required.
- To cite references. *Note:* References cited in the table may be given as in the text, with superscript reference numbers. However, to indicate that the entire table (or column within the table) was based on data from another source, the following footnote form should be used: "Data from Kaufman and Berstein.[3]"
- To give credit for reproduction of the table. If the entire table has been reprinted, with permission, from another source, and if that source is one of the listed references, credit should be given in a footnote to the table as follows: "From James.[10]" If a table is reproduced, with permission, from another source that is *not* one of the listed references, credit should be given in the acknowledgments (see 2.8.4, Acknowledgments, Reproduction of Figures and Tables).

Système International (SI) units: All 10 AMA journals used a dual reporting system for SI and conventional units before going to sole use of SI units (see 11.11, Abbreviations, Units of Measure, and 15.1, Units of Measure, SI Units). If both sets of units are used, the following guidelines may assist in the presentation of both SI and conventional units in tables.

- List the unit of measure following a comma in the table column heading or stub, with a clear indication of which units apply to values inside and outside of parentheses.

    Serum urea nitrogen, mg/dL (mmol/L)

    In this example, and the ones in this section that follow, the conventional units will be listed outside parentheses and the SI units inside parentheses.

- Then list the appropriate values, with the converted form in parentheses, in the body of the table.

    15.5 ± 0.8 (5.5 ± 0.02)

    Here 15.5 ± 0.8 mg/dL represents the conventional value and 5.5 ± 0.02 mmol/L, the SI value.

- If the numerical value is the same in SI and conventional units, give only one numerical value in tables.

    Sodium, mEq/L (mmol/L): 142.3.

    In this case the conversion factor from milliequivalents per liter to millimoles per liter is 1.00. One column (or row) of numbers, without parenthetical repetition, is sufficient.

2.13.7 *Capital Letters.*—For table titles and column headings, use the capitalization style used for titles (see 2.1.6, Titles and Subtitles, Capitalization). For each column or row entry, capitalize the first word. If it is preceded by a number or percent, capitalize the first letter of the word (eg, 10% Strength).

2.13.8 *Punctuation.*—As with numbers and abbreviations, rules for punctuation are relaxed in tables in the interest of space (see 6.0, Punctuation). Virgules may be used to present dates (eg, 10/20/86 for October 20, 1986). Hyphens may be used to present ranges (eg, 60-90 for 60 to 90).

2.13.9 *Abbreviations and Numbers.*—Within the body of the table and in column headings, units of measure and numbers normally spelled out (see 15.0, Units of Measure, and 16.0, Numbers and Percentages) may be abbreviated (See 11.11, Abbreviations, Units of Measure) to save space. For example, a column describing a patient's history may list "Patient had 5 or 6 seizures, occurring 5-6 wk apart." But do not combine spelled-out words with abbreviations for units of measure; use "1st wk" or "First Week" as a column heading, but *not* "First wk."

2.13.10 *Zeros and Ellipses.*—Use a zero to indicate "none" in answer to the implied question "how much?" or "how many?" Use ellipses to indicate that no data were available or that the category of data is not applicable. Except in matrices, avoid the use of a blank space as a table entry as it creates ambiguity.

Do not add zeros after the decimal point to make neat, same-sized table entries. This would indicate more precise calculations than were actually performed. (See 17.3, Statistics, Significant Digits.)

2.13.11 *Totals.*—Totals and percentages in tables should correspond to values given in the text and should be checked for accuracy. In some cases, discrepancies due to rounding error (see 17.4, Statistics, Rounding Off) may be noted in a footnote. True totals, ie, totals that represent sums of other values *given in the table*, are set boldface (see Table 18). In such cases, the word *Total* is also set boldface. When *Total* is the table stub, it should be set flush left. If the stub includes additional words (eg, Total No. of Patients), these words should all be set boldface and follow the capitalization style used in titles.

Table 18.—Incidence of Occult Primary Melanoma		
Source, y	No. (%) With Occult Primary Melanoma	Total No. of Melanomas
Lane et al,[4] 1958	22 (4.0)	554
Pack and Miller,[5] 1961	29 (2.4)	1190
Charalambidis and Patterson,[6] 1962	8 (3.2)	250
Das Gupta et al,[7] 1963	37 (3.7)	992
Smith and Stehlin,[8] 1965	40 (8.7)	461
Shah and Goldsmith,[9] 1972	97 (6.0)	1552
Baab and McBride,[10] 1975	98 (4.0)	2446
Nathanson,[11] 1976	16 (5.6)	284
Total	**347** (4.5)	**7729**

In this case, 347 and 7729 are set boldface because they represent the sum of the items given in the table in the columns above them. However,

(4.5) is not set boldface because it is the total percent but does *not* represent the sum of the items in the column above.

2.14 **Appendixes.**—The use of appendixes is discouraged in AMA publications. If the material in question is essential to understanding the article, it may be handled as a table or figure or integrated into the text, whichever is appropriate to the individual case. If the appendix material is, rather, an adjunct to the text (eg, derivation of a mathematical formula that, although it may interest a small number of readers, is not required to comprehend the text), a repository service such as that provided by the National Auxiliary Publication Service (NAPS) (see 2.15) may be the appropriate place for the material. If one of these courses is followed, the editor must, of course, renumber any remaining tables, figures, and/or references as appropriate.

2.15 **National Auxiliary Publications Service (NAPS).**—The American Society for Information Science (ASIS) provides a repository for material such as auxiliary tables, graphs and charts, computer printouts, bibliographies, and complex formulas that are adjuncts to articles published in scholarly or technical journals but that would require too many journal pages to publish in full. The availability of the deposited materials is announced at the time the relevant article is published, so that the reader may order copies. Materials are supplied in either microfiche or hard copy (photocopy). This service is operated for ASIS by Microfiche Publications. All inquiries about depositing or retrieving materials should be directed to ASIS/NAPS, c/o Microfiche Publications, PO Box 3513, Grand Central Station, New York, NY 10163-3513.

2.15.1 *How to Make Deposits of Adjunctive Materials in NAPS.*—In most cases, the copy editor of the AMA journal makes the deposit. (The AMA pays the deposit fee for its authors.) The deposit fee or purchase order is accompanied by a signed deposit form (available from NAPS). This form provides copyright clearance. The materials to be deposited accompany the purchase order or deposit fee and the deposit form (see 2.15.2, Format of Materials to Be Deposited). On receipt of these materials, NAPS will send to the depositor 10 microfiche duplicates of the deposited materials and the NAPS document number assigned to the deposit. They will retain the material sent.

2.15.2 *Format of Material to Be Deposited.*—The following guidelines are suggested by NAPS:

- Standard-size (21.6 × 27.9 cm [8½ × 11 in]) paper is recommended, although oversized sheets can be processed.

- All pages should be numbered in their proper sequence, beginning with page 1.
- Copy should not be smaller than elite or 10-point typewriter type.
- Material should be the original or clear enough to be legible when reduced for microfiche or photocopy.
- If necessary, several deposits related to the same article may be batched into a single deposit and assigned one NAPS number as long as they do not exceed 98 pages. *Note:* In this case, however, the reader who wishes to purchase any part of this deposit must pay for the *entire* deposit.

2.15.3 *How to Announce the Availability of a Deposit.*—Published articles for which there is supplementary material deposited with NAPS must contain a footnote giving the NAPS document number and the cost of obtaining a copy of the document. (See 2.8.6, Acknowledgments, National Auxiliary Publications Service [NAPS] or Other Supplementary Information.)

3.0 Legal and Ethical Considerations

3.1 Duplicate Publication.—Duplicate publication is the simultaneous or subsequent republication—*unbeknownst to the editors*—of essentially the same article in two or more journals (or other printed media). Duplication occurs when there is significant overlap in one or more of the elements of an article, eg, in a study, materials and methods, graphic and illustrative material, discussion, and conclusions. Duplicate publication differs from *parallel publication*, in which the editors of two journals may *mutually agree* to publish the same material. For example, the editors of an English-language journal and a non–English-language journal may agree to publish the same article in translated form for the benefit of different audiences, at short intervals from each other, with the English-language journal usually having primacy of publication and therefore holding the copyright.

The editors of *JAMA* and the AMA specialty journals have adopted the following policy to prevent the practice of duplicate publication.

At the time an article is submitted, the author(s) must inform the editor in the event that any part of the material (1) is under consideration by another journal or (2) has been or is about to be published elsewhere. In the latter case, the author(s) should provide the editor with a copy of the previous article, so that the editor may determine whether the two are in fact duplicative.

All authors are required to sign a copyright release form stating that the material is original and has not been published elsewhere, in whole or in part (see 3.3, Copyright).

If a case of duplicate publication is suspected, the editor (possibly with the benefit of additional expert opinion) will consult the editor of the other journal in which the material appeared. If they agree that duplication has occurred, the editor will so inform the author(s) and ask for an explanation. The editor may then elect to publish a notice of duplicate publication in a subsequent issue of the journal (Fig 1 provides an example of such a notice; wording would, of course, be contingent on the actual circumstances in each case). Other measures, including legal action for copyright infringement and/or notifying the dean or director or other officer of the offending author's institution, are within the editor's prerogative.

Notice of Duplicate Publication

The article "Prevalence of Measles in Day-care Centers" by I. M. Shadey, MD, published in the November 4, 1985, issue of THE JOURNAL,[1] is virtually identical to an article by the same author, describing the same three cases in similar words, published in the *Journal of Improbable Results*, September 1985.

In June 1985, the author had sent THE JOURNAL a copyright notice assigning "all copyright ownership to the AMA" and shortly after submission, but well before either publication, received a letter of acceptance from THE JOURNAL. Dr Shadey, pleading ignorance of both the ethics of scientific publication and copyright law, offers his sincere apologies.

1. Shadey IM. Prevalence of measles in day-care centers. *JAMA*. 1985;254:0000-0000.

Figure 1.

Duplicate publication constitutes a violation of copyright law and of the ethics of scientific publishing. When in doubt about the common source, overlapping, or coincidence of data in articles based on the same study, *the author(s) should inform and consult the editor.*

3.2 Fraud and Plagiarism.—Fraud and plagiarism are deliberate attempts to deceive. Fraud in science may range from the fabrication of data to the manipulation of real data to achieve a predetermined desired result. Although scientists have long been aware of the dangers of forging, "cooking," or "trimming" data (Babbage 1969, as cited by Schiedermayer and Siegler 1986), recent highly publicized incidents of fraudulent research have put editors and investigators on their guard (Knox 1983; Relman 1983).

In plagiarism, an author passes off as his or her own the ideas, language, data, graphics, or even scientific protocols created by someone else, whether published or unpublished. Plagiarism of published work violates copyright laws as well as standards of honesty and collegial trust and may be subject to penalty imposed by a court should the holders of the copyright bring suit. Four common kinds of plagiarism have been identified (Northwestern University): (1) direct verbatim lifting of passages, (2) rewording ideas from the original in the purported author's own style, (3) paraphrasing the original work without attribution, and (4) noting the original source of only *some* of what is borrowed.

The common characteristic of all these kinds of plagiarism is the failure to attribute words, ideas, or findings to their true author(s). Such failure to acknowledge a source properly may on occasion be caused by careless note taking or ignorance of the canons of research, and coincidences of ideas can occur. The best defense against charges of fraud and plagiarism is careful note taking and documentation of all data observed and sources used. Those who peer review manuscripts that are similar to their own unpublished work are especially at risk for charges of plagiarism. If a reviewer foresees such a potential conflict of interest, he or she should consider returning the manuscript to the editor unreviewed, as *JAMA* advises in the letter that accompanies each manuscript sent out for review (Southgate 1987).

Fraud and plagiarism are difficult to detect; there may be many more cases than have been discovered (Stewart and Feder 1987). Detection is often accidental and the result of the alertness of coworkers, the editorial staff, the peer reviewers, other authors of the same manuscript, or the readers.

Because fraud and plagiarism violate the trust that must underlie all scientific communication, editors of the AMA journals will respond strongly to documented instances of fraud or plagiarism. In the case of published work, the journal will publish an announcement and the author or purported author will be asked to prepare a statement of explanation or retraction. (See 21.3.1, On-line Resources, MEDLINE.)

In the case of unpublished work in which fraud or plagiarism is suspected and for which some persuasive evidence exists, the editor will ask the senior author for a written explanation. If an explanation is not provided or is unsatisfactory, the author's organizational superior may be contacted.

3.3   Copyright.—The first major statutory revision of US copyright law in almost 70 years became effective January 1, 1978. The new law clarifies the status of copyright ownership by requiring explicit agreements to vary the basic assumption that copyright belongs to the creator of the work from the instant of its creation. Under the old law, it was often unclear when an author or artist had in fact transferred copyright to a publisher. If the parties did not enter into a written agreement, the courts looked to their correspondence, course of dealing, custom of the trade, etc, and attempted to determine the parties' intent. This arrangement was often unsatisfactory for authors because it led to uncertainty about what rights had specifically been conveyed to the publisher.

The following summary of a complex field of legal specialization is intended only to alert authors and editors to some of the problems of copyright. Authors submitting papers to AMA journals should familiarize themselves with the practices set forth here and are urged to consult private counsel if in doubt.

The journals published by the AMA are copyrighted by the AMA according to the provision of the Copyright Revision Act of 1976 (the present US copyright law, effective January 1, 1978) and are the property of the AMA.

3.3.1   *Copyright Transfer.*—The present law provides that copyright of a work vests initially in the author(s) of the work. Each copyright assignment must be submitted prior to review and decision of the AMA to publish that work. The author(s) of the work must affirm that the work submitted has not been previously transferred or assigned to a third party and that the work has not been otherwise encumbered. In the event the work is published by the AMA, the author agrees to transfer copyright to the AMA. If the AMA does not publish the work, the copyright reverts to the author(s).

The authors of a "joint work" are co-owners of copyright in the work. A joint work is a work prepared by two or more authors with the intention that their contributions be merged into inseparable or interdependent parts of a unitary whole. To transfer copyright of a joint work to a publisher, a copyright assignment must be executed by each of the authors.

Figure 2 is a sample copyright assignment form. Although this copyright form is used generally by *JAMA* and the AMA specialty journals, it may not be appropriate in all circumstances and should be modified as needed.

Re: MS # 113—Macroscopic Cysts . . .

Dear Dr Brown:

Your manuscript is being reviewed and considered for publication in *JAMA*.

In compliance with the Copyright Revision Act of 1976, effective January 1, 1978, the American Medical Association, in consideration of having reviewed, edited, and accepted your submission for publication, now requests that each author sign a copy of this form before publication of the manuscript. Such signature shall evidence the mutual understanding between the American Medical Association and the undersigned author hereby transferring, assigning, or otherwise conveying all copyright ownership, including any and all rights incidental thereto, exclusively to the American Medical Association.

The author(s) warrant(s) that he/she/they is (are) the author(s) and sole owner(s) of the work submitted; that it is original and unpublished; that the work has not been previously transferred, assigned or otherwise encumbered; and that the author(s) has/have full power to grant such rights. In addition, the undersigned author(s) hereby grant(s) to the AMA the right to edit, revise, abridge, condense, and translate the work.

Sincerely yours,

Author(s) signature(s)   Date signed

_____   _____

_____   _____

_____   _____

_____   _____

_____   _____

_____   _____

Figure 2.

3.3.2   *US Government Works.*—A major exception to the requirement of obtaining written copyright assignment is US government works. The Copyright Act provides that the US government may not hold copyright of the works it prepares. Thus, if a work was prepared by an officer or employee of the US government as part of that person's official duties, the work is the property of the US government. Since copyright cannot be obtained in such a government work, no assignment from the author is necessary. What constitutes a work of a government employee as part of the person's official duties is not always clear. It is advisable to obtain a signed statement from the author or authors representing that a work is a US government work (see Fig 3).

Re: MS #5610
Title: The ABCs of Medicine

Author(s): Doe, Smith, and Jones

The above article, which has been submitted to *The Journal of the American Medical Association*, fits the description in the US Copyright Act of 1976 of a "US government work." It was written as a part of my (our) official duties as government officer(s) or employee(s). Therefore, it cannot be copyrighted. The article is freely available to you for publication without a copyright notice, and there are no restrictions on its use, now or subsequently. I (we) retain no rights to the article.

Author(s) signature(s)   Date signed

_____   _____
_____   _____
_____   _____
_____   _____
_____

Figure 3.

3.3.3 *Works Made for Hire.*—Another major exception to the requirement of obtaining written copyright assignment under the new act is a "work made for hire." No written assignment is required for a work made for hire since copyright ownership automatically is vested in the hiring party. Works made for hire generally fall into two categories. The first category is a work prepared by an employee within the scope of his or her employment duties. The second category comprises certain specially ordered or commissioned works. In the case of the second category, although a written copyright assignment is not necessary, the parties must expressly agree beforehand in a signed written instrument that the work should be considered a work made for hire. In the case of a work made for hire, the employer or other person for whom the work was prepared is considered the author for purposes of copyright laws and owns the copyright of the work. (This party holds the copyright for 75 years from the year of first publication or for 100 years from the date of the work's creation.)

3.3.4   *Copyright Notice and Registration.*—Under the present copyright law, copyright of a particular work automatically comes into being the moment the work is fixed in tangible form. (The copyright remains valid for the author's life plus 50 years.) Note that generally it is the fact of publication with a proper copyright notice that preserves copyright in a particular work. The 1976 act provides that the word or symbol "Copyright" (or "Copr.") or © followed by the year of first publication and the name of the copyright owner constitutes proper copyright notice. Under the 1976 act, copyright notice is affixed to copies "in such manner and location as to give reasonable notice of the claim of copyright."

Registration and deposit of a work with the Copyright Office in Washington, DC, are provided for under the provisions of the 1976 act. Failure to do so, however, does not affect the copyright owner's rights in that property. It is, however, a prerequisite to bringing suit for copyright infringement.

To be copyrightable, literary work must be an original work of authorship. The AMA generally requires that the manuscripts it accepts for publication be original and not previously published in any form.

3.3.5   *Copying and Reproducing.*—To copy or reproduce an entire work without authorization from the copyright owner constitutes copyright infringement. The Copyright Revision Act of 1976 provides remedies for this violation of the law. However, a reasonable type and amount of copying is permitted as a "fair use" of a copyrighted work.

What constitutes fair use of copyrighted material in a given case is a question of fact, taking into account four primary factors: (1) the purpose and character of the use, including whether such use is of a commercial nature or is for nonprofit educational purposes; (2) the nature of the copyrighted work; (3) the amount and substantiality of the portion used in relation to the copyrighted work as a whole; and (4) the effect of the use on the potential market for or value of the copyrighted work.

If a portion of a copyrighted work is to be used in a subsequent work and such use is not fair use, written permission must be obtained from the copyright owner. Examples of such portions include the printed text, or illustrations such as charts, diagrams, or photographs. It is not permissible to use an article in its entirety unless permission to do so is obtained in writing. In all cases, the matter should carry a proper credit.

Works in the public domain (where there is no copyright therein) may be quoted from freely. The copyright notice on a work gives notice of its copyright. If there is doubt about the copyright status of a particular work, an inquiry should be directed to the author, publisher, or US Copyright Office.

3.3.6 *Publishing Symposium Discussions.*—When symposia papers are published, transcripts of discussion, which consist of questions posed to the presenters of papers and the presenters' responses, often accompany them and are printed at the end of the article in a separate section entitled "Discussion." The discussants' comments and questions also require copyright transfer (see Fig 4).

COPYRIGHT TRANSFER

Re: Ms #

In consideration of the American Medical Association ("AMA") reviewing and editing the transcript and text of my discussion on the subject of _____ _____ given at the _____, and other good and valuable consideration, receipt of which is hereby acknowledged, I do hereby represent that I am the owner of the copyright of the text of my discussion and that it has not been previously published, assigned or otherwise encumbered and I hereby transfer such copyright to the AMA and irrevocably authorize the AMA, its successors, and assigns and licensees, to edit, copyright, use, publish and sell for any lawful purpose whatsoever, the transcript and/or text of my discussion.

Date: _____

(Signature) Name: _____

Street Address: _____

City: _____

Phone: _____

Figure 4.

3.3.7 *Reprints.*—The copyright owner has a right to attach conditions to giving permission such as requiring proper credit and copyright notice. The copyright owner may refuse permission altogether. Permission is usually granted by the AMA without charge or royalty to scholarly authors to use portions (text, figures, or tables) of articles or other written works published in *JAMA* and the AMA specialty journals. It is AMA policy to require submission of a letter of consent from the author when requesting reprint permission.

Permission to reprint an article must be obtained from the AMA even by its author. When a work copyrighted by the AMA is published by authority of the AMA, notice of copyright must be placed on all publicly distributed copies. The form of the credit may vary depending on the nature of the work. No general rule can cover all possible situations, but the following should be considered: Use the word "Copyright" and/or the symbol © followed by the year of first publication of the work, the name of the copyright owner, and the established wording approved for reprint credit notices.

3.3.8 *Derivative Works and Compilations.*—Under the Copyright Revision Act of 1976, a new version of a copyrighted work that has been produced by or with the consent of the copyright owner is copyrightable. Examples of such derivative works include translations, abridgements, adaptations, and works republished with new material. A new or revised edition of a work already copyrighted may be copyrighted again, but the new copyright applies only to materials added in the new edition and is effective only if there is substantial original new work in the new edition or revision. The existing copyright of materials retained in a subsequent edition is not affected, and copyright of the new material will not extend the life of copyright of the old material.

A compilation is a work composed of preexisting material arranged in such a way that the resulting work is original in presentation and organization. Compilations may include various works, including articles, books, or other publications. A compilation may be copyrighted as an original work, but only to the extent of material prepared by the compiler. A compilation copyright does not extend the life of copyright in any of the copyrighted materials in the compilation. Similarly, it does not confer copyright on any materials in a compilation for which copyright is unavailable.

3.3.9 *International Copyright.*—There is no "international copyright" that will automatically protect an author's writings throughout the world. Most countries do offer protection to foreign works, and these conditions have been greatly simplified by international copyright treaties and conventions. Copyright relations between the United States and other countries are based on bilateral treaties, presidential proclamations regarding copyright protection for nationals for other countries, and various international conventions to which the United States has acceded.

Under the Universal Copyright Convention, to which the United States is a signatory, protection in all participating nations is obtained by publication in any one of them provided the proper copyright notice is used (the symbol ©, the year of first publication, and the name of the copyright owner) placed in a manner and location that gives reasonable notice of the claim of copyright.

An author who wishes copyright protection in a particular country should find out the extent of protection of foreign works in that country. If possible, this should be done before the work is published anywhere, since protection may often depend on facts existing at the time of first publication of the work.

3.4   **Informed Consent.**—To protect the safety and dignity of human subjects in experimental investigations, academic institutions and grant-giving agencies have in recent years come to require that the nature and purpose of all procedures, and their attendant possible risks, be fully explained to potential subjects in advance.

In accordance with these ethical guidelines, *JAMA* and the AMA specialty journals require that authors of manuscripts describing experimental investigation of human subjects state formally *in the "Methods" section of the manuscript* that an appropriate institutional review board approved the project and/or informed consent was obtained from all adult participating subjects and from parents or legal guardians for minors. (Note that this differs from statements of financial interest or support, which should appear in the acknowledgments. See 2.8.1, Acknowledgments, Financial Support, and 2.8.2, Acknowledgments, Proprietary Statement.)

4.0 Editorial Assessment and Processing

Major biomedical journals receive thousands of manuscripts each year, and as their rejection letters state, they can publish only a small fraction of these. Ultimately, the most important question for medical editors is, *which?* To help them decide, they call on their own knowledge and judgment of validity, professional interest, and priority, and those of their consultants, or "peer reviewers."

But another important question for medical editors and the journal's staff is, *how?* How will the manuscripts chosen be published? In what category will they be placed? How will they be edited? How will they be laid out on the page? What other articles will be published at the same time? Journal procedures vary, of course, but in following a manuscript from submission to eventual publication at *JAMA*, this section offers some idea of how these publishing decisions are made.

(The AMA journals are now making a step-by-step transition to electronic publishing. It will eventually be possible to receive manuscripts on floppy disks or in another computer-compatible format, to edit on-screen, and to transmit them electronically to a printer. This account will describe the established publishing process, in which paper, pencil, and mailbags are not yet obsolete, since it better represents the workings of most scientific journals.)

4.1   Assignment to Category.—Submitted manuscripts are logged in as they arrive and read for the first time by the deputy editor or one of the senior editors, who categorizes them according to their subject, length, and style. At *JAMA*, for instance, an account of a multicenter clinical trial of a treatment would probably be called an Original Contribution; a report of a few cases of a disease would probably be a Brief Report; and a personal account of its emotional consequences for the patient and the family would be A Piece of My Mind. All of *JAMA*'s editorial categories are formalized, but some other journals invent new categories to fit the subject of a particular article. (See 1.0, Types of Articles.)

Once categorized, the manuscripts are assigned to editors, most of whom are physicians, according to their specialties and areas of interest and responsibility in the journal. These editors have the authority to reject manuscripts without consultation. Manuscripts that make it past this first cut undergo additional peer review.

4.2   **Peer Review.**—As used in scientific publishing, the term *peer review* refers to the long-standing practice of submitting manuscripts to acknowledged experts inside or outside the editorial office for their considered opinions and recommendations on publication. Often reviewers provide comments and suggestions intended to be sent directly to authors, but their primary responsibility is to advise the editors.

The practice of peer review varies to some degree from journal to journal. At *JAMA*, for instance, the only accepted articles not routinely sent to review are invited editorials commenting on an article and stories about the cover art, although other journals allow a freer rein to the editors' judgment. However, the use of some regular form of peer review on most scientific articles is the distinguishing characteristic of a reputable and scientifically useful journal.

A considerable number of discussions of peer review have been published (eg, Lock 1985; *Sci Technol Hum Values* 1985; Harnad 1983). The majority accept the system as faulty, but nevertheless the best available means of maintaining the quality of journals and, through journals, scientific disciplines. Editors often observe that even authors of manuscripts that do not reach publishable standards may profit from the reviewers' comments on the work's substance and methods.

Some critics, however, have suggested that the peer review process excessively legitimates an insiders' network that limits scientific originality (Horrobin 1982) or is suspiciously random in its outcome (Cole, Cole, and Simon 1981). In recent years, there have been a number of widely publicized incidents in which plagiarized or fraudulent work has been published, or in which authors have attempted (or achieved) multiple publications of the same article. These serious ethical lapses in the research community have inspired increased editorial awareness of the extreme care, even wariness, that the peer review process demands of both editors and reviewers. (See also 3.1, Duplicate Publication, and 3.2, Fraud and Plagiarism.) Many discussions of these issues in peer review conclude that too little is known about the actual workings and effects of the practice (Bailar and Patterson 1985; Lock 1985; Rennie 1986), and that empirical study of this process that has been taken so much for granted is needed.

Editors, of course, act as the first judges of submitted manuscripts. Those that the editors find promising are sent to consultants in the relevant field—at *JAMA*, usually two consultants (Lundberg and Carney 1986). Many journals encourage separate sets of comments for the author and for the editor. The former often offer specific criticisms or points of information; the latter, an overall assessment of quality and suitability for the journal. The editor's cover letter reminds reviewers that the manuscript is confidential material protected by copyright law and asks them to return the manuscript unreviewed should they perceive that they would have any conflict of interest in reviewing it (Southgate 1987).

Manuscripts are accepted if reviews by reliable reviewers are encouraging and if the editors agree, after discussion at a formal manuscript meeting, that the manuscript is both important and suitable for *JAMA*. Even with strongly positive reviews in hand, no manuscript is accepted by any editor alone; thus, no guarantees can or should be made to authors at any stage during the review process, no matter how confident the editor may be of the manuscript's quality and interest.

4.3   **Copy Editing.**—Once discussed in a manuscript meeting and formally accepted by the chair (the chief editor or a designate), a manuscript is copy edited. At *JAMA*, copy editors correct grammar, spelling, and usage, query ambiguities and inconsistencies, verify totals in tables, prepare copy for rebuilding of line art, designate type size for preparation of the layout, and edit to the AMA style, subject to the author's approval. Technical deficiencies not resolved during peer review (for instance, artwork that will not reproduce, values not converted to SI units, incomplete copyright waiver forms, or lack of permission for material reprinted from another source or for use of a patient's photograph) are also followed up and resolved by the copy editor. Substantial deletions or drastic changes are dealt with earlier by the senior editor, in consultation with the author.

4.4   **Layout.**—The layout department estimates the length of the printed article, sizes and crops the figures, rebuilds line art, and orders photocopies of figures. A "dummy" layout is created, showing breaks (if any) in the title and placement of tables, figures, and flush left headings. This layout gives the author a preview of the article's final appearance in the journal and also serves as a blueprint for the printer in making up the page proof.

The copy-edited manuscript, with the proposed layout, a letter from the copy editor with queries (for instance, about incomplete references or unclear abbreviations), and a reprint order form, is sent first to the senior editor for review (for *JAMA* articles) and then to the author before it is sent to the printer. (If the manuscript has been scheduled for extremely rapid publication, the copy-edited typescript is sent simultaneously to the editor and the author, and the copy editor coordinates any changes they make.) Changes made in the text at this point are fairly easily accommodated. Once the manuscript is set in type, however, changes become much more expensive and logistically difficult to arrange.

4.5   **Typesetting/Proofreading.**—Once the author has approved and returned the copy-edited manuscript and layout, and the copy editor has made the requested changes and dealt with the answers to queries, the manuscript, layout, and figures are sent to the senior production assistants. They designate type face and check that the manuscript and the layout correspond with one another before sending the manuscript to the printer for typesetting and page makeup. The page proofs are sent to the senior editor and the chief editor for review, while proofreaders check them against the original copy-edited manuscript. The copy editor will also send the author a proof-read copy of the proofs if the author specifically requests them when returning the copy-edited manuscript. Any changes made at this stage are sent to the printer by the production assistant. When there have been many changes, revised proofs may be requested from the printer.

4.6   **Advertising.**—The advertising division, which is administratively entirely separate from all editorial functioning, sells space for advertising. Advertisements must be assigned a specific position within an issue. The staffs of the AMA journals take care to ensure that there is no accidental link between advertisements and articles—for instance, that no advertisement for an antihypertension medication appears next to a report of research on hypertension. The AMA journals do *not* endorse any commercial products and scrupulously avoid any editorial content or structure that could imply such an endorsement.

4.7   **Makeup.**—For each issue, the production department gives the chief editor a list of manuscripts available for selection for that issue or subsequent issues. Once he or she has selected the editorial material for an issue, the senior production assistant merges the editorial and the advertising material, prepares the pages for the printer, and organizes the table of contents. This made-up issue is reviewed one final time before it is sent to the printer, along with instructions needed to produce the issue. Photographic negatives are prepared and proofread against the final copy before the issue is released for printing.

4.8   **Reprints.**—If reprints have been ordered, they will be shipped 6 to 8 weeks after the article appears in print. More reprints may be ordered at any time by contacting the Reprints staff.

4.9   **Corrections.**—Unfortunately, mistakes sometimes appear in print; fortunately, authors or readers usually call them to the journal's attention, and corrections can be published. In *JAMA*, corrections are printed at the end of the Letters to the Editor column. If the staff is notified quickly, the reprint film can be corrected before reprints are printed.

4.10   **Index.**—Although easily searched computerized databases may ultimately supplant them to some extent, indexes, organized by subject and author's surname, are published regularly in most medical journals. At *JAMA*, they appear in the last issues of June and December, at the end of the volume. New volumes begin with the first issues in July and January.

2

STYLE

Chapter 5

5.0 Grammar

A clear understanding of grammar is basic to good writing. There are many excellent grammar books that provide a detailed discussion of specific points (see 21.1, Resource Bibliography, References, and 21.2, Resource Bibliography, Additional Readings). In this section, the focus is on common grammatical errors.

5.1 **The Sentence.**—A sentence must contain a minimum of a subject and a verb; it usually contains modifiers as well. Sentence fragments omit a subject or verb. Occasionally writers will use sentence fragments intentionally, for effect:

> Dogs, undistinguishable in mire. Horses, scarcely better; splashed to their very blinkers. (Dickens, *Bleak House*)

> Her affect signaled depression. Utter depression.

More frequently, however, these fragments are unintentional:

> The clinical spectrum of disease varying according to the population and age group under study.

5.2 **The Paragraph.**—A paragraph is a group of sentences (or, occasionally, a single sentence) that presents a thought or several related thoughts. It should be long enough to stand alone but short enough to hold the reader's attention and then direct that attention to the next step in the development of the manuscript.

5.3   Punctuation

5.3   Punctuation.—Punctuation is an important element in the composition of a sentence. (See 6.0, Punctuation, for specific punctuation marks.) When punctuation is incorrectly placed or omitted, the reader is given unclear or confusing signals or no signals at all.

5.4   Modifiers.—An adjective modifies a noun or a pronoun. An adverb modifies a verb, adjective, or another adverb. Clauses or phrases may serve as adjectives or adverbs. (A clause is a group of words with a subject and predicate within a compound or complex sentence. A phrase is a group of words without a subject or predicate, usually introduced by a preposition or conjunction.) Failure to make clear what is modified or to identify the actor results in ambiguous and, often, outright ridiculous statements.

5.4.1   *Misplaced Modifiers.*—Misplaced modifiers result from a failure to make clear who or what is being modified. This illogical or ambiguous placement of a word or phrase can usually be avoided by placing the modifying word or phrase appropriately close to the word it modifies.

> *Unclear:* Dr Young treated the patients using antidepressants. [Ambiguity makes two meanings possible.]
> *Better:* By using antidepressants, Dr Young treated the patients. *Or:* Dr Young treated the patients who were using antidepressants.

> *Unclear:* It was raining, and John went to feed the cows with his umbrella.
> *Better:* It was raining, and John went with his umbrella to feed the cows.

The word *only* poses particular problems. It must be placed immediately before the word or phrase it modifies for the meaning to be clear. Note the three different meanings achieved by placement in the examples below:

> Only I saw John.
>
> I only saw John.
>
> I saw only John.

5.4.2   *Dangling Participles.*—A participle is a verb form used as an adjective. A dangling participle implies an actor but fails to specify who or what that actor is. The following examples of dangling participles illustrate the problem:

> *Avoid:* Organized into 13 chapters, the reader will benefit from an extensive appendix. (The participle appears to refer to "the reader"; however, it is the *book* that is organized into 13 chapters.)
> *Better:* The reader of this 13-chapter book will benefit from an extensive appendix.

> *Avoid:* Dietary therapy slows the return of hypertension after stopping prolonged medication. (This states that dietary therapy not only

86

slows the return of hypertension but also stops prolonged medication.)

Better: Dietary therapy slows the return of hypertension after prolonged medication is stopped.

Avoid: Before undertaking an exercise program or engaging in heavy physical labor, a physician should be consulted. ("A physician" is erroneously implied to be the actor, the one undertaking an exercise program or engaging in heavy physical labor.)

Better: Anyone about to undertake an exercise program or engage in heavy physical labor should consult a physician.

5.5   **Parallel Construction.**—One device used to build a sentence or emphasize a point is parallel construction. This device may rely on accepted clues (either/or, neither/nor, not only/but also, both/and). In this usage, the correlative conjunctions are often misplaced. Be sure that all elements of the parallelism that appear on one side of the coordinating conjunction are matched by corresponding elements on the other side.

Avoid: The compleat physician has not only mastered the science of medicine but also its art.

Correct: The compleat physician has mastered not only the science of medicine but also its art.

Avoid: Either you may clear the table or wash the dishes.

Better: You may either clear the table or wash the dishes.

Avoid: They debated between going to either the movie or to the play.

Correct: They debated between going either to the movie or to the play.

Parallel construction is also useful in presenting series or in making comparisons. In these usages, the elements of the series or of the comparison should be parallel structures, ie, nouns with nouns, prepositional phrases with prepositional phrases.

Avoid: The text was written for interns, residents, and to help them teach their students.

Correct: The text was written for interns, residents, and students. *Or:* The text was written to help interns and residents teach their students.

Avoid: When an operation is designed to improve function rather than extirpation of an organ, surgical technique becomes paramount.

Correct: When an operation is designed to improve function rather than to extirpate an organ, surgical technique becomes paramount.

Avoid: There was a long delay between the purchase of an x-ray machine and when it started to be widely used.

Correct: There was a long delay between the purchase of an x-ray machine and its widespread use.

5.6   Nouns.—Nouns are one of the two essential ingredients of most sentences. They may serve as subjects or objects. Some would contest the use of nouns as modifiers.

5.6.1   *As Modifiers.*—Although the English language permits nouns to be used as modifiers, overuse can lead to a lack of clarity. Purists may demand more strict rules on usage, but, as with the use of nouns as verbs (see 9.3, Correct and Preferred Usage, Back-formations), judgment and common sense take into account the inevitable process of linguistic change while participating, reasonably, in that change.

Avoid	*Preferred*
diabetes patient	patient with diabetes
depression episode	depressive episode

It is advisable to use no more than one noun modifier per noun for the sake of clarity.

Avoid: lung cancer chest roentgenograms
Better: chest roentgenograms showing lung cancer

Avoid: Medicare physician payment reform
Better: reform of Medicare payment to physicians

5.6.2   *Modifying Gerunds.*—When a noun or pronoun is used before a gerund (a verb form ending in *-ing* that is used as a noun), it takes the possessive. (See also 6.11, Punctuation, Apostrophe.)

The toxicity of the drug was not involved in the patient's dying so suddenly.

5.6.3   *Involving Time or Money.*—Nouns involving time or money, when used as possessive adjectives, also take the possessive. (See also 6.11.6, Apostrophe, Units of Time and Money as Possessive Adjectives.)

After 4 months' therapy, the child's condition improved.

5.7   Pronouns.—Pronouns replace nouns. In this replacement, the antecedent must be clear and the pronoun must agree with the antecedent in both number and gender.

Avoid: The authors unravel the complex process of gathering information about diethylstilbestrol and disseminating it. (Antecedent unclear)
Correct: The authors unravel the complex process of gathering and disseminating information about diethylstilbestrol.

Avoid: When the time comes for magnetic resonance imaging, it will be widely recognized. (Antecedent unclear)
Correct: When the time comes, magnetic resonance imaging will be widely recognized.

Avoid: In cases of child abuse, one parent is usually involved. They were often abused themselves.

Correct: Cases of child abuse usually involve only one parent. Often these parents were themselves abused as children.

Avoid: There are several factors militating against full reimbursement, yet it is hotly contested by some health planners.

Correct: There are several factors militating against full reimbursement, yet they are hotly contested by some health planners.

5.7.1 *Personal Pronouns.*—Care must be taken with personal pronouns to use the correct case, subjective or objective. Difficulty often arises when pronouns are used after prepositions or after the verb *to be*. Below are several examples of correct usage:

Give the award to whomever you prefer. (Objective case: the object of "you prefer")

Give the award to whoever will benefit most. (Subjective case: the subject of "will benefit")

Whom did you consult? (Objective case: the object of "did consult")

Who was the consultant on this case? (Subjective case: the subject of the sentence)

He is one of the patients whom Dr Rundle is treating. (Objective case: the object of "is treating")

He is one of the patients who is receiving the placebo. (Subjective case: the subject of "is receiving")

Avoid the use of pronouns ending in *-self* or *-selves* as subjects.

Avoid: George, Herbert, and myself attended the lecture.
Better: George, Herbert, and I attended the lecture.

5.7.2 *Relative Pronouns.*—Relative pronouns may be used in subordinate clauses to refer to previous nouns. The word *that* introduces a *restrictive* clause, one that is essential to the meaning of the sentence. *Which* introduces a *nonrestrictive* clause, one that merely adds more information but is not essential to the meaning; *which* clauses are preceded by commas. Two examples of correct usage follow:

This is the house that Jack built. (Restrictive)

This house, which Jack built, sold for $150 000. (Nonrestrictive)

As with misplaced modifiers, the incorrect use of *that* and *which* frequently leads to ridiculous statements:

Avoid: He had had stridor since birth, which initially was mild and positional but later became continuous.

> *Better:* He had had stridor since birth that initially was mild and positional but later became continuous.
>
> *Still better:* Since birth he had had stridor that initially was mild and positional but later became continuous.

5.8 **Verbs.**—Verbs express an action, an occurrence, or a mode of being. They have voice, mood, and tense.

5.8.1 *Voice.*—In the active voice the subject does the acting; in the passive voice, the subject is acted on. In general, the active voice is preferred, except in instances in which the interest concerns what is acted on.

> The 45-year-old man had been shot in the lower intestine and was brought to the emergency department within 10 minutes.

5.8.2 *Mood.*—Verbs may have one of three moods: the indicative (the most common), the imperative (used for requesting or commanding), and the subjunctive. The last-mentioned causes the most difficulty. Although once in common use, the subjunctive is now used primarily for expressing a wish (I wish it *were* possible), a supposition (If I *were* to accept the position, . . .), or a condition contrary to fact (If I *were* younger, . . .). This mood occurs in fairly formal situations and usually involves past (*were*) or present (*be*) forms.

> *Past form:* If we were to operate, the patient's prognosis would be excellent.
>
> *Present form:* The patient insisted she be admitted immediately.

In some cases, the subjunctive will be used where it is incorrect, eg, where matters of fact—not supposition—are discussed.

> Therefore, we determined whether there had been [not the subjunctive, *were*] a tendency to deviate from the prescribed regimen.
>
> We investigated to see if his leg was [not the subjunctive, *were*] set incorrectly.

5.8.3 *Tense.*—Tense indicates the time relation of a verb: past, present, future, past perfect, present perfect, and future perfect. It is important to choose the verb that expresses the time that is intended. It is equally important to maintain uniformity of tense.

As Day notes in *How to Write and Publish a Scientific Paper*, it is customary to use the present tense to refer to previously published work (thereby showing respect for that work, since the present tense implies a statement of fact):

> Kilgallen's assay results demonstrate the highest sensitivity and specificity to date.

Within an article the past tense is used to refer to the results of the study being described:

Group 1 had a seropositivity rate of 50%.

We examined the patient after he had been bitten by a dog.

In general, tense must be used consistently:

Incorrect: There were no false negatives in group 1, but there are three in group 2.

However, tenses may and will vary in a single article, dictated by context and judgment. For instance, one might use the present tense in the "Results" section of a paper in analyzing data from the same paper given, as noted above, in the past tense:

Group 1 had 90 true positives and 10 false negatives, which gives a sensitivity of 90%.

Even when mixing tenses, however, consistency is still the rule:

Incorrect: I found it difficult to accept Dr Smith's contention in chapter 3 that the new agonist has superior pharmacokinetics and was therefore more widely used.

Correct: I found it difficult to accept Dr Smith's contention in chapter 3 that the new agonist has superior pharmacokinetics and is therefore more widely used.

5.8.4   *Double Negatives.*—Two negatives used together constitute a double negative. In some cases this is necessary to express the desired meaning:

I couldn't not go.

It was not an uncommon occurrence in ward B.

In other cases, used improperly, the double negative expresses exactly the opposite of what is intended:

I can't hardly keep penicillin in stock.

5.8.5   *Split Infinitives.*—Since the dictum against splitting infinitives is still strong, it is best to try to avoid doing so. However, in attempting to avoid split infinitives, writers may create problems of ambiguity. These can usually be corrected by rewording the sentence.

Avoid: They sought to express clearly different points of view. [In attempting to avoid a split infinitive, the writer has created ambiguity as to what *clearly* modifies.]

Better: They sought to express different points of view clearly. *Or:* They sought to express points of view that were clearly different.

Avoid: He vowed to vigorously promote exercising. [Here the split in-finitive makes clear that it is the *promotion* that is vigorous. In attempting to avoid the split infinitive the writer must keep that link intact as the movement of *vigorously* in either direction would change the meaning.]

He vowed vigorously to promote exercising. [Here *vigorously* modifies *vowed.*]

He vowed to promote exercising vigorously. [As in the example above, this modification introduces ambiguity. It is unclear whether it is the exercising or the promotion that is vigorous.]

Better: He vowed to be vigorous in his promotion of exercise.

5.8.6   *Contractions.* —A contraction is a word made up of two words combined into one by omitting one or more letters. An apostrophe shows where the omission has occurred. Contractions are usually avoided in formal writing.

Note: It's and *its* are frequently interchanged—and always erroneously. *It's* is the contraction of *it is*, and *its* is the possessive form of the pronoun *it.* (See also 6.11, Punctuation, Apostrophes.)

5.9   Subject-Verb Agreement. —The subject and verb must agree; use a sin-gular subject with a singular verb and a plural subject with a plural verb. However, this simple rule is often violated. The guidelines outlined below will help ensure proper usage.

5.9.1   *Intervening Phrase.* —Plural nouns take plural verbs and singular nouns take singular verbs, even if a plural phrase follows the subject.

A review of all patients with grade 3 tumors was undertaken in the university hospital.

Where the intervening phrase is introduced by *together with, as well as,* or similar phrases, the singular verb is preferred.

The editor, as well as the reviewers, believes that this article is ready for acceptance.

The patient, together with her physician and her family, makes this decision.

5.9.2   *False Singulars.* —A few nouns are used so frequently in the plural that the plural has come to be used as a singular noun. This usage is still incorrect. Frequently treated in this way are the plurals *criteria, phenom-ena,* and *media* (in both senses). The singulars, which should be used when the singular is intended, are *criterion, phenomenon,* and *medium,* respectively. (Likewise, *data* is a plural noun and takes a plural verb. When the singular is intended, *item of data, fact, datum, finding,* or a similar alternative can substitute.)

5.9.3   *False Plurals.* —Some nouns, by virtue of ending in a ''plural'' -*s* form, are mistakenly taken to be plurals even though they should be treated as singular and take a singular verb (eg, *measles*, *mumps*, *mathematics*).

5.9.4   *Parenthetical Plurals.*—When an *s* or *es* is added to a word parenthetically to express the possibility of a plural, the verb should be singular, since the *s* or *es* is parenthetical. However, in most instances today grammarians prefer to avoid this construction and change to the plural noun.

> The name(s) of the editor(s) of the book in reference 2 is unknown.

5.9.5   *Collective Nouns.*—A collective noun is one that names a group. When the group is regarded as a unit, the singular verb is the appropriate choice:

> The couple owns property near the Canadian border.
>
> The paramedic crew helps respond to these emergency calls.
>
> Twenty percent of her time is spent on administration.

When the group is instead being treated as a unit composed of individual members, the plural verb is correct:

> The couple were no longer living together.
>
> The surgical team were from all over the country.
>
> Ten percent of the staff work flexible hours.
>
> The majority of patients who suffer brain death are to be found on the neurosurgical, neurological, and cardiac services of general hospitals.
>
> The graduating class were preparing to go their separate ways.
>
> The committee are opening their agenda books and preparing to begin work.

5.9.6   *Compound Subject.*—When two words or two groups of words, usually joined by *and* or *or*, are the subject of the sentence, the singular or plural verb form may be appropriate, depending on whether the words joined are singular or plural and on the connectors used.

Compound subject joined by and: With *and*, a plural verb is usually preferable. A singular verb should be used if the two elements are thought of as a unit (ham and eggs, lox and bagels, bread and butter, dilatation and curettage) or refer to the same person (our friend and host) or thing.

Compound subject joined by or *or* nor: With a compound subject joined by *or* or *nor*, the plural verb is correct if both elements are plural; if both elements are singular, the singular verb is correct. When one is singular and one is plural, the better choice for the verb form is that of the closer noun.

5.9   Subject-Verb Agreement

Both plural: Neither staphylococci nor streptococci were responsible for the infection.

Both singular: Neither a false positive nor a false negative is definitive.

Mixed: Neither the hospital nor the physicians were responsible for the loss.

5.9.7   Shift in Number of Subject and Resultant Subject-Verb Disagreement.— In elliptical constructions involving the verb, ie, when a verb is omitted as understood, if the number of the subject changes, the ellipsis (omission) is incorrect.

Incorrect: Her tests were run and her chart updated.
Correct: Her tests were run and her chart was updated. *Or:* Her test was run and chart updated.

Incorrect: The rocks underfoot are slippery and the current strong.
Correct: The rocks underfoot are slippery and the current is strong.

5.9.8   Subject and Predicate Nominative Differ in Number.—When the subject and the predicate nominative differ in number, follow the number of the *subject* in selecting the singular or plural verb form.

Incorrect: The factor that showed the most abnormality were the red blood cells.
Correct: The factor that showed the most abnormality was the red blood cells.

Avoid this by rephrasing:

The red blood cells showed the most abnormality.

5.9.9   Every/Many a.—When *every* or *many a* is used before a word or series of words, use the singular.

Many a teacher has experienced such emotions.

Every resident has had such an encounter with a patient.

5.9.10   One of Those.—In clauses following *one of those*, the plural is always correct.

Dr Hyatt is one of those researchers who prefer the library to the laboratory.

5.9.11   Number.—*The number* is singular and *a number of* is plural.

The number who responded was surprising.

A number of respondents were verbose in their answers.

The same is true of *the total* and *a total of*.

5.9.12 *Indefinite Pronouns.*—Most indefinite pronouns express the idea of quantity and share properties of collective nouns (see 5.9.5, Subject-Verb Agreement, Collective Nouns). Some (eg, *each, either, neither, one, no one, everyone, someone, anybody, somebody*) always take the singular; some (eg, *several, few, both, many*) always take the plural. And some (eg, *some, any, none, all,* and *most*) may take either the singular or the plural, depending on the referents. Usually the best choice is to use the singular verb when the pronoun refers to a singular word and the plural verb when the pronoun refers to a plural word.

Singular referent:	Some of my time is spent wisely.
Plural referent:	Some of his calculations are difficult to follow.
Singular referent:	Most of the manuscript was typed with a justified right-hand margin.
Plural referent:	Most of the manuscripts are edited on computer terminals.

6.0 Punctuation

To indicate a break or pause in thought, to set off material, or to introduce a new but connected thought, commas, semicolons, or colons can be used. Each has specific uses, and the strength of the break in thought determines which mark to choose.

6.1   **Comma.**—Commas are the least forceful of the three marks. There are definite rules for using commas; however, usage is often subjective. Some writers and editors use the comma frequently to indicate what they see as a natural pause in the flow of words. However, commas can be overused; of late the trend is to use them sparingly. A safe rule of thumb is to follow the accepted rules and use commas only when breaks are needed for the sense or readability of the sentence and to avoid confusion or misinterpretation.

6.1.1   *Separating Groups of Words.*—The comma is used to separate phrases, clauses, and groups of words and to clarify the grammatical structure and the intended meaning.

Use a comma after opening dependent clauses (whether restrictive or not) or long opening adverbial phrases (however, a comma is not essential if the introductory phrase is short).

> If you insist on being abusive, we shall leave.

Use commas to set off nonrestrictive subordinate clauses (see 5.7.2, Pronouns, Relative Pronouns) or nonrestrictive participial phrases.

> The Smiths, who had been standing in line for more than an hour, abandoned all hope of getting front-row seats.
>
> The bathrobe, dripping wet, was the one I wanted.
>
> The numbness, which had been apparent for 3 days, disappeared after drug therapy.

Use a comma to avoid an ambiguous or awkward juxtaposition of words.

> I think his rib must be cracked, because he coughed. (*But:* He coughed because his rib was cracked; his rib cracked because he coughed.)

Inside, the fire burned steadily.

Peace is a daily, a weekly, a monthly process, gradually changing opinions, slowly eroding old barriers, quietly building new structures. (John F. Kennedy)

Use commas to set off appositives. (*Note:* Commas precede and follow the apposition.)

Two friends, John Smith and Perry White, sold us the car.

The battered-child syndrome, a clinical condition in young children who have received serious physical abuse, is a frequent cause of permanent injury or death.

6.1.2   *Series.*—In a simple coordinate series of three or more terms, separate the elements by commas.

Each patient was given a 21-item, seven-point, self-administered questionnaire to complete.

A conjunction before the last term should be preceded by a comma.

Magenta, taupe, and forest green were the predominant colors in the dress.

Neither the physician, the nurse, nor the family could induce the patient to take his medication daily.

While in the hospital, these patients required neuroleptics, maximal observation, and seclusion.

6.1.3   *Names of Organizations.*—When an enumeration occurs in the name of a company or organization, the comma is usually omitted before the ampersand. However, follow the punctuation used by the individual firm, except in references. (See 2.10.27, References, Publishers.)

Smith, Kline & French Laboratories

Little Brown & Co

6.1.4   *Setting Off* viz, ie, eg.—Use commas to set off *viz, ie, eg,* and the expanded equivalents, *namely, that is,* and *for example.*

The most important tests, viz, white blood cell count and hematocrit, were unduly delayed.

The use of standardized scores, eg, Z scores, has no effect on statistical comparisons.

(*Note:* If the clause that follows these terms or their equivalents is independent, precede the clause with a semicolon.)

Our own work consisted of a double-blind study that compared continuous with cyclic estrogen treatment; ie, estrogens for 4 weeks were compared with estrogens for 3 weeks followed by placebo for 1 week.

6.1.5   *Separating Clauses Joined by Conjunctions.*—Use commas to separate main clauses joined by coordinating conjunctions (*and, but, or, nor, for*).

> Plasma lipid and lipoprotein concentrations were unchanged after low-intensity training, but high-intensity training resulted in a reduction in triglyceride levels.
>
> No subgroup of responders could be identified, and differences between centers were so great that no real comparison was possible.

Clauses introduced by *yet* and *so* and subordinate conjunctions (eg, *while, where, since, after*) are preceded by a comma.

> He gathered up his belongings and packed his bag, yet could not find the courage to go.
>
> I consulted the vice president, since the president was not available.

If both clauses are short, punctuation can be omitted.

> You may leave or you may stay.
>
> I have Bright's disease and he has mine. (S. J. Perelman)

6.1.6   *Setting Off Parenthetical Expressions.*—Use commas to set off parenthetical words, phrases, questions, and other expressions that interrupt the continuity of a sentence, eg, *therefore, moreover, on the other hand, of course, to tell the truth, nevertheless, after all, consequently, to say the least, however.*

> The real issue, after all, was how to find the money for the new stadium.
>
> We should take care not to make the intellect our god; it has, of course, powerful muscles, but no personality. (Einstein)
>
> However, much as I try, I cannot understand Bayes' theorem. (*But:* However much I try, I cannot understand Bayes' theorem.)
>
> Therefore, he drew the correct conclusion. (*But:* He therefore drew the correct conclusion.)

In scientific text, one often encounters the following parenthetical construction:

> Her platelet count was 100×10^9/L (normal, 150×10^9/L).

6.1.7   *Setting Off Degrees and Titles.*—Academic degrees, titles, and *Jr* and *Sr* are set off by commas when they follow the name of a person.

> Berton Smith, Jr, MD, and Priscilla Armstrong, MD, PhD, interpreted the roentgenographic findings in this study. (*But:* Marshall Field IV; Pope John Paul II [See 16.2.6, Numbers and Percentages, Roman Numerals.])

6.1 Comma

> Harold Washington, mayor of Chicago, attended the neighborhood rally.

6.1.8   Addresses.—Use commas to separate the elements in an address. (*Note:* Commas are not used before the ZIP code.)

> This year, the editorial board meeting will be held in the Board Room, American Medical Association, 1101 Vermont Ave NW, Washington, DC 20420.

6.1.9   Dates.—In dates and similar expressions of time, use commas according to the following examples. Note that no commas are used when the month and year are given without the day.

> The first issue of *The Journal of the American Medical Association* was published on Saturday, July 14, 1883.

> Steven's rhinoplasty was scheduled for August 19, 1985, with postoperative evaluation on September 30, 1985.

> December 1941 was a time to fear.

> They were married on New Year's Day, 1967.

6.1.10   Numbers.—Do not separate digits with a comma to indicate thousands. (See 16.0, Numbers and Percentages.)

> 5034   12 345   615 478   9 473 209

Occasionally, a comma may be used to separate adjacent unrelated numerals if neither can be expressed easily in words. Usually, it is preferable to reword the sentence or spell out one of the numbers.

> By December 1983, 3064 cases of AIDS had been reported nationwide.

> (*Better:* By December 1983, a total of 3064 cases of AIDS had been reported nationwide.)

> NASA reported that in the year 2000, 2000 active satellites would orbit the earth.

> (*Better:* NASA reported that 2000 active satellites would orbit the earth in the year 2000.)

> In 1983, 27% of all surgical procedures in this institution were performed on an outpatient basis.

> (*Better:* In 1983, of all surgical procedures performed in this institution, 27% were done on an outpatient basis.)

6.1.11   Units of Measure.—Do not use a comma between two units of the same dimension.

> 3 years 4 months old   3 lb 4 oz

6.1.12   Placement.—The comma is placed inside quotation marks (see 6.6.5,

Quotation Marks, Placement) and before superscript citation of references and footnote symbols.

6.1.13 *To Indicate Omission.*—Use a comma to indicate omission or to avoid repeating a word when the sense is clear.

> Three patients could not be studied: in one, treatment was too short; in two, too long.

> A plus indicates present; a minus, absent.

6.2 **Semicolon.**—Semicolons represent a more solid break in thought than commas do. Generally, semicolons are used to separate two independent clauses. Often a comma will suffice if sentences are short; but when the main clauses are long and joined by coordinating conjunctions or conjunctive adverbs, especially if one of the clauses has internal punctuation, a semicolon is the mark to use.

6.2.1 *Separating Independent Clauses.*—Use a semicolon to separate independent clauses in a compound sentence when no connective word is used. (In most instances it is equally correct to use a period and make two sentences.)

> The conditions of 52% of the patients improved greatly; 4% of the patients were dropped from the study.

However, if clauses are short and similar in form, use a comma.

> Seventy grafts were patent, five were occluded.

Use a semicolon between main clauses joined by a conjunctive adverb (eg, *also, besides, furthermore, then, however, thus, hence, indeed, yet*) or a coordinating conjunction (*and, but, or, for, nor*) if one of the clauses has internal punctuation or is quite long.

> The word *normal* is often used loosely; indeed, it is not easily defined.

> This consideration is important in any research; yet it is often overlooked, if not denied.

> The patient's fever had subsided; however, his condition was still critical.

6.2.2 *Enumerations.*—For clarity, use semicolons between items in a complex or lengthy enumeration within a sentence. (In a simple series with little or no internal punctuation, use commas.)

> A number of questions remain unresolved: (1) whether beverages that contain caffeine are an important factor in arrhythmogenesis; (2) whether such beverages can trigger arrhythmias de novo; and (3) whether their arrhythmogenic tendency is enhanced by the presence and extent of myocardial impairment.

There was, to be sure, a decent assortment of male champions: for example, Byeong-Keun Ahn, of Korea, in lightweight judo; Juha Tiainen, of Finland, in the hammer throw; and Mauro Numa, of Italy, in the men's individual foils.

6.3   Colon.—The colon is the strongest mark of a decided pause or break in thought. It separates two main clauses in which the second clause amplifies or explains the first.

We begin with a single tenet: all men are created equal.

6.3.1   *When Not to Use a Colon.*—Do not use a colon if the sentence is continuous without it.

You will need enthusiasm, organization, and a commitment to your beliefs.

Do not use a colon to separate a preposition or a verb (including *to be* in all of its manifestations) from its object (or predicate nominatives). Do not use a colon after *because*.

6.3.2   *Introducing Quotations or Enumerations.*—Use a colon to introduce a formal or extended quotation.

Harold Johnson, MD, chair of the committee, said: ''The problems we face in developing a new vaccine are numerous, but foremost is isolating the antigen.''

Use a colon to introduce an enumeration, especially after anticipatory phrasing such as *thus, as follows, the following.*

The following ingredients will be needed: eggs, salt, pepper, and milk.

Laboratory studies yielded the following values: hemoglobin, 119 g/L; erythrocyte sedimentation rate, 104 mm/h; calcium, 4.22 mmol/L; phosphorus, 1.81 mmol/L; and creatinine, 270 μmol/L.

If more than one grammatically independent statement follows the colon, they may be treated as separate sentences and the initial words may or may not be capitalized if the statement is a complete sentence. However, if the sentence to follow is in quotes, the first word is capitalized.

The following rules apply to manuscript preparation: (1) Submit an original typescript and two high-quality copies. (2) Type all copy double-spaced on heavy-duty white bond paper. (3) Provide ample margins. (4) Do not justify the right-hand margin. (5) Do not use a dot matrix printer.

6.3.3   *Numbers.*—Use a colon to separate chapter and verse numbers in biblical references, hours and minutes in expressions of time, and parts of numerical ratios.

The reading for today is Genesis 3:28.

The flight to Paris was scheduled for 2:35 PM.

The chemicals were mixed in a 2:1.5 ratio.

6.3.4 *References.*—In references, use a colon (1) between title and subtitle; and (2) for periodicals, between volume and page numbers. (See also 2.10, References.)

6.4   Question Mark, Exclamation Point, Period

6.4.1 *Question Mark.*—The primary use of the question mark is to end interrogative sentences.

How long has he been practicing medicine?

If this symphony were a work of the 1930s, not the 1980s, would we hear it differently today? And should we?

In dates: Use the question mark to show doubt about specific data.

Catiline (108?-62 BC) lived during the time of Cato the Younger.

Placement: Place the question mark inside the end quotation mark (see 6.6.5, Quotation Marks, Placement), the closing parenthesis, or the end bracket when the mark is part of the material being quoted or that is parenthetic.

The wine steward asked the patron, "Would you like to have the bottle of Bordeaux uncorked before your dinner?"

The chapter on interpretation asks the question, "Can I be wrong?"

In declarative sentences that contain a question, place the question mark at the end of the interrogative statement.

Why did I bother to come to this party? she wondered.

The first section of the book, "What Medical Advances Made Open Heart Surgery Possible?" is certain to interest medical historians. (Note that the question mark, like the exclamation point [see 6.4.2, Exclamation Point, Placement] is never combined with other question marks, exclamation points, periods, or commas; thus, the need for a second comma is obviated in this example.)

6.4.2 *Exclamation Point.*—Exclamation points indicate emotion, an outcry, or a forceful comment. Try to avoid their use except in direct quotations and in rare and special circumstances. They are more common in less formal articles such as book reviews or editorials, when added emphasis is essential.

Beware!

If you cannot accept the gold standard (within reason, that is, nothing is perfect!), then you should question whether the diagnostic data are worth capturing. (Sackett DL, Haynes BR, Tugwell P. *Clinical Epidemiology.* Boston, Mass: Little Brown & Co; 1985:49)

I think of the noon whistle as a wake-up call: You, weeding your tomato patch, wake up!

Placement: Note that, when it completes the emphasized material, the exclamation point goes inside the end quotation mark, parenthesis, or bracket. (Note that the exclamation point, like the question mark [see 6.4.1, Question Mark, Placement] is never combined with another exclamation point, question mark, period, or comma; thus, the need for a comma is obviated in the first example.)

"Let the buyer beware!" his listeners shouted back as one.

The frightened child cried, "Don't leave me here all alone!"

Factorial: In mathematical expressions, the exclamation point is used to indicate a factorial.

$$5! = 5 \times 4 \times 3 \times 2 \times 1$$

6.4.3   *Period.*—Periods are the most common end-of-sentence punctuation marks. Use a period at the end of a declarative or imperative sentence, at the end of each footnote and each legend, and after an indirect question not requiring an answer.

Where, indeed, is the Osler of today.

Wasn't it odd that the occasion for this public outburst about what was going on in US schools was the publication of a dictionary.

Placement: The period precedes ending quotation marks and reference citations.

The child is rated in seven areas, such as "progressing very well" or "could be doing better."

We followed the methods of Wilkes et al.[5]

Enumerations: Use a period after the arabic numeral, when enumerating paragraphed items. (See also 16.1.5, Numbers and Percentages, Enumerations.)

Decimals: Use the period as a decimal indicator (see 16.2.1, Numbers and Percentages, Decimals).

$r = .75$ 0.123% .32 caliber

Introductory expressions: AMA style uses a period after a run-in sidehead, after the opening words in letters to the editor, and in numerical designation of figures and tables (ie, in figure legends and table titles). (See 2.6.1, Headings, Subheadings, and Side Headings, Levels of Headings; 2.11, Legends; and 2.13.5, Tables, Table Titles.)

> **Diagnoses.**—Each patient was seen within 24 hours of his first acute attack.

> Fig 1.—Cystourethrogram demonstrates an intrapelvic filling defect.

> Table 2.—Patients Presenting Without Lymphoma

Symbols and abbreviations: Omit the period from titles, running feet, scientific and chemical symbols, abbreviations (see 2.1, Manuscript Preparation, Titles and Subtitles, and 11.0, Abbreviations).

> NaCl   Al   *t* test

Multiplication: The period in raised position shows multiplication. (See also 15.1.3, Units of Measure, Multiplication Sign vs Times Dot, and 18.3.2, Mathematical Composition, Simplifying.)

6.5 **Dashes.**—Dashes as another form of internal punctuation convey a particular meaning or emphasize and clarify a certain section of material within a sentence. Compared with parentheses, dashes convey a less formal "aside."

There are four types of dashes of varying length: the *em* dash, the most common; the *en* dash; the *2-em* dash; and the *3-em* dash. When typing a manuscript, use two hyphens to indicate an em dash (—) and one for an en dash (–), which the editor will mark for the typesetter.

6.5.1 *Em Dash.*—Em dashes are used to indicate a sudden interruption or break in thought in a sentence. It is best to use this mode sparingly; do not use an em dash when another punctuation mark will suffice.

> All of these factors—age, severity of symptoms, psychic preparation, and choice of anesthetic agent—determine the patient's reaction.

An em dash may be used to separate a referent from a pronoun that is the subject of an ending clause.

> Osler, Billings, and Jacobi—these were the men he tried to emulate.

Introductory and closing expressions: AMA style uses an em dash in the following instances:

1. After the opening words in Letters to the Editor.

> *To the Editor.*—   *In Reply.*—

2. Before the designation "ED." in an editor's note.

> *These comments have been abstracted from two letters.*—ED.

3. After sideheads and after numerical designation in table titles and figure

legends. (See 2.6.1, Headings, Subheadings, Side Headings, Levels of Headings; 2.11, Legends; and 2.13.5, Tables, Table Titles.)

Fibrinolysis.—Increase in spontaneous fibrinolytic activity was noted.

CASE **4.**—A 4-year-old girl was first seen on August 20, 1984.

Fig 2.–Three months later, new lesions had appeared.

Table 2.—Incidence of Bleeding Episodes

Running foot: AMA style uses an em dash before volume numbers and authors' names in the running foot (see 2.4, Manuscript Preparation, Running Feet).

6.5.2 **En Dash.**—The en dash is longer than a hyphen but half the length of the em dash.

The en dash shows relational distinction in a hyphenated or compound modifier, one element of which consists of two words or a hyphenated word, or when the word being modified is a compound.

Winston-Salem–oriented group

physician-lawyer–directed section

anti–basement membrane glomerulonephritis

phosphotungstic acid–hematoxylin stain

post–World War I

multiple sclerosis–like symptoms

6.5.3 **2-Em Dash.**—The 2-em dash may be used to separate independent statements in a paragraph.

These items were noted: Graham Smith, MD, was the youngest member of this class; he was certified by the American Board of Pediatrics in 1951, and he won the Judson Prize in 1960.——Pearson Jones, MD, was licensed by reciprocity, is in general practice, and has never published his findings, despite extensive personal research.——Francine Piedicue, MD, started her graduate work at the age of 38 and has served as a missionary in West Africa since receiving her MD degree in 1976.

6.5.4 **3-Em Dash.**—The 3-em dash is used to show exclusion of information in the text. (It is not used in references.)

Our study began in N———, noted for its casual life-style.

I admire Dr ——— too much to expose him in this anecdote.

6.6 **Quotation Marks.**—Quotation marks are used to indicate that material is taken directly from another source, ie, material that is being quoted. There are definite rules to follow in using quotation marks.

6.6.1 *Quotations.*—Use quotation marks to enclose a direct quotation of no more than four typewritten lines from textual material or speeches (see also 6.6.12, Block Quotations). When the quotation marks enclose conversational dialogue, there is no limit to the length that may be set in run-on format.

In all quoted material, follow the wording, spelling, and punctuation of the original exactly. Whenever possible, verify the quotation from the original source. The only time this does not apply is when the quoted material, although a complete sentence or part of a complete sentence in its original source, is now used as part of another complete sentence. Then the capital letter in the quoted sentence would be omitted.

Similarly, in legal material any change in initial capital letters from quoted material should be indicated by placing the change in brackets. (See 6.9.1, Brackets, Insertions in Quotations.)

To indicate an omission in quoted material, use ellipses. (See 6.7, Ellipses.)

To indicate editorial interpolation in quoted material, use brackets. (See 6.9.1, Brackets, Insertions in Quotations.) Use [*sic*] after a misspelled word or an incorrect or apparently absurd statement in quoted material to indicate that this is an accurate rendition of the original source. However, when quoting material from another era that uses now obsolete spellings, use *sic* sparingly. Do not use *sic* with an exclamation point. (*Note:* The use of *sic* is not limited to quoted material; in other instances, it means that any unusual or bizarre appearance in the preceding word is intentional, not accidental.)

6.6.2 *Dialogue.*—With conversational dialogue, enclose the opening word and the final word in quotation marks.

"Please do not close the door just yet."

"Okay, if you insist, I won't."

6.6.3 *Titles.*—Within titles (this includes titles of references and tables) and within centered heads, use single quotation marks.

The 'Sense' of Humor

6.6.4 *Single Quotation Marks.*—Use single quotation marks when quoting material that appears in material that is already enclosed in quotation marks.

He looked at us and said, "As my father always told me, 'Be a good listener.' "

6.6.5 *Placement.*—Place closing quotation marks outside commas and periods, inside colons and semicolons. Place question marks, dashes, and exclamation points inside quotation marks only when they are part of the quoted material. If they apply to the whole statement, place them outside the quotation marks.

Why bother to do autopsies at all if the net result is invariably "edema and congestion of the viscera"?

The clinician continues to ask, "Why did he die?"

"I'll lend you my camping stove for the weekend retreat"—then she remembered the last time she had lent it out and said, "On second thought, I'll be needing it myself."

(*Note:* If a single word or short phrases are quoted, do not separate by commas: He said he had had his "fill of it all" and was "content" to leave.)

6.6.6   *Omission of Opening or Closing Quotation Marks.*—The opening quotation mark should be omitted when an article beginning with a stand-up or drop two-line initial capital letter also begins with a quotation. It is best, however, to avoid this construction.

D octors need some patients," a sage had said.

When excerpting long passages that consist of several paragraphs, use the opening double quotation marks before each passage and closing quotation marks only at the end of the final passage. (See also 6.7, Ellipses, and 6.6.12, Block Quotations.)

6.6.7   *Coined Words, Slang.*—Coined words, slang, and words or phrases used ironically or facetiously may be enclosed in quotation marks at first mention. Thereafter, omit quotation marks.

This bone acts as the fulcrum or "nut" and thus causes the "flattop" talus in the victim of the "nutcracker" treatment.

They called him a "square" because he preferred classical music to jazz.

It has been said that shoes and latrines are the best "medicine" for ancylostomiasis (hookworm disease).

A note should be made on the subject of "apologetic" quotation marks. Quotation marks used around words to give special effect or to indicate irony, although not out of date, are often unnecessary and offensive to the intelligent reader.

In such instances when irony or special effect is intended, skillful preparation can take the place of using these quotes. Resort to the apologetic quote or the quote used to express irony only after such attempts have failed.

The title of this book may come as something of a shock to those of us who have considered "socialized medicine" practically a "dirty word" for all of our professional lives.

6.6.8   *Common Words Used in a Technical Sense.*—Enclose in quotation marks a common word used in a special technical sense when the context does not make the meaning clear. (See also 6.6.9, Definition of Foreign Words.)

> In many publications, ''running feet'' on left-hand pages face the ''gutter'' at the bottom of the page.

> Both the subjects and the investigators in the first testing period were ''blind.''

6.6.9   *Definition of Foreign Words.*—Enclose in quotation marks the definition of a foreign word or phrase if it follows the word or phrase.

> Hysterical patients may exhibit an attitude termed *la belle indifference* (''beautiful indifference,'' ''total unconcern'') toward their condition.

6.6.10   *Titles.*—In the text, use quotation marks to enclose titles of short poems, essays, lectures, radio and television programs, songs, parts of published works (chapters, articles in a periodical), papers read at meetings, dissertations, and theses, and parts of the same article (eg, the ''Results'' section).

6.6.11   *Indirect Discourse, Discussions.*—With indirect discourse, do not use quotation marks.

> He said he would go home earlier.

Do not use quotation marks with yes or no.

> His answer to the question was no.

In interview or discussion formats, when the speaker(s) is set off do not use quotation marks.

> Dr Brown: xxxxxxxxxxxxxxxxxxxxxxxxxxxxxxxxxx
> xxxxxxxxxxxxxxxxxxxxxxxxxxxxxxxxxxxxxxxxxx

> Dr Smith: xxxxxxxxxxxxxxxxxxxxxxxxxxxxxxx

6.6.12   *Block Quotations.*—If the quoted material is longer than four typewritten lines from textual material or speeches, the material should be set off in blocks, ie, use reduced type and eliminate the quotation marks. Paragraph indents are generally not used unless the quoted material is known to be the beginning of a paragraph. AMA style uses a 4-point space both above and below these longer quotations.

If the block quotation appears in a section to be set in reduced type, do not reduce the type size of the quoted material further.

If another quotation, regardless of how long it is, appears within a block quote, use double quotation marks around the quote within the quote.

6.7   **Ellipses.**—Ellipses are three spaced dots (. . .) generally used to indicate

6.7 Ellipses

omission of one or more words, lines, paragraphs, or data from quoted material (this omission being the *ellipsis*). Excerpts from the following paragraph will be used to demonstrate the use of ellipses.

> In *Fruit Displayed on a Stand* (cover), exhibited in 1882, Caillebotte depicts a traditional subject in a manner far removed from the traditional cornucopian flow of fruit. Instead, he shows a stark, rectangular grid lit by centers of rounded forms, brilliantly colored. Vivid oranges, reds, and purples, light greens, creamy violets, and color-flecked gold are cupped within areas of crinkly blue-white paper, the cooler shades in the center separating the hotter tones, preventing them from spilling into each other (*JAMA*. 1985;254:1000).

6.7.1 Omission Within a Sentence.—If the ellipsis occurs within a sentence, ellipses represent the omission. Note that a space precedes and follows the ellipses.

> Instead, he shows a . . . grid lit by centers of rounded forms, brilliantly colored.

In some such instances, additional punctuation may be used on either side of the ellipses if it helps the sense of the sentence or better shows the omission.

> Instead, he shows a stark, rectangular grid . . ., brilliantly colored.

6.7.2 Omission at the End of a Sentence.—If the ellipsis occurs at the end of a sentence, but before a new sentence begins, ellipses follow the final punctuation mark, the final punctuation mark being set close to the word preceding it, although this word is not the final word in that sentence.

> In *Fruit Displayed on a Stand* (cover), exhibited in 1882, Caillebotte depicts a traditional subject in a manner far removed from the traditional. . . . Instead, he shows a stark, rectangular grid lit by centers of rounded forms, brilliantly colored.

6.7.3 Omission Between Sentences.—If the ellipsis occurs between two complete sentences, ellipses follow the final punctuation mark of the first sentence, the final punctuation mark being set close to the preceding word.

> In *Fruit Displayed on a Stand* (cover), exhibited in 1882, Caillebotte depicts a traditional subject in a manner far removed from the traditional cornucopian flow of fruit. . . . Vivid oranges, reds, and purples, light greens, creamy violets, and color-flecked gold are cupped within areas of crinkly blue-white paper, the cooler shades in the center separating the hotter tones, preventing them from spilling into each other.

110

If a sentence is omitted after a sentence that already ends in an ellipsis, no additional dots are needed, ie, the three spaced dots following the preceding incomplete sentence are sufficient.

> In *Fruit Displayed on a Stand* (cover), exhibited in 1882, Caillebotte depicts a traditional subject. . . . Vivid oranges, reds, and purples, light greens, creamy violets, and color-flecked gold are cupped within areas of crinkly blue-white paper, the cooler shades in the center separating the hotter tones, preventing them from spilling into each other.

6.7.4 *Grammatically Incomplete Expressions.*—The sentence preceding as well as that following the ellipses should be a grammatically complete expression. However, three dots and *no* period may be used at the end of a sentence to indicate that it is purposely grammatically incomplete.

> Complete the sentence ''When I return, I plan to . . .'' in 20 words or less.

6.7.5 *Omissions in Verse.*—Use one line of em-spaced dots to indicate omission of a full line or several consecutive lines of verse.

6.7.6 *Omissions Between or at the Start of Paragraphs.*—With material in which several paragraphs are being quoted and omissions of full paragraphs occur, a period and three dots at the end of the paragraph preceding the omitted material is sufficient to indicate this omission of one or more intervening paragraphs.

> xxxxxxxxxxxxxxxxxxxxxxxxxxxxxxxxxxxxxxxxxxxxxxxxxxxxxxxx
> xxxxxxxxxxxxxxxxxxxxxxxxxxxxxxxxxxxxxxxxxxxxxxxxxxxxxx
> xxxxxxxxxxxxxxxxx. . . .

If the first sentence of the paragraph being quoted is omitted, begin that paragraph with three ellipses dots and a paragraph indention to indicate that this is not the opening sentence of that paragraph.

> . . . xxxxxxxxxxxxxxxxxxxxxxxxxxxxxxxxxxxxxxxxxxxxxxxxxx
> xxxxxxxxxxxxxxxxxxxxxxxxxxxxxxxxxxxxxxxxxxxxxxxxxxxxxxxx
> xxxxxxxxxxx.

6.7.7 *Change in Capitalization.*—The first word following the end punctuation mark and the ellipses should use the original capitalization, particularly in legal and scholarly documents. This facilitates finding the material in the original source and avoids any change of meaning. If a change in the original capitalization is made, brackets should be used around the letter in question. (See also 6.6.1, Quotation Marks, Quotations, and 6.9.1, Brackets, Insertions in Quotations.)

> [H]e shows a stark, rectangular grid lit by centers of rounded forms, brilliantly colored.

6.7   Ellipses

6.7.8   *Omission of Ellipses.*—Ellipses are not necessary at the beginning and end of a quotation if the quoted material is a complete sentence from the original.

> In a 1985 *JAMA* cover story, Martha Bier wrote, "Instead, he shows a stark, rectangular grid lit by centers of rounded forms, brilliantly colored."

Omit ellipses within a quotation when the omitted words occur at the same place as a bracketed editorial insertion. (See also 6.9.1, Brackets, Insertions in Quotations.)

> [Caillebotte] shows a stark, rectangular grid lit by centers of rounded forms, brilliantly colored."

6.7.9   *Ellipses in Tables.*—In tables, ellipses may be used to indicate that no data were available or that a specific category of data is not applicable. (See also 2.13.10, Tables, Zeros and Ellipses.)

6.8   Parentheses

6.8.1   *Supplementary Expressions.*—Use parentheses to indicate supplementary explanations, identification, direction to the reader, or translation. (See also 6.9, Brackets, and 6.5, Dashes.)

As a rule, it should be possible to delete the parenthetical material without affecting the meaning or structure of the sentence.

> A known volume of fluid (100 mL) was injected.
>
> The changes were not significant ($P > .05$).
>
> One of us (B.O.G.) saw the patient in 1985.
>
> Asymmetry of the upper part of the rib cage (patient 5) and pseudoarthrosis of the first and second ribs (patient 8) were incidental anomalies (Table 3).
>
> Of the 761 hospitalized patients, 171 (22.5%) were infants (younger than 2 years).
>
> In this issue of THE JOURNAL (p 1037), a successful transplant is reported.
>
> The restaurant's acclaimed *bûche de Noël* ("yule log") was prepared by its French-born pastry chef.

If there is a close relationship between the parenthetical material and the rest of the sentence, commas are preferred to parentheses.

> James, although exhausted, continued to run at the pace he had set earlier in the race.

If the relationship in thought following the expressions *namely* (*viz*), *that is* (*ie*), and *for example* (*eg*) is incidental, use parentheses instead of commas.

112

He weighed the advice of several committee members (namely, Jones, Burke, and Easton) before making his proposal.

6.8.2   *Punctuation Marks With Parentheses.*—Use no punctuation before the opening parenthesis except in enumerations (see 6.8.5, Enumerations).

Any punctuation mark can follow a closing parenthesis, but only three punctuation marks, namely, the period, the question mark, and the exclamation point, may precede it.

The discussion on parentheses lasted 2 hours (A final draft was yet to be written. That would come later.) and did not resolve the question.

After what seemed an eternity (It took 2 hours!), the discussion on parentheses ended.

The discussion on the parentheses section lasted 2 hours (Can you believe it?) and we still did not resolve the issue.

The discussion on parentheses took up most of the meeting time (namely, 2 hours); parentheses will be discussed further next week.

(Note that, in these above examples, when the parenthetical material is a complete sentence, terminal punctuation is placed inside the closing parenthesis.)

6.8.3   *Identifying Numbers or Letters.*—When an item identified by letter or number is referred to later by that letter or number only, enclose the letter or number in parentheses.

You then follow (3), (5), and (6) to solve the puzzle.

If the category name is used instead, adopt the open style.

Steps 1, 2, and 3 must be done slowly.

6.8.4   *Insertion of Location.*—When the proper name of an institution, organization, or publication includes a place name, the state may be identified parenthetically, except in specific addresses. (See also 11.4, Abbreviations, Local Addresses, and 11.5, Abbreviations, States, Territories, and Possessions.)

Winter Park (Fla) Memorial Hospital

Springfield (Mass) *Republican*

When the proper name includes the name of a county, do not abbreviate the state name.

Cook County (Illinois) Sanitary District

6.8.5   *Enumerations.*—For division of a short enumeration that is run in and indicated by numerals or lowercase italic letters, enclose the numerals or letters in parentheses. (See also 16.1.5, Numbers and Percentages, Enumerations.)

> The calligraphy instructor told us to bring (1) paper, (2) an india ink pen, and (3) ink to our next class.

6.8.6   *References in Text.*—Use parentheses to enclose all or part of a reference given in the text. (See also 2.10.2, References, References Given in Text.)

> The case was originally reported in the *Archives of Surgery* (1975;148:343-346).

> The legality of this practice was questioned more than a decade ago (*Br Med J*. 1963;2:394-396).

6.8.7   *In Legends.*—In legends, use parentheses to identify a case or patient. (See also 2.11.5, Legends, Patient Identification.)

> Fig 6.—Facial paralysis on the right side (patient 3).

> Fig 2.—Fracture of the left femur (case 7).

The date, if given, is similarly enclosed.

> Fig 2.—Fracture of the left femur (case 7, October 23, 1985).

For photomicrographs, give the magnification and the stain, if relevant, in parentheses.

> Fig 3.—Marrow aspiration 14 weeks after transplantation (Wright's stain, original magnification ×600).

6.8.8   *Reprint Address.*—In the address for reprint requests and reader correspondence, indicate in parentheses the author who can be reached at this address. (See also 2.3.7, Footnotes, Reprint Address.)

> Reprint requests to 469 Prospect Dr, Peekskill, NY 10566 (Dr Smith).

6.8.9   *Trademarks.*—If the author provides a trademark for a drug or equipment, enclose the trademark in parentheses immediately after the first use of the nonproprietary name in the text and in the synopsis-abstract. (See also 12.6.3, Drugs, Trademarks, and 12.8, Nomenclature, Equipment and Reagents.)

> Treatment included oral administration of indomethacin (Indocin), 25 mg three times a day.

6.8.10   *Abbreviations.*—If used five or more times in the text, specialized abbreviations (as specified in 11.10, Abbreviations, Clinical and Technical Terms) are enclosed in parentheses immediately after first mention of the term, which is spelled out in full.

6.8.11   *Explanatory Footnotes.*—Explanatory footnotes may be incorporated into the text by means of parentheses. In such instances, terminal punctuation occurs before the closing parentheses, the sentence(s) within the parentheses being a complete thought but only parenthetical to the text.

Parenthetical expressions within a parenthetical expression are enclosed in brackets. (*But:* In mathematical expressions, parentheses go *inside* brackets. See also 6.9.2, Brackets, Within Parentheses.)

> (Antirejection therapy included parenteral antithymocyte globulin [ATGAM], at a dosage of 15 mg/kg per day.)

6.8.12 ***Parenthetical Plurals.***—Parentheses are often used around the letters *s* or *es* to express the possibility of a plural when singular or plural could be meant. (See also 5.9.4, Subject-Verb Agreement, Parenthetical Plurals.)

> The name(s) of the editor(s) of the book in reference 2 is unknown.

(*Note:* If this construction is used, the verb should be singular, since the *s* is parenthetical. In most instances today, grammarians prefer avoiding this construction and changing to the plural noun.)

6.9   Brackets

6.9.1 ***Insertions in Quotations.***—Brackets are used to indicate editorial interpolation within a quotation and to enclose corrections, explanations, or comments in material that is quoted. (See also 6.6.1, Quotation Marks, Quotations; 6.7.7, Ellipses, Change in Capitalization; and 6.7.8, Ellipses, Omission of Ellipses.)

> "Enough questions had arisen [these are not described] to warrant medical consultation."
>
> Thompson stated, "Because of the patient's age and debility, *surgery* was postponed [italics added]."
>
> "The following year [1947] was a turning point."

Note: Use *sic* in brackets to indicate an error or peculiarity in the spelling or grammar of the preceding word. As with apologetic quotation marks (see 6.6.7, Quotation Marks, Coined Words, Slang), use *sic* with discretion.

> "The plural [*sic*] cavity was filled with fluid."
>
> "Breathing of the gas is often followed by extraordinary fits of extacy [*sic*]."

6.9.2 ***Within Parentheses.***—Use brackets to indicate parenthetical expressions within parenthetical expressions.

> A nitrogen mustard (mechlorethamine [Mustargen] hydrochloride) was one of the drugs used.

6.9   Brackets

6.9.3   *In Formulas*.—In chemical and mathematical formulas, parentheses are generally used for the innermost units, with brackets added if necessary. (See also 18.3, Mathematical Composition, Simplifying.)

1-$\left(10\text{-}\{3\text{-}[4\text{-}(2\text{-hydroxyethyl})\text{-}1\text{-piperazinyl}]\text{propyl}\}\text{-}10H\right.$
$\left.\text{phenothiazine-2-yl}\right)$-1-propanone carphenazine

When a parenthetical or bracketed insertion in the text contains a formula in which parentheses or brackets appear, the characters within the formula should be left as given unless that would place two identical characters immediately adjacent to each other. To avoid adjacent identical characters, change parentheses to brackets or brackets to parentheses in the formula as needed.

The chemical name of pyroxamine maleate (3-[(p-chlorophenylbenzyl)oxy]-1-methylpyrrolidine maleate) is a good example.

The equation suggested by this phenomenon ($t = d[r_1 - r_2]$) can be applied in a variety of circumstances.

6.10   Virgule (Solidus).—The virgule is a diagonal line used to represent *per*, *and*, or *or* and used to divide material (eg, numerator and denominator in fractions; month, day, and year in dates [only in tables and figures]; lines of poetry).

6.10.1   *Used to Express Duality*.—With he/she, change the virgule construction where the gender is to be specified; substitute the word *or* for the virgule.

Tom and Kate said they were coming. Now I need to know whether he or she [not he/she] will be bringing the extra chairs.

If the gender is unspecified and does not matter, retain the virgule construction.

This French recipe is one that any cook can master whether or not he/she has experimented with nouvelle cuisine.

(*Note:* The trend today is toward rephrasing such sentences and using the plural to avoid sexist language; eg, ''This recipe is one that cooks can master whether or not they have experimented with nouvelle cuisine.'' [See 9.10, Correct and Preferred Usage, Sexist Language.])
    Often the virgule construction is used to imply a duality, eg, the physician/patient experience, in which the virgule implies the physician and patient are the same person.
    But, when two separate individuals are implied in a relationship, change the virgule to another punctuation mark or word.

One often reads about the physician-patient relationship in medical literature. [Here it is the relationship between the physician and the patient.]

They decided to sign up for the father and son bowling league.

6.10.2 *Used to Mean* **Per.**—In the "per" construction, use a virgule only when (1) the construction involves units of measure (including time), *and* (2) at least one element includes a specific numerical quantity, *and* (3) the element immediately adjacent on each side is either a specific numerical quantity or a unit of measure. In such cases, the units of measure should be abbreviated in accordance with 11.11, Abbreviations, Units of Measure. (See also 16.2.5, Numbers and Percentages, Proportions and Rates.)

> The hemoglobin level was 140 g/L.
>
> The leukocyte count was 4.2×10^9/L.
>
> Blood volume was 80 mL/kg of body weight.
>
> Serum carotenoids measured 3 U/mL. Respirations were 60/min.
>
> (*But:* Pulse rate was 98 beats per minute [because beat is not considered a unit of measure per se].)

Do *not* use the virgule in a "per" construction (1) when a prepositional phrase intervenes between the two elements, (2) when neither element contains a specific numerical quantity, or (3) in nontechnical expressions.

> 4.5 mmol of potassium per liter
>
> (*Avoid:* 4.5 mmol/L of potassium)
>
> expressed in milliliters per minute
>
> 2 days per year

6.10.3 *In Dates.*—Use the virgule in dates only in tables and figures to save space (month/day/year) (see 2.13.8, Tables, Punctuation).

6.10.4 *In Equations.*—In equations that are set on line and run into the text rather than centered and set off (see 18.3, Mathematical Composition, Simplifying), use the virgule to separate numerator and denominator.

> The "stacked" fraction $y = \dfrac{r_1 + r_2}{p_1 - p_2}$ is written as $y = (r_1 + r_2)/(p_1 - p_2)$

Note that when the virgule is used for this purpose, parentheses and brackets must often be added to avoid ambiguity.

6.10.5 *Phonetics, Poetry.*—The virgule is also used to set off phonemes and phonetic transcription and to divide run-in lines of poetry.

> /d/ as in *dog*
>
> . . . cold-breathed earth/earth of the slumbering and liquid trees/earth of the mountains misty-topped.

6.11   Apostrophe

6.11.1 *To Show Possession.*—Use the apostrophe to show the possessive case of nouns and indefinite pronouns in accordance with the following examples (see also 13.1, Eponyms, Possessive Form):

Caesar's Palace	Jones' bones (one Jones)
a child's wants	the Joneses' bones (two or more Jones)
men's ties	everyone's answer
Marx's theories	

(*Note:* If a singular or plural word does not end in *s*, add *'s* to form the possessive.)

6.11.2 *Possessive Pronouns.*—Do not use *'s* with possessive pronouns: his, hers, ours, its, yours, theirs, whose.

The car is hers.

Give the review of the book its due.

(*Note:* Do not confuse the contraction of *it is* (it's) with the possessive of *its*; eg, "It's a beautiful day.")

6.11.3 *Possessive of Compound Terms.*—Use *'s* after only the last word of a compound term.

father-in-law's tie	physician-in-chief's decision
mothers-in-law's letters	Secretary of Health's ruling
someone else's carton	

6.11.4 *Joint Possession.*—When joint possession is being shown with nouns, or with an organization's or business firm's name, use the possessive form only in the last word of the noun or name.

Food and Drug Administration's policy

Farrar, Straus & Giroux's books

Merck Sharp & Dohme's drug inserts

Centers for Disease Control's Task Force

Hammond and Horn's study

(*Exception:* When one of the words is a possessive pronoun, the others take the possessive as well: I presented the intern's and my workup. *But:*

When possession is individual, each noun takes the possessive form: Jane's and Ken's baseball bats.)

6.11.5 *Using Apostrophes to Form Plurals.*—Do not use an apostrophe to indicate the plural of a name. Do not use an apostrophe in the name of an organization in which the qualifying term is used as an adjective rather than a possessive. (Of course, always follow the official name.)

> The Chicago Cubs
>
> Veterans Administration
>
> Rainbow Babies Hospital
>
> Childrens Hospital (*But:* Children's Memorial Hospital)

Use *'s* to indicate the plural of letters, signs, or symbols spoken as such, or words referred to as words when *s* alone would be confusing. Note the italics with the inflectional ending in roman type for words, letters, and numbers but not for symbols and signs.

> He uses too many *and*'s.
>
> Mind your *p*'s and *q*'s.
>
> There are nine +'s on the page.
>
> His *l*'s looked like *7*'s.

Do not use an apostrophe to form the plural of an all-capital abbreviation or of numerals (including years).

> ECGs   EEGs   IQs   WBCs   RBCs
>
> A woman in her 40s
>
> During the late 1970s

6.11.6 *Units of Time and Money as Possessive Adjectives.*—However, with units of time (minute, hour, day, month, year, etc) used as possessive adjectives, an *'s* is added. The same holds true for monetary terms (see also 5.6.3, Nouns, Involving Time or Money):

> a day's wait
>
> an hour's wait
>
> 5 days' hard work
>
> a few hours' time
>
> several months' time
>
> 80 cents' worth of licorice

6.11   Apostrophe

6.11.7 *Prime.*—Do not use an apostrophe where a prime sign is intended. Do not use a prime sign as a symbol of measurement.

> The methyl group was in the 5′ position.

6.12   Hyphen.—Hyphens are connectors. The hyphen connects words permanently or temporarily. Certain compound words always contain hyphens. Such hyphens are called *orthographic*. Examples are seen in the compound words *merry-go-round*, *free-for-all*, and *mother-in-law*. For temporary connections, hyphens help prevent ambiguity, clarify meanings, and indicate word breaks at the end of a line.

In general, when not otherwise specified, hyphens should be used only as an aid to the reader's understanding, primarily to avoid ambiguity. For capitalization of hyphenated compounds in titles, subtitles, subheads, and table heads, see 8.4.2, Capitalization, Hyphenated Compounds.

6.12.1 *Temporary Compounds.*—Hyphenate temporary compounds according to the following:

Hyphenate a compound that contains a noun (as object) and a present participle that together serve as an adjective.

> decision-making methods (*But:* methods of decision making)

Hyphenate a compound adjectival phrase when it precedes the noun it modifies.

> all-or-nothing situation (*But:* The situation was all or nothing.)
>
> step-by-step instructions (*But:* The instructions were step by step.)
>
> up-to-date schedule (*But:* The schedule was up to date.)
>
> end-to-end anastomosis (*But:* The anastomosis was end to end.)

Hyphenate an adjective-noun compound when it precedes and modifies another noun.

> upper-class values (*But:* Values were upper class.)
>
> third-floor apartment (*But:* The apartment was on the third floor.)
>
> low-quality fabric (*But:* The fabric was of low quality.)
>
> well-publicized event (*But:* The event was well publicized.)

(*Note:* In most instances *high-* and *low-* adjectival compounds are hyphenated.)

Hyphenate a combination of two nouns used coordinately as a unit modifier when preceding the noun but not when following.

albumin-globulin ratio (*But:* ratio of albumin to globulin)

the Binet-Simon Test (*But:* the test of Binet and Simon)

Hyphenate a combination of two nouns of equal participation used as a single noun. (See also 6.10.1, Virgule [Solidus], Used to Express Duality.)

player-manager   author-critic

soldier-statesman   physician-poet

actor-director

Hyphenate most compound nouns containing a preposition. Follow the latest edition of *Webster's New Collegiate Dictionary*.

a tie-in   a tie-up   a go-between   a looker-on

a hand-me-down

(*But:* an onlooker, a passerby, a handout, a workup, a makeup)

Hyphenate a compound in which a number is the first element and the compound precedes the noun it modifies.

18-factor blood chemistry analysis

two-way street

ninth-grade reading level

1-cm increments

Hyphenate two or more adjectives used coordinately or as conflicting terms whether they precede the noun or follow as a predicate adjective.

He had manic-depressive episodes.

His psychosis was manic-depressive.

The false-positive test results were noted.

The test results were false-positive.

We performed a double-blind study.

The test we used was double-blind.

Hyphenate color terms where the two elements are of equal weight.

blue-gray eyes

blue-black lesions (lesions were blue-black) (*But:* bluish gray fabric)

Hyphenate compounds formed with the prefixes *all-*, *self-*, and *ex-* whether they precede or follow the noun.

self-assured salesperson   all-powerful ruler

He needs self-respect.   My ex-husband called.

(*Note:* With the prefix *vice*, follow the latest edition of *Webster's New Collegiate Dictionary*, eg, vice-chancellor, vice-consul, *but* vice president, vice admiral.)

Hyphenate compounds made up of the suffixes *-type, -elect*, and *-designate.*

Hodgkin's-type lymphoma

Valsalva-type maneuver

chair-elect

secretary-designate

Hyphenate most contemporary adjectival *cross-* compounds (check the dictionary for absolute accuracy; there are exceptions, eg, crossbred, crosshatched, crossmatched).

cross-country race

cross-city competition

cross-eyed cat

Hyphenate *adjectival* compounds with *quasi*. (*Note:* Noun compounds formed with *quasi* are not hyphenated.)

quasi-legislative group   quasi-diplomatic efforts

quasi diplomat

Hyphenate some compounds in which the first element is a possessive. Consult the latest edition of *Webster's New Collegiate Dictionary*.

bird's-eye view   crow's-feet   bull's-eye

Hyphenate all prefixes preceding a proper noun, a capitalized word, a number, or an abbreviation.

anti-American demonstration   pro-Israeli forces

un-American activities   pseudo-Christian

anti-Iranian movement   pre-Victorian era

post-1945 clothing   pre-RBC trials

Hyphenate compound numbers from 21 to 99 and compound cardinal and ordinal numbers when written out, as at the beginning of a sentence. (See 16.1, Numbers and Percentages, Usage.)

Thirty-six patients were examined.

Sixty-fifth birthdays are often celebrated with flair.

One hundred thirty-two people died in the plane crash.

Hyphenate fractions used as adjectives.

A two-thirds majority was needed.

The flask was three-fourths full.

(*But:* Do not hyphenate spelled-out common fractions used as nouns: Three fourths of the questionnaires were returned.)

When two or more hyphenated compounds have a common base, omit the base in all but the last. In unhyphenated compounds written as one word, repeat the base.

first-, second-, and third-grade students

10- and 15-year-old boys

(*But:* preoperative and postoperative treatment, *not* pre- and postoperative treatment)

6.12.2   *Clarity.*—Use hyphens to avoid ambiguity. If a term could be misleading without a hyphen, hyphenate it.

a small-bowel constriction (constriction of the small bowel)

a small bowel constriction (a small constriction of the bowel)

an old-car salesperson (a salesperson of old cars)

an old car salesperson (a car salesperson who is old)

man-eating plants (a plant that eats humans)

man eating plants (a man eating plants)

Use a hyphen after a prefix when the unhyphenated word would have a different meaning.

re-treat   re-creation   re-formation

Occasionally, a hyphen is used after a prefix or before a suffix to avoid an awkward combination of letters, such as two of the same vowel or three of the same consonant (with exceptions noted in 6.12.5, When Not to Use Hyphens). Follow the latest edition of *Webster's New Collegiate Dictionary*.

semi-independent   hull-less   ultra-atomic

de-emphasize   intra-abdominal   bell-like

(*But:* microorganism; cooperation; reenter)

6.12   Hyphen

In complex modifying phrases that include suffixes or prefixes, hyphens and en dashes are sometimes used to avoid ambiguity. (See also 6.5.2, Dashes, En Dash.)

non–self-governing   non–group-specific blood

non–brain-injured subjects   manic-depressive–like symptoms

6.12.3   *Expressing Ranges and Dimensions.* —In expressing dimensions, use hyphens and spacing in accordance with the following examples. In the text, do not use hyphens to express ranges (eg, in 5% to 10% of the group). (*Note:* There is a distinction between the terms *to* and *through* when expressing ranges. *To* indicates up to but not including; *through* implies up to and including; eg, their ages ranged from 3 to 5 years, 5 to 7 years; *but* their ages ranged from 3 through 5 years, 6 through 7 years.)

in a 10- to 14-day period   10 to 14 days' duration

a 3×4-cm strip   a strip measuring 3×4 cm

a 5- to 10-mg dose   a dose of 5 to 10 mg

in a 5-, 10-, or 15-mg dose   a dose of 5, 10, or 15 mg

a 3-cm-diameter tube   a tube 3 cm in diameter

(*But:* Figs 4 through 6; Tables 3 through 5)

6.12.4   *Word Division.* —Use hyphens to indicate division of a word at the end of a line (follow the latest edition of *Webster's New Collegiate Dictionary* or *Dorland's* or *Stedman's* medical dictionaries).

6.12.5   *When Not to Use Hyphens.* —Rules also exist for when *not* to use hyphens. The following common prefixes are not joined by hyphens.

ante-, anti-, bi-, co-, contra-, counter-, de-, extra-, infra-, inter-, intra-, micro-, mid-, non-, over-, pre-, post-, pro-, pseudo-, re-, semi-, sub-, super-, supra-, trans-, tri-, ultra-, un-, under-

antivivisectionist	midaxillary	posttraumatic
repossess	nonresident	coauthor
overproduction	coidentity	coexistence
coworker	postoperative	ultramicrotome
transsacral	nonnegotiable	

(*But:* co-opt, intra-aortic)

124

The following suffixes are always joined without a hyphen, with exceptions noted in 6.12.2, Clarity: *-fold, -hood, -less, -like, -wise.*

twofold	womanhood	manhood	shoeless
barklike	clockwise		

Some combinations of words are commonly read together as a unit. As such combinations come into common usage, the hyphen tends to be omitted.

birth control methods	open heart surgery
public health officials	bone marrow biopsy
medical school students	urinary tract infection
social service agency	amino acid levels

Do not hyphenate names of disease entities used as modifiers. (*But:* Follow *Dorland's*, eg, small-cell carcinoma [see also 6.12.2, Clarity].)

grand mal seizures	hyaline membrane disease
basal cell sarcoma	sickle cell disease
sickle cell trait	

Do not use a hyphen after an adverb ending in *-ly* even when used in a compound modifier preceding the word modified.

the clearly stated purpose	a highly developed species

Do not hyphenate names of chemical compounds used as adjectives.

sodium chloride solution	tannic acid test

(*But:* hematoxylin-eosin stain)

Most combinations of proper adjectives derived from geographic entities are not hyphenated.

Central Americans	the Far East	Latin Americans
Far Eastern customs	Central American customs	

(*But:* Scotch-Irish ancestry)

Do not hyphenate Latin expressions or foreign phrases used in an adjectival sense. Most of these are treated as separate words; a few are joined without a hyphen. Follow the latest edition of *Webster's New Collegiate Dictionary*.

an a priori argument	per diem employees

6.12   Hyphen

    prima facie evidence   postmortem examination

    an ex officio member   antebellum South

    in vivo specimens   carcinoma in situ

Do not hyphenate modifiers in which a letter or number is the second element.

    grade A eggs   study 1 protocol   type I diabetes

6.12.6   Compound Official Titles.—Hyphenate compound designations of office as follows:

    secretary-treasurer   acting secretary

    honorary chair

    (*But:* past vice president, executive vice president, past president)

6.12.7   Special Combinations.—Special combinations may or may not necessitate the use of hyphens. Consult *Dorland's, Stedman's, Saunder's,* and the latest edition of *Webster's New Collegiate* dictionaries.

T wave	T-shirt	γ-globulin
T square	*t* test	Mann-Whitney *U* Test
T tube	B cell	B-cell helper
T-cell marker	I beam (I-shaped beam)	

126

7.0 Plurals

7.1 **Abbreviations.**—With units of measure, use the same abbreviation for singular and plural forms. (See 11.11, Abbreviations, Units of Measure.) For most all-capital abbreviations, the plural is formed by adding *s*.

RBCs   WBCs   HMOs   PSROs   EEGs   IQs   ECGs

Do not use the abbreviation or its plural form to denote a person by title or status.

Three physicians reported the cases. (*Not:* Three MDs reported the cases.)

7.2 **Collective Nouns.**—Collective nouns may take verbs that are singular or plural, depending on the intended meaning. (See also 5.9.5, Subject-Verb Agreement, Collective Nouns.)

A number of subjects were unavailable for follow-up.

The number of controls was small.

The majority rules.

The majority were cured.

(*Note:* With units of measure always use a singular verb: Five milliliters was injected.)

7.3 **Compound Nouns.**—For compound nouns written as one word, add *s* to form the plural.

teaspoonful   teaspoonfuls

For compound nouns formed by a noun and a modifier, form the plural by making the noun plural. Follow the lastest edition of *Webster's New Collegiate Dictionary* when in doubt.

mother-in-law   mothers-in-law

attorney-general   attorneys-general

coup d'etat   coups d'etat

man-of-war   men-of-war

7.3   *Compound Nouns*

Some compound nouns form the plural irregularly.

tie-up	tie-ups
2-month-old	2-month-olds
merry-go-round	merry-go-rounds

7.4   Latin and Greek vs English.—Follow the latest edition of *Webster's New Collegiate Dictionary* or *Dorland's* or *Stedman's* medical dictionaries. Use the English form, rather than the Latin or Greek form, for the plural whenever such form is available. Be aware, however, that rarely is there a difference in meaning with the variant forms:

The book had both subject and author indexes.

The book was rated on numerous indices.

(In mathematics, *indices* is always the preferred spelling.)

alga	algae
appendix	appendixes (although appendices is acceptable)
cannula	cannulas
corpus delicti	corpora delicti
cranium	craniums (although crania is acceptable)
criterion	criteria
formula	formulas
genus	genera
humerus	humeri
maxilla	maxillae
phenomenon	phenomena
sequela	sequelae
trabecula	trabeculae
vertebra	vertebrae

7.5   Microorganisms.—For organisms use the lowercase plural form for those that have a common designation. Consult the latest edition of *Dorland's* or *Stedman's* medical dictionaries. (See 12.16.1, Nomenclature, Genus and Species.)

Bacillus	bacilli
Staphylococcus	staphylococci
Streptococcus	streptococci

For some organisms that do not have a common plural designation, add the word *organisms* or *species* to indicate a plural use. (See 12.16.1, Nomenclature, Genus and Species.)

7.6   **Other Plurals.**—For the plural of numbers, letters, signs, and symbols, see 6.11.5, Apostrophe, Using Apostrophes to Form Plurals.

Chapter 8

8.0 Capitalization

Words are capitalized sparingly but conventionally in the scientific publications of the AMA. When a common noun is capitalized in the singular as part of a proper name or in a title, it is generally not capitalized in the plural.

8.1 **Proper Nouns.**—Capitalize proper nouns; follow the most recent edition of *Webster's New Collegiate Dictionary* and *Webster's New International Dictionary.*

8.1.1 *Geographic Names.*—Capitalize geographic names for political divisions (except numbered designations), cities, townships, counties, states, countries, continents, islands, peninsulas, straits, bodies of water, mountain chains, streets, parks, forests, canyons, dams, specific locations, and accepted designations for regions.

Mississippi River	Pacific Ocean	Lake Erie
the Great Lakes	Hudson Bay	the West Coast
the Bay Area	Kettle Moraine	

(*But:* Mississippi and Missouri rivers; Atlantic and Pacific oceans)

New York City	Mexico City (*But:* Quebec city)	
North Pole	British Isles	Central America
United Kingdom	Isle of Wight	the Orient
Straits of Gibraltar	New Trier Township	Cook County
the Black Forest	the Badlands	the Green Mountains
Hoover Dam	Forty-second Street	the Iron Curtain
the Loop [Chicago]	Fisherman's Wharf	Estes National Park

New York State (*But:* the state of New York)

(*Note:* the fifth precinct; the 23rd congressional district)

Expanded compass directions are not capitalized when indicating general directions or locations, although they are capitalized when used as accepted designations for regions and when part of geographic designations.

> She lives in the Far East, in central China. Her home is east of Chongqing (Chungking) but not as far east as Wuhan.
>
> He is a westerner. He lives in the West, 15 miles west of Salt Lake City, Utah.
>
> Go due north, then northwest. (*But:* ENE, SSW)
>
> North Carolina   West Berlin   North Korea (*But:* southern France, northern Illinois)

There is a current trend to write nouns and adjectives derived from compass directions in lowercase.

> midwesterner   southern-style cooking   eastern influence

8.1.2   *Sociocultural Designations.*—Capitalize proper names of languages, peoples, races, political parties, religions, and religious denominations and sects. Do not capitalize the common nouns following these designations. Do not capitalize political doctrines. Do not capitalize *white* or *black* as a designation of race.

the English language	Sanskrit	French people
Orientals	Europeans	Mohawks
of Spanish ancestry	Jew	Protestant
Hispanic community	a Baptist church (*But:* First Baptist Church)	

> Although she has been a member of the Republican party for years, at one time she was a Democrat. She nonetheless has always endorsed the principles of democracy in our republican form of government. She is democratic in her attitudes toward social equality.

8.1.3   *Events, Awards, Legislation.*—Capitalize the names of historical events and periods, special events, awards, treaties, and official names and specific parts of adopted laws and bills. Do not capitalize common nouns and adjectives in proposed laws, bills, or amendments that have not passed.

Russian Revolution	New York Marathon	Kentucky Derby
Purple Heart	World War II	Nobel Prize
Geneva Convention	Medicare	Medicare Act
Fifth Amendment	Battle of Gettysburg	Social Security Act
Louisiana Purchase	Bill of Rights	Civil Rights Law

Public Law 89-74   Title XVIII

Congressional Medal of Honor

Pfizer Biomedical Research Award

(*But:* King-Anderson bill; Medicare law; premarital laws)

8.1.4   *Words Derived From Proper Nouns.*—Most words derived from proper nouns are not capitalized. Follow the boldface entries in the most recent edition of *Webster's* for nonmedical terms; follow *Dorland's* and *Stedman's* medical dictionaries or *Saunder's Dictionary and Encyclopedia of Laboratory Medicine and Technology* for medical terms. (See also 12.8, Nomenclature, Equipment and Reagents; 12.16.1, Nomenclature, Genus and Species; and 12.16.2, Nomenclature, Viruses.)

india ink	*Candida*	candidiasis
Mendel	mendelian	parkinsonian
addisonian	*Schistosoma*	schistosomiasis
brussels sprouts	plaster of paris	

(*Note:* Although *Webster's* is a useful standard, there are instances where words derived from proper nouns have become part of common usage and are not capitalized; eg, arabic numerals, roman numerals, turkish coffee, roman candles.)

8.1.5   *Eponyms.*—When an eponym is included in the name of a disease, syndrome, sign, position, or similar designation, capitalize the eponym but not the common noun. Consult the most current editions of *Dorland's* and *Stedman's* medical dictionaries, *Current Medical Information and Terminology*, and the *Illustrated Dictionary of Eponymic Syndromes and Diseases and Their Symptoms.* (See also 13.0, Eponyms.)

Raynaud's disease	Babinski's sign	Marfan's syndrome
Gram's stain	Trendelenberg's position	

8.1.6   *Proprietary Names.*—Capitalize trademarks and proprietary names of drugs and brand names of manufactured products and equipment. Do not capitalize generic names or descriptive terms. The common noun after a brand name is not capitalized. (See also 12.6, Nomenclature, Drugs; and 12.8, Nomenclature, Equipment and Reagents.)

Smith-Corona typewriter	Peter Pan peanut butter
Xerox copies	Macintosh computer
Dacron implant	Teflon-coated

8.1.7   *Organisms.*—Capitalize the name of a genus when used in the singular,

133

with or without a species name. Do not capitalize when used in the plural or as an adjective. Do not capitalize the name of a species, variety, or subspecies. Do capitalize class, order, family, and tribe. (See also 12.16.1, Nomenclature, Genus and Species.) For capitalization of virus names, see 12.16.2, Nomenclature, Viruses.

8.1.8   *Seasons, Deities, Holidays.*—Do not capitalize the names of the seasons. Do capitalize the designations of specific deities and personifications.

the Almighty	Mother Nature	God	Allah
the Holy Spirit			

Capitalize recognized holiday and calender events.

Easter	Passover	Fourth of July	St Patrick's Day
Holy Week	Thanksgiving	New Year's Eve	

8.1.9   *Tests.*—The exact titles of published and unpublished tests are capitalized. The word *scale* or *test* is not capitalized when used to refer to a subscale of a test.

Advanced Vocabulary Test   Wechsler Adult Intelligence Scale

Minnesota Multiphasic Personality Inventory Depression scale
[this is a subscale of the MMPI]

Hamilton Depression Rating Scale   Hopkins Symptom Checklist

Draw-a-Man Test   Bayley Scales of Infant Development

(*But:* Bayley Scales consist of three tools: Mental scale, Motor scale, and Infant Behavior record. Only the Mental and Motor scales were used.)

When a test name is specific to its inventor (be it a statistical or a psychological test), the words following the inventor's name are capitalized. If the words following the inventor's name are more general, they usually are not capitalized. Also, if the test is not being referred to by its exact name, or if its name is being used in an abbreviated form, do not capitalize.

Fisher's Exact Test   Newman-Keuls Test

Wechsler Intelligence Scale for Children

Pearson Product-Moment Correlation Coefficient

(*But:* Pearson correlation coefficient)

Goodenough-Harris Drawing Test

(*But:* The Goodenough-Harris test was used.)

Kuder-Richardson reliability   Kuder-Richardson coefficient vocabulary test   Stroop color test

Hamilton score   (*But*: Student's *t* test)

8.2   **Titles and Degrees of Persons.**—Capitalize the title of a person when it precedes the person's name but not when it follows the name.

> Chairman John W. Smith (*But:* John W. Smith was named chairman.)
>
> Prime Minister Thatcher addressed the US Congress. Later in the week the prime minister will meet with the president.

In addition, institutions and organizations, when referring to themselves and their officers in abbreviated form, often use capitals.

Capitalize academic degrees when abbreviated but not when written out. (See also 11.1, Abbreviations, Academic Degrees and Honors, and 11.6, Abbreviations, Names and Titles of Persons.)

8.3   **Official Names.**—Capitalize the official titles of conferences, congresses, postgraduate courses, organizations, institutions, business firms, and governmental agencies, and their departments and other divisions. Do not capitalize a conjunction, article, or preposition of three letters or less, except when it is the first or last word in a title or subtitle. In institution names, do not capitalize *the* unless it is part of the official title.

> Family Service Association of America
>
> The Johns Hopkins Hospital
>
> *The Journal of the American Medical Association*
>
> *The New England Journal of Medicine*
>
> the Federal Bureau of Investigation
>
> Pharmaceutical Products Division, Baxter Laboratories, Inc
>
> The Robert Wood Johnson Foundation

the Girl Scouts of America	Chicago Lying-In Hospital
Cambridge University	Trans World Airlines
Quaker Oats Corporation	Supreme Court
Interstate Commerce Commission	New York Academy of Sciences
Chicago Board of Education	Congress
Department of Labor	House of Representatives

> Tufts University School of Medicine
>
> the Third International Congress on Poliomyelitis
>
> the 10th Annual Surgical Symposium of the Association of Veterans Administration Hospitals

the Insect Allergy Committee of the American Academy of Allergy

the Federation of State Medical Boards in the United States

the Illinois State Senate

the International Subcommittee on Viral Nomenclature

the Ad Hoc Committee on Evaluation of Experimental Trials

But: an ad hoc committee	the federal government
congressional reports	the committee
the department	the university
the corporation	the company
the association	the army
the navy	the armed forces
naval service	federal courts
state senators	the congressman
the board of health	the board of trustees

Institutions and organizations when referring to themselves and their officers in abbreviated form often use capitals. For example, at the AMA:

the Board of Trustees	the Board
the House of Delegates	the House
the Association	

the Department of Continuing Medical Education

the Department

the Committee on Allied Health Education and Accreditation

the Committee

the President of the AMA	the President

(*But:* the trustees; the delegates)

A singular noun that is capitalized as part of the official name is usually not capitalized in the plural.

Department of Pediatrics *but* departments of pediatrics and neurology

(*Exception:* From the Departments of Medicine and Pediatrics, University of Tennessee College of Medicine, Memphis.)

However, when the plural of a common noun is part of the title of an organization or institution, it should be capitalized.

136

National Institutes of Health   Centers for Disease Control

Vanderbilt University Affiliated Hospitals

(*But:* Michael Reese and Northwestern Memorial hospitals have programs on prenatal care.)

8.4   **Titles and Headings.**—Capitalize major words in titles, subtitles, and headings of publications, parts of publications, musical compositions, plays (stage and screen), radio and television programs, movies, paintings, works of art, and names of ships, airplanes, and monuments. Do not capitalize a conjunction, article, or preposition of three letters or less, except when it is the first or last word in a title or subtitle.

the *Merrimac*   the Tomb of the Unknown Soldier

Golden Globe   Truman Memorial Library

Oscar   *Tartuffe*

Busse Highway   the *Kitty Hawk*

Seurat's *Sunday Afternoon on the Grande Jatte*

Calder's *Baseball Bat*   Verdi's *The Four Seasons*

Samuel Barber's *Adagio for Strings* op 11

"General Hospital"   "Family Ties"

Navy Pier

Do capitalize a two-letter verb, for example, *go, do, am, is, be.*

What Is Sarcoma?   We Do Need to Treat Mild Hypertension

Where the World Will Be in the Year 2001

With dual verbs, such as *follow up,* do capitalize both parts in a title.

Following Up the Diabetic Patient

8.4.1   *In References.*—In listed references, follow 2.10.10, References, Titles; 2.10.11, References, Foreign-Language Titles; and 2.10.12, References, Subtitles, for capitalization of titles and subtitles of articles, parts of books, bulletins, and pamphlets, in English or in a foreign language.

8.4.2   *Hyphenated Compounds.*—In titles, subtitles, table heads, centerheads, sideheads, and line art, do not capitalize the second part of a hyphenated compound in the following instances:

● If either part is a hyphenated prefix or suffix (see 6.12.1, Hyphens, Temporary Compounds).

Re-treat   Self-preservation

Anti-infective Drugs	Intra-abdominal Surgery
Intra-arterial Embolism	Vaso-occlusive Disease

- If both parts together constitute a single word (if in doubt about hyphenation of such terms, consult the current edition of *Webster's*, or *Dorland's* or *Stedman's* medical dictionaries).

Long-term	Follow-up Studies
X-ray Films	Part-time Help
End-expiratory Pressure	Small-cell Carcinoma In Situ

(*But:* Auditory Brain-Stem Response; Low-Level Radioactive Waste; Drug-Resistant Diseases)

Note: Capitalize the word that follows a Greek letter (see 14.2, Greek Letters, Capitalization After a Greek Letter), a number, or a small capital letter in titles, subtitles, table heads, centerheads, sideheads, and line art:

β-Blockers	1,25-Dihydroxycholecalciferol

8.5   First Word of Statements, Quotations, or Subtitles.—Capitalize the first word (1) of a formal statement following a colon (see 6.3.2, Colon, Introducing Quotations or Enumerations); (2) after the word *resolved* in a resolution; (3) of a direct quotation (but see 6.6.1, Quotation Marks, Quotations); and (4) of a question or a statement inserted in a sentence but not in quotation marks. (*But:* See also 6.6.1, Quotation Marks, Quotations, concerning legal quotations.)

(*Note:* In the case of the question, this can be left up to the author's personal style. Generally, with a more formal question, the first word will take a capital letter.)

After a colon, capitalize the first word (1) in book titles (see 2.10.10, References, Titles; however, the first word in subtitles of journal articles is *not* capitalized) and, often, (2) in the text when the following enumeration or explanation contains two or more independent clauses. (See also 6.3.2, Colon, Introducing Quotations or Enumerations.)

For capitalization in quoted material, follow the quotation exactly. Usually the first word of a direct quotation should be capitalized, especially if it is formally presented as a quotation.

> The report noted: "A candidate may be admitted after completing 2 years of medical school."

If the quotation is run into the sentence, however, a lowercase letter on the first word might be preferable. (See also 6.6.1, Quotations Marks, Quotations.)

The report noted that ''a candidate may be admitted after completing 2 years of medical school.''

If a sentence fragment is being quoted, do not capitalize the first word.

The committee agree with the report that candidate admission requires ''completing 2 years of medical school.''

8.6   **Acronyms.**—Do not capitalize the words from which an acronym is derived.

intelligence quotient (IQ)

enzyme-linked immunosorbent assay (ELISA)

Exception: When words forming the acronym are proper names, use capitals as described in 8.3, Official Names.

National Broadcasting Company (NBC)

8.7   **Designators.**—When used as specific designation, with or without numerals, capitalize *Table*, *Figure*, *Fig*, and *Figs*.

as shown in the Table

as seen in compact bundles (Figure)

summarized in Table 2

as illustrated in Figs 2 through 7

cultures yielded *Candida* (Fig 3)

Note: When a table or figure is cited in a paragraph with its number designation and is then referred to again in that paragraph, the capital letter as well as the numeral designation can be deleted provided no other tables or figures are cited in the intervening material.

In Table 5 one can see the distribution of the patient population. This table also shows the prevalence of disease in this group.

Do not capitalize the following words, even when used as specific designations:

case	fraction	notes	section
chapter	grade	page	series
chromosome	grant	paragraph	stage
column	group	part	type
experiment	lead	patient	volume
factor	method	phase	wave

Chapter 9

9.0   Correct and Preferred Usage

We offer this section on correct and preferred usage to help authors and
editors avoid common errors and infelicities and, we hope, to encourage
sensitivity to their use of language. (See also 5.0, Grammar, and 12.0,
Nomenclature.) The section is intended less to proscribe than to clarify
the meanings of or describe distinctions between frequently misused words.
Beyond that, we always entreat authors to avoid words and phrases that
are unnecessarily elaborate, trendy, euphemistic, or dry. Scientific investigations and clinical care are sometimes dull and confusing, and often
seem endless, but that need not be true of written accounts of what they
reveal.

9.1   Commonly Misused Words and Phrases

abort, terminate—*Abort* means "to stop a process in the early stages." A
pregnancy, not a fetus or a woman, may be aborted. We prefer the synonym
terminate, which is less likely to be misused.

acute, chronic—These terms should be reserved for descriptions of symptoms, conditions, or diseases. Avoid the use of *acute* and *chronic* to
describe patients, parts of the body, treatment, or medication.

Incorrect	*Correct*
chronic therapy	long-term therapy
chronic marijuana users	acute myocardial infarction
	chronic alcoholism
	long-term marijuana users

(*But: Acute abdomen* is a specific medical condition. Also, *acute* pain can
indicate both quality [sharp] and time.)

adopt, adapt—To adopt means to take and use as one's own; to adapt
means to modify to fit a particular circumstance or requirement.

The American Medical Association adopted Système International units in
1985 as standard units of measurement.

The method described for the larger sample was adapted for groups of 50
or fewer.

affect, effect—*Affect*, as a verb, means to have an influence on; *effect*, as a verb, means to bring about or cause. The two cannot be used interchangeably.

> Ingesting massive doses of vitamin C may affect his recovery [ie, influence it in some way, possibly negative].

> Ingesting massive doses of vitamin C may effect his recovery [ie, produce it].

Affect, as a noun, means the subjective aspect of an emotion; the term is often used as part of psychiatric diagnostic terminology. *Effect*, as a noun, means result.

> Mr Z's general lack of affect was considered to be an effect of his father's disappearance 20 years earlier.

aged, age, teenaged, teenage—The adjective form *aged*, not the noun *age*, should be used to designate a person's age. Similarly, we prefer *teenaged* to *teenage*. However, a precise age should be given whenever possible.

> The patient, aged 65 years, showed symptoms of senile dementia of the Alzheimer type.

> The teenaged victims of tinnitus spent an average of 4½ hours a day listening to their portable stereo headphones.

> *Better*: The patients, aged 14, 16, and 17 years, complained of a constant ringing in the ears.

aggravate, irritate—When an existing condition is made worse, more serious, or more severe, it is *aggravated*. When tissue is caused to be inflamed or sore, it is *irritated*. An irritation may be aggravated, but an aggravation cannot be irritated.

although, though—*Although* is preferable to *though* as a complete conjunction, since *though* in this construction is an abbreviation and thus inappropriate for a formal publication. *Though* is correct in the adverbial construction, though.

> Although the analysis was done correctly, the fundamental terms of the investigation were too narrow to be interesting.

among, between—*Among* usually pertains to general collective relations in a group of more than two, *between* to the relation between one thing and one or more other things. For instance, a treaty may be made *between* four powers, since each is defining a relationship with each of the others, but peace may exist *among* them.

> The patients shared the library books equally among themselves.

Between you and me, we are certain to find the key variable among those
we have examined.

apt, likely, liable—*Apt* denotes a volition or habitual tendency, and should
not be used in regard to an inanimate object; *likely* merely denotes probability, and thus is more inclusive than *apt*; *liable* denotes the possibility
of risk or disadvantage to the subject.

The child is apt to cry when he is frustrated.

The computer system is likely to go down unexpectedly if it is overloaded.

(*Note:* To write "The system is apt to go down . . ." implies that the
computer is capable of habitual tendencies or volitions—an implication
that the cautious writer may wish to avoid given the present limitations of
artificial intelligence.)

Patients receiving immunosuppressant drugs are liable to get fungal infections.

assure, ensure, insure—These words are used synonymously in many
contexts, but there are distinctions. *Assure* means to inform positively and
implies removal of doubt and suspense (*assure* the subjects that their results
will be held in complete confidence). *Ensure* means to make sure, certain,
or safe (*ensure* the statistical power of the study). *Insure* means taking
precautions beforehand, to meet foreseen contingencies (*insure* his life).

biopsy—*Biopsy* means the procedure of removing and examining tissue,
cells, or fluids from the living body. The word should not be used as a
verb. Observations are made on the biopsy specimen, not on the biopsy
itself.

Incorrect:	The mass was biopsied.
Correct:	A biopsy of the mass was done.
Incorrect:	Biopsy was negative.
Correct:	The results of the biopsy were negative.

case, patient, subject, control—In biological research, a *case* is a particular
instance of a disease. A *patient* is a particular person under medical care.
A *research subject* is one with a particular characteristic or behavior examined in a scientific investigation. A *control subject* is one who does not
share the characteristic of interest in an investigation. The subjects in the
experimental group are compared with the control subjects to determine
the effect of the characteristic. In case-control studies, it is appropriate to
refer to *case patients* and *control patients*, or *patients in the case group*.

A *case* is evaluated, documented, and reported. A *patient* is admitted
for treatment, examined, given medication, and discharged. A *research
subject* is recruited, selected, sometimes subjected to experimental con-

ditions, observed, and thanked. (See **observe, follow** and **examine, evaluate**.)

classic, classical—In most scientific writing, the adjective *classic* generally means "authentic," "authoritative," or "typical" (the *classic* symptoms of myocardial infarction include chest pain, nausea, and diaphoresis). In contrast, *classical* has to do with the humanities or the fine arts (a *classical* column, unlike a medieval column or pier, is strictly defined and self-sufficient).

compare—One thing or person is usually compared *with* another when the aim is to examine similarities or differences in detail. A thing is compared *to* another when a single striking similarity (or dissimilarity) is observed, or when a thing of one class is likened to one of another class, without analysis.

> The sodium levels of the patients in the control group were compared with those of the patients in the study group.
>
> *But:* "Shall I compare thee to a summer's day?"

compose, comprise—Although the two are often used interchangeably, *comprise* is not synonymous with *compose*. *Comprise* means "to be composed of" or simply "include"; it takes the active voice where *compose* takes the passive voice. Thus one can say that the whole is composed of its parts and comprises its parts.

> The "quack" medication *comprises* several highly toxic ingredients.
>
> The "quack" medicine *is composed of* several highly toxic ingredients.

As a rule of thumb, never use *of* with *comprise*.

continual, continuous—In modern usage, *continual* means "to recur at frequent intervals," while *continuous* means "going on without pause or interruption."

> The elderly patient with emphysema coughed continually.
>
> His breathing was eased by a continuous flow of oxygen through the respirator.

delivery—A neonate is delivered, but a woman is delivered *of* a neonate.

describe, report—Patients or cases are *described*; only cases are *reported*. (See **case, patient, subject, control**; **manage**; **diagnose, evaluate, identify**.)

develop—To say "the patient developed a fever" is jargon. Use the verb in its more correct intransitive mode: "the fever developed in the patient."

diagnose, evaluate, identify—All these terms apply to conditions, syndromes, diseases, and pathogens. Patients as such are not diagnosed, evaluated, or identified (unless, of course, their names are actually unknown). (See **case, patient, subject, control** and **manage**.)

die of, die from—Persons die *of*, not *from*, specific diseases or disorders.

> He died of pneumonia.

Conceivably, a victim in a play could die *from* act II to act IV (in the sense of passing time), but he would die *of* injuries resulting from the villain's knife thrust, gunshot, or garrote.

dilate, dilatate—*Dilate* means "to stretch or expand," while the noun form *dilation* means "the act of dilating." The would-be verb *dilatate* is an incorrect back-formation from the noun *dilatation*, which refers to "the condition of being stretched or expanded." (See 9.3, Back-formations.)

disk, disc—Use *disc* when referring to the optic *disc*; use *disk* when referring to all else, including computer *disk*.

disinterested, uninterested—Although these two words are increasingly treated as synonyms in both written and spoken English, their differences in meaning are sufficiently useful to be worth preserving. To be *disinterested* is to lack a wish for personal advantage in the situation at hand; to be *uninterested* is to be unconcerned, indifferent, or inattentive. A disinterested judge is admirable; an uninterested judge is not.

doctor, physician—*Doctor* is a more general term than *physician*, since it legitimately includes people holding the degrees of PhD, DO, DDS, EdD, DD, DPH, DBA, etc. Thus, the term *physician* should be used when it refers specifically to a medical doctor.

document, report—Although these terms are often used synonymously, *document* has a specific meaning that it is useful to retain. Authors who state that they are *documenting* their findings imply that they are providing factual support for their conclusions or hypotheses with some form of direct evidence (such as patient records). As a rule, a study's conclusions are not *documented* but simply *reported* in a publication.

dose, dosage—A *dose* is the quantity to be administered at one time, or the total quantity administered. *Dosage* implies a regimen; it is the regulated administration of individual doses, and is usually expressed as a quantity per unit of time.

> The patient received an initial dose of 50 mg and thereafter a dosage of 25 mg three times a day for 6 days, or until he had received a total dose of 500 mg over the course of treatment.

due to, owing to—These terms are not synonymous, but the differences are subtle enough to elude even the most pedantic stylebook authors. *Due to* or *caused by* are used in adjectival phrases, *owing to* or *because of* in adverbial phrases. The use of *due to* in both situations can sometimes alter a sentence's meaning.

> Victims tend to enter abusive relationships due to intrapsychic conflicts.

(Because *due to* is used in an adjectival sense, "intrapsychic conflicts" characterizes the relationships. *Caused by* could be substituted, and the meaning would be retained. *That are* could be inserted before *due to* without changing the sentence's meaning.)

> Victims tend to enter abusive relationships owing to intrapsychic conflicts.

(Because *owing to* is used in an adverbial sense, "intrapsychic conflicts" characterizes the entrance into abusive relationships. *Because of* could be substituted and the meaning would be retained. However, if *that are* were inserted before *owing to*, the sentence's meaning would change.)

Clue to usage: The phrase "coughs due to colds" is a good paradigm for the use of *due to.* If "because of" sounds right, use it or "owing to"; if "caused by" is intended, use it or "due to."

efficacy, efficacious; effective, effectiveness—Although all refer to effectiveness of some kind, they have different shades of meaning. *Efficacy* and *efficacious*, applied to medications, mean "sure to have the desired or intended effect." *Effective* and *effectiveness*, however, mean "having an effect in a particular instance."

It is thus possible that a medication could be *effective* at one time, although not generally *efficacious*. Alternatively, it could be generally *efficacious* but occasionally not *effective.*

endemic, epidemic—These similar terms may be confused, but the difference is key in epidemiology as well as lexicography. *Endemic* conditions or diseases are ones that are usually prevalent in a particular place or among a particular people. *Epidemic* conditions break out suddenly in a defined area and are (usually) temporary. A *hyperendemic* condition is one that is prevalent at a very high level; a *pandemic* condition is one that is epidemic over a wide geographic area.

> Until the discovery of vaccination, smallpox was endemic to western Europe.

> The study reported an epidemic of legionnaires' disease among the participants at eight conferences.

> Parasitism is hyperendemic in Third World populations.

> Fourteenth-century Europe suffered from pandemic bubonic plague.

etc—Use *etc* or *and so on* with discretion. Such terms are often superfluous and are used simply to extend the author's list of examples. Because *etc* is not itself an example, it can be omitted. When, in other instances, omission would be detrimental, substitute more specific phrasing such as *and other methods* or *and other factors*. *Etc* may be used in a noninclusive listing when a complete list would be unwieldy *and* its content is obvious to the reader.

> *Incorrect*: A first-aid kit should include aspirin, emetics, self-adhesive bandages, etc.
>
> *Correct*: Cough arising from irritation of pharyngeal mucosa can be managed with demulcents and sialagogues (hard candy, cough drops, etc).

Do not use *etc* when the listing is preceded by *eg* or *for example*.

Use a comma before *etc* when it is preceded by more than one term but not when preceded by one term only.

etiology—*Etiology* has a broader meaning than either *origin* or *cause* and should not be used synonymously with these terms. *Etiology* refers to the study of all the possible causes, separate or related, of a condition or a disease.

> The etiology of cancer is a maze of unknowns.
>
> *But*: The cause of heart failure was acute myocardial infarction.

examine, evaluate—Patients are *examined*; conditions or diseases are *evaluated*. (See **case, patient, subject, control**.)

Note that *evaluable*, used to mean "capable of being evaluated," is not a word, according to *Webster's New Collegiate Dictionary*. An alternative is *assessable*.

fever, temperature—*Fever* is a condition in which body temperature rises above normal. It is not informative to say that a person has a temperature. Everyone has a temperature, either normal or abnormal. A patient may have a *temperature* (not *fever*) of 39.5°C. The following forms are also correct:

> The patient has a fever (temperature, 39.5°C).
>
> The patient is febrile (temperature, 39.5°C).

fewer, less—The words *fewer* and *less* are not interchangeable. Use *less* for volume or mass (quantity) and *fewer* for number (individual persons and things).

> If fewer than 20 persons attend the meeting and sign the petition, there will be less support for the proposition.

imply, infer—To *imply* is to suggest or to indicate or express indirectly. To *infer* is to conclude or to draw conclusions from facts, statements, or indications.

> Her physical appearance implies that she is healthy, but after reviewing her chart I infer that she may have aplastic anemia.

> These statistics imply a decrease in production, from which I infer an increase in staff vacancies.

incidence, prevalence—These two terms are often confused with one another. *Incidence* is the rate of occurrence of *new* cases of a disease or condition. In contrast, *prevalence* is the measure of *existing* number of cases.

The *incidence* is the ratio of the number of new cases of a condition to the total number of persons in the population at risk for the condition during a specified period.

> The incidence of toxic shock syndrome in 1980 was 15 cases per 100 000 menstruating women.

The *prevalence* is the proportion of existing cases of a condition in the population at risk at a specified point in time.

> The prevalence of Alzheimer's disease in Medicare patients in 1970 was only 3%.

> The prevalence of tuberculosis in hospitalized patients was 2% on September 12, 1987.

infection, infestation—An *infection* involves an immune response by the host to an invading organism. Frequently, although not always, *infections* are caused by endoparasites (that is, those living within the host's body). However, ectoparasites and some endoparasites (for instance, intestinal worms) produce an *infestation*, a case in which there is no immune response by the host, although the presence of the parasite may damage the host's health.

> The infection was caused by *Salmonella enteritidis*.

> The dog was infested with lice.

> The dog was infected with worms.

malignant, malignancy—The term *malignant* as applied to neoplasms implies the properties of anaplasia, invasion, and metastasis. The term *malignancy* should not be used as a synonym for a specific tumor; properly speaking, it refers to a more general state of progressive virulence, or the quality of being malignant. Use *malignant neoplasm* instead.

manage—Just as we try to avoid other dehumanizing usages (see **case, patient, subject, control** and **diagnose, evaluate, identify**), we generally prefer to say that cases are *managed* but patients are *cared for* or *treated*. However, we accept the construction ''the management of patients with *X*'' when it refers to a general treatment protocol.

militate, mitigate—These two words are often confused, but they are not synonymous. As is suggested by its shared root with *military, militate* means to have force as evidence; it is usually used with *against. Mitigate* means to moderate, abate, soften.

> The leukocytosis militates against that diagnosis.

> The analgesic did much to mitigate the patient's pain.

morbidity, morbidity rate; mortality, mortality rate; fatality rate, case-fatality rate—*Morbidity* describes the condition of being diseased. *Morbidity rate* (or *attack rate*) is the number of cases of a specific disease divided by the total population at risk for that disease.

> Morbidity due to peptic ulcer is an increasing health problem among the young.

> The morbidity rate of influenza in the general population has declined since World War I.

Mortality describes the number of deaths from a particular condition. *Mortality rate* is the number of deaths in a particular population divided by the size of that population at the same time.

> Cancer has one of the highest mortality rates of any disease in the United States today.

Fatality rate gives the percentage of those with a particular condition who will eventually die of that condition.

> The fatality rate of AIDS is 100%—that is, everyone who has AIDS will eventually die.

The term *case-fatality rate* gives the percentage of those with a condition who die of that condition in a given period.

> The case-fatality rate of AIDS in this city was 40% last year—that is, 40% of the people who had AIDS died.

negative, positive; normal, abnormal—Examinations and laboratory tests are not negative, positive, normal, or abnormal in themselves. These adjectives apply to observations, results, or findings.

Cultures, tests for microorganisms, tests for specific reactions, and reactions to tests may be negative or positive. Other tests focus on a pattern of activity rather than a single feature, and in these only a range of normal and abnormal results is possible. Such tests include electroencephalograms and electrocardiograms and modes of imaging such as isotope scans, roentgenograms, and computed tomographic scans.

Incorrect:	The throat culture was negative.
Correct:	The throat culture was negative for β-hemolytic streptococci.
Incorrect:	The physical examination was normal.
Correct:	The results of the physical examination were normal.
Incorrect:	The electroencephalogram was positive.
Correct:	The electroencephalogram showed abnormalities in the alpha wave activity.

observe, follow—Cases are *followed*. Patients are not *followed* (unless they are being trailed by a private investigator) but *observed*. However, either cases or patients may be *followed up*. (See **case, patient, subject, control**.)

-ology—This suffix, derived from the Greek *logos*, meaning "word," "idea," or "thought," denotes *science of* or *study of*. Terms with this suffix, like *pathology, morphology, histology*, are general and abstract nouns, and should not be used to describe concrete particular items. (See also **etiology**.)

Incorrect:	The pathology was located in the upper part of the gastrointestinal tract.
Correct:	The pathologic lesion was located in the upper part of the gastrointestinal tract.
Incorrect:	The histology was small-cell carcinoma of the lung.
Correct:	The histologic diagnosis was small-cell carcinoma of the lung.

on, upon—*Upon* in all of its uses means *on*. Except in direct quotations and acceptable poetic forms, *upon* should be routinely changed to *on*.

operate, operate on—Only Dr Frankenstein *operates* a patient. All other surgeons *operate on* a patient, or *perform operations on* a patient. Similarly, patients are not *operated* but are *operated on*.

Incorrect:	The operated group recovered quickly.
Correct:	The surgical group recovered quickly.
Preferred:	The group that underwent the operation recovered quickly.

over, under—The correct use of these words depends on the context in which they appear.

Periods of time: In some ambiguous constructions, *over* may mean either *more than* or *for (a period of)*. In such cases, *over* should be avoided and the more precise term used.

Ambiguous: The cases were followed up over 2 years.

Preferred: The cases were followed up for more than 2 years.

Preferred: The cases were followed up for a period of 2 years.

Age: When referring to age groups, *over* and *under* should be replaced by the more precise *older than* and *younger than*.

Ambiguous: We studied all the members of the control group over 65 years.

Preferred: We studied all the members of the control group older than 65 years.

Units: When referring to units, *over* and *under* should be replaced by *more than* and *less than*. The symbols < and > are appropriate in tables and figures but not in a manuscript's text, except parenthetically.

Ambiguous: Over 300 people died during the epidemic.

Preferred: More than 300 people died during the epidemic.

problematic—*Problematic* means "puzzling, questionable, open to debate," not "full of problems."

put on, place—The awkward and unclear jargon phrase "to put/place a patient on a drug" conjures up an image of a person in a hospital gown being made to sit on top of a small plastic bottle. Medications are *prescribed* or patients are *given* medications; therapy or therapeutic regimens are started.

Incorrect: The patient with depression was put on imipramine.

Correct: Imipramine was prescribed for the patient with depression.

Correct: The patient with depression was given imipramine.

Correct: A therapeutic regimen of daily moderate doses of imipramine was begun.

quantitate, quantify, measure—Although the use of *quantitate* as a back-formation from *quantitative* seems to be increasing, it is an example of jargon that can almost always be replaced with the clearer and less pretentious *measure* (and sometimes even *count*). *Quantify* is also a synonym for *measure*, but it has the additional implication that assigning a numerical value to the substance discussed is difficult or novel.

The patient's weight was measured at three different times during the experiment.

We have developed a method of scoring responses to the Thematic Apperception Test to quantify the degree of psychopathological ideation.

This ratio of faulty test to acceptable test made it possible to quantify the quality of the laboratory's performance.

regime, regimen—A *regime* is a form of government, a social regulation, or a period of rule. A *regimen* is a systematic plan (diet, therapy, medication) designed to improve and maintain the health of a patient.

His initial regimen for hypertension included prazosin hydrochloride, 1 mg twice a day.

repeat, repeated—*Repeat* is a noun or a verb and should not be used in place of the adjective *repeated. Repeated* implies multiple repetitions. For the sake of precision and clarity, the exact number should be given.

Incorrect:	A repeat electroencephalogram was obtained.
Possible but misleading:	A repeated electroencephalogram was obtained.
Preferred:	A second electroencephalogram was obtained.
Preferred:	Two subsequent electroencephalograms showed no abnormalities.

respective, respectively—*Respective* and *respectively* indicate a one-to-one correspondence that may not otherwise be obvious between members of two series. The distinction is meaningless and should not be used when only one series, or none at all, is listed.

Incorrect:	The three Victorian patients were given their respective sedatives.
Incorrect:	The three Victorian patients were given laudanum, morphine, and brandy, respectively.
Correct:	Mrs Grace Poole, Mr Jonathan Harker, and Miss Anna O. were given laudanum, morphine, and brandy, respectively.

roentgen, x-ray, roentgenogram, radiograph, radiology—*Roentgen* (R) is a unit of x- or gamma radiation that is now used only infrequently. An *x-ray* is a roentgen ray—that is, electromagnetic radiation above about 10 keV in energy, capable of penetrating tissue.

A *roentgenogram* is a film image made by means of roentgen rays, in a process known as *roentgenography.* (More specific terms such as *venogram* or *arthrogram* are, of course, entirely acceptable.) According to

Dorland's, roentgenogram is synonymous with *x-ray film* or *roentgeno-graph*, but not with *x-ray*. In the AMA journals, we prefer the term *roentgenogram*.

Roentgenology, the study of the diagnostic use of roentgen radiation, is a branch of *radiology*, the science of radiant energy and radiant substances in general.

Use *radiograph* as a more general term to describe all images produced by means of ionizing radiation: roentgenograms, computed tomographic scans, or radioactive isotope scans. (Note that images made by ultrasound or magnetic resonance imaging, which are not forms of ionizing radiation, are not radiographs.)

According to *Dorland's, radiogram* is synonymous with *radiograph*, but it has a second meaning of "a message sent by radio waves." To avoid confusion, the term *radiograph* should be used.

suspicious of, suggestive of, suspicious for—To be *suspicious of* is to distrust. To be *suggestive of* is to give a suggestion or indication of. Thus, the two phrases are not synonymous, and care should be taken to avoid confusing them, lest a phrase imply that a test result can show paranoid characteristics.

> *Incorrect:* The roentgenogram was suspicious of tuberculosis.
> *Correct:* The roentgenogram was suggestive of tuberculosis.

toxic, toxicity—*Toxic* means pertaining to or caused by a poison or toxin. *Toxicity* is the quality, state, or degree of being poisonous. A patient is not toxic. A patient does not have toxicity.

> The antineoplastic agent carmustine is a very toxic drug.
>
> A drug has a toxic effect on a patient.
>
> A patient is in a toxic condition.
>
> The toxicity of the drug must be considered.
>
> A patient has a toxic reaction.

use, utilize, usage—*Use* is almost always preferable to *utilize*, which has the specific meaning "to turn to a practical use or account," suggesting the discovery of a new use for something. However, even where this meaning is intended, *use* would be acceptable.

> The chimpanzee utilized a long reed to dig the ants out of the anthill.

Usage refers to a practice or procedure, usually a linguistic one. For the broader sense in which there is no reference to a standard of practice, *use* is also the correct noun form.

> To say "between you and I" defies all rules of correct usage.

9.1 Commonly Misused Words and Phrases

> Jane Goodall described the chimpanzee's use of the reed as a tool.

As a rule of thumb, then, avoid *utilize* and be wary of *usage*. Use *use*.

while—Authorities disagree on the proper use of *while*. Some regard it as a purely temporal conjunction meaning only *during the time that*; others allow the nontemporal use of it as a synonym for *although* or *whereas*. We accept the broader meaning.

However, all agree that the useful meanings of *while* end there. The term should not be weakened by being used as a convenient alternative to *and* or *but*, in what Fowler (1968) has called "elegant variation." Such use may make the sentence self-contradictory, implying that events happening at different times happened at the same time.

Possible:	The first set of laboratory results was positive, while the second set confirmed the diagnosis.
Preferred:	The first set of laboratory results was positive, and the second set confirmed the diagnosis.
Possible:	Four children were severely injured, while the adults were only bruised.
Preferred:	Four children were severely injured, but the adults were only bruised.

9.2 Redundant, Expendable, and Incomparable Words

9.2.1 *Redundant Words.*—A redundancy is a term or phrase that unnecessarily repeats words or meanings of words. Here are some common redundancies that should be avoided (redundant words are italicized):

consensus *of opinion*	rough *in texture*
bright red *in color*	hematocrit *reading*
fuse *together*	fewer *in number*
large (small) *in size*	contemporaneous *in age*
lenticular *in shape*	outside *of*
two halves	estimated at *about*
soft *in consistency*	own *personal* view
in order to, *in order* that	sum *total*
sour (sweet, bitter) *tasting*	2 *out* of 12
skin rash	period *of time*
tender *to the touch*	oval *in shape*
whether *or not*	all *of*
interval *of time*	

9.2.2 *Expendable Words.*—Some words and phrases can usually be omitted without affecting meaning, and doing so often improves the readability of a sentence:

> in other words
> it goes without saying
> it is important to note that

154

needless to say
it may be said that
it was found that
it was demonstrated that

Quite, very, and *rather* are often overused and misused and can easily be deleted in many instances. (See also 9.1, Commonly Misused Words and Phrases, *etc.*)

Beware of *in terms of:* usually *in, of,* or *for* will suffice.

9.2.3   *Incomparable Words.*—Some words are regarded by grammarians as "absolute" adjectives, those not possessing a comparative or superlative form. One often sees expressions like "a rather unique case" and "a very unique perspective." Some words considered incomparable and needing no superlative or comparative modifier are listed below:

ambiguous	infinite
complete (*But:* almost complete)	perfect (*But:* nearly perfect)
comprehensive	pregnant
equal	supreme
eternal	total
fatal (*But:* almost fatal)	unanimous
final	unique
preferable	original
dead	

9.3   Back-formations.—This term refers to the transformation of nouns into verbs, often seen in technical as well as informal writing. *Diagnose*, for example, is a mid–19th-century back-formation from *diagnosis*. (See 9.1, Commonly Misused Words and Phrases, *diagnose, evaluate, identify* and *dilate, dilatate*.) A recent back-formation now in standard use is *dialyze* (from dialysis). A back-formation not presently acceptable is *diurese* (from diuresis). Any use of back-formations should be checked against a dictionary.

> *Correct:*   The patient was given diuretics.
> *Incorrect:*   The patient was diuresed.

9.4   Medicalese and Jargon.—Words or phrases that are peculiar to conversations among medical personnel are generally inappropriate in scientific writing. Examples of expressions and their corrected forms are given here. (See also 9.1, Commonly Misused Words and Phrases, *-ology*.)

Jargon	*Correct Form*
4+ albuminuria	proteinuria (4+) *or* urine reaction for protein was 4+
blood sugar	blood glucose [query author]
cardiac diet	diet for patients with cardiac disease

Jargon	*Correct Form*
clinical material (meaning patients)	patients in the study
congenital heart	congenital heart disease, anomaly
hyperglycemia of 150 mg	hyperglycemia (8.265 mmol/L)
jugular ligation	jugular vein ligation *or* ligation of the jugular vein
left heart failure	left ventricular failure [query author]
prepped	prepared
psychiatric floor	psychiatric ward, department, service
emergency room	emergency department
skull series	skull roentgenographic series
urinary infection	urinary tract infection *or* infection of the urinary tract
upper respiratory infection	upper respiratory tract infection

In describing drugs, *intravenous, oral, parenteral, topical,* and *rectal* are acceptable terms when these are the usual or intended routes of administration. Except for systemic chemotherapy, however, drugs are usually neither systemic nor local but are given for systemic or local effect.

Some topical ointments produce systemic effects.

Parenteral penicillin is often preferred to oral penicillin.

Intravenously injected heroin is often contaminated.

The following terms should be changed to preferred forms:

Avoid	*Use*
Caucasian	white
colored, Negro	black
expired, succumbed	died
osteopath, osteopathy	osteopathic physician, osteopathic medicine
sacrificed	killed
therapy of (a disease or condition)	therapy for
treatment for (a disease or condition)	treatment of

Colloquialisms and vulgarisms should be avoided in scientific writing;

however, exceptions may be made occasionally in editorials, informal articles, and the like.

9.5   **Age and Sex Referents.**—*Neonates* or *newborns* are people from birth to 1 month of age.

Infants are people aged 1 month to 2 years (24 months).

Children are people aged 2 to 13 years. Sometimes, *children* may be used more broadly to encompass people from birth to 13 years of age. They should be referred to as *boys* or *girls*.

Adolescents are people aged 13 through 17 years. They may also be referred to as *teenagers* or as *boys* or *girls*.

Adults are people 18 years of age or older and should be referred to as *men* or *women*.

Whenever possible, a patient should be identified as a man, woman, boy, girl, or infant, not as a male or female. Occasionally, however, a study group may comprise children and adults of both sexes. Then, the use of *male* and *female* as nouns is appropriate.

9.6   **Body Parts.**—Authors often err in referring to such things as the "right heart," "left chest," and "left neck." Generally, these terms can be corrected by inserting a phrase such as "part of the" or "side of the."

> the right side of the heart
>
> left side of the chest *or* left hemithorax
>
> (*But:* proximal jejunum and distal esophagus; ascending [right] and descending [left] colon)

The *upper extremity* comprises the upper arm (extending from the shoulder to the elbow), the forearm (from elbow to wrist), and the hand. The *lower extremity* comprises the thigh (extending from the hip to the knee), the leg (from the knee to the ankle), and the foot. Therefore, references to upper arm, lower arm, and upper and lower leg are often ambiguous. When such references appear in a manuscript, the author should be queried.

9.7   **Clock Referents.**—Occasionally, reference to a locus of insertion, position, or attitude is given in terms of a clockface orientation, as seen by the viewer.

> *Avoid:*   The needle was inserted into the left eye at 9 o'clock.
> *Use:*   The needle was inserted into the left eye at the 9-o'clock position.

Note: The terms *clockwise* and *counterclockwise* can also be misleading. The plane of reference should be specified if the usage is ambiguous.

9.8   Laboratory Values.—Usually, in reports of clinical or laboratory data, the substance per se is not reported; rather, a value is given that was obtained by measurement of a substance or some function or constituent of it. For example, one does not report "blood" but rather blood pressure, blood cell count, or bleeding time. Some other correct forms are as follows:

> differential blood cell *count*
>
> hemoglobin *level*
>
> agglutination *titer*
>
> prothrombin *time*
>
> pulse *rate* (beats per minute)
>
> sedimentation *rate* (per hour)
>
> total serum cholesterol *value*
>
> rise in antibody *level*
>
> creatinine *level* or *clearance*
>
> serum phosphorus *concentration*
>
> rise in bilirubin *level* or *increase* in bilirubin

In reports of findings from clinical examination or laboratory studies, data may be enumerated without repeating *value, level*, etc, in accordance with the following example:

> Laboratory studies disclosed the following values: sodium, 128 mmol/L; potassium, 4.0 mmol/L; hematocrit, 0.28; phosphate, 0.48 mmol/L; serum urea nitrogen, 27 mmol/L of urea; creatinine, 760 μmol/L; and total calcium, 2.54 mmol/L.

9.9   Articles.—The article *a* is used before aspirate *h* (*a* historic occasion) and nonvocalic *y* (*a* ubiquitous organism). Acronyms are preceded by *a* or *an* according to the *sound* following (*a* UHF station, *an* HMO plan).

a dog (*d* sound)   a history (*h* sound)
a WCTU poster (*d* sound)   an ultraviolet source (*u* sound)
a hematocrit (*h* sound)   an honor (*o* sound)
an MS degree (*e* sound)

9.10   Sexist Language.—The objectivity of science lends itself to language usage that recognizes neither sex as preeminent. However, problems frequently exist for authors and editors in determining appropriately neutral terminology. The editors of AMA publications support the use of sex-neutral language where appropriate, but that does not mean sex should never be specified. Sex can be designated when discussing a specific person or whenever pertinent. The careful writer and editor should select terms that avoid bias, suit the material, and do not intrude on the reader's attention.

9.10.1 *Personal Pronouns.*—The creation of common-gender pronouns (eg, "s/he," "shem," "shim," "himorher," "himmer," "he'er") unduly emphasizes the problem without really solving it. Over the years editors of AMA publications have implemented an unwritten policy for cases where grammatical gender specificity is irrelevant: Try to reword the sentence to use the plural pronoun, neutral noun equivalent, or a change of voice; or use "he or she" ("him or her," "his or her[s]").

Avoid	*Better*
The physician and his office staff can do much to alleviate a patient's nervousness.	Physicians and their office staff can do much to alleviate a patient's nervousness. [plural]
	The physician and the office staff can do much to alleviate a patient's nervousness. [neutral noun equivalent]
One must allocate her time effectively.	People must allocate their time effectively. [plural]
	Time must be allocated effectively. [change of voice]

Note: In an effort to avoid both sex-specific pronouns and awkward sentence structure, some grammarians advocate the use of plural pronouns with singular indefinite antecedents (eg, Everyone allocates [note singular verb] their [instead of "his or her"] time), particularly in informal writing and dialogue. Editors of AMA journals recognize this trend but prefer that agreement in number be maintained in formal scientific writing. (See 5.9, Grammar, Subject-Verb Agreement.)

Incorrect:	One must allocate their time.
	Everyone must allocate their time.
Correct:	One must allocate one's time.
Or:	One must allocate time.
	Everyone must allocate time.

9.10.2 *Nouns and Adjectives.*—Choosing a neutral noun equivalent may be more difficult. Although some common terms lend themselves well to "generic" alternatives, others do not. For example, *chairman* and *chairwoman may* be changed to *chair* or *chairperson* (where appropriate); *salesman, saleswoman,* and *saleslady* to *salesperson* or *sales clerk*; *policeman* and *policewoman* to *police officer*; *fireman* to *firefighter*; *mailman* to *letter carrier*; *spokesman* and *spokeswoman* to *spokesperson.* However, attempts to change other terms border on the ridiculous, as in *personslaughter* for *manslaugh-*

ter. Choose sex-neutral terms that do not call attention to themselves by sounding strained.

Many terms, such as *physician* and *astronaut*, are sex-neutral and do not require modification (eg, female physician, female astronaut) unless the sex of the person or persons described is relevant to the discussion (eg, a study of only female physicians or female astronauts).

When a specific person is being discussed, specify sex.

> The astronaut underwent thorough preflight training. Her debriefing was equally rigorous.

In a general case, be sex-neutral.

> *Change:*   The astronaut undergoes thorough preflight training. His debriefing is equally rigorous.
>
> *To:*   The astronaut undergoes thorough preflight training and a debriefing that is equally rigorous.
>
> *Or:*   Astronauts undergo thorough preflight training. Their debriefing is equally rigorous. [Or simply, ''Debriefing is equally rigorous.'']

Baron's *Grammar and Gender* (1986) and *Grammar and Good Taste: Reforming the American Language* (1982) contain excellent historical and contemporary discussion and suggest guidelines for appropriate textual usage. Miller and Swift (1980) suggest reasonable sex-neutral alternatives. The stylebook of the American Psychological Association delineates some of the problems of sexist language (ambiguity of referent, stereotyping, introduction of bias) and, by specific examples, suggests ways to avoid them.

10.0 Foreign-Language Words and Phrases and Accents (Diacritics)

10.1 Foreign-Language Words and Phrases

10.1.1 *Use of Italics.*—Some foreign words and phrases have become part of standard English usage (eg, in vivo, in vitro). Those that have not, ie, that do not appear in the most recent edition of *Webster's New Collegiate Dictionary* or in standard medical dictionaries, should be italicized.

> *Çao gio* (coin rolling) bruises have been reported as an example of apparent child abuse among Vietnamese refugees.
>
> *Ua mau ke ea o ka aina i ka pono* (the life of the land is established in righteousness) is the motto of Hawaii.

10.1.2 *Translation.*—Foreign-language titles mentioned in text may be translated or not, at the author's discretion. If the original title is used, an English-language translation should be given parenthetically except in cases where the work is well known (translating Pascal's *Pensées* as *Thoughts*, for example, is unnecessary).

Note that this rule varies somewhat from that governing foreign-language titles in references (see 2.10.11, References, Foreign-Language Titles).

10.1.3 *Capitalization and Punctuation.*—Foreign-language words should be capitalized and foreign-language phrases punctuated according to that language's standard of correctness. Follow foreign-language dictionaries and *The Chicago Manual of Style*, 13th ed, chap 9. (See 10.2, Accents [Diacritics].)

10.2 Accents (Diacritics).

—Accent marks tend to be superfluous for persons whose first language is English. Words once spelled with marks (eg, coöperation, rôle, naïve) now are written and printed without them. The current trend toward omission of accent marks is given further impetus by the limitations of computer typesetting, by the additional cost in time and effort for marking copy, and by the increased likelihood of error when accents are used. Late-edition dictionaries give optional forms for words to show that they may or may not include accents (eg, resume/resumé/résumé; facade/façade).

10.2 Accents (Diacritics)

Accents marks should be retained in proper names. Otherwise, however, such marks normally should be omitted, except in instances where current usage continues their inclusion. If an author is consistent about use of accents with given terms, however, the accents may be retained. Accents may be omitted from the following terms:

Angstrom [Ångstrom]

cafe au lait [café au lait]

Accents are used appropriately:

- To show pronunciation:

    lues (lü-ēz)

- To show correct spelling in original language:

    Köln (Cologne)

- In quotations:

    "L'utilité du vivre n'est pas en espace, elle est en l'usage . . ."—Montaigne [The value of life lies not in the length of days, but in the use we make of them.]

- In terms in which the accent is retained in current use:

    garçon

    Möbius strip [alternative form: Moebius]

    tête-à-tête

Accents should be clearly marked on copy. Although for most typefaces the diaeresis and umlaut are indistinguishable, each should be marked correctly. (The diaeresis is used to indicate that the vowel under it is pronounced in a separate syllable.)

Name	Example
acute	le déluge
breve	Omskiĭ
cedilla	garçon
circumflex	tête-bêche
diaeresis	dadaïsme
dot	faùst
grave	après
macron	gignōskein

162

Name	*Example*
ring	Ångstrom
slash	København
tilde	mañana
umlaut	für
wedge	Československà

3

TERMINOLOGY

Chapter 11

11.0 Abbreviations

Webster's New Collegiate Dictionary defines an abbreviation as a shortened form of a written word or phrase used in place of the whole. An acronym is a word formed from the initial letter or letters of each of the successive parts or major parts of a compound term (eg, ELISA). An initialism is an acronym formed from initial letters (eg, DHHS).

The editors of the AMA's scientific publications strongly discourage the use of abbreviations, acronyms, and initialisms in their journals, with the exception of internationally approved and accepted units of measure and some well-recognized clinical, technical, and general terms and symbols.

The editors believe such overuse can be confusing and ambiguous for readers and stress that such abbreviations should be used only to clarify the content of an article. In this era of rapid technologic advances in telecommunications in the United States and abroad, it is essential that clarity be maintained.

The abstracts of many thousands of scientific articles are republished each year in English- and non–English-language journals. *JAMA* and several of the AMA's specialty journals are translated into other languages, and the English-language editions of these journals are distributed to more than 135 countries. The potential for incorrect translation of abbreviations and for confusion among non–English-speaking editors and readers of these and other journals is considerable.

11.0   *Abbreviations*

Many medical and scientific journals publish instructions for authors that give guidelines on the use of abbreviations, ranging from "limit of four per manuscript" to "use only approved abbreviations." Authors, copy editors, and others involved in preparing scientific manuscripts should use good judgment, flexibility, and common sense when considering the use of abbreviations or acronyms, while at the same time conforming to specified guidelines. Abbreviations that some may consider universally known may be obscure to others. So-called author-invented abbreviations should be avoided. See specific entries in this section and 12.0, Nomenclature, for further guidance in correct usage of abbreviations.

11.1   Academic Degrees and Honors.—Abbreviate the following academic degrees in bylines as well as in the text and elsewhere at first mention. (*But:* See 11.6, Names and Titles of Persons.) Note that these abbreviations are to be used only with the full name of a person. (*But:* June is a doctor of medicine and also holds a PhD in biochemistry.)

Generally, US honorary designations (eg, FACP) are not used in bylines.

With the exceptions noted below, degrees below a master's are generally not listed in bylines or elsewhere. Verify any unusual degrees with the author.

ART	accredited record technician
BS, BCh, BC, CB, or ChB	bachelor of surgery
CNM	certified nurse midwife
CRTT	certified respiratory therapy technician
DC	doctor of chiropractic
DCh or ChD	doctor of surgery
DDS	doctor of dental surgery
DMD	doctor of dental medicine
DME	doctor of medical education
DMSc	doctor of medical science
DO or OD	doctor of optometry
DO	doctor of osteopathy
DPH or DrPH	doctor of public health
DPM	doctor of podiatric medicine
DSW	doctor of social work
DVM or DMV	doctor of veterinary medicine
DVMS	doctor of veterinary medicine and surgery
EdD	doctor of education
FCGP	fellow of the College of General Practitioners
FCPS	fellow of the College of Physicians and Surgeons

FFA	fellow of the Faculty of Anaesthetists
FFARCS	fellow of the Faculty of Anaesthetists of the Royal College of Surgeons
FNP	family nurse practitioner
FP	family practitioner
FRACP	fellow of the Royal Australian College of Physicians
FRCGP	fellow of the Royal College of General Practitioners
FRCOG	fellow of the Royal College of Obstetricians and Gynaecologists
FRCP	fellow of the Royal College of Physicians
FRCPC	fellow of the Royal College of Physicians of Canada
FRCP(Glasg)	fellow of the Royal College of Physicians and Surgeons of Glasgow *qua* Physician
FRCPE or FRCP(Edin)	fellow of the Royal College of Physicians of Edinburgh
FRCPI or FRCP(Ire)	fellow of the Royal College of Physicians of Ireland
FRCR	fellow of the Royal College of Radiologists
FRCS	fellow of the Royal College of Surgeons
FRCSC	fellow of the Royal College of Surgeons of Canada
FRCSE or FRCS(Edin)	fellow of the Royal College of Surgeons of Edinburgh
FRCS(Glasg)	fellow of the Royal College of Physicians and Surgeons of Glasgow *qua* Surgeon
FRCSI or FRCS(Ire)	fellow of the Royal College of Surgeons of Ireland
FRCVS	fellow of the Royal College of Veterinary Surgeons
FRS	fellow of the Royal Society
JD	doctor of jurisprudence
LLB	bachelor of laws
LLD	doctor of laws
LLM	master of laws
LPN	licensed practical nurse
LVN	licensed visiting nurse
LVN	licensed vocational nurse
MA or AM	master of arts
MB or BM	bachelor of medicine
MBA	master of business administration

11.1   *Academic Degrees and Honors*

MBBS or MB,BS	bachelor of medicine, bachelor of surgery
MD or DM	doctor of medicine
ME	medical examiner
MEd	master of education
MFA	master of fine arts
MN	master of nursing
MPH	master of public health
MPharm	master in pharmacy
MRCP	member of the Royal College of Physicians
MRCS	member of the Royal College of Surgeons
MS, MSc, or SM	master of science
MS, MSc, SM, MCh, or MSurg	master of surgery
MT	medical technologist
MTA	medical technical assistant
MT(ASCP)	registered medical technologist (American Society of Clinical Pathologists)
NP	nurse practitioner
OTR	registered occupational therapist
PA	physician's assistant
PhD or DPhil	doctor of philosophy
PharmD, DP, or PD	doctor of pharmacy
PharmG	graduate in pharmacy
PT	physical therapist
RN	registered nurse
RPh	registered pharmacist
RPT	registered physical therapist
RTR	recreational therapist, registered
ScD, DSc, or DS	doctor of science
VMD	veterinary medical doctor

11.2   Military Services and Titles.—An abbreviation of a military service follows a name; that of a military title precedes a name: COL Adrian Locke, MC, USA.

11.2.1   *Military Services*

Air National Guard Medical Corps	MC, ANG
Army National Guard Medical Corps	MC, ARNG
US Air Force Medical Corps	MC, USAF
US Army Medical Corps	MC, USA
US Navy Medical Corps	MC, USN
US Air Force	USAF
US Army	USA
US Coast Guard	USCG
US Marine Corps	USMC

US Navy	USN
US Air Force Reserve	USAFR
US Army Reserve	USAR
US Coast Guard Reserve	USCGR
US Marine Corps Reserve	USMCR
US Naval Reserve	USNR

11.2.2 Military Titles

US Army

General of the Army	GA
General	GEN
Lieutenant General	LG
Major General	MG
Brigadier General	BG
Colonel	COL
Lieutenant Colonel	LTC
Major	MAJ
Captain	CPT
First Lieutenant	1LT
Second Lieutenant	2LT
Chief Warrant Officer	CW
Warrant Officer	WO

US Navy and Coast Guard

Admiral	ADM
Vice Admiral	VADM
Rear Admiral	RADM
Captain	CAPT
Commander	CDR
Lieutenant Commander	LCDR
Lieutenant	LT
Lieutenant (Junior Grade)	LTJG
Ensign	ENS
Chief Warrant Officer	CWO

US Air Force and Marine Corps

General	Gen
Lieutenant General	Lt Gen
Major General	Maj Gen
Brigadier General	Brig Gen
Colonel	Col
Lieutenant Colonel	Lt Col
Major	Maj
Captain	Capt
First Lieutenant	1st Lt
Second Lieutenant	2nd Lt

11.3   Days of the Week, Months, Eras.—Generally, days of the week and months are not abbreviated. In tables and figures, however, to conserve space when necessary, use the following three-letter abbreviations:

| Monday | Mon |
| Tuesday | Tue |

Wednesday	Wed
Thursday	Thu
Friday	Fri
Saturday	Sat
Sunday	Sun

January	Jan
February	Feb
March	Mar
April	Apr
May	May
June	Jun
July	Jul
August	Aug
September	Sep
October	Oct
November	Nov
December	Dec

The manuscript was received in late December 1987 and accepted for publication on February 5, 1988, after minor revisions. Because of the importance of its topic, the article was published on Friday, February 26.

Occasionally, scientific manuscripts may contain discussion of eras. Abbreviations for eras are set in small capitals with no punctuation. Figures are used for years and words for centuries through the ninth (see 16.0 and 16.1, Numbers and Percentages, Usage). The more common era designations are AD (*anno Domini*, in the year of our Lord), BC (before Christ), CE (common era), and BCE (before the common era). The abbreviation AD precedes the year number, and BC, CE, and BCE follow it.

Cyrus I was king of Anshan in the late seventh century BCE.

Cuneiform was invented probably by the Sumerians before 3000 BC.

"The Dark Ages" is a general term for the centuries of decline in Europe from AD 500 to 1000, after the fall of the Roman Empire.

11.4   Local Addresses.—Use the following abbreviations when *complete* local addresses are given:

Air Force Base	AFB
Army Post Office	APO
Avenue	Ave
Boulevard	Blvd
Building	Bldg
Circle	Cir
Court	Ct
Drive	Dr
East	E
Fleet Post Office	FPO
Fort	Ft (*but:* Fort Dearborn [query author])

Highway	Hwy
Lane	Ln
Mount	Mt (*but:* Mount Sinai [query author])
North	N
Northeast	NE
Northwest	NW
Parkway	Pkwy
Place	Pl
Post Office	PO
Road	Rd
Route	Rte
Rural Free Delivery	RFD
Rural Route	RR
Saint	St (*but:* Sault Ste Marie [query author])
South	S
Southeast	SE
Southwest	SW
Square	Sq
Street	St
Terrace	Terr
West	W

When the plural form is used in the text, do not abbreviate, for example, *streets* or *avenues*. Abbreviate *building* (Bldg) only when a building number or room number is given. Do not abbreviate *room*. Do not use periods or commas with *N, S, E, W*, or their combinations.

Occasionally there may be exceptions. For example, "One IBM Plaza" and "One Magnificent Mile" are not only addresses but also proper names of buildings or office centers (see also 16.3 and 16.3.1, Numerals, Addresses). The editor should use his or her own judgment and verify unusual addresses with the author.

11.5 **States, Territories, and Possessions.**—Names of states and US territories and possessions should be spelled out in full when they stand alone. When state names follow the name of a city, abbreviations should be used, without periods. Use postal codes for states only when using ZIP codes. Do not abbreviate a state name after a county name.

Chicago, Ill
Chicago, IL 60610
Cook County, Illinois

State or Possession	*Abbreviation*	*Postal Code*
Alabama	Ala	AL
Alaska	Alaska	AK
American Samoa	American Samoa	AS
Arizona	Ariz	AZ
Arkansas	Ark	AR

171

11.5   States, Territories and Possessions

California	Calif	CA
Canal Zone	Canal Zone	CZ
Colorado	Colo	CO
Connecticut	Conn	CT
Delaware	Del	DE
District of Columbia	DC	DC
Florida	Fla	FL
Georgia	Ga	GA
Guam	Guam	GU
Hawaii	Hawaii	HI
Idaho	Idaho	ID
Illinois	Ill	IL
Indiana	Ind	IN
Iowa	Iowa	IA
Kansas	Kan	KS
Kentucky	Ky	KY
Louisiana	La	LA
Maine	Me	ME
Maryland	Md	MD
Massachusetts	Mass	MA
Michigan	Mich	MI
Minnesota	Minn	MN
Mississippi	Miss	MS
Missouri	Mo	MO
Montana	Mont	MT
Nebraska	Neb	NE
Nevada	Nev	NV
New Hampshire	NH	NH
New Jersey	NJ	NJ
New Mexico	NM	NM
New York	NY	NY
North Carolina	NC	NC
North Dakota	ND	ND
Ohio	Ohio	OH
Oklahoma	Okla	OK
Oregon	Ore	OR
Pennsylvania	Pa	PA
Puerto Rico	Puerto Rico	PR
Rhode Island	RI	RI
South Carolina	SC	SC
South Dakota	SD	SD
Tennessee	Tenn	TN
Texas	Tex	TX
Utah	Utah	UT
Vermont	Vt	VT
Virginia	Va	VA
Virgin Islands	Virgin Islands	VI
Washington	Wash	WA
West Virginia	WVa	WV
Wisconsin	Wis	WI
Wyoming	Wyo	WY

At first mention in the text and elsewhere, the name of the appropriate state or country should follow the name of a city, in accordance with the following examples.

> Investigators from the Centers for Disease Control, Atlanta, Ga, were called in to determine the source of the *Salmonella* outbreak in Chicago, Ill.

> In May 1986 several thousand prominent workers met in Paris, France, to share information about and discuss research into the acquired immuno-deficiency syndrome.

However, there are instances where naming the state may be redundant or awkward.

> Studies were carried out at the University of Pennsylvania School of Medicine, Philadelphia [unnecessary to add "Pa"].

> The young peregrine falcons were raised atop a University of Chicago (Ill) campus building [unnecessary to say "University of Chicago, Chicago, Ill"].

Note: The abbreviation "US" may be used as a modifier but should be expanded to "United States" in all other contexts.

> The authors stratified all counties in the United States as urban or rural according to US census data.

11.6   **Names and Titles of Persons.**—Given names should not be abbreviated in the text or in bylines except by using initials, when so indicated by the author. (The copy editor should verify the use of initials with the author. Some medical publishers prefer to use only initials, instead of given names.) Do not use Chas., Geo., Jas., Wm., etc, except when such abbreviations are part of the formal name of a company or organization that regularly uses such abbreviations (see 11.7, Business Firms).

Initials used in the text to indicate names of persons (usually coauthors of an article) should be followed by periods and set close within parentheses.

> We have looked at several pooled γ-globulin preparations for which one or more donors were known to be seropositive and have failed to recover infective virus (P.D.M., unpublished observations).

> Pathologic material was reviewed by two of us (P.R.M. and R.J.L.), using the classification system of Lukes and Collins.

Senior and *Junior* are abbreviated when they are part of a name. The abbreviations follow the surname and are set off by commas. (*But:* See 2.10.8, References, Authors, and 16.2.6, Forms of Numbers, Roman Numerals.)

Peter M. Forsythe, Jr, MD, did his landmark research in collaboration with James Philips, Sr, at the National Institutes of Health.

(*But:* John Paul II, Marshall Field IV)

Most titles of persons are abbreviated only when they precede the full name (first name [or initials] and surname). Spell titles out (1) when used before a surname alone, (2) at the beginning of a sentence, and (3) when used after a name (in that instance, the title will *not* be capitalized). (*But:* See also 11.2, Military Services and Titles.)

Alderman Bauler
Ald Paddy Bauler
Paddy Bauler, alderman of the 43rd ward of Chicago

Assistant Professor Garducci
Asst Prof Peter Garducci
Peter Garducci, assistant professor, Department of Medicine

Father Doyle
Fr Raymond Doyle
Raymond Doyle, SJ

Governor Thompson
Gov James R. Thompson
"Big Jim" Thompson, governor of Illinois

Representative Bolger
Rep Margaret S. Bolger
Margaret Bolger, representative from the state of Montana

Senator Simon
Sen Paul Simon (D, Ill)
Paul Simon, senator from Illinois

Sister Monica
Sr Monica Sobieski
Monica Sobieski, SJC, mother superior

Superintendent Smith
Supt H. B. Smith
Hannah B. Smith, superintendent of schools

Colonel Todd
COL John Todd, MC, USA
Dr Todd, colonel in the army

Exception: President is not abbreviated and is always capitalized, except when following a name (see also 8.2, Capitalization, Titles and Degrees of Persons):

President John F. Kennedy
President Kennedy
John F. Kennedy, president of the United States

the president of the United States
the president

The following social titles are always abbreviated when preceding a surname, with or without first name or initials: *Dr, Mr, Messrs, Mrs, Mmes, Ms,* and *Mss.* Note that in most instances, the title *Dr* should be used only after the specific academic degree has been mentioned and only with the surname.

> Arthur L. Rudnick, MD, PhD, gave the opening address. At the close of the meeting, Dr Rudnick was named permanent chairperson of the committee on sports injuries.

The Reverend, Reverend, or *Rev* is used only when the first name or initials are given with the surname. When only the surname is given, use *the Reverend Mr* (or *Ms* or *Dr*), *Mr* (or *Ms* or *Dr*), or *Father* (Roman Catholic, sometimes Anglican). Never use *the Reverend Brown, Reverend Brown,* or *Rev Brown.*

> the Reverend Joseph P. Fitzmaurice; the Reverend Katharine Burke
>
> the Reverend Dr Fitzmaurice; the Reverend Ms Burke
>
> Rev Joseph P. Fitzmaurice; Rev Katharine Burke

11.7   Business Firms.—In running text, use the name of a company exactly as the company uses it, but omit the period after *Co, Inc, Corp,* or *Ltd.* However, to conserve space in footnotes and references, abbreviate *company, corporation, brothers, incorporated, limited,* and *and* (using an ampersand), without punctuation, even if the company expands them, in accordance with the following examples. (See also 2.10.27, References, Publishers, and 12.8, Nomenclature, Equipment and Reagents.)

> John B. Ross & Co Inc
>
> Richardson-Merrell Inc
>
> Gale-Sharpe Corp
>
> Williams & Wilkins Co
>
> Smith Kline & French Laboratories
>
> The Upjohn Co
>
> Mead Johnson & Co
>
> Merrill Lynch Pierce Fenner & Smith Inc
>
> Boehringer Ingelheim Ltd
>
> CIBA-GEIGY Corp
>
> WB Saunders Co
>
> JB Lippincott Co

11.8   Agencies and Organizations.—The names of many agencies and organizations (eg, associations, government agencies, research institutes, broadcasting companies) are often known by their abbreviations rather than by their full names. Many of these organizations have identical acronyms (eg, AHA for both American Heart Association and American Hospital Association). Therefore, to avoid confusion, the names of all such organizations should be expanded at first mention in the text and other major elements of the manuscript (abstract, tables, legends, acknowledgments) with the abbreviation following immediately in parentheses.

The following are some commonly known associations and organizations.

AAAS
American Association for the Advancement of Science

AABB
American Association of Blood Banks

AAMC
Association of American Medical Colleges

AAP
Association of American Physicians

ADAMHA
Alcohol, Drug Abuse, and Mental Health Administration

AFCR
American Federation for Clinical Research

AFIP
Armed Forces Institute of Pathology

AHA
American Heart Association
American Hospital Association

AMA
American Medical Association

AMSA
American Medical Student Association

AMWA
American Medical Women's Association
American Medical Writers Association

ANSI
American National Standards Institute

AOA
American Osteopathic Association

ARC
American Red Cross

CDC
Centers for Disease Control

DHHS
Department of Health and Human Services

FDA
Food and Drug Administration

HCFA
Health Care Financing Administration

IOM
Institute of Medicine

NAS
National Academy of Sciences

NASA
National Aeronautics and Space Administration

NCHS
National Center for Health Statistics

NCI
National Cancer Institute

NCNR
National Center for Nursing Research

NEI
National Eye Institute

NHLBI
National Heart, Lung, and Blood Institute

NIA
National Institute on Aging

NIAID
National Institute of Allergy and Infectious Diseases

NIAMSD
National Institute of Arthritis and Musculoskeletal and Skin Diseases

NICHD
National Institute of Child Health and Human Development

NIDDK
National Institute of Diabetes and Digestive and Kidney Diseases

NIDR
National Institute of Dental Research

NIEHS
National Institute of Environmental Health Sciences

NIGMS
National Institute of General Medical Sciences

NIH
National Institutes of Health

NIMH
National Institute of Mental Health

NINDS
National Institute of Neurological Disorders and Stroke

NIOSH
National Institute for Occupational Safety and Health

NISO
National Information Standards Organization

NLM
National Library of Medicine

NMA
National Medical Association

NRC
National Research Council
Nuclear Regulatory Commission

OSHA
Occupational Safety and Health Administration

PAHO
Pan American Health Organization

PHS
Public Health Service

SSA
Social Security Administration

UN
United Nations

VA
Veterans Administration

WHO
World Health Organization

WMA
World Medical Association

11.9   **Names of Journals.**—In reference listings, abbreviate names of journals according to the current *Index Medicus*. These names are also italicized. (See also 2.10.14, References, Names of Journals.) The following is a selection of commonly referenced journals and their abbreviations (note that the article *The* has been omitted, as in *The Journal of . . .*).

AJR: American Journal of Roentgenology
AJR

American Family Physician
Am Fam Physician

American Journal of Cardiology
Am J Cardiol

American Journal of Clinical Nutrition
Am J Clin Nutr

American Journal of Clinical Pathology
Am J Clin Pathol

American Journal of Digestive Diseases
Am J Dig Dis

American Journal of Diseases of Children
AJDC

American Journal of the Medical Sciences
Am J Med Sci

American Journal of Medicine
Am J Med

American Journal of Nursing
Am J Nurs

American Journal of Obstetrics and Gynecology
Am J Obstet Gynecol

American Journal of Ophthalmology
Am J Ophthalmol

American Journal of Pathology
Am J Pathol

American Journal of Physical Medicine and Rehabilitation
Am J Phys Med Rehabil

American Journal of Psychiatry
Am J Psychiatry

American Journal of Public Health
Am J Public Health

American Journal of Surgery
Am J Surg

American Journal of Tropical Medicine and Hygiene
Am J Trop Med Hyg

American Review of Respiratory Disease
Am Rev Respir Dis

Anaesthesia
Anaesthesia

Anesthesia and Analgesia
Anesth Analg

Anesthesiology
Anesthesiology

Annals of Emergency Medicine
Ann Emerg Med

Annals of Internal Medicine
Ann Intern Med

Annals of Otology, Rhinology, and Laryngology
Ann Otol Rhinol Laryngol

11.9   Names of Journals

Annals of Surgery
Ann Surg

Annals of Thoracic Surgery
Ann Thorac Surg

Annual Review of Medicine
Annu Rev Med

Archives of Dermatology
Arch Dermatol

Archives of Disease in Childhood
Arch Dis Child

Archives of Environmental Health
Arch Environ Health

Archives of General Psychiatry
Arch Gen Psychiatry

Archives of Internal Medicine
Arch Intern Med

Archives of Neurology
Arch Neurol

Archives of Ophthalmology
Arch Ophthalmol

Archives of Otolaryngology–Head and Neck Surgery
Arch Otolaryngol Head Neck Surg

Archives of Pathology and Laboratory Medicine
Arch Pathol Lab Med

Archives of Physical Medicine and Rehabilitation
Arch Phys Med Rehabil

Archives of Surgery
Arch Surg

Arthritis and Rheumatism
Arthritis Rheum

Blood
Blood

Brain
Brain

British Heart Journal
Br Heart J

British Journal of Obstetrics and Gynaecology
Br J Obstet Gynaecol

British Journal of Radiology
Br J Radiol

British Journal of Rheumatology
Br J Rheumatol

British Journal of Surgery
Br J Surg

British Medical Journal
Br Med J

British Medical Journal [Clinical Research Edition]
Br Med J Clin Res

CA: A Cancer Journal for Clinicians
CA

Canadian Medical Association Journal
Can Med Assoc J

Cancer
Cancer

Chest
Chest

Circulation
Circulation

Clinical Orthopaedics and Related Research
Clin Orthop

Clinical Pediatrics (Philadelphia)
Clin Pediatr (Phila)

Clinical Pharmacology and Therapeutics
Clin Pharmacol Ther

Clinical Toxicology
Clin Toxicol

Critical Care Medicine
Crit Care Med

Current Problems in Surgery
Curr Probl Surg

Diabetes
Diabetes

Digestive Diseases and Sciences
Dig Dis Sci

Disease-a-Month
Dis Mon

Endocrinology
Endocrinology

Gastroenterology
Gastroenterology

Geriatrics
Geriatrics

Gut
Gut

11.9   Names of Journals

Heart and Lung
Heart Lung

Hospital Practice (Office Edition)
Hosp Pract Off

Hospitals
Hospitals

Journal of Allergy and Clinical Immunology
J Allergy Clin Immunol

Journal of the American Dietetic Association
J Am Diet Assoc

Journal of the American Medical Association
JAMA

Journal of Bone and Joint Surgery. American Volume
J Bone Joint Surg Am

Journal of Bone and Joint Surgery. British Volume
J Bone Joint Surg Br

Journal of Clinical Endocrinology and Metabolism
J Clin Endocrinol Metab

Journal of Clinical Investigation
J Clin Invest

Journal of Clinical Pathology
J Clin Pathol

Journal of Family Practice
J Fam Pract

Journal of Gerontology
J Gerontol

Journal of Immunology
J Immunol

Journal of Infectious Diseases
J Infect Dis

Journal of Laboratory and Clinical Medicine
J Lab Clin Med

Journal of Laryngology and Otology
J Laryngol Otol

Journal of Medical Education
J Med Educ

JNCI: Journal of the National Cancer Institute
JNCI

Journal of Nervous and Mental Disease
J Nerv Ment Dis

Journal of Neurosurgery
J Neurosurg

Journal of Nursing Administration
J Nurs Adm

Journal of Obstetrics and Gynaecology of the British Commonwealth
J Obstet Gynaecol Br Commonw

Journal of Oral and Maxillofacial Surgery
J Oral Maxillofac Surg

Journal of Oral Surgery
J Oral Surg

Journal of Pediatrics
J Pediatr

Journal of Thoracic and Cardiovascular Surgery
J Thorac Cardiovasc Surg

Journal of Toxicology, Clinical Toxicology
J Toxicol Clin Toxicol

Journal of Trauma
J Trauma

Journal of Urology
J Urol

Lancet
Lancet

Mayo Clinic Proceedings
Mayo Clin Proc

Medical Clinics of North America
Med Clin North Am

Medical Letter on Drugs and Therapeutics
Med Lett Drugs Ther

Medicine (Baltimore)
Medicine (Baltimore)

Milbank Quarterly
Milbank Q

Morbidity and Mortality Weekly Report
MMWR

Neurology
Neurology

New England Journal of Medicine
N Engl J Med

New York State Journal of Medicine
NY State J Med

Nursing Clinics of North America
Nurs Clin North Am

Nursing Outlook
Nurs Outlook

Nursing Research
Nurs Res

Obstetrics and Gynecology
Obstet Gynecol

Orthopedic Clinics of North America
Orthop Clin North Am

Pediatric Clinics of North America
Pediatr Clin North Am

Pediatrics
Pediatrics

Physical Therapy
Phys Ther

Plastic and Reconstructive Surgery
Plast Reconstr Surg

Postgraduate Medicine
Postgrad Med

*Proceedings of the National Academy of Sciences
of the United States of America*
Proc Natl Acad Sci USA

Progress in Cardiovascular Diseases
Prog Cardiovasc Dis

Public Health Reports
Public Health Rep

Radiologic Clinics of North America
Radiol Clin North Am

Radiology
Radiology

Rheumatology and Rehabilitation
Rheumatol Rehabil

Southern Medical Journal
South Med J

Surgery
Surgery

Surgery, Gynecology and Obstetrics
Surg Gynecol Obstet

Surgical Clinics of North America
Surg Clin North Am

Urologic Clinics of North America
Urol Clin North Am

Western Journal of Medicine
West J Med

11.10   Clinical and Technical Terms.—This compilation of common clinical and technical terms and their abbreviations is not intended to be all-encompassing but is provided as an aid to the stylebook user. There are many excellent published listings of abbreviations and acronyms, to which the reader is referred (see 21.2, Resource Bibliography, Additional Readings).

These terms should always be expanded at first mention. Use common sense and good judgment in deciding whether to abbreviate them and other terms. For example, if "toxic shock syndrome" appears only once or twice in an article, spell it out; if the article concerns toxic shock syndrome and the term is used many times (perhaps five or more times), expand the term at first mention with the abbreviation immediately following in parentheses. Abbreviate it thereafter, except at the beginning of a sentence. Apply this concept to each element of the manuscript. (See 2.0, Manuscript Preparation, and 11.0, Abbreviations. See also specific sections [eg, 12.0, Nomenclature, and 17.5, Statistics, Commonly Used Statistical Symbols and Tests] for additional guidelines for correct use of specialized terms and their abbreviations.)

ACTH	Use *corticotropin* (previously adrenocorticotropic hormone).
ADH	antidiuretic hormone
ADP	adenosine diphosphate
ADPase	adenosine diphosphatase
AFP	α-fetoprotein
AIDS	acquired immunodeficiency syndrome
ALT	alanine aminotransferase (previously SGPT)
AMP	adenosine monophosphate
ANA	antinuclear antibody
APB	atrial premature beat
ARDS	adult respiratory distress syndrome
AST	aspartate aminotransferase (previously SGOT)
ATP	adenosine triphosphate
ATPase	adenosine triphosphatase
BCG	bacille Calmette-Guérin (*but:* BCG vaccine [do not expand as drug])
BP	blood pressure
BSA	body surface area
BTPS	body temperature, pressure, saturated
C	complement (eg, C1, C2, . . . C9)
cAMP	cyclic adenosine monophosphate
CBC	complete blood cell (add *count*)
CEA	carcinoembryonic antigen
CFT	complement fixation test
cGMP	cyclic guanosine monophosphate
CI	confidence interval
CK	creatine kinase
CK-BB	creatine kinase–BB (BB designates the isozyme)
CK-MB	creatine kinase–MB

185

CK-MM	creatine kinase–MM
CMV	cytomegalovirus
CNS	central nervous system
COPD	chronic obstructive pulmonary disease
CPR	cardiopulmonary resuscitation
CRF	corticotropin-releasing factor
CSF	cerebrospinal fluid
CT	computed tomography, computed tomographic
dAMP	deoxyadenosine monophosphate (deoxyadenylate)
D&C	dilation and curettage
DDT	dichlorodiphenyltrichloroethane (chlorophenothane)
DE	dose equivalent
DEV	duck embryo vaccine
dGMP	deoxyguanosine monophosphate (deoxyguanylate)
DIC	disseminated intravascular coagulation
DIF	direct immunofluorescence
DNR	do not resuscitate
DRG	diagnosis related group
EBV	Epstein-Barr virus
ECG	electrocardiogram, electrocardiographic
ECT	electroconvulsive therapy
ED	effective dose
ED_{50}	median effective dose
EEE	eastern equine encephalomyelitis
EEG	electroencephalogram, electroencephalographic
EIA	enzyme immunoassay
EIS	Epidemic Intelligence Service (Centers for Disease Control)
ELISA	enzyme-linked immunosorbent assay
EMG	electromyogram, electromyographic
EMIT	enzyme-multiplied immunoassay technique
ENG	electronystagmogram, electronystagmographic
EOG	electro-oculogram, electro-oculographic
ESP	extrasensory perception
ESR	erythrocyte sedimentation rate
ESRD	end-stage renal disease
EST	electroshock therapy
EVR	evoked visual response
FEV	forced expiratory volume
FEV_1	forced expiratory volume in 1 second
FSH	follicle-stimulating hormone
FTA	fluorescent treponemal antibody
FTA-ABS	fluorescent treponemal antibody absorption (add *test*)
FVC	forced vital capacity
GDP	guanosine diphosphate
GFR	glomerular filtration rate
GI	gastrointestinal
GLC	gas-liquid chromatography
GMP	guanosine monophosphate (guanylate, guanylic acid)
GMT	geometric mean titer

GnRH	gonadotropin-releasing hormone (*gonadorelin* as diagnostic agent)
Hbco	carboxyhemoglobin
HBO	hyperbaric oxygen
Hbo$_2$	oxyhemoglobin, oxygenated hemoglobin
HbS	sickle cell hemoglobin
HBV	hepatitis B virus
hCG	human chorionic gonadotropin (do not abbreviate as drug)
HDL	high-density lipoprotein
HDL-C	high-density lipoprotein cholesterol
HIV	human immunodeficiency virus
HMO	health maintenance organization
HPF	high-power field
HPLC	high-pressure liquid chromatography
HSV	herpes simplex virus
HTLV	human T-cell lymphotropic virus, human T-cell leukemia virus

ID	infective dose
Ig	immunoglobulin (eg, IgA, IgG, IgM; see 12.12.3, Nomenclature, Immunoglobulins)
IM	intramuscular, intramuscularly
IND	Investigational New Drug
IOP	intraocular pressure
ISG	immune serum globulin
ITP	idiopathic thrombocytopenic purpura
IUD	intrauterine device
IV	intravenous, intravenously
IVP	intravenous pyelogram

LAV	lymphadenopathy-associated virus
LD	lethal dose
LD$_{50}$	median lethal dose
LDH	lactate dehydrogenase
LDL	low-density lipoprotein
LDL-C	low-density lipoprotein cholesterol
LH	luteinizing hormone
LHRH	luteinizing hormone–releasing hormone (*gonadorelin* as diagnostic agent)
LSD	lysergic acid diethylamide

MCH	mean corpuscular hemoglobin
MCHC	mean corpuscular hemoglobin concentration
MCV	mean corpuscular volume
MD	muscular dystrophy
MEC	mean effective concentration
MIC	minimum inhibitory concentration
MMPI	Minnesota Multiphasic Personality Inventory
MRI	magnetic resonance imaging
mRNA	messenger RNA
MS	multiple sclerosis

NANB	non-A, non-B (add *hepatitis*)

11.10   Clinical and Technical Terms

NDA	New Drug Application
NF	*National Formulary*
NK	natural killer (add *cells*)
NSAID	nonsteroidal anti-inflammatory drug
NS	not significant
NTP	normal temperature and pressure
OR	odds ratio
PAS	periodic acid–Schiff
PEEP	positive end-expiratory pressure
PET	positron emission tomography
PID	pelvic inflammatory disease
PKU	phenylketonuria
PPD	purified protein derivative (tuberculin)
PSRO	professional standard review organization
PT	prothrombin time
PTA	percutaneous transluminal angioplasty
PTT	partial thromboplastin time
PUVA	oral psoralen with long-wave UV radiation in the A range (photochemotherapy)
RAM	random access memory
RAST	radioallergosorbent test
RBC	red blood cell
REM	rapid eye movement (sleep)
ROM	read-only memory
RR	relative risk
RSV	respiratory syncytial virus
SCID	severe combined immunodeficiency disease
SEM	scanning electron microscope
SIADH	syndrome of inappropriate secretion of antidiuretic hormone
SIDS	sudden infant death syndrome
SLE	systemic lupus erythematosus; St Louis encephalitis
sp g	specific gravity (use with a number)
STD	sexually transmitted disease
T_3	triiodothyronine
T_4	thyroxine
TCD_{00}	tissue culture dose
TIBC	total iron-binding capacity
TPA	tissue plasminogen activator
TPN	total parenteral nutrition
TRH	thyrotropin-releasing hormone (*protirelin* as diagnostic agent)
tRNA	transfer ribonucleic acid
TSH	thyrotropin (previously thyroid-stimulating hormone)
TSH-RF	thyroid-stimulating hormone–releasing factor
TSS	toxic shock syndrome
TTP	thrombotic thrombocytopenic purpura
USAN	*United States Adopted Names*
USP	*United States Pharmacopeia*

VEP	visual evoked potential
VER	visual evoked response
VHDL	very-high-density lipoprotein
VLDL	very-low-density lipoprotein
VPB	ventricular premature beat
WAIS	Wechsler Adult Intelligence Scale
WBC	white blood cell
WEE	western equine encephalomyelitis

The following abbreviations may be used without expansion. (See also 2.13.6, Tables, Setup; and 17.5, Statistics, Commonly Used Statistical Symbols and Tests.)

AC	alternating current
DC	direct current
DNA	deoxyribonucleic acid
F	French (add *catheter*) (use only with a number, eg, 12F)
HLA	human leukocyte antigen
IQ	intelligence quotient
m-	meta- (use only in chemical formulas or names)
o-	ortho- (use only in chemical formulas)
OD	oculus dexter (right eye) (use only with a number)
OS	oculus sinister (left eye) (use only with a number)
OU	oculus unitas (both eyes) or oculus uterque (each eye) (use only with a number)
p-	para- (use only in chemical formulas or names)
Pa_{CO_2}	carbon dioxide pressure (tension), arterial
Pa_{O_2}	oxygen pressure (tension), arterial
P_{CO_2}	carbon dioxide pressure (tension)
pH	hydrogen ion concentration; negative logarithm of hydrogen ion activity
P_{O_2}	oxygen pressure (tension)
RNA	ribonucleic acid
UHF	ultrahigh frequency
UV	ultraviolet
VDRL	Venereal Disease Research Laboratory (test)
VHF	very high frequency

11.11 **Units of Measure.**—On July 1, 1986, the AMA adopted the use of the International System of Units (SI units, Système International d'Unités) in *JAMA* and the nine specialty journals (*JAMA*. 1986;255:2329-2339). For 1 year, conventional units of measure continued to be used with the corresponding SI conversion following immediately in parentheses. Beginning July 1, 1987, the reverse occurred, with SI units as the primary measurement and conventional units in parentheses. As of July 1, 1988, only SI units are being used.

Use the following abbreviations and symbols with a numerical quantity in accordance with guidelines in 15.0, Units of Measure. (See also 6.10, Punctuation, Virgule [Solidus].)

acre	acre
ampere	A
angstrom	Convert to nanometers (1 Å = 0.1 nm).
atmosphere, standard	atm
bar	bar
barn	b*
becquerel	Bq
Bessey-Lowry unit	Bessey-Lowry unit
billion electron volts	GeV*
Bodansky unit	BU*
British thermal unit	BTU
calorie	Convert to joules (1 calorie = 4.2 J).
candela	cd*
Celsius	C (Use closed up with degree symbol, eg, 40°C.)
centigram	cg
centimeter	cm
centimeters of water	cm H_2O
centipoise	cp
coulomb	C*
counts per minute	cpm
counts per second	cps
cubic centimeter	cm^3 (Use milliliter for liquid and gas measure.)
cubic foot	cu ft
cubic inch	cu in
cubic meter	m^3
cubic micrometer	μm^3
cubic millimeter	mm^3 (Use microliter for liquid and gas measure.)
cubic yard	cu yd
curie	Ci
cycles per second	Use hertz.
dalton	d
day	$d^\dagger$

---

*Expand at first mention, without giving abbreviation parenthetically. Abbreviate thereafter (*but:* see 15.3.3, Units of Measure, Beginning of Sentence, Title, Subtitle).
†Use only in a virgule construction and in tables and line art.

decibel	dB
decigram	Convert to grams (1 decigram = 0.1 g).
deciliter	dL
decimeter	Convert to meters (1 decimeter = 0.1 m).
diopter	D*
disintegrations per minute	dpm*
disintegrations per second	dps*
dram	dram
dyne	dyne
electron volt	eV
electrostatic unit	ESU*
equivalent	Eq
equivalent roentgen	equivalent roentgen
farad (electric capacitance)	F
Fahrenheit	F (Use closed up with degree symbol, eg, 99°F.)
femtogram	fg
femtoliter	fL
femtomole	fmol
fluid ounce	fl oz
foot	ft
foot-candle	ft-c*
foot-pound	ft-lb
foot-lambert	foot-lambert
gallon	gal
gas volume	gas volume
gauss	G
grain	grain
gram	g
gravity (acceleration due to)	g (Use closed up to preceding number, eg, 200g.)
gray	Gy
henry	H*
hertz	Hz
horsepower	hp
hour	h†
immunizing unit	ImmU*
inch	in
international benzoate unit	IBU*
international unit	IU
joule	J
kelvin	K
kilocalorie	Convert to kilojoules (1 kcal = 4.2 kJ).

kilocurie	kCi
kilodalton	kd
kiloelectron volt	keV
kilogram	kg
kilohertz	kHz
kilojoule	kJ
kilometer	km
kilovolt	kV
kilovolt-ampere	kVA
kilovolt (constant potential)	kV(cp)*
kilovolt (peak)	kV(p)*
kilowatt	kW
King-Armstrong unit	King-Armstrong unit
knot	knot
liter	L
lumen	lumen
lux	lux
megacurie	MCi
megacycle	Mc
megahertz	MHz
megaunit	megaunit
meter	m
metric ton	metric ton
microampere	μA
microcurie	μCi
microfarad	μF*
microgram	μg
microliter	μL
micrometer	μm
micromicrocurie	Use picocurie.
micromicrogram	Use picogram.
micromicrometer	Use picometer.
micromole	μmol
micron	Use micrometer.
micromolar	μmol/L
micronormal	μN
micro-osmole	μOsm
microunit	μU
microvolt	μV
microwatt	μW
mile	mile
miles per hour	mph
milliampere	mA
millicurie	mCi
millicuries destroyed	mCid*
milliequivalent	mEq
millifarad	mF*
milligram	mg
milligram-element	mg-el*
milli–international unit	mIU

milliliter	mL
millimeter	mm
millimeters of mercury	mm Hg
millimeters of water	mm H$_2$O
millimicron equivalent (physical)	nmEq*
millimole	mmol
millimolar	mmol/L
million electron volts	MeV
milliosmole	mOsm
millirem	mrem
milliroentgen	mR
millisecond	ms[†]
milliunit	mU
millivolt	mV
milliwatt	mW
minute (time)	min[†]
molar	mol/L
mole	mol
month	mo[†]
mouse unit	MU*
nanocurie	nCi
nanogram	ng
nanometer	nm
nanomolar	nmol/L
nanomole	nmol
newton	N
normal (solution)	N
ohm	Ω
osmole	osm
ounce	oz
outflow (weight)	C*
parts per million	ppm
pascal	Pa
picocurie	pCi
picogram	pg
picometer	pm
pint	pt
pound	lb
pounds per square inch	psi
pounds per square inch absolute	psia*
pounds per square inch gauge	psig*
prism diopter	PD, Δ*
quart	qt
rad	Convert to gray (1 rad = 0.01 Gy).
radian	radian
rat unit	RU*
revolutions per minute	rpm

roentgen	R
roentgen equivalents man (or mammal)	rem
roentgen equivalents physical	rep
Saybolt seconds universal	SSU*
second	s†
siemen	siemen
sievert	Sv
square centimeter	cm²
square foot	sq ft
square inch	sq in
square meter	m²
square millimeter	mm²
Svedberg flotation unit	Sf*
tesla	T
tonne (metric ton)	tonne
torr	Use millimeters of mercury.
tuberculin unit	TU
turbidity-reducing unit	TRU*
unit	U
volt	V
volume	vol
volume per volume	vol/vol
volume percent	vol%
watt	W
week	wk†
weight	wt
weight per volume	wt/vol
weight per weight	wt/wt
yard	yd
year	y†

11.12   Elements and Chemicals.—In general, the names of chemical elements and compounds should be expanded in the text and elsewhere in accordance with the guidelines for clinical and technical terms (*but:* see 12.6, Nomenclature, Drugs, and 12.13, Nomenclature, Isotopes). However, in some circumstances it may be helpful or necessary to provide the chemical symbols or formulas—in addition to the expansion—for clarification or explanation, especially if the compound under discussion is new or relatively unknown, if no nonproprietary term exists, or if the name is long and complex. For example:

Isorhodeose (6-deoxy-D-glucose [$CH_3(CHOH)_4CHO$]) is a sugar derived from cinchona bark.
(Use ''isorhodeose'' thereafter in the manuscript.)

The chemical compound 2,3,7,8-tetrachlorodibenzo-*p*-dioxin (TCDD, or dioxin) is often referred to as the most toxic man-made chemical known.

(Use "TCDD" or "dioxin" thereafter [TCDD is more specific, since there is more than one form of dioxin].)

3,4-Methylenedioxymethamphetamine (MDMA, "ecstasy"), a synthetic analogue of 3,4-methylenedioxyamphetamine, has been the center of recent debate over its potential for abuse vs its use as a psychotherapeutic agent. (Use "MDMA" or "ecstasy" thereafter [depending on the sense of the sentence].)

Names such as "sodium lauryl sulfate" certainly are easier to express and understand (and, for the printer, easier to set in type) than "$CH_3(CH_2)_{10}CH_2OSO_3Na$." Similarly, "oxygen," "carbon dioxide," and "water" do not take up much more space than "O_2," "CO_2," and "H_2O" and hence should remain expanded throughout a manuscript, unless specific measurements are under discussion.

The venous CO_2 pressure is always greater than arterial CO_2 pressure; specifically, Pv_{CO_2}/Pa_{CO_2} is greater than 1.0 except when Po_2 plus Pco_2 is measured. Nevertheless, the CO_2 levels should be carefully measured.

Water consists of hydrogen and oxygen.

Repeated serum chemistry studies confirmed a low serum sodium [not "Na"] level of 131 mmol/L and a serum potassium [not "K"] level of 4.8 mmol/L.

The expansion of such symbols as Na^{++} or H^+ would be cumbersome, since these symbols have a specific meaning for the reader. And in creative pieces, the flavor of the writing might be lost if, for example, the editor arbitrarily changed "CO_2" to "carbon dioxide" or vice versa ("What's his CO_2?").

Chemical symbols and formulas also must be carefully marked for the printer, especially when expressing chemical bonds. There are three types: single, double, and triple. These bond formations are commonly seen in organic and biochemical compounds.

$$H_3—CH_3 \qquad H_2C{=}CH_2 \qquad HC{\equiv}CH$$

The editor and the author should consider guidelines for established terminology, the manuscript's subject matter and technical level, the context in which the term appears, and the journal's audience in determining whether to expand or abbreviate such terms.

Chapter 12

12.0 Nomenclature

"A rose by any other name is not a rose" (Patterson and Sommers 1981). T4 is not T_4 is not T-4. Proper naming may not be sufficient to ensure identity, but it is necessary. Systems of nomenclature in medicine and science have as their goal the consistent, correct, and stable (Patterson and Sommers 1981) naming of entities. Does A exist? Is it what we think? Does it deserve its own name? Is A the same as B, or do the two require different names? How best might A and B be named?

In describing the work of the International Committee on Coagulation Factor Nomenclature, Dr Rosemary Biggs wrote, "An impenetrable confusion was cleared away, apparent disagreements were often shown to be conflicts of terminology not of fact, and a much freer exchange of information was made possible" (Biggs 1976). The last, especially, is certainly a goal of medical journals, and it can be argued that a single entity deserves a single name.

Numerous nomenclature committees exist in medicine, as ad hoc national or international bodies or as work units of associations and other extant groups—often "born in the midst of a fulminating controversy . . . and nurtured in the grumbling aftermath" (Melnick 1971). While attempting to achieve correctness and consistency, they must also take into account tradition (familiar old names and "the ruins of previous systems" [Melnick 1971]), future needs of the field (with which familiar old names often conflict), and the possibly inherent human tendencies to enumerate and abbreviate.

Usually, a report entitled "Nomenclature" presents rules for naming the elements of a given field. This Nomenclature section, however, is meant not to generate but rather to reflect the nomenclature in various areas of medicine. It is hoped that amidst the hodgepodge of numbers and letters, superscripts and subscripts, a useful selection of familiar but not quite accessible terms, or simply confusing ones, has been included.

The Nomenclature section will present style, along with examples and definitions. Sometimes, consistency or ease of use (eg, the limited capacity of many computers to display subscripts or superscripts [Shows et al 1979]) has been behind recommendations. However, forms difficult to recreate on typewriters or computer printers (eg, superscript italics) remain in many official nomenclature systems, and authors can see 20.0, Copy Editing and Proofreading Marks, to learn how to indicate such forms manually. Copy editors are responsible for marking copy clearly for the typesetter and will consult with authors about terminology as needed (see 4.3, Editorial Assessment and Processing, Copy Editing).

All systems of nomenclature try for logic and meaning, but, in truth, whether to hyphenate or italicize, despite the surprisingly strong feeling such decisions sometimes evoke, may be arbitrary. Recognizing this and the constant evolution of medical subject matter, including nomenclature, the Nomenclature section is not meant as a definitive source, but rather as a guide. A common theme throughout will be *context*, which must always be made clear. For, while a hyphen may identify a bone (T-4), only additional prose can distinguish a hormone from an electrode (T_4) or a tumor from a lymphocyte (T4)!

12.1   Blood Groups.—Blood group terminology uses single letters (eg, group A) or dual letters (eg, AB, Le), often with a letter or number as a superscript or subscript. If a subscript letter or number is part of an antigen symbol, it becomes a superscript in the symbol for the gene (eg, A_1 antigen; A^1 gene). If a superscript letter is part of an antigen symbol, it remains a superscript in the symbol for the gene (eg, Fy^a antigen; Fy^a gene).

The following are some of the more commonly used blood group systems (see also 12.9.3, Genetics, Human Gene Nomenclature).

- ABO system
    Antigens: A, A_1, A_2, A_x, B
    Phenotypes: A_1, A_2, A_1B, A_2B, O
    Genotypes: A^1O; A^1A^1; A^1B; OO
    Sample expressions: ABO antigens, A cell, type AB recipient, type O donor
- Lewis system
    Antigens: Le^a, Le^b, Le^x
    Phenotypes: Le(a−b+); Le(a+b−); Le(a−b−)
    Genotypes: *Lele*; *LeLe*; *lele*
    The Lewis type of a red blood cell depends on the uptake of Lewis antigens from the plasma.
- Ii system
    Antigens: I, i
    Phenotypes: I+, i+
- MNSs system
    Antigens: M, N, S, s, M_2, U, Mi^a
    Phenotypes: M+N+, M+N−, M−N+, S+
    Genotypes: *MN, MM, NN, MSNs*

- P system
  - Antigens: P, p, P_1, pk
  - Phenotypes: P+, p_1+
- Rh system (*Note:* The system is Rh, *not* Rhesus.)
  - Antigens: D, C, E, c, e
    - (Rh1, Rh2, Rh3, Rh4, Rh5)*
  - Phenotypes: D-positive (Rh positive)
    - D-negative (Rh negative)
  - Genotypes: *DCe/DCe* (R^1R^1)
    - *DcE/dce* (R^2r)
    - *dce/dce* (*rr*)
- Kell system
  - Antigens: K, k, Kp^a, Kp^b, Js^a, Js^b
    - K1, K2, K3, K4, K5, K6
  - Phenotypes: K+k+, Kp(a−b+), Js(a−b+)
    - K:1, K:2, K:−3, K:4, K:−5, K:6
  - Genotypes: *Kk*, Kp^bKp^b, Js^bJs^b
    - K^1, K^2, K^{-3}, K^4, K^{-5}, K^6
- Lutheran system
  - Antigens: Lu^a, Lu^b
  - Phenotypes: Lu(a+b−), Lu(a−b+), Lu(a+b+)
  - Genotypes: Lu^aLu^a, Lu^bLu^b, Lu^aLu^b
- Duffy system
  - Antigens: Fy^a, Fy^b
  - Phenotypes: Fy(a+b−), Fy(a−b+), Fy(a−b−)
  - Genotypes: Fy^aFy^a, Fy^bFy^b, *FyFy*
- Kidd system
  - Antigens: Jk^a, Jk^b
  - Phenotypes: Jk(a+b−), Jk(a−b+), Jk(a+b+)
  - Genotypes: Jk^aJk^a, Jk^bJk^b, Jk^aJk^b
- Secretor system
  - Secretors of ABH antigens have a secretor (*Se*) gene. Their genotypes may be *SeSe* or *Sese*.

12.2   Cancer Staging

12.2.1 *Cancer Stage.*—Cancer stages are expressed using capital roman numerals:

stage I	stage III
stage II	stage IV

---

*An Rh phenotype can be described with letters or with numbers.

The term *stage 0* indicates carcinoma in situ.

Letter and numerical on-line suffixes may be added to subdivide cancer stages, as in the following examples:

stage IA	stage II3
stage IE	stage IVA
stage IS	stage IVB

12.2.2   *The TNM System.*—Authors will frequently use and editors frequently encounter a system used in the staging of cancer known as the ''TNM system.'' The TNM classification is put forth by the American Joint Committee on Cancer (AJCC) and the Union Internationale Contre le Cancer, and the third edition of the AJCC *Manual for Staging of Cancer* (see 21.1, Resource Bibliography, References) presents the stages of cancer as defined by TNM criteria. The TNM symbols follow.

- T: tumor (indicates size or involvement)

    T is followed by numerical or other on-line suffixes, eg,

    TX: tumor size or involvement cannot be assessed

    T0: no evidence of a primary tumor

    Tis: in situ tumor

    T1, T2, T3, T4: size, involvement, or other characteristics of the tumor

    (*Note:* The numbers following T indicate increasing size or involvement but do not refer to specific sizes for all tumors. For example, for one type of tumor, T1 may indicate size less than 2 cm, for another, size less than 0.75 mm, and for another, confinement within the underlying mucosa.)

- N: node (indicates regional lymph node involvement)

    NX: regional lymph node involvement cannot be assessed

    N0: no involvement of regional lymph nodes

    N1, N2, N3: increasing regional lymph node involvement according to criteria that vary for different tumor types

- M: metastasis (indicates extent of metastasis)

    MX: extent of metastasis cannot be determined

    M0: no metastasis

    M1: distant metastasis present

    Site of metastasis may be indicated by such three-letter abbreviations as PUL (pulmonary), OSS (osseous), or HEP (hepatic).

12.2.3   *The TNM System and Cancer Staging.*—Various combinations of T, N, and M criteria are used to define cancer stages. For example, stage I is defined as T1, N0, M0 for many types of cancer.

The combinations that define particular stages differ among the myriad types of cancer. For example, in laryngeal cancer, stage II is defined as T2, N0, M0, while in colon cancer, stage II is defined as T3, N0, M0.

More than one combination of T, N, and M criteria may constitute the definition of a stage, eg, in a given cancer stage II may be defined as T3, N0, M0 *or* T1, N1, M0 *or* T2, N1, M0 *or* T3, N1, M0.

12.2.4 *Other Staging Indicators.*—Other criteria are used as adjuncts to the T, N, and M criteria in defining cancers and sometimes in assessing stage; these are indicated by capital letters as follows.

grade	GX, G1, G2, G3
lymphatic invasion	LX, L0, L1, L2
venous invasion	VX, V0, V1, V2
residual tumor	RX, R0, R1, R2
host performance	H0, H1, H2, H3, H4 (This represents the AJCC scale; other scales of host performance may be used.)
scleral invasion	SX, S0, S1, S2

Lowercase prefixes to the T, N, M, and other symbols may be used to indicate the mode of determining criteria for tumor description and staging; these are as follows.

c	clinical classification
p	pathologic classification
r	retreatment classification
a	autopsy staging
y, yp	classification during or following multimodality treatment

Examples: cTNM, pT3

The T, N, M, and other symbols used in cancer staging may be followed by suffixes in addition to the common X, 0, and numerals; the following are additional examples.

T1a	T2a	N1a
T1b	T3a	N2b
T1c	T3b	pN1a
T1a1	T4a	pN1biv
T1a2	T2(m)	M1a

Terms such as "stage I cancer," "TNM system," and "T1, N1, M0" are widely recognized and may be used in articles without further definition. The additional suffixes and prefixes given above, however, should be defined by the author, as they are less familiar and may be confused with other systems of nomenclature.

12.3   Cardiology

12.3.1   *Electrocardiographic Terms.*—Note the use of capitals, lowercase letters, subscripts, and hyphens in the following examples of electrocardiographic terms.

Leads: Leads are designated as follows:

standard (bipolar) leads	I, II, III
augmented limb leads	aVR, aVL, aVF
precordial leads	V_1, V_2, V_3, V_4, V_5, V_6, V_7, V_8, V_9
right precordial leads	V_{3R}, V_{4R}, V_{5R}, etc
ensiform cartilage lead	V_E
third interspace leads	$3V_1$, $3V_2$, $3V_3$, etc
esophageal leads	E_{15}, E_{24}, E_{50}, etc

The abnormality appeared in leads V_3 through V_6 [not V_3-V_6 or V_{3-6}].

Recording terminology: Capital letters are used to describe electrocardiographic deflections in general. For example:

Improper paper speed will spuriously alter the QRS configuration [*not* qrs configuration].

For specific deflections, capitals may indicate larger waves and lowercase letters smaller waves; in practice, this most often applies to the Q, R, and S waves.

Pathologic Q waves occur in myocardial infarction; the q wave in aVF in this case indicated inferior wall infarction. The Rr′ pattern in lead V_3 may indicate early repolarization.

Tracing terms: The following are examples of some tracing terms:

P wave	U wave
Ta wave	QS wave, qs wave
Q wave, q wave	QRS complex, configuration, axis, etc
R wave, r wave	ST segment, depression, etc (*not* S-T segment)
S wave, s wave	ST-T segment, elevation, etc (*not* S-T-T)
R′ wave, r′ wave	QT interval, prolongation, etc (*not* Q-T)

S′ wave, s′ wave	QT_c (corrected QT interval)
T wave	PR interval, segment, etc (*not* P-R)
J-junction, J-point	

QRS axis: When QRS axis is specified, it is given with a plus or minus sign followed by the number of degrees in arabic numerals, eg, $+60°$, $-30°$.

12.3.2 *Heart Sounds and Murmurs.*—Descriptions of cardiac auscultatory findings mention heart sounds and murmurs.

Heart sounds: Four heart sounds and four components are commonly abbreviated in discussions of cardiac auscultatory findings; numerical subscripts are used:

S_1	first heart sound
	M_1: mitral valve component
	T_1: tricuspid valve component
S_2	second heart sound
	A_2: aortic valve component
	P_2: pulmonic valve component
S_3	third heart sound
S_4	fourth heart sound

In describing actual, specific findings in a given patient, the heart sound abbreviations may be used:

The presence of an audible S_3 was consistent with the patient's ventricular aneurysm.

However, sound names should be written out in general discussion of heart sounds:

Third heart sounds are suggestive of ventricular aneurysm.

Other terms, although often seen in abbreviated form, especially on phonocardiographic tracings, should be written out in full in text and defined in figure legends. The following are some examples, and some are redundant:

EC	ejection click
SC	systolic click
E	ejection sound
NEC	nonejection click
OS	opening snap
SS	summation sound
W	whoop
C	click
AOC	aortic opening click

AEC	aortic ejection click
PEC	pulmonary ejection click

Murmurs: In both specific discussions of patients and general discussions of cardiac auscultation, murmur names and descriptions should be written out rather than abbreviated (eg, systolic murmur [SM], diastolic murmur [DM], systolic ejection murmur [SEM]). When murmur names are abbreviated in figures, they should be defined in the legend.

Other murmur names commonly encountered are the following:

LSM	late systolic murmur
PSM	pansystolic murmur
ESM	ejection systolic murmur
IDM	immediate diastolic murmur
DDM	delayed diastolic murmur
ASM	atrial systolic murmur
CM	continuous murmur

Murmurs are graded from soft (low grade) to loud (higher grade). Systolic murmurs may be graded from 1 to 6, diastolic from 1 to 4. Murmur grades are written in arabic numerals.

12.4   Clotting Factors.—An international system of nomenclature, completed in the early 1960s, clarified coagulation factor terminology and, as Dr Rosemary Biggs has observed, scientific findings in coagulation (Biggs 1976).

Roman numerals are always used for plasma coagulation factors.

The following table indicates preferred terms and synonyms. Authors are encouraged to use terms from columns 1 *or* 2 or, if other terms are used, to use the term from column 1 parenthetically after first mention. Common abbreviations appear here, but their use should conform to guidelines in 11.10, Abbreviations, Clinical and Technical Terms. There is no currently designated factor VI.

Factor No.	*Descriptive Name*	*Synonym(s)*
factor I	fibrinogen	. . .
factor II	prothrombin	prethrombin
factor III	tissue factor	thromboplastin tissue thromboplastin tissue extract
factor IV	calcium	calcium ion Ca^{2+}

factor V	proaccelerin	labile factor accelerator globulin (AcG) Ac globulin thrombogen
factor VII	proconvertin	stable factor serum prothrombin conversion accelerator (SPCA) autoprothrombin I
factor VIII	antihemophilic factor	AHF antihemophilic globulin (AHG) antihemophilic factor A platelet cofactor 1 thromboplastinogen
factor IX	plasma thromboplastin component	PTC Christmas factor antihemophilic factor B autoprothrombin II platelet cofactor 2
factor X	Stuart factor	Prower factor Stuart-Prower factor autoprothrombin III thrombokinase
factor XI	plasma thromboplastin antecedent	PTA antihemophilic factor C
factor XII	Hageman factor	glass factor contact factor
factor XIII	fibrin stabilizing factor	FSF Laki-Lorand factor (LLF) fibrinase plasma transglutaminase fibrinoligase

A lowercase *a* designates the activated form of a factor, eg, IXa. Activation is indicated with a solid arrow

$$X \longrightarrow Xa,$$

and action on another factor, with a dashed arrow

$$XIIa \dashrightarrow XI$$
$$IX \xrightarrow{\;Ca^{2+}\;} IXa.$$

Factor VIII and von Willebrand factor, which are closely associated, have their own specialized nomenclature, which has recently undergone modification. The International Committee on Coagulation and Thrombosis has put forth the following changes:

Old	New
factor VIII:C	factor VIII
factor VIII:CAg	factor VIII:Ag or VIII:Ag
von Willebrand factor	vWF
factor VIII:RAg	vWF:Ag
VIII:RCoF	ristocetin cofactor

Although the terms on the right are currently preferred, the nomenclature is complicated and is dictated by theory and biochemical measurement. Some writers may prefer to retain the older terminology, but, if possible, the newer preferred terms should always be indicated.

Arabic numerals are used to designate platelet factors, eg, platelet factor 3, PF 3.

12.5   Diabetes Mellitus

12.5.1 *Disease Terminology.*—The types of diabetes mellitus currently recognized are as follows:

Preferred Term	Older Terms
type I or insulin-dependent	juvenile
type II or non–insulin-dependent	maturity- or adult-onset
impaired glucose tolerance (non-diagnostic fasting blood glucose level, glucose tolerance between normal and diabetic)	chemical or latent
secondary, eg, pancreatic disease	
gestational	

The genetic and immunologic aspects of diabetes mellitus are areas of intense investigation. (See sections 12.9 and 12.12.2 for genetics and HLA nomenclature, respectively.) The following terms relate to the autoimmune destruction of β-cells:

islet cell surface (or cytotoxic) antibodies
islet cell (cytoplasmic) antibodies

The measurement of glycosylated hemoglobin is an important tool in the diagnosis and management of diabetes mellitus. The predominant glycosylated hemoglobin is HbA_{1c}. Others include HbA_{1a1}, HbA_{1a2}, and HbA_{1b}. Total glycosylated hemoglobin is not abbreviated.

12.5.2 *Insulin Terminology.*—Insulin terminology can be a source of clinically important confusion. Difficulties arise with regard to insulin concentrations and types. Insulin concentrations are as follows:

U100	contains 100 U/mL (the most commonly used concentration)
U40	contains 40 U/mL
U80	contains 80 U/mL (no longer available in the United States)
U500	contains 500 U/mL (for use in severe insulin resistance)

Insulin types in common use today include the following:

Preferred Term	*Other Terms*
insulin injection	regular insulin, crystalline zinc
insulin injection, human	regular insulin, human

Note that the insulins above, being the only ones that can be administered intravenously, are called "injections" by the United States Adopted Names Council. Those below are suspensions.

Preferred Term	*Other Terms*
insulin zinc suspension, prompt	semilente insulin
insulin zinc suspension	Lente insulin
insulin zinc suspension, extended	ultralente insulin
insulin suspension, isophane	NPH insulin
insulin suspension, isophane, human	NPH insulin, human
insulin suspension, protamine zinc	PZI

Human insulin is prepared from recombinant DNA technology or synthetic modification of porcine insulin. The specific technique used should not be appended to the insulin term unless the technique itself is important in context, as, for example, in "Insulin injection, human (recombinant DNA origin), is one result of new technologies in medicine."

Insulin is formed by the cleavage of C peptide, the connecting peptide, from proinsulin.

12.6   **Drugs.**—Drugs may be referred to by several types of name.

The *nonproprietary name* is the *generic name* of a drug and is the established, official name for a drug entity. It is in the public domain and, therefore, may be used without restrictions. In the United States, the drug manufacturer is required by law to use the nonproprietary name in advertising, labels, and brochures.

In the United States, nonproprietary names for new chemical entities of potential medicinal use are selected by the United States Adopted Names (USAN) Council. The council follows established rules and guidelines in coining new nonproprietary names; "stems" are frequently incorporated into new designations to establish a chemical and/or pharmacologic relationship to related older drugs, eg:

ranitidine, cimetidine
lorazepam, diazepam

On the international level, the USAN Council cooperates with the World Health Organization Nomenclature Committee to select one identical nonproprietary name for each new drug entity.

The manufacturer's name for a drug (or other product) is called a *trademark*. *Trade name* is a broader term, which, as defined by the Trademark Act of 1946, may apply to "any titles lawfully adopted and used by persons, firms, associations, corporations, companies, unions." A trade name (as opposed to a trademark) thus identifies a manufacturer but not necessarily a product. Note that trademarks for a compound can differ in the United States and overseas.

The term *brand name* is often used interchangeably with *trademark*. The term *proprietary name* is also used.

A *code name* is a temporary designation assigned to a product by the manufacturer, such as a number (*code number*) or number-letter combination (*code designation*), used for an as yet unnamed drug. In contrast to trademarks, the code names for compounds are usually identical regardless of location, ie, United States and overseas.

The *chemical name* describes a drug in terms of its chemical structure.

Nonproprietary names best identify particular drugs, because of the attributes mentioned above and for general nomenclatural reasons (see 12.0, Nomenclature). A trademark, however, often acquires a familiarity that equals or exceeds that of the nonproprietary name of a product. The policy as reflected in the following guidelines is meant to take familiarity of drug trademarks into account, while using the nonproprietary name preferentially to avoid confusion and ambiguity.

The guidelines below are primarily addressed to AMA editors, who will work with authors to arrive at precise and unambiguous terminology for drugs mentioned in manuscripts.

12.6.1 *Nonproprietary Names.*—The nonproprietary (generic) name of a drug should be used throughout a manuscript. Formally adopted nonproprietary names are given in *AMA Drug Evaluations*, *United States Pharmacopeia (USP)*, *National Formulary (NF)*, and *USAN and the USP Dictionary of Drug Names*.

Available to editors of AMA scientific publications is the AMA International Drug Nomenclature Edit Copy, an updated printout of drug nomenclature prepared by the AMA Department of Medical Terminology, Division of Drugs and Toxicology. The printout provides an alphabetical, cross-indexed listing of the formally approved nonproprietary names, code names, US and foreign trademarks, and trivial names or synonyms.

Substitution of nonproprietary name: When an author uses a drug name other than the preferred nonproprietary name, the editor should substitute the preferred nonproprietary name given in the drug printout and bring the substitution to the author's attention as follows:

If the author has given only part of the nonproprietary name, the editor should substitute the full nonproprietary name and bring the change to the author's attention (see 12.6.2, Two-Word Names).

If the author has used a synonym or trivial name and/or trademark, the preferred nonproprietary name should be used, and the author's term(s) may appear in parentheses after first mention of the preferred name in the text and synopsis-abstract.

> leucovorin calcium (citrovorum factor)
> dactinomycin (Cosmegen)
> ascorbic acid (cevitamic acid; Cebid)

See also 12.6.3, Trademarks.

If the author has used the chemical name or code name, the nonproprietary name should be substituted and the change brought to the author's attention. The author may wish to retain the chemical name or code name in parentheses.

> triamterene (SK&F 8542)
> triamterene (2,4,7-triamino-6-phenylpteridine)
> fluorouracil (5-fluorouracil)

If the author uses a foreign nonproprietary name, and the drug printout gives a US preferred name, use the latter; the author may retain the foreign name in parentheses at first mention.

> albuterol (salbutamol)

Drugs with no nonproprietary name: For those drugs that have no adopted nonproprietary name in the drug printout, *USAN Dictionary*, or the *International Nonproprietary Names*, editors should consult the Department of Medical Terminology staff. Such drugs may have had names approved since issuance of the latest printout. If not, it is likely that the Division of Drugs will recommend an alternate nonproprietary name that is likely to be approved in the future, if available.

If an author uses a chemical or code name for a new, unlisted drug, that use should be called to the attention of the AMA Division of Drugs and verified. In addition, a useful reference for chemical names is *The Merck Index* (latest available edition), which uses the approved nonproprietary name when available as the primary name and also includes chemical names, code names, trademarks, and trivial names where known and available.

Combination products: In the case of combination products (mixtures), give the names of the active ingredients, which can be obtained from the drug printout.

> pseudoephedrine hydrochloride and triprolidine hydrochloride (Actifed)
> povidone and hydroxyethylcellulose (Adsorbotear)

An author, however, might wish to provide a more detailed description, or an author or editor may find that including the names of the active ingredients at each mention may prove unwieldy; then the trademark may be used throughout the manuscript after the first mention.

> Adsorbotear (a sterile solution containing water-soluble polymers, 1.67% povidone, hydroxyethylcellulose, 0.004% thimerosal, and 0.1% edetate disodium)

Note: The prefix *co-* (as in co-trimoxazole) is a British approach to naming some combination products and is not used in AMA publications; instead, such a product would be described as follows:

> a combination product of sulfamethoxazole and trimethoprim [first mention]
> sulfamethoxazole-trimethoprim [acceptable for subsequent mentions]

Abbreviations: Abbreviations are acceptable after first mention for multiple-drug regimens (see also 11.10, Abbreviations, Clinical and Technical Terms):

> methotrexate, vincristine sulfate (Oncovin), prednisone, and procarbazine (MOPP)

In some cases of single drugs, an abbreviation not clearly related to the nonproprietary name of the drug may be included parenthetically for the sake of reader familiarity, but use the approved nonproprietary name throughout the manuscript.

> semustine (MeCCNU)
> *or* semustine (methylcyclohexylchloroethyl nitrosourea [MeCCNU])

12.6.2   *Two-Word Names.*—Drugs often contain both an active and an inactive moiety, for reasons such as chemical stability or physiologic effect (eg, absorbability), or, occasionally, two active moieties. Examples of such drugs are salts, esters, and complexes. For purposes of medical text editing, the following is an aid to recognition.

Salts may contain sodium, potassium, chloride, hydrochloride, sulfate, mesylate, or fumarate.

> ampicillin sodium
> acyclovir sodium
> sodium chloride
> medazepam hydrochloride
> benztropine mesylate
> morphine sulfate

Quaternary ammonium salts usually have the suffix -*ium* on the first word of the name.

> atracurium besylate
> alcuronium chloride
> octonium bromide

Esters include other -*ates*. An ester can have a one-, two-, or three-word nonproprietary name. Three-word names are used for compounds forming both a salt and an ester.

> pivampicillin [the pivalate ester of ampicillin]
>
> clomegestone acetate
> hydrocortisone valerate
> testosterone cypionate
>
> methylprednisolone sodium phosphate

Complexes may contain the word *complex* or a second word ending in -*ex*.

> bisacodyl tannex
> nicotine polacrilex

The drug name will consist of two (sometimes more) words. The inactive moiety is part of the nonproprietary name. The same active moiety may be the entire name of one drug but only part of the name of another drug.

> tetracycline
> tetracycline hydrochloride
> tetracycline phosphate complex

Use the complete name of a drug at first mention in each element of the manuscript—text, synopsis-abstract, legends, and tables—and elsewhere in contexts involving dosage. If in doubt regarding the form of the drug used, ask the author for more information. In titles, inclusion of the inactive moiety is usually not necessary. However, there may be reasons to include it, eg, comparison of two forms of a drug. Consult authors and the AMA Department of Medical Terminology as necessary regarding drug names in titles.

The inactive moiety is not included when referring to a drug used in cultures of microorganisms.

12.6.3 *Trademarks.*—Authors are encouraged to provide the trademark as well as the nonproprietary name of a mentioned drug, especially when the drug has been used therapeutically, both to indicate the exact preparation used and for reader familiarity.

12.6 Drugs

Trademarks use initial capitals, except for a few oddities (eg, pHisoHex; consult *USAN Dictionary*). In mentioning trademarks in the text, follow the examples given here. Note that when the inactive moiety is included in both the nonproprietary name and the trademark, the inactive moiety is given only once, as in the second example:

> penicillin G potassium (Pentids)
> hydralazine (Apresoline) hydrochloride

If a foreign trademark is given, it should be noted in parentheses at first mention, together with the comparable US product:

> phenprocoumon (Marcumar [Canada]; Liquamar, comparable US
>   product)

Trademarks should be avoided in titles and subtitles of articles except in (1) adverse reaction reports and (2) comparisons of the same drug formulated by different manufacturers.

When the author uses only nonproprietary names, ask the author to specify the trademark of any drug actually used in treatment.

12.6.4 Special Drug Classes of Interest

Insulins: See 12.5.2, Diabetes Mellitus, Insulin Terminology.

Interferons: Use the nonproprietary names and trademarks given in the drug printout or the *USAN Dictionary*. The following classification schema conforms to the recommendations of the International Interferon Nomenclature Committee:

> internationally accepted nonproprietary class name: interferon

The following are names of general classes of compounds or single compounds before a specific nonproprietary name has been assigned; note spelling out of Greek letters:

interferon alfa	(formerly leukocyte or lymphoblastoid interferon; sometimes abbreviated IFN-α; note phonetic *f*)
	(This unusual orthography is for the *nonproprietary* drug name and is an internationally accepted term whose spelling is more congenial to a variety of languages; when referring to interferon outside of the therapeutic context, ie, when the nonproprietary name is not being used, then "alpha" is acceptable, eg "the alpha interferons.")
interferon beta	(formerly fibroblast interferon; sometimes abbreviated IFN-β)
interferon gamma	(formerly immune interferon; sometimes abbreviated IFN-γ)

Individual pure, identifiable compounds with nonproprietary names include the following; note the use and order of hyphen, arabic numeral, and lowercase letter:

> interferon alfa-2a
> interferon alfa-2b
> interferon gamma-1a
> interferon gamma-1b

The following are names of mixtures of interferons from natural sources; note "n" *preceding* the arabic numeral:

> interferon alfa-n1
> interferon alfa-n2

Steroids: Occasionally, an author may state that a patient was treated with "steroids" without identifying the drug or stating the dosage. Since different corticosteroids have different effects, and because there is controversy about the dosage in various therapeutic situations, the author should be asked to name the drug and give the dosage.

Thyroid and other endocrine drugs: Hormones such as the thyroid hormones provoke nomenclatural confusion, as they appear in three contexts: the in vivo, physiologic, or native hormone; in tests of organ function; and as therapeutic agents (see also 12.7, Endocrinology). The adopted nonproprietary names are usually not the same as the names of the native hormones, and, unfortunately, are often not as well known to authors. Thus, it is recommended that when the *therapeutic* or *diagnostic* name for a given hormone is used, the native hormone name be retained textually or parenthetically, as in the following examples:

> levothyroxine sodium (levorotatory isomer of thyroxine [T_4])
> liothyronine sodium (levorotatory isomer of triiodothyronine [T_3])
> dextrothyronine sodium (dextrorotatory isomer of triiodothyronine [T_3])
> liotrix (mixture of levothyroxine sodium and liothyronine sodium)
> thyroid, USP
>
> *Note:* Native thyroid hormones should be referred to as *thyroxine* and *triiodothyronine* at first mention and later may be referred to as T_4 and T_3, respectively (the latter terms being given initially in parentheses).
>
> thyroglobulin
> thyrotropin (thyroid-stimulating hormone [TSH])
> somatropin (human growth hormone)
> protirelin (synthetic thyrotropin-releasing hormone)
> corticotropin, purified (corticotropin [previously adrenocorticotropic
>   hormone, ACTH] extract)
> cosyntropin (synthetic corticotropin analogue)
> gonadotropin, chorionic (human chorionic gonadotropin)

12.6   Drugs

Vitamins: The familiar letter names of most vitamins are reserved for the substances as found in food and in vivo. The same vitamins, when given therapeutically, have other nonproprietary names. The following table is a guide; consult the drug printout or other source for more complete information.

Native Vitamin	Drug Name
vitamin B_1	thiamine hydrochloride
vitamin B_2	riboflavin
vitamin B_6	pyridoxine hydrochloride
vitamin B_{12}	cyanocobalamin
vitamin C	ascorbic acid
vitamin D_2	ergocalciferol
vitamin D_3	cholecalciferol
vitamin K_1	phytonadione
vitamin K_3	menadione

A special note on the vitamin D's: The terms in the right-hand column above are the usual active ingredients of preparations containing D vitamins. There are also various terms referring to *native* metabolites of vitamin D:

Calcifediol is the preferred nonproprietary name for 25-hydroxycholecalciferol, also known as 25-hydroxyvitamin D_3, or $25(OH)D_3$.

Calcitriol is the preferred nonproprietary name for 1,25-dihydroxycholecalciferol, also known as 1,25-dihydroxyvitamin D_3, or $1,25(OH)_2D_3$.

12.7   Endocrinology.—For the most part, endocrine terminology is straightforward (see 12.6.4, Drugs, Special Drug Classes of Interest). However, investigation and testing of the hypothalamic-pituitary axis is an area of endocrinology in which confusion may occur. Substances produced by the hypothalamus act through stimulation or inhibition of pituitary function.

12.7.1   *Hypothalamic Hormones.*—The US Adopted Names Council, working with the World Health Organization Expert Committee on Nonproprietary Names for Pharmaceutical Substances, has chosen the suffix *-relin* to denote stimulatory hypothalamic peptide hormones and the suffix *-relix* for inhibitory ones. Because few names have been formally approved at this writing, the following list is illustrative rather than inclusive.

Native Substance	Diagnostic/Therapeutic Agent
Hypothalamic Hormones, Stimulatory	
thyrotropin-releasing hormone (TRH)	protirelin

214

| luteinizing hormone–releasing hormone (LHRH) (or gonadotropin-releasing hormone [GnRH]) | buserelin, gonadorelin, histrelin, lutrelin, nafarelin |
| growth hormone–releasing factor (GHRF) | somatorelin |

Hypothalamic Hormones, Inhibitory

| growth hormone release-inhibiting factor (somatostatin, GHRIF) | detirelix |

Note: The suffix -*tropin*, indicating an ability to change or redirect, is preferred to -*trophin*, which indicates a relationship to nutrition.

Some readers will not be familiar with the new nonproprietary names. Therefore, parenthetical inclusion of the native substance at first mention is encouraged.

After venipuncture, protirelin (thyrotropin-releasing hormone) was injected.

12.7.2   *Pituitary Hormones.*—The suffix -*actide* will be used in the future for nonproprietary names of synthetic corticotropins. Currently available compounds include the following:

Native Substance	*Diagnostic Agent*
corticotropin (ACTH)	seractide, cosyntropin, corticotropin
growth hormone (GH), somatotropin	somatrem, somatropin
follicle-stimulating hormone (FSH), luteinizing hormone (LH)	urofollitropin, menotropins (LH and FSH)
arginine vasopressin (AVP)	vasopressin

12.8   Equipment and Reagents.—To avoid appearing to endorse particular products or implying that a particular brand is somehow an essential part of a treatment or an investigation, nonproprietary names or descriptive phrasing should be used in preference to brand names and trademarks. However, if several brands of the same product are being compared, brand names and manufacturers' names should be given. If the brand name or manufacturer's name is critical to the replication of the study, it should be included parenthetically after the descriptive phrasing. Occasionally it will be desirable to include the manufacturer's or supplier's name and location parenthetically as well. Authors should be routinely requested to provide this information for any reagents, antibodies, enzymes, or probes used in their investigations.

Brand Name	Nonproprietary Name
Scotch tape	cellophane tape
Xerox machine	photocopier
Silastic	silicone elastomer
Epon	epoxy resin
Band-Aid	adhesive bandage

Note that brand (proprietary) names but not nonproprietary names should be capitalized. (See 8.1.6, Capitalization, Proprietary Names.) The registered trademark symbol ® is not used.

A complex system or piece of equipment may be identified by a brand name if the descriptive phrasing is either much more cumbersome or less familiar, with some notation that other types are available. In this case, use the descriptive phrasing at first mention, with the trademark following in parentheses, and then use the trademark thereafter.

Use a suitable mask with carbon dioxide absorber (eg, Ohio-Heidbrink No. 36).

Some hearing loss may result from use of a portable radio or cassette player equipped with headphones (Walkman-style) played at high decibel levels.

If equipment or apparatus is provided free of charge by the manufacturer, this fact should be included in the acknowledgments. (See 2.8.1, Acknowledgments, Financial Support.)

If a device is described as "modified," the modification should be explained or an explanatory reference cited.

12.9   **Genetics.**—This section on genetic nomenclature will deal with terminology found in medical manuscripts, that often, but not always, describes human systems. Abbreviations found throughout this section should be used in accordance with the guidelines in 11.0, Abbreviations.

The section is arranged approximately in order of increasing size of the elements described, from the molecular to the microscopic to the macroscopic: DNA, RNA, and amino acids; restriction enzymes; human genes; oncogenes; chromosomes; animal genes and chromosomes; and mouse strains.

12.9.1   *DNA, RNA, and Amino Acids.*—The nucleic acids—deoxyribonucleic acid (DNA) and ribonucleic acid (RNA)—and the amino acids are the biochemical constituents of genetics and have their own nomenclature and preferred symbols. The following is meant to be in conformity with International Union of Biochemistry nomenclature, but is not exhaustive. For further details, consult the instructions for authors of the *Journal of Biological Chemistry*, which appear in the first issue of each year.

DNA: DNA is the embodiment of the genetic code and is contained in the chromosomes of humans and animals. It is a polymer of four nucleotides, which contain the bases thymine, cytosine, adenine, and guanine.

A codon is a sequence of three nucleotides in a DNA molecule, which codes for an amino acid or biosynthetic message. In codons, a one-letter designation is used for each nucleotide, named for the base in that nucleotide, eg, T, C, A, and G. Examples of codons are CAT, ATC, and ATT.

The abbreviation for complementary DNA is cDNA. Double-stranded DNA and single-stranded DNA are commonly abbreviated dsDNA and ssDNA, respectively.

RNA: Functionally associated with DNA is RNA. It contains the three bases cytosine, adenine, and guanine, but, instead of the thymine found in DNA, RNA contains the base uracil (U). Examples of RNA codons include CAU, UUG, and AUU.

There are several well-known types of RNA, and the following abbreviations are standard (use of the expanded term, however, should not be discouraged):

mRNA	messenger RNA
tRNA	transfer RNA
rRNA	ribosomal RNA
hnRNA	heterogeneous RNA
snRNA	small nuclear RNA

Types of RNA may be further specified:

mRNA-1

$\text{tRNA}^{\text{fMet}}$ tRNA^{Met}	tRNA specific for methionine
tRNA^{Ala}	tRNA specific for alanine
$\text{fMet-tRNA}^{\text{fMet}}$	*N*-formylmethionyl-tRNA
$\text{Met-tRNA}^{\text{Met}}$	methionyl-tRNA

Amino acids: The following table gives the amino acids of proteins and their preferred three- and single-letter symbols:

alanine	Ala	A
arginine	Arg	R
asparagine	Asn	N
aspartic acid	Asp	D
cysteine	Cys	C
glutamine	Gln	Q
glutamic acid	Glu	E
glycine	Gly	G
histidine	His	H
isoleucine	Ile	I

leucine	Leu	L
lysine	Lys	K
methionine	Met	M
phenylalanine	Phe	F
proline	Pro	P
serine	Ser	S
threonine	Thr	T
tryptophan	Trp	W
tyrosine	Tyr	Y
valine	Val	V

12.9.2 *Restriction Enzymes.*—Restriction enzymes (or restriction endonucleases) are special enzymes that cleave DNA at specific sites. They are named for the organism from which they are isolated, usually a bacterial species or strain. As originally proposed, their names consist of a three-letter term, italicized and beginning with a capital letter, taken from the organism of origin (eg, *Hpa* for *Haemophilus parainfluenzae*), followed by a roman numeral, which is a series number (eg, as in *Hpa* I, *Hpa* II). In some cases, the number is preceded by a lowercase letter or a capital letter (roman), and/or an arabic numeral, which refers to the strain of bacterium, in which case there is no space between the series number and the organism term, eg, *Eco*RI, *Hin*fI, *Sau*96I, *Sau*3AI). If there is *no* strain designation, then the series number is separated from the rest of the restriction enzyme by a space.

Many variations in the form of the names of these enzymes have appeared, eg, *Hin* d III, *Hin* dIII, *Hind* III, *Hind* III. It is currently recommended that italics and spacing be given as noted in the preceding paragraph, to differentiate the species name, strain designation, and enzyme series number. The following table gives examples:

Enzyme Name	*Organism of Origin*
Acc I	*Acinetobacter calcoaceticus*
Bal I	*Brevibacterium albidum*
*Bam*HI	*Bacillus amyloliquefaciens* H
*Bst*EII	*Bacillus stearothermophilus*
Dpn I	*Streptococcus* (diplococcus) *pneumoniae* M
*Eco*RI	*Escherichia coli* RY13
*Eco*RII	*Escherichia coli* R245
Hae II	*Haemophilus aegyptius*
*Hinc*II	*Haemophilus influenzae* Rc
*Hind*III	*Haemophilus influenzae* Rd
*Hin*fI	*Haemophilus influenzae* Rf
Msp I	*Acinetobacter calcoaceticus* (*Moraxella* species 3416)
*Sau*3AI	*Staphylococcus aureus* 3A
*Sau*96I	*Staphylococcus aureus* 96

Sst I	*Streptomyces* stanford
Xba I	*Xanthomonas campestris* (*Xanthomonas badrii*)
Xho I	*Xanthomonas campestris* (*Xanthomonas holicola*)

12.9.3 *Human Gene Nomenclature.*—Efforts to standardize human gene nomenclature are relatively recent, and, in the case of the genes in the HLA and blood group systems, traditional forms persist and are officially recognized. The International Committee on Standardizing Human Gene Nomenclature has developed an all-capital, on-line (no subscripts or superscripts), all-roman system known as the International System for Human Gene Nomenclature (ISGN). The committee recommendations are presented here but are not given exhaustively nor are they universally accepted. Hence, caution is advised in making any changes in a manuscript without consulting the author and/or the publications of the International Committee (see 21.1, Resource Bibliography, References).

Gene or locus symbol: Genes are the molecular units of heredity, loci their location (eg, within the chromosome), and alleles their alternative forms. The main form of a gene and its locus have the same symbol, which is usually recognizable as an abbreviation for the gene name or a quality of the gene.

Gene (and locus) symbols usually have three or four characters, all capital letters, or all capitals plus an arabic numeral. The entire term is italicized (or underlined in typescript):

HPRT	hypoxanthine phosphoribosyltransferase
PHP	panhypopituitarism
CF	cystic fibrosis

The first character is always a capital letter:

G6PD [not *6GPD*]   glucose-6-phosphate dehydrogenase

There are no superscripts or subscripts—all characters of the term are on line:

CA1 [traditionally *CA^1*]   carbonic anhydrase

Likewise, there are no hyphens or spaces:

GLO1 [traditionally *GLO-1*]   glyoxalase I

It is currently preferred that within gene symbols, roman numerals be changed to arabic numerals and Greek letters to English letters ''and placed at the end of the gene symbol'' (although such placement is not always effected):

FUCA1 [traditionally *αFUC*]   alpha-L-fucosidase 1, tissue

B2M [traditionally $\beta_2 m$] β_2-microglobulin

Allele symbols: The International Committee recommends that allele symbols consist of the gene symbol plus asterisk plus allele designation, but traditional notations for alleles tend to persist, eg,

HBB*6V (*Hbβ^{s6val}*, traditional).

If clear in context, the allele symbol may be used in a shorthand form that omits the gene symbol and includes only the asterisk and the allele designation that follows, eg, **6V*.

Exceptions: As noted above, the HLA and blood group systems in humans incorporate exceptions to the aforementioned rules for gene symbols. Hyphens are preserved in the case of HLA genes, and italics are not mandatory (although context—genotypic or phenotypic—should be clear). While the International Committee now recommends all capital letters for blood groups, researchers in the field may prefer to retain the capital-lowercase combinations. The following are examples of gene symbols from these systems (see also 12.1, Blood Groups, and 12.12.2, Human Leukocyte [HLA] and Other Histocompatibility Antigens).

HLA-A	major histocompatibility complex, class I antigens
HLA-B	
HLA-C	
HLA-D	major histocompatibility complex, class II antigens
HLA-DR	
Do, DO	Dombrock blood group
Fy, FY	Duffy blood group
Ii, II	Ii blood group
Jk, JK	Kidd blood group
Le, LE	Lewis blood group
Lu, LU	Lutheran blood group
Rd, RD	Radin blood group
Rh, RH	Rh blood group
Sc, SC	Scianna blood group
Se, SE	ABH secretion
Sf, SF	Stoltzfus blood group
Ss, SS	Ss blood group
Xg, XG	Xg blood group
Xk, XK	Kell blood group precursor

Genotype terminology: Genotype terms consist of one or more expressions of allele symbol pairs. Allele groupings may be indicated by placement above and below a horizontal line or on line. Note in the following examples (Shows et al 1971) the different uses of virgules (/), semicolons, spaces, and commas:

$\dfrac{ADA*1}{ADA*2}$ or $ADA*1/ADA*2$	*Horizontal line, virgule* separate alleles of the same gene.
$\dfrac{ADA*1}{ADA*2}, \dfrac{ADH1*1}{ADA*2}, \dfrac{ADH1*1}{ADH1*1}$; $\dfrac{AMY*A}{AMY1*B}$	*Semicolons* separate pairs of alleles at different loci, on *different chromosomes*.

or

$ADA*1/ADA*2$; $ADH1*1/ADH1*1$; $AMY*A/AMY1*B$

$\dfrac{AMY1*A\ \ PGM1*2}{AMY1*B\ \ PGM1*1}$	Single *space* represents alleles together on the same *chromosome* (above horizontal line) from alleles together on another chromosome (*phase known*).
$\dfrac{AMY*A\ \ PGM1*1}{AMY1*B, PGM1*2}$	*Commas* indicate alleles above and below line are on same *chromosome* pair, but not on which chromosome of the pair specifically (*phase unknown*).
$G6PD*A/Y$ or $G6PD*A$	Special form for hemizygous males.

Phenotype terminology: The phenotype term derives from the genotype term, but no italics are used, and, instead of asterisks, spaces are used. Genotypes usually contain pairs of symbols while phenotypes contain single symbols. The following examples are from Shows et al (1987):

Genotype	*Phenotype*
*ADA*1/ADA*1*	ADA 1
*ADA*1/ADA*2*	ADA 1-2
*C2*C/C2*QO*	C2 C,QO
*HBB*A/HBB*6V*	HBB A,S [traditional, Hb A/S]
*ABO*A1/ABO*O*	ABO A1
*CF*N/CF*R*	CF NR
*G6PD*A/Y*	G6PD A

12.9.4 *Oncogenes.*—Oncogenes are written as three-letter, italicized, lowercase terms, which are usually taken from the names of the viruses with which these genes are associated (eg, *mos* is associated with Moloney sarcoma virus, *abl* with Abelson leukemia virus, *myb* with avian myeloblastosis, *sis* with simian sarcoma virus, *src* with Rous sarcoma virus).

abl mos fes myb myc erb ras sis src

Commonly, the oncogene contains one of two prefixes, which indicate the source or location of the gene: *v-* for virus or *c-* for the oncogene's cellular or chromosomal counterpart (known as a proto-oncogene and given in all capitals in the ISGN):

c-*abl* (or *ABL*)	c-*mos* (or *MOS*)	c-*erb* (or *ERB*)
v-*abl*	v-*mos*	v-*erb*

12.9 Genetics

Additional oncogene expressions with variations in prefixes, suffixes, and superscripts seen commonly include the following:

ras^H	H-*ras*	Ha-*ras*	(all equivalent)
H-*ras*-1	Ha-*ras*-1		(both equivalent)
K-*ras*-2	Ki-*ras*-2		(both equivalent)
erb B	*erb* B	*erb-b*	(all equivalent)
N-*ras*			
N-*myc*			
B-*lym*			

It is best to avoid using an oncogene expression with a prefix at the beginning of a sentence, since it would then be uncertain whether the prefix would under other circumstances still be capitalized:

Avoid: "C-*abl* was discovered in . . . ."

Better: "The proto-oncogene c-*abl* was discovered in . . . ."

12.9.5 Human Chromosomes.—Human chromosomes are numbered from 1 to 22. There are two additional chromosomes, the sex chromosomes X and Y. Chromosomes are also divided into groups:

Group	*Chromosomes*
A	1-3
B	4, 5
C	6-12, X
D	13-15
E	16-18
F	19, 20
G	21, 22, Y

One may speak of a chromosome by number or by group, eg:

chromosome 14
a chromosome in group D
a group D chromosome

Chromosome bands: Chromosome bands are elicited by special staining methods, which are referred to as follows:

Band	*Stain*
Q-banding, Q bands	quinacrine
G-banding, G bands	Giemsa
R-banding, R bands	reverse-Giemsa
C-banding, C bands	constitutive heterochromatin
N-banding, N bands	nucleolar organizing region

Chromosomes contain long and short arms (Fig 1). The long arm is designated by *q* and the short arm by *p*:

    17p   short arm of chromosome 17
    3q   long arm of chromosome 3
    Xq   long arm of X chromosome

These arms are divided into regions, from 1 to 4, depending on their length:

    4q3   region 3 of long arm of chromosome 4

The regions are divided into bands:

    11q23   chromosome 11, long arm, band 23 (region 2, band 3)
    11q23.3   band in above subdivided: new band is 23.3
    20p11.23   chromosome 20, short arm, band 11.23 (region 1, band 1, subdivision 23)

Karyotype: A karyotype is a short term describing an individual's chromosome complement, ie, the number of chromosomes plus the sex chromosomes present. Normal human karyotypes are 46,XX and 46,XY.
  The following are examples of abnormal karyotypes:

    45,X or 45,XO   48,XXX
    47,XXY   47,XX
    47,XYY   47,XY

A virgule is used to indicate more than one karyotype in an individual:
    46/47
    45,X/46,XX (alternatively, X/XX)
An individual with more than one karyotype may be a *mosaic* or a *chimera*, which should be specified in the text and, with a three-letter abbreviation, at first mention of the karyotype, eg,
    mos45,X/46,XY
    chi45,XX/46,XY

Chromosome rearrangements: Terms that specify chromosome rearrangements generally incorporate a chromosome band designation plus additional symbols specifying the type of rearrangement. Commonly encountered rearrangement symbols are the following:

    t   translocation
    r   ring form
    i   isochromosome
    inv   inversion
    ins   insertion
    del   deletion
    dup   duplication
    ter   terminal
    s   satellite

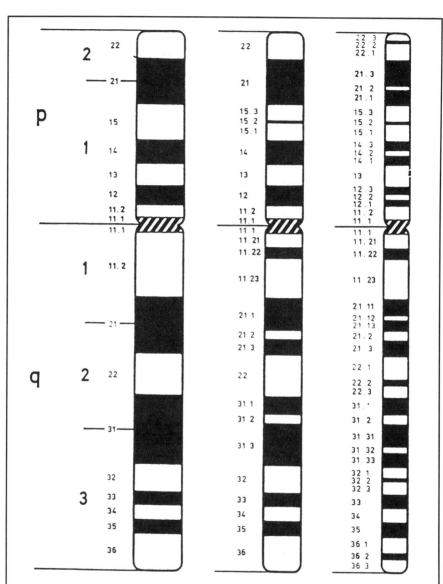

Fig 1.—Schematic diagram of one long and short arm of chromosome 7 (from Harnden DG, Lindsten JE, Buckton K, Klinger HP. An international system for human cytogenetic nomenclature: high resolution banding [1981]/ISCN [1981]. *Cytogenet Cell Genet*. 1981;31:14. Used by permission of S Karger AG, Basel, Switzerland.).

:	break
::	break and join
→	from-to
+	addition
−	deletion

The following are examples of chromosome rearrangement terms:

t(14q21q)
Xqi
5p−   [*part* of 5p missing]
−5p   [*all* of 5p missing]
t(DqGq)
+14p   [*all* of 14p added]
14p+   [addition *to* 14p]
inv(2)(p13p24)
46,XX,r(18)
46,XX,del(1)(pter→q21:)
t(9q+22q)
t(9;22)(q34;q11)

Philadelphia chromosome: The term *Philadelphia chromosome*, the name given to a particular chromosome rearrangement found in chronic myelogenous leukemia, is well established. It can be abbreviated as "Ph chromosome" or, if clear in context, "Ph." Although it is often seen with appendages, eg, Ph^1, Ph1, Ph$_1$, or Ph′, they are not necessary, and Ph is the current acceptable form.

12.9.6 *Animal Genetic Terms.*—Like the terms for human genes and their loci, animal gene names are short (two to four characters), descriptive, and italicized. They differ in that they may be all lowercase (recessive gene) or have an initial capital letter only (dominant gene), and they may contain hyphens and, occasionally, superscripts.

Examples of genes from the mouse are the following:

a	*Ea-8*	*Ea-1*
bt-2	*Akvp*	*Ea-2*
Crm	*c*	*Ly-4*
ru-2	*Xt*	*Lyb-2*
Hct	*Igh-1*	*Lyt-1*
Al	*H-1*	*Xld-1*
Ce-1	*H-2*	*cw^{thd}*
Ce-2		

Animal alleles: Whereas with human gene terms, alleles are indicated by the gene term plus asterisk plus allele term, all on line, alleles in animals are indicated by the gene term plus the allele designation as an italicized superscript, eg, *Pgm-1^a*, *H-2^a*, *c^{ch}*, *d^{+2J}*, *Igk-Ef1^a*. Alleles do not always

225

have superscripts, and the context in addition to the term itself should clarify whether the gene, locus, or allele is under discussion, eg, *B*, *Ca*, *nu*.

Animal phenotype symbols are capitalized and in roman type. Examples from the mouse are as follows:

Gene/Locus	*Phenotype*
Gpi-1	GPI-1A, GPI-1B, GPI-AB
Pgm-2	PGM-B
Ldh-1^a/Ldh-1^a	LDH-A$_4$^{a}

Animal chromosomes: Although chromosomal nomenclature is similar for animals and humans, there are two main differences. Animals contain different numbers of chromosomes than do humans. The rearrangement terms are given with capital letters or initial capitals, eg:

T	translocation
Rb	Robertsonian translocation
In	inversion
Is	insertion
Ms	monosomy
Dp	duplication
Df	deficiency
R	ring
Cen	centromere

Terms often include suffixes indicating the person or institution of discovery and numbers indicating the series, eg, T37H is the 37th translocation found at Harwell, In5Rk the fifth inversion found by Roderick.

Mouse strains: Names of inbred strains of mice are frequently encountered in discussions of genetics. Such names consist of capital letters or combinations of letters and numbers, which may be followed by a virgule and then by a substrain symbol, which may be a number, letter, or number-letter combination. Letters indicating substrains are usually capitalized, except for six standard lowercase abbreviations for strain-isolating method, but exceptions exist in the case of two well-known strains of mouse, the BALB/c and C57BR/cd strains.

The strains themselves are largely derived from crosses dating back to the early 20th century and even older lines, and the names reflect abbreviations for characteristics such as albino (''alb'') or lines designated simply by letters, eg, C.

Examples of mouse strain designations follow:

DBA/1 DBA/2 A/He CBA/J C57BL/6J CBA/HN

Standard abbreviations of strain-isolating methods are as follows:

e   egg transfer
f   foster-nursing
h   hand-rearing
o   ovary transplant
p   freeze preservation
fh   fostered on hand-reared

12.10 **Globulins.**—Globulins are a family of proteins precipitated from plasma or serum. They may be further fractionated into many subgroups. Use Greek letters and subscript numerals (where applicable) in designating globulins and globulin fractions.

α-globulin α_1-globulin α_2-globulin

β-globulin γ-globulin

12.11 **Hepatitis.**—The major types of viral hepatitis now recognized are hepatitis A; hepatitis B; non-A, non-B hepatitis; and delta hepatitis. Terms such as *infectious hepatitis*, *short-incubation-period hepatitis*, *long-incubation-period hepatitis*, and *serum hepatitis* are no longer useful in designating types of viral hepatitis; however, their use may be appropriate, depending on the context, eg, historical discussions of hepatitis. This is also true for the designations MS-1 and MS-2, except when they refer to infections caused by the extant strains of those names.

Abbreviations used for hepatitis A include the following:

HAV   hepatitis A virus
anti-HAV antibody to HAV

Important hepatitis B antigens and antibodies include the following; note use of capitals, lowercase letters, numbers, hyphens, and virgules:

HBV   hepatitis B virus
HBsAg   hepatitis B surface antigen
  HBsAg/adr   examples of subdeterminants of HBsAG
  HBsAg/ayr
  HbsAg/adw1-4
HBcAg   hepatitis B core antigen
HBeAg   hepatitis B e antigen
  HBeAg/1   components of HBeAg
  HBeAg/2
  HBeAg/3
anti-HBs, HBsAb antibody to HBsAg

anti-HBc, HBcAb	antibody to HBcAg
anti-HBe, HBeAb	antibody to HBeAg
HBIG	hepatitis B immune globulin

The following terms are associated with delta hepatitis, a form of hepatitis B:

delta virus (preferred)	δ virus
delta agent (preferred)	δ agent
delta-Ag	delta antigen
anti-delta	antibody to delta antigen

12.12   Immunology

12.12.1   *Complement.*—The term *complement* refers to a group of factors involved as a system in antigen-antibody reactions and inflammation. Current nomenclature is based largely on the 1968 World Health Organization bulletin "Nomenclature of Complement."

Most of the complement factors are designated by a capital C. Other complement factors exist that are designated by the capital letters B, P, and D. The designation C replaced C′, which was discontinued in 1968. Also discontinued are the terms β_1C, β_1E, β_1H, etc.

Suffixes: Various suffixes further define complement.

Components of complement are designated with C and a number on line, eg:

C1   C2   C7   C9

Fragments of complement components are designated with C (or other capital letter) plus number and lowercase letter, usually *a* or *b*.

C4a   C5b   Bb

The subunits of C1 are as follows:

C1q   C1r   C1s

Inactive complement fragments are designated with C plus number, lowercase letter, and *i*, eg:

C4bi

Complement inactivators are designated with C plus number, lowercase letter, and *INA*, eg:

C3bINA

Other conventional expressions: Further conventions govern complexes of complement components.

All the elements of a complement complex are written in a series without spaces, eg:

C3bBb   C4b2a

Although some authors place commas within such an expression (eg, C4b,2a), notation without commas is less ambiguous and should be used.

A bar over the suffix(es) designates activated complement, eg:

$\overline{\text{C4}}$ $\overline{\text{C423}}$ $\overline{\text{C4b2a}}$

The term "CH_{50}" denotes an assay for total complement, the *CH* referring to hemolytic complement and the subscript *50* to 50% lysis, an end point of the assay.

12.12.2 *Human Leukocyte (HLA) and Other Histocompatibility Antigens*

HLA: Human leukocyte antigens appear on virtually all nucleated cells of human tissues including white blood cells and on platelets. Just as red blood cell antigens determine one's blood type (see 12.1, Blood Groups), HLA antigens determine one's tissue type (HLA type).

The term *HLA* signifies both human leukocyte antigens and the segment of the human genome that codes for these antigens. For historical reasons, it is proper, and not redundant, to refer to "HLA antigens" (the "A" originally was a simple letter designation and does not stand for "antigen").

The seven recognized loci of the HLA complex are designated as follows (note placement of hyphen):

HLA-A HLA-B HLA-C HLA-D HLA-DR HLA-DQ HLA-DP

(*DR* signifies "D-related.") The first three are also known as the class I loci/antigens and the last four as the class II loci/antigens.

Antigenic specificities of the major HLA loci are indicated with numbers following the major locus letter, eg:

HLA-A1   HLA-B27   HLA-DR1

Often, a *w* appears in the specific HLA designation, eg:

HLA-Aw19   HLA-DRw10

The *w* stands for "workshop" and indicates that the antigen/locus in question is of provisional status, as determined by the International Workshop on HLA. When provisional status becomes official status, the "w" is omitted from the term, eg, HLA-DRw1 becomes HLA-DR1.

To find current antigen status, check the reports of the International Histocompatibility Testing Workshops and the World Health Organization nomenclature committee on leukocyte antigens, published at intervals in the *Bulletin of the World Health Organization.*

Parenthetical numbers may be part of the term for an HLA antigen; these indicate subspecificities or "splits" of the antigen (and its gene) such that two antigens (or alleles) are recognized instead of one.

HLA-A23(9), HLA-A24(9); HLA-B49(21), HLA-Bw50(21)

These examples indicate, respectively, that A23 and A24 are splits of HLA-A9, and that B49 and Bw50 are splits of HLA-B21.

The HLA haplotype is "the combination of alleles at each [HLA] locus on a single chromosome" (Schwartz 1987, p 58). Each person possesses two such haplotypes and thus has two HLA antigens determined by each major locus, ie, two HLA-A antigens, two HLA-B antigens, etc. When HLA typing is done, the HLA antigens are determined without respect to haplotype and are given as the phenotype.

A1, A3, B5, B8, Cw1, Cw3, DR2, DR3

If the HLA types of the parents or siblings are known, it may be possible to determine the two HLA haplotypes. In this situation, an alternate form of expression, known as the genotype, can be given. In this form, the two haplotypes are expressed as two series of HLA specificities, separated by a virgule.

A1, B8, Cw1, DR3/A3, B5, Cw3, DR2

On occasion, it may be possible to type only one antigen from a given locus. For example, if only DR3 can be typed at the DR locus, the phenotype is given as follows:

A1, A2, B8, B27, Cw4, Cw5, DR3,-

(Note use of hyphen and spacing.)

The individual either may have an untypeable DR antigen, or may have two identical DR3 antigens. In the former case, the genotype would be given as follows:

A1, B8, Cw4, DR3/A2, B27, Cw5,-

In the latter case, the genotype is expressed as follows:

A1, B8, Cw4, DR3/A2, B27, Cw5, DR3

Just as red blood cell types are important in transfusion, HLA types are important in tissue transplantation; host and donor tissues should be compatible. In keeping with these principles, the following terms are used interchangeably: *leukocyte antigens, transplantation antigens,* and *histo-compatibility* (*histo* meaning "relating to tissue") *antigens.*

Other histocompatibility antigens: HLA antigens represent only one part of a genetic region known as the major histocompatibility locus, often abbreviated MHC. Other HLA antigens and components of this locus are as follows:

> class III loci (complement loci):
> C2
> C4
> properdin factor B (BF)

(See also 12.12.1, Complement.)

The terms *MB, DC, MT, DS,* and *SB,* formerly used for class II loci, are outmoded and should no longer be used.

The following are examples of alleles/antigenic specificities of these other regions of the major histocompatibility locus; note use of asterisks (*QO* designates a deficiency allele):

> BF*F   BF*S   BF*F1   BF*S1
>
> C2*C   C2*A   C2*QO
>
> C4A   (formerly "Rogers")
>   C4A*1
>   C4A*QO
>
> C4B   (formerly "Chido")
>   C4B*1
>   C4B*QO

Some authors use italics to distinguish HLA genotype from phenotype. This is a useful, but not mandatory, convention. In general, especially when italics are not used for genotype, authors should attempt to make clear through context whether genotype or phenotype is being discussed. (See also 12.9.3, Human Gene Nomenclature.)

> HLA-A1   vs   *HLA-A1*

Additional HLA-related terminology: The following terms are provided as a reference. When writing for a general medical audience, it is preferable to use expanded forms.

> The HLA-DR antigens are also referred to as "Ia-like" antigens.
>
> MLR signifies "mixed leukocyte reaction."
>
> PLT signifies "primed leukocyte typing."
>
> CREG stands for cross-reactive group, as in A1-CREG, A2-CREG, B15-CREG.

12.12.3 *Immunoglobulins.*—The classes of immunoglobulins are IgG, IgM, IgA, IgD, and IgE.

The immunoglobulin molecule can be broken into various fragments, designated as follows:

Fab
Fc
$F(ab')_2$
Fd'
Fd
Fv

The immunoglobulin molecule itself contains the following components and subcomponents:

heavy chain, also designated as   H chain
light chain   L chain
constant region   C
variable region   V

Heavy chains: The following heavy chains are associated with the respective classes of immunoglobulin: γ (IgG), μ (IgM), α (IgA), δ (IgD), and ϵ (IgE).

There are four subclasses of IgG: IgG1, IgG2, IgG3, IgG4; the corresponding heavy chains are designated $\gamma1$, $\gamma2$, $\gamma3$, and $\gamma4$.

Similarly, there are two subclasses of IgA (IgA1, IgA2) and two subclasses of IgM (IgM1, IgM2); the corresponding heavy chains are $\alpha1$ and $\alpha2$, and $\mu1$ and $\mu2$.

Light chains: There are two types of light chain, κ and λ; both types are associated with all five immunoglobulin classes. The four subtypes of λ are $\lambda1$, $\lambda2$, $\lambda3$, and $\lambda4$.

The following form is used to designate immunoglobulins containing a single type of light chain:

IgG-κ, IgG-λ
IgM-κ, IgM-λ
IgA-κ,
IgA-λ

Variable and constant regions: Domains are designated in terms of variable and constant regions of the light and heavy chains:

V_L
C_L
V_H
C_H1
C_H2
C_H3
C_H4

Hypervariable regions are designated L_V1, L_V2, L_V3; H_V1, H_V2, H_V3. Subgroups of the variable region are as follows:

$V_H I$, $V_H II$, $V_H III$, $V_H IV$
$V_\kappa I$, $V_\kappa II$, $V_\kappa III$, $V_\kappa IV$
$V_\lambda I$, $V_\lambda II$, $V_\lambda III$, $V_\lambda IV$, $V_\lambda V$, $V_\lambda VI$

SC stands for the *secretory component*, associated with the IgA found in secretions.

12.12.4 *Lymphocytes and Monoclonal Antibodies.*—The two types of lymphocyte commonly recognized are the *T lymphocyte* and the *B lymphocyte*. These are often referred to as the *T cell* and the *B cell*. Note that no hyphen appears in these expressions, unless used adjectivally (eg, *T-cell lymphoma*). (Historically, the *T* and *B* come from the terms *thymus-derived* and *bursa [of Fabricius]–derived*, respectively. However, these are no longer spelled out.)

In the context of leukocyte typing and lymphocyte differentiation, the prefixes *pre-* and *pan-* are encountered; examples are included here for guidance on hyphenation. Capitalize only if it is clear that a commercial preparation is referred to:

pre-B cell
pan-B antibodies
pan-B plus B-progenitor
pan-T lymphocyte
pan-thymocyte

T lymphocytes: The majority of T lymphocytes are grouped into two subsets, according to function:

- helper/inducer T lymphocytes
  (also known as helper cells, helper T lymphocytes, etc)

- cytotoxic/suppressor T lymphocytes
  (also known as suppressor cells)

When the ratio of helper to suppressor T cells is referred to, use a hyphen and not a virgule, ie, helper-suppressor ratio (not helper/suppressor ratio). Surface antigens of T lymphocytes are expressed as follows:

T1	T3
T4	T6
T8	T9
T10	T11

Monoclonal antibodies to the surface antigens of T lymphocytes are often designated by the commercially available preparations used in the study of T-cell subsets. These are not treated as brand names. Commonly encountered are the following (note the style for capitalization, numbering, and spacing):

- The OK series (produced by Ortho Pharmaceutical Corporation, Raritan, NJ): OKT1, OKT3, OKT4, OKT6, OKT8, OKT9, OKT10, OKT11

- The Leu series (produced by Becton Dickinson & Co, Mountain View, Calif): Leu-1, Leu-2a, Leu-2b, Leu-3a, Leu-3b, Leu-4, Leu-5, Leu-6, Leu-7, Leu-8, Leu-9, Leu-10, Leu-11a, Leu-12, Leu-14, Leu-15, Leu-M1, Leu-M4, Leu-M9—also referred to with the prefix *anti–*, eg, anti–Leu-1, anti–Leu-2

- The Lyt series (New England Nuclear, Boston, Mass): Lyt-1, Lyt-2, Lyt-3

- Other T-cell–associated antibodies: 17F12, T101, SC1, A50, NA1/34

T-lymphocyte monoclonal antibodies may be expressed in various combinations and with superscript plus signs and minus signs. A virgule implies probable identity of the antibodies on either side; superscript plus and minus signs, presence or absence in a particular T-cell subset:

$T1^+$, $T3^+$, $T4^+$, $T11^+$
$T8^-$
$OKT1^+$
$OKT3/Leu-4^+$

B lymphocytes: The following are representative monoclonal antibodies reactive with human B lymphocytes:

BA-1
B1
B2
FMC1
FMC7
PI153/3

Other B-lymphocyte–associated surface markers are as follows:

SmIg	surface membrane immunoglobulin
CIg	cytoplasmic immunoglobulin
$C\mu$	cytoplasmic μ heavy chain (actually associated with pre–B lymphocytes)
Ia antigens and other HLA antigens	correspond to the HLA-DR locus (see also 12.12.2, Human Leukocyte [HLA] and Other Histocompatibility Antigens)
Iak	a mouse antigen
complement receptors	eg, C3b, C3d, C4 (see also 12.12.1, Complement)
Fc receptors	(see 12.12.3, Immunoglobulins)

Other monoclonal antibodies and cell markers:

OKM1/Mo1
Mo2
63D3
D5D6
Mac-120
D5
TA-1
1/12/13
MY3
MY4
5F1, 1G10
E (sheep erythrocyte; also used in the term *E rosette*)
CALLA (common acute lymphoblastic leukemia antigen); also expressed cALLA, but all-capital term is preferred; CALL$^+$ and CALL$^-$, rather than CALLA$^+$ and CALLA$^-$, are used to express presence or absence of antigen
TdT (the enzyme terminal deoxynucleotidyltransferase)
p24/BA-2
RFB-1
J-5

Clusters of differentiation are a system involving monoclonal antibodies to determine human leukocyte differentiation. There are currently several dozen such clusters. While a complicated nomenclature involving parenthetic suffixes exists—eg, CD10(nT,nB;gp100)J5—usually clusters can be referred to more simply with CD plus a numeral or a numeral and a letter, eg:

CD1a, CD2, CD10, CD45R

A lowercase *w* ("workshop": International Workshop and Conference on Human Leukocyte Differentiation Antigens [see 21.1, Resource Bibliography, References]) signifies a provisional cluster, eg:

CDw13, CDw14

12.13 **Isotopes.**—Isotope numbers are used in AMA publications principally in connection with radioactive drugs. When an isotope number is given for an element named by itself rather than as part of the name of a chemical compound, follow 12.13.1.

The official nonproprietary names of radiopharmaceuticals have a style that differs from standard chemical nomenclature; when the isotope number appears as part of the name of a compound, follow 12.13.2 if the compound has an approved nonproprietary drug name.

When a compound does not have an approved nonproprietary name, guidelines are intended to conform to standard chemical nomenclature; follow 12.13.3 and consult publications of the International Union of

Biochemistry and the International Union of Pure and Applied Chemistry (books and journals, eg, *European Journal of Biochemistry*, *Pure and Applied Chemistry*) and *Chemical Abstracts* for further information.

Chemical formulas are often given in standard medical dictionaries. For those that are not, consult *USAN and the USP Dictionary of Drug Names* for drugs (published annually by the US Pharmacopeial Convention, Inc, Rockville, Md) and the *Merck Index* (Merck & Co, Inc) or *Handbook of Chemistry and Physics* (CRC Press) for other compounds.

12.13.1 *Elements.*—When an isotope is mentioned by itself rather than as part of the name of a chemical compound (drug, diagnostic agent, or other compound), there are two correct ways to name it.

- When the name of the element is spelled out, the isotope number follows the name in the same typeface and type size (not as a superscript or subscript). The number is not preceded by a hyphen, even in the adjectival use. This is the preferred form for first mention of an isotope in the text or synopsis-abstract.

  Who first discovered uranium 235?

  Substances labeled with iodine 125 generally have the same uses as those containing iodine 131.

- When the element symbol rather than the spelled-out name of an element is used, the isotope number *precedes* the symbol as a *superscript*; the first example below mentions an isotope by itself as a general term and in the nonproprietary name of a radiopharmaceutical (see also 12.13.2, USAN Assigned to Radioactive Pharmaceuticals).

  In its use as a drug (in the form of a colloid), radioactive gold (^{198}Au) should be referred to by its approved nonproprietary name: gold Au 198.

  Of the 13 known isotopes of iodine, ^{128}I is the only one that is not radioactive.

Do not use the symbol representing a single element as an abbreviation for a compound (eg, do not abbreviate sodium arsenate As 74 as ^{74}As).

12.13.2 *USAN Assigned to Radioactive Pharmaceuticals.*—The United States Adopted Names applicable to radioactive pharmaceuticals are composed of the name of the basic compound serving as the carrier for the radioactivity, the symbol for the radioactive isotope, and the isotope number. Element symbols are useful components of the nonproprietary name because (1) they are internationally approved and recognized; (2) they specify the radioactive element in chemically, but not grammatically, redundant names (eg, sodium pertechnetate Tc 99m); and (3) several radioactive isotopes of a given element may be in use. (Such unambiguous labeling is in accordance with recommendations of the US Food and Drug Administration.) For drug nomenclature, consult the most recent edition of *USAN and the USP Dictionary of Drug Names* and the *AMA International Drug Nomenclature Edit Copy* (the "drug printout" prepared by the AMA Department of Medical Terminology; see also 12.6.1, Drugs, Nonproprietary Names). The isotope number appears in the same type (not superscript) as the rest of the drug name, and it is not preceded by a hyphen (*but:* see 12.13.4, Trademarks).

> iodohippurate sodium I 131 (not radioactive iodohippurate sodium or ^{131}I-labeled iodohippurate sodium)
> sodium iodide I 125
> cyanocobalamin Co 60
> gallium citrate Ga 67
> fibrinogen I 125
> iodinated I 131 aggregated serum albumin
>
> *Exception:* The approved nonproprietary name *tritiated water* omits the element symbol and isotope number (see also 12.13.6, Hydrogen Isotopes).

In general, follow the guidelines for terminology in 12.6, Drugs. Use the nonproprietary name at first mention when referring to a radiopharmaceutical administered to a patient. Afterward, a shorter term may be used, eg, iodinated albumin, gallium scan. In general discussions, a more colloquial term may be used.

> Technetium is used in scans of several body systems. Technetium sulfur colloid is used for lung imaging. In one study 50 patients underwent lung imaging with technetium Tc 99m sulfur colloid. No patients suffered ill effects attributable to ^{99m}Tc–sulfur colloid.

(*Note:* At the beginning of a sentence, the name rather than the element symbol should be used.)

Readers will note in preceding sections that expanded terms, rather than chemical formulas (eg, $Na_3^{74}AsO_4$), have been used. Not only is this consistent with pharmaceutical labeling, as discussed previously, this is currently preferred AMA style for clarity. In descriptions of chemical reactions, chemical nomenclature is, of course, acceptable (see also 11.12, Abbreviations, Elements and Chemicals).

12.13.3 *Compounds Without Approved Names.*—A compound not having an approved nonproprietary drug name may be referred to in any of several descriptive ways.

> glucose labeled with radioactive carbon (^{14}C)
>
> glucose tagged with carbon 14

amikacin labeled with iodine 125

After first mention, the name of such a substance can be abbreviated. Use the superscript form of the isotope number to the left of the element symbol. Enclose the isotope symbol in brackets and close up with the compound name if the isotope element is normally part of the compound.

[^{14}C]glucose (*not* glucose C 14)

Use *no* brackets and separate the element and compound name with a hyphen if the compound does not normally contain the isotope element.

^{125}I-amikacin

If uncertain as to whether the isotope element is normally part of a compound, consult the sources of chemical formulas mentioned at the beginning of this section (12.13).

12.13.4 Trademarks.—In trademarks, isotope numbers usually appear in the same position as in approved nonproprietary names, but they are usually joined to the rest of the name by a hyphen, and they are not necessarily preceded by the element symbol. Follow the *AMA International Drug Nomenclature Edit Copy*, *USAN Dictionary*, *AMA Drug Evaluations*, and the usage of individual manufacturers.

Iodotope I-131   Cobatope-57

Glofil-125   Hippuran I 131

12.13.5 Uniform Labeling.—The abbreviation "ul" (for "uniformly labeled") may be used without expansion in parentheses:

[^{14}C]glucose (ul)

Similarly, terms such as *carrier-free*, *no carrier added*, or *carrier added* may be used. In general medical publications, these terms should not be abbreviated, as not all readers will be familiar with them.

12.13.6 Hydrogen Isotopes.—Two isotopes of hydrogen have their own specific names, *deuterium* and *tritium*, which should be used instead of "hydrogen 2" and "hydrogen 3." In the text, the specific names are also preferred to the symbols ^{2}H or D (for deuterium, which is stable) and ^{3}H (for tritium, which is radioactive). The two forms of heavy water (D_2O and $^{3}H_2O$) should be referred to by the approved nonproprietary names *deuterium oxide* and *tritiated water*.

12.13.7 Metastable Isotopes.—The abbreviation *m*, as in krypton Kr 81m (approved nonproprietary name), stands for "metastable." It should never be dropped, as the term without the *m* then designates a different radionuclide isomer.

12.14 Neurology

12.14.1 *Cranial Nerves.*—Use roman numerals when designating cranial nerves, but ordinals when the adjectival form is used:

Cranial nerves II, III, and VI are protected by . . .

The second, third, and sixth cranial nerves are protected by . . .

English names are preferred to Latin:

Nerve	English Name	Latin Name
I	olfactory	olfactorius
II	optic	opticus
III	oculomotor	oculomotorius
IV	trochlear	trochlearis
V	trigeminal	trigeminus
VI	abducens	abducens
VII	facial	facialis
VIII	acoustic	vestibulocochlearis
IX	glossopharyngeal	glossopharyngeus
X	vagus	vagus
XI	accessory	accessorius
XII	hypoglossal	hypoglossus

12.14.2 *Electroencephalographic (EEG) Terms.*—The following are symbols employed for the electrodes used in electroencephalography (see Fig 2). They are the terms used in placement according to the "10-20 System" and are widely employed and recognized. Capital letters refer to anatomic areas (primarily of the skull, which do not necessarily coincide with the brain areas from which the electrodes register impulses). Subscripts refer to relative electrode positions; odd numbers are for electrodes placed on the left side, even numbers for electrodes placed on the right side, and z for midline ("zero") electrodes.

frontal pole or prefrontal electrodes	F_{pz}, F_{p1}, F_{p2}
frontal electrodes	F_z, F_3, F_4
parietal electrodes	P_z, P_3, P_4
central electrodes	C_z, C_3, C_4
anterior temporal electrodes	F_7, F_8
midtemporal electrodes	T_3, T_4
posterior temporal electrodes	T_5, T_6
occipital electrodes	O_z, O_1, O_2
nasopharyngeal electrodes	P_{g1}, P_{g2}
earlobe electrodes	A_1, A_2

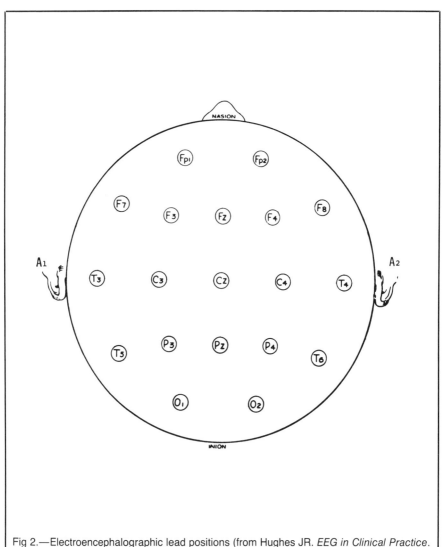

Fig 2.—Electroencephalographic lead positions (from Hughes JR. *EEG in Clinical Practice*. Boston, Mass: Butterworths; 1982:2; reprinted with permission of Butterworths, ©1982).

Additional electrodes and other placement systems may be used, eg,

C_5, F_1, P_2

In figures showing EEGs, electrode symbols will usually be paired, either beside, above, or above and below a tracing (Fig 3).

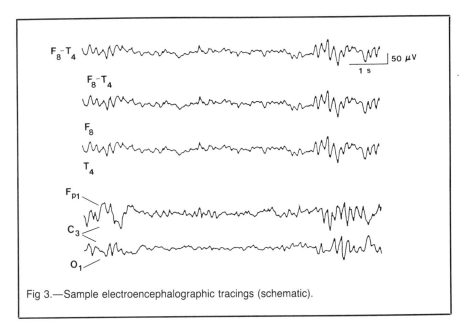

Fig 3.—Sample electroencephalographic tracings (schematic).

Authors should include with tracings a time marker and an indicator of voltage, as in the top tracing above.

Descriptions of EEG potentials include many qualitative terms and frequencies. The following are but a few of numerous terms:

> alpha waves, beta rhythms, slow waves, slow transients, spindles, spike and wave pattern, spike and dome complex, paroxysms, sharp waves, delta brush, frontal sharp transient, mu pattern, lambda rhythm (Note that the Greek letters are spelled out in these terms.)

Frequency is given in cycles per second (c/s) or the equivalent term hertz (Hz). The latter is preferred in AMA scientific publications.

> background rhythm of 8 to 10 c/s
> 60-Hz artifact
> a theta frequency of 5 to 7.5/s
> 14/s spindles

12.15 Obstetric Terms.—In obstetrics, the letters G, P, and A or Ab, accompanied by numbers, are used to indicate an individual's obstetric history; the letters stand for *gravida, para,* and *aborta*. G3, P2, A1 would indicate three pregnancies, two births of viable offspring, and one abortion. In published articles, however, it is preferable to write out the expression, eg, gravida 3, para 2, aborta 1.

Alternatively, ''TPAL'' terminology may be used, standing for *term infants, premature infants, abortions,* and *living children.* Often, four numbers separated by hyphens simply are recorded: 3-1-1-4 would indicate three term infants, one premature infant, one abortion, and four living children. However, the text of a manuscript should define the numerical expressions and not give the numbers alone.

A *nulligravida* (also expressed gravida 0) is a woman who has had no pregnancies; a *primigravida* (gravida 1) has had one pregnancy; a *secundigravida* (gravida 2) has had two pregnancies; and a *nullipara* (para 0) has had no deliveries of viable offspring.

The *Apgar score* is an assessment of a newborn's physical well-being based on pulse, breathing, color, tone, and reflex irritability, each of which is rated 0, 1, or 2. Usually the Apgar score is reported as two numbers, from 0 to 10, separated by a virgule, reflecting assessment at 1 minute and 5 minutes after birth. In general medical journals, however, it is best to specify the time intervals, especially as, occasionally, the Apgar score may be assessed at another interval as well, eg, at 10 minutes.

> *Ambiguous:*   Apgar of 9/10
>
> *Preferred:*   Apgar score of 9/10 at 1 and 5 minutes

The score is named after the late Virginia Apgar, MD, and thus is *not* printed all in capital letters as though for an acronym (although versions of such an acronym have been created as a mnemonic device).

12.16   Organisms

12.16.1 *Genus and Species*

Specific terms/species names: For the correct names of microbial genera and species, including plurals, consult any of the following:

> *Approved Lists of Bacterial Names,* edited by Skerman, McGown, and Sneath (1980) and subsequent lists of valid names published in the *International Journal of Systematic Bacteriology* (appropriate sources to be searched for names that are valid according to the international code for nomenclature of bacteria);
>
> *Bergey's Manual of Systematic Bacteriology,* edited by Krieg and Holt (comprehensive reference source of bacterial nomenclature and taxonomy);
>
> *Manual of Clinical Microbiology,* edited by Lennette (published by the American Society for Microbiology);
>
> *Principles and Practice of Infectious Diseases,* edited by Mandell, Douglas, and Bennett (one of several major textbooks that reflect medical usage).

After first mention of the singular form in the text, abbreviate genus name (without a period) when used with species except when the species is other than that given at first mention. Another genus may be mentioned in the

242

interim. Do not abbreviate species name.

Italicize species, variety or subspecies, and genus when used in the singular. Do not italicize genus name when used in the plural. Do not italicize the name of a class, order, family, or tribe.

Capitalize genus in the singular, genus abbreviation, class, order, family, and tribe. In the text, do not capitalize species, variety, or subspecies, or plural forms of a genus name. In titles, capitalize the plural of genus names, but do not capitalize name of species or subspecies (see also 8.1.7, Capitalization, Organisms).

Sometimes, a subspecies name is given in addition to the genus-species term, as in the following examples:

> *Campylobacter fetus* subsp *venerealis*
> *Campylobacter fetus* subsp *fetus*
>
> *Campylobacter fetus jejuni* was shown to be two species, *C jejuni* and *C coli*.

Likewise, the abbreviation "var" is acceptable when discussing varieties or variants of species.

A hyphenated species name implies two species that are indistinguishable in the context in which they are mentioned; neither is a subspecies of the other. For example, the two species *Mycobacterium avium* and *Mycobacterium intracellulare* may be referred to as *Mycobacterium avium-intracellulare*.

General terms: Many bacteria and other organisms possess traditional generic or plural designations; however, if the correct generic or plural cannot be determined, add the word "organisms" to the italicized genus name (see also 7.5, Plurals, Microorganisms); the following are examples:

Salmonella enteritidis	*Mycobacterium tuberculosis*
Salmonella typhimurium	*Mycobacterium kansasii*
salmonellae	mycobacteria
Treponema pallidum	*Escherichia coli*
Treponema genitalis	*Escherichia aurescens*
treponemes	*Escherichia* organisms
Staphylococcus aureus	*Proteus vulgaris*
Staphylococcus epidermidis	*Proteus mirabilis*
staphylococci	*Proteus* organisms
the staphylococcus	*Chlamydia trachomatis*
Streptococcus pneumoniae	chlamydia
Streptococcus mutans	
streptococci	*Chlamydia trachomatis* and *Chlamydia*
the streptococcus	*psittaci*
	chlamydiae
Pseudomonas aeruginosa	
pseudomonads	

The abbreviations "sp" and "spp" both stand for *species* and are used when the genus is certain but the species cannot be determined. For instance, if the author knows that a skin test reaction occurs with *Toxocara* organisms but is uncertain about whether the reaction results from the presence of *Toxocara canis* or *Toxocara cati*, the author may write *Toxocara* sp (or *Toxocara* spp) to show the uncertainty.

However, the expanded term *species* would, when following a genus name, have the connotation not of uncertainty but of reference to the genus as a whole; for example: "*Toxocara* species are infectious agents transmissible by household pets."

As this is a fine and sometimes blurred distinction, in both of the above situations, the expanded term *species* is preferred.

In texts dealing with infectious conditions, it is important to distinguish between the infectious agent and the condition. Infectious agents, infections, and diseases are not equivalent:

Incorrect:	*Haemophilus influenzae* may be a life-threatening disease.
Better:	*Haemophilus influenzae* infection may be life threatening.
Preferred:	Infection with *Haemophilus influenzae* may be life threatening.

Incorrect:	*Chlamydia trachomatis* is often an overlooked disease.
Inelegant:	*Chlamydia trachomatis* disease is often overlooked.
Preferred:	Disease caused by *Chlamydia trachomatis* is often overlooked.

The suffixes *-osis* and *-iasis* are used to indicate disease caused by particular classes of infectious agents or types of infection, eg, "treponematosis," "dermatophytoses" (plural form), "amebiasis."

12.16.2 *Viruses.*—For a listing of official virus terms, consult the most recent summary report of the International Committee on Taxonomy of Viruses (ICTV), whose reports have been published in the journal *Intervirology.*

Ideally, internationally agreed-on terms are used, but in practice, vernacular terms are frequently encountered. The genus-species combination familiar in bacterial and higher organism nomenclature is not used for viruses.

In official terms, there are three standard endings:

-idae (family)
 (eg, *Herpesviridae, Adenoviridae, Reoviridae*)

-inae (subfamily)
 (eg, *Oncovirinae*)

-virus (genus)
 (eg, *Reovirus, Rotavirus*)

The endings *-idae* and *-inae* are reliable indicators of official terms for family or subfamily, but the *-virus* ending might signify either a vernacular or an official term. Note that *virus* is usually a closed-up suffix in official terms but often a separate word in vernacular terms.

As with other organisms, names for higher viral classifications (eg, family, subfamily) are capitalized (see also 8.1.7, Capitalization, Organisms). Viral family and subfamily names are also italicized. However, viral genus names, unlike those for other organisms (see 12.16.1, Genus and Species), are not usually capitalized and italicized, unless it is clear that the official terminology is being used.

Many virus names are combinations of specific words (eg, *echovirus* [*e*nteric *c*ytopathic *h*uman *o*rphan *virus*], papovavirus [*pa*pilloma *po*lyoma *va*cuolating agent *virus*]. At one time capitalization reflected this (eg, ECHOvirus, PaPoVa virus). However, the trend is now to lowercase usage.

Viruses of humans: The following is a list of virus names frequently encountered in medical texts and is meant as a guide to acceptable common terminology. For a more extensive table with official terms, see Virus Names Appendix.

> herpesvirus
> herpes simplex virus 1
> herpes simplex virus 2
> varicella-zoster virus
> cytomegalovirus
> Epstein-Barr virus
>
> influenza virus [see also next paragraph]
>
> eastern equine encephalomyelitis virus
> arbovirus group B
> yellow fever virus
> tickborne encephalitis virus
> rubella virus
>
> paramyxovirus
> mumps virus
> parainfluenza 1
> measles virus
> respiratory syncytial virus
>
> retroviruses
>
> poliovirus 1, poliovirus 2, poliovirus 3
> enterovirus 68, 69, etc
> echovirus 1, echovirus 2, etc
> coxsackievirus A1, A2, B1, etc
> rhinovirus 1A

> hepatitis B virus [see also 12.11, Hepatitis]
> hepatitis A virus
> Marburg virus
> Ebola virus

In medical publications, terms for the three types and various strains of influenza virus often contain appended suffixes (Melnick 1982, p 219). Strains of influenza A are often identified by antigenic subtypes, defined by the surface antigens hemagglutinin and neuraminidase, eg:

> influenza A(H1N1)   [hemagglutinin subtype 1, neuraminidase subtype 1]

As of 1982 there were 12 recognized subtypes of hemagglutinin (H1 through H12) and nine subtypes of neuraminidase (N1 through N9). (HO and HSW have been reclassified as H1.)

Only influenza A employs the H and N suffix, but the three types of influenza virus, A, B, and C, may also contain suffixes with terms for the host of origin (if nonhuman), geographic origin, strain number, and year of isolation, separated by virgules (and followed by the H and N designations in parentheses in the case of influenza A).

> influenza A/PR/8/34(H1N1)   influenza B/Mass/3/66
> influenza A/USSR/90/77(H1N1)   influenza B/Singapore/79
> influenza A/Port Chalmers/1/73(H3N2)

Along with a special subcommittee of the International Committee on Taxonomy of Viruses, AMA journals prefer the term *human immunodeficiency virus* (HIV) for the virus implicated in the acquired immunodeficiency syndrome. Occasionally, at a specific author's request, other names for the virus may be included parenthetically after the first mention of HIV, namely:

> human T-cell lymphotropic virus type III *or*
> human T lymphotropic virus type III (HTLV-III)
>
> lymphadenopathy-associated virus (LAV)
>
> AIDS-associated retrovirus (ARV)

Human T-cell lymphotropic virus type I and HTLV-II continue to be referred to as such.

Subtypes of HIV are now being recognized, most recently at this writing, HIV-2. This virus is *not* considered equivalent to HTLV-II, but rather to HTLV-IV, LAV-2, and SBL666-9 (Swedish Biological Laboratories).

Note the use of *roman* numerals in the HTLV series and *arabic* numerals in the other series.

Other new virus names are emerging that could create further confusion in this area, for example, HBLV (herpes B lymphotropic virus) or HV-6 (herpesvirus type 6). Authors should be specific and use expanded forms of virus names at first mention; editors should make suggestions per style guidelines but should not make changes in virus names without consulting the author.

Phages: Phages are viruses that infect bacteria; *phage* is an accepted term, shortened from "bacteriophage." Phage groups or genera are sometimes referred to with terms such as *T-even phages, actinophages, T7 phage group.* Specific bacteriophages tend to be referred to as "phage x," *x* being a letter (usually roman or lowercase Greek), number, or letter-number combination, eg "phage λ." Other examples include the following:

phage α3	phage μ2
phage φ149	phage ZG/3A
phage MY	phage dφ3
phage φX174	phage 6
phage Bam35	phage fd
T4 phage	
T5 phage	

12.17   Pulmonary and Respiratory Terminology.—Despite the familiarity of many of the abbreviations and symbols of pulmonary-respiratory medicine, authors and editors are encouraged to expand all terms at first mention.

Two sets of abbreviations tend to appear in pulmonary-respiratory medicine: *symbols* used in physiology and *acronyms* from pulmonary function testing. While the contexts of physiology and pulmonary function testing overlap, the distinction between the symbols and acronyms is offered as a way to become familiar with the abbreviations and their style.

12.17.1 *Symbols.*—The following groupings of the *symbols* of pulmonary physiologic terminology are primarily adapted from West (1985); the symbols and groupings are consistent with the approved nomenclature of the Committee on Respiratory Physiology of the International Union of Physiological Sciences (IUPS) and the Publications Committee of the American Physiological Society (1986).

Primary symbols are the first terms of an expression and are set on line:

C	concentration of gas in blood
F	fractional concentration of a dry gas
P	pressure or partial pressure
Q	volume of blood
Q̇	volume of blood per unit time (blood flow; perfusion)
S	saturation of hemoglobin with oxygen
V	volume of gas
V̇	volume of gas per unit time (gas flow)
D	diffusing capacity
R	gas exchange ratio

Secondary symbols for gas phase traditionally follow the primary symbol as small capitals:

A	alveolar
B	barometric
DS	dead space
E	expired
I	inspired
L	lung
T	tidal
ET	end-tidal

Secondary symbols for blood phase are traditionally lowercase letters that follow the secondary symbol for gas phase:

b	blood, in general
a	arterial
c	capillary
c′	pulmonary end-capillary
i	ideal
v	venous
v̄	mixed venous

Gas abbreviations are traditionally the last element of the term, given as small capitals (*note:* in IUPS terminology, these are given as subscripts):

O_2	oxygen
CO_2	carbon dioxide
N_2	nitrogen
CO	carbon monoxide

These symbols are combined in various ways to derive the terms of pulmonary and respiratory physiology. Common examples are the following:

P_{CO_2}	partial pressure of carbon dioxide
Pa_{CO_2}	partial pressure of carbon dioxide, arterial
P_{O_2}	partial pressure of oxygen
Pa_{O_2}	partial pressure of oxygen, arterial

(*Note:* The above four terms may be given without expansion at first mention; see also 11.10, Abbreviations, Clinical and Technical Terms.)

$P_{A_{O_2}}$	partial pressure of oxygen in the alveoli
$P\bar{v}_{O_2}$	partial pressure of oxygen, mixed venous blood
P_B	barometric pressure
$P_{A_{O_2}} - Pa_{O_2}$	alveolar-arterial difference in partial pressure of oxygen (preferred to AaD_{O_2})
Sa_{O_2}	saturation with oxygen, arterial blood
$F_{I_{O_2}}$	fraction of inspired oxygen
$\dot{V}/\dot{Q}$	ventilation-perfusion ratio (also $\dot{V}_A/\dot{Q}$)
$\dot{V}_{O_2}$	oxygen consumption per unit time
$\dot{V}_{O_2}max$	maximum oxygen consumption

V̇E	expired volume per unit time
CaO$_2$	oxygen concentration, arterial
Cc′O$_2$	oxygen concentration, pulmonary end-capillary blood
FEN$_2$	fractional concentration of nitrogen in expired gas
VT	tidal volume
VDS	volume of dead space

12.17.2 *Acronyms*.—The following are some common acronyms for entities referred to in pulmonary function testing; they should always be expanded at first mention:

FEV	forced expiratory volume
FEV$_1$	forced expiratory volume in 1 second
FVC	forced vital capacity
FIVC	forced inspiratory vital capacity
FEF$_{25\%-75\%}$	forced expiratory flow, mid–expiratory phase (formerly mid–maximal expiratory flow, MMEFR; midflow; mid–maximal flow, MMF; or mid–expiratory flow rate, MEFR)
FEF$_{200-1200}$	forced expiratory flow between 200 and 1200 mL of FVC
FRC	functional residual capacity
VC	vital capacity
IVC	inspiratory vital capacity
TLC	total lung capacity
CC	closing capacity
RV	residual volume
CV	closing volume
ERV	expiratory reserve volume
IRV	inspiratory reserve volume
MVV	maximum voluntary ventilation
CL	lung compliance
sGaw	specific airway conductance
Raw	airway resistance

In the alphabet soup of pulmonary-respiratory nomenclature, certain letters often stand for more than one entity. For instance, capital C stands for *concentration* in the context of gas exchange and for *closing* and/or *capacity* in pulmonary mechanics, and may also stand for *compliance* in the latter context. Moreover, the above lists are simplified from the IUPS nomenclature and are not exhaustive. Therefore, authors and editors should be cautious in expanding terms and should not assume that the letters in the above lists always stand for the terms indicated.

12.18   Vertebrae, Dermatomes, and Spinal Nerves.—For preferred terminology, consult *Dorland's Illustrated Medical Dictionary*, *Stedman's Medical Dictionary*, *Blakiston's Gould Medical Dictionary*, *Nomina Anatomica*, or any reputable anatomy text.

In manuscript texts, legends, and tables, specific designations of vertebrae and intervertebral spaces may be abbreviated without first being written out, if no confusion results. Abbreviate in accordance with these examples:

Vertebra	Abbreviation	Space
second cervical vertebra	C-2	C2-3
second thoracic vertebra	T-2	T2-3
second lumbar vertebra	L-2	L2-3
second sacral vertebra	S-2	S2-3

The same abbreviations are used for dermatomes and spinal nerves. It should always be clear which is being referred to, ie, vertebra, dermatome, or spinal nerve.

13.0 Eponyms

Eponyms are phrases or names derived from or including the name of a person or place. In medical writing, eponyms are used most often for conditions or diseases, tests, methods, and procedures.

In the area of diseases or conditions, eponyms historically have indicated the name of the describer or discoverer of the disease (eg, Hodgkin's disease), that of the person found to have the disease (eg, Christmas disease), or the location in which the disease was found to occur (eg, Lyme disease). With the first of these, the possessive form (*-'s*) was always used, and with the latter two the nonpossessive was used to make the distinction. However, these distinctions are beginning to fade.

13.1 **Possessive Form.**—At present, there is considerable debate over the retention or deletion of the possessive with eponyms. Although there seems to be a trend toward dropping the possessive, feelings on this point are still strongly divided, and therefore, we recommend following current usage as represented in the latest editions of *Dorland's* or *Stedman's* medical dictionaries. Along with the usage found in the dictionaries, several traditional rules of thumb can still be kept in mind concerning the use of eponyms: (1) when two or more names are involved, the *-'s* is not used (eg, Niemann-Pick disease, Stanford-Binet Test); (2) when the eponymous term derives from a location, drop the possessive (eg, Lyme disease) (current usage as reflected in the medical dictionaries can be seen to support these two items); (3) capitalize the eponym but not the noun or adjective that accompanies it (eg, Down's syndrome) (see 8.1.5, Capitalization, Eponyms); and (4) if *the*, *a*, or *an* is used before the name, an apostrophe and *s* (even if given in the sources listed) should *not* be used (eg, Wilms' tumor, *but* the Wilms tumor; Preyer's reflex *but* the Preyer reflex).

13.2 **Eponymous vs Noneponymous Terms.**—Eponyms often were a result of the describer's name or the location of the condition's detection being more widely recognized at the time of discovery of the condition than the actual disease processes found to be involved later on. To insist on the use of the noneponymous term only seems arbitrary and contrary to the purpose of scientific writing, which is to disseminate information that can be quickly understood by all. The majority of readers would be familiar with the term *Paget's disease* and would have to go through less strenuous mental acrobatics to recognize the condition than if osteitis deformans were used. Yet there are those who argue that the complete descriptive definition and understanding of the disease entity are thus missed when an eponym is used. This is readily seen in the case of Paget's disease: although most people *are* familiar with the term, there is actually more than one type of Paget's disease (eg, Paget's disease of the bone, Paget's disease of the nipple). Therefore, for educational purposes one may consider putting the less familiar noneponymous term or phrase in parentheses after first mention of the widely recognized and accepted eponymous term, eg, Parkinson's disease (paralysis agitans).

14.0 Greek Letters

Greek letters in copy should be marked for the typesetter's attention by writing, in the margin, the letters "GK" followed by the universal code numbers in the following list. Alternatively, use the name of the character itself.

| | β-adrenergic | | | κ light chain |
| | γ-globulin | | ΔT | δβ-thalassemia |

1	A	Alpha		18	Σ	Sigma		36	μ	mu
2	B	Beta		19	T	Tau		37	ν	nu
3	Γ	Gamma		20	Υ	Upsilon		38	ξ	xi
4	Δ	Delta		21	Φ	Phi		39	o	omicron
5	E	Epsilon		22	X	Chi		40	π	pi
6	Z	Zeta		23	Ψ	Psi		41	ρ	rho
7	H	Eta		24	Ω	Omega		42	σ	sigma
8	Θ	Theta		25	α	alpha		43	ς	sigma
8a	O	Theta		26	β	beta		44	τ	tau
9	I	Iota		27	γ	gamma		45	υ	upsilon
10	K	Kappa		28	δ	delta		46	φ	phi
11	Λ	Lambda		29	ε	epsilon		46a	φ	phi
12	M	Mu		30	ζ	zeta		47	χ	chi
13	N	Nu		31	η	eta		48	ψ	psi
14	Ξ	Xi		32	θ	theta		49	ω	omega
15	O	Omicron		33	ι	iota		50	ϑ	theta
16	Π	Pi		34	κ	kappa				
17	P	Rho		35	λ	lambda				

Greek letters are frequently used in statistical formulas and notations, in mathematical composition, in certain chemical names for drugs, and in chemical and technical terms (see 11.10, Abbreviations, Clinical and Technical Terms; 12.6.4, Nomenclature, Special Drug Classes of Interest; 12.10, Nomenclature, Globulins; 12.12.3, Nomenclature, Immunoglobulins; 17.0, Statistics; and 18.0, Mathematical Composition).

14.1 **Greek Letter vs Word.**—AMA publications prefer the use of Greek letters over words, unless usage dictates otherwise. Consult *Dorland's* and *Stedman's* medical dictionaries for general terms. If the Greek letter, rather than the word, is found in either of these sources for the item in question, use the letter in preference to the word. For chemical terms, the use of

14.1   *Greek Letter vs Word*

Greek letters is almost always preferred. For electroencephalographic terms, the word is used (see 12.14.2, Nomenclature, Electroencephalographic [EEG] Terms). For drug names that contain Greek letters, consult the sources listed in 12.6, Nomenclature, Drugs, for preferred usage. In some cases, when the Greek letter is part of the word, as in *betamethasone*, of course the Greek letter is spelled out. In other cases, however, the approved nonproprietary name takes the word, not the Greek letter, eg, beta carotene. (*Note:* The chemical name would be β,β-carotene, however.)

14.2   Capitalization After a Greek Letter.—In titles and subtitles (except in references), centered heads, side heads, table column heads, and line art and at the beginning of sentences, the first non-Greek letter following a Greek letter should be capitalized. Do not capitalize the Greek letter itself, unless, of course, the capital is specifically intended.

Title:	Liver Disease in α_1-Antitrypsin Deficiency
Table title:	Table 1.—Effectiveness of Various β-Blockers in Migraine
Beginning of a sentence:	β-Hemolytic streptococci were identified. Δ^1-3,4-*trans*-Tetrahydrocannabinol is one of two psychomimetically active isomeric principles in cannabis.

254

4

MEASUREMENT AND QUANTITATION

15.0 Units of Measure

After a transitional period of dual reporting of clinical laboratory measurements in conventional and Système International (SI) units, AMA publications are using SI units for most of these measurements (see exceptions noted in 15.1, SI Units; see also 11.11, Abbreviations, Units of Measure). Medical journals and their editorial staff members, as well as authors, must take responsibility for this conversion process. With the publication of the American National Metric Council's document in January 1987, more journals are moving to the use of SI reporting, either alone or with conventional units.

AMA journals will still be making some exceptions, however, for use of English units; eg, a discussion of a dietary regimen may be given in calories, with portions described in cups and ounces; an informal essay may speak of "miles"; idioms such as "an ounce of prevention is worth a pound of cure" will remain unchanged.

15.1   **SI Units.**—In 1954, the General Conference on Weights and Measures adopted a rationalized system based on the meter, kilogram, second, ampere, degree kelvin, and candela. In 1960, the system was given the title International System of Units, Système International (SI units).

In May 1977, the 30th World Health Assembly recommended that SI units be used in medicine. Many medical journals throughout the world

15.1   SI Units

have adopted SI units, even though some journals in the United States continue to report some measurements in the traditional metric system.

"The . . . SI is the most up-to-date version of the metric system and replaces all earlier versions of that system. . . . The short-term goal [of conversion to SI] is to correct the present confused measurement system and improve test-result communication within and between countries." (McQueen 1986) The SI is based on seven fundamental units (Table 1) from which others derive (Table 2) and that refer to seven basic properties or quantities measured.

Table 1.—Base Units of SI		
Physical Quantity	**Base Unit**	**SI Symbol**
Length	meter	m
Mass	kilogram	kg
Time	second	s
Amount of substance	mole	mol
Thermodynamic temperature	kelvin	K
Electric current	ampere	A
Luminous intensity	candela	cd

Table 2.—Representative Derived Units		
Derived Unit	**Name and Symbol**	**Derivation From Base Units**
Area	square meter (m^2)	m^2
Volume	cubic meter (m^3)	m^3
Force	newton (N)	$kg \cdot m \cdot s^{-2}$
Pressure	pascal (Pa)	$kg \cdot m^{-1} \cdot s^{-2}$ (N/m^2)
Work, energy	joule (J)	$kg \cdot m^2 \cdot s^{-2}$ (N·m)
Density	kilogram per cubic meter (kg/m^3)	kg/m^3
Frequency	hertz (Hz)	s^{-1}

Prefixes (eg, *kilo-*, *milli-*, *micro-*) are combined with the base units to express multiples and submultiples thereof. The factors are powers of 10, with exponents that are simple multiples of 3 (Table 3). Note that those prefixes such as *hecto-*, *deca-*, *deci-*, and *centi-* that represent powers that are *not* multiples of 3 do not conform and hence are usually avoided in scientific writing.

Table 3.—Multiples and Submultiples of SI Units		
Factor	**Prefix**	**Symbol**
10^{18}	exa	E
10^{15}	peta	P
10^{12}	tera	T
10^9	giga	G
10^6	mega	M
10^3	kilo	k
10^{-3}	milli	m
10^{-6}	micro	μ
10^{-9}	nano	n
10^{-12}	pico	p
10^{-15}	femto	f
10^{-18}	atto	a

15.1.1 *Exponents.*—The SI reporting style uses exponents rather than the abbreviations "cu" and "sq."

sq m   becomes m^2

cu m   becomes m^3

15.1.2 *Commas in Numbers.*—No commas are used in numbers. In numbers of four digits, the digits are set closed up. In numbers of five or more digits, a half-space is used where previously a comma would have appeared. No commas or spaces are used in numbers containing decimal points, even in numbers of five or more digits.

1,000	becomes	1000
10,000	becomes	10 000
2492.7201	remains	2492.7201

15.1.3 *Multiplication Sign vs Times Dot.*—In most cases the times dot is preferred to the multiplication sign (see also 18.3.2, Mathematical Composition, Expressing Multiplication and Division). Some exceptions include expressions of area (eg, a 1.23×3.5-m^2 space) or volume (eg, a $5.2 \times 3.7 \times 6.9$-$m^3$ cube), matrixes (eg, 2×2 table), magnification ($\times 30\ 000$), or scientific notation (eg, 3.6×10^9/L).

15.1.4 *Space Between Numeral and Unit of Measure Symbol.*—With the exception of the percent sign, the degree sign (angles), and the °C symbols,

257

a space should appear between the arabic numeral and the unit of measure symbol.

15.1.5 *Percentage Replaced by Values Expressed as a Fraction of One.*—In many instances, most notably those of mass fraction, volume fraction, and relative quantities, the unit of percentage has been replaced by values expressed as a fraction of one.

> *hematocrit:*   40% becomes 0.40
> *differential cell count:* 30% band cells becomes band cells, 0.30

15.1.6 *Units of Time.*—Although the recommended abbreviations for minute, week, and month remain min, wk, and mo, respectively, the abbreviations for hour, day, and year become h, d, and y. *But* these abbreviations should be used only in tables, line art, and virgule (solidus) construction.

15.1.7 *SI Units With One-to-One Conversion During Dual Reporting.*—To report both SI and conventional units clearly in cases of one-to-one conversion, the following guidelines are suggested:

In text: Repeat the number in parentheses, along with the unit of measure.

> 20 mmol/L (20 mEq/L)

In table headings or stubs and line art: Give the units of measure and then list the numerical value only once, ie, do not give the same number in a table entry once inside parentheses and once outside parentheses.

15.1.8 *Number of Significant Digits.*—Note that in the conversion table to SI units (15.10, Conversion Tables, Table 4), limiting the number of significant digits is recommended. Round off (see 17.4, Statistics, Rounding Off) in accordance with these recommendations.

15.1.9 *Pascal, Katal, pH, and Kelvin.*—At the present time, the SI units *pascal* and *katal* are being held in abeyance. Blood pressure and oxygen pressure are still being reported in millimeters of mercury (mm Hg) and centimeters of water (cm H_2O). Enzyme activity is still being reported in international units. The pH scale is being retained. And although kelvin is the SI unit for thermodynamic temperature, temperatures will continue to be reported in degrees Celsius as the kelvin has limited application in medicine.

15.1.10 *SI and Radiology.*—Convert the *rad* to the *gray* (Gy) as follows:

> 1 rad = 0.01 Gy (1 Gy = 100 rad)

15.1.11 *SI and Energy.*—Convert the *calorie* and *kilocalorie* to the *joule* (J) and *kilojoule* (kJ) as follows:

> 1 calorie = 4.2 J
>
> 1 kilocalorie = 4.2 kJ

SI units are becoming the standard of the future, and medical scientists and practicing physicians still using familar metric units should learn the new SI units (also see 15.10, Conversion Tables, Table 5, for conversion from English units to metric units). This section should not be considered the final word on SI. There will be further information on an ongoing basis as we progress toward complete conversion.

15.2   **Quantities.**—Use arabic numerals for all quantities (one or more) with units of measure (see 16.3.10, Numbers and Percentages, Units of Measure).

15.3   **Abbreviations.**—Most units of measure are abbreviated when used with numerals or in a virgule construction. (Abbreviations and specifications for their use are given in 11.11, Abbreviations, Units of Measure.)

15.3.1   *Time.*—Do not abbreviate units of time, except in tables, line art, and virgule construction.

15.3.2   *Plurals.*—Use the same abbreviation for singular and plural forms:

> 1 L   6 L (not 6 Ls)
>
> 1 mm   2 mm (not 2 mms)

15.3.3   *Beginning of Sentence, Title, Subtitle.*—When a unit of measure follows a number at the beginning of a sentence, a title, or a subtitle, it too must be written out, even though the same unit of measure is abbreviated elsewhere in the same sentence.

> Fifteen milligrams (not *Fifteen mg* or *15 mg*) of the drug was administered at 9 PM and 25 mg at 3:30 AM.

15.3.4   *Specialized Abbreviations.*—Follow the instructions in 11.11, Abbreviations, Units of Measure, for spelling out specialized abbreviations at the first mention.

15.3.5   *Names and Symbols.*—Do not mix spelled-out names and symbols; eg, use newton·meter or N·m, but not newton·m or N·meter; use mmol or millimole, but not mmole or millimol. (*Note*: With numbers it is preferable to use the abbreviations rather than the words.) *But*: See also 15.4.1, Virgule.

15.4 Punctuation.—No periods are used with abbreviations of units of measure. Also, no punctuation is used between units of the same dimension, eg, time with time.

> 9 years 5 months

15.4.1 *Virgule.*—Use only one virgule (/) per expression, to avoid ambiguity; eg, if there are two units of measure, a virgule is correct and unambiguous; if there are more than two units of measure in the expression, use dot products and negative exponents to avoid ambiguity. (See 18.3.2, Mathematical Composition, Expressing Multiplication and Division.)

> 6 mL/kg per minute or 6 mL·kg^{-1}·min^{-1} (*not* 6 mL/kg/min)

15.4.2 *Hyphen.*—Use hyphens to join a unit of measure and the number associated with it when these are used as adjectives. (See 6.12.1, Hyphen, Temporary Compounds.)

> an 8-L container   a 10-mm strip

For use of hyphens in spelled-out numbers, see 16.1.1, Numbers and Percentages, Beginning a Sentence, and 16.2.2, Numbers and Percentages, Fractions.

15.5 Subject-Verb Agreement.—Treat units of measure as collective singular nouns, not plural.

> Five milligrams was [not *were*] given immediately.

15.6 Dosage.—Drug dosages will continue to be expressed in *conventional metric units*, although it is possible that, at some time in the future, drug dosages will also be expressed in SI units. Avoid *teaspoonfuls* and the apothecary *ounces*, *drams*, and *grains*. In some instances, *drops* is acceptable.

> The drug was given intravenously, 0.1 L of a 2% solution at a rate of 30 drops per minute.

15.7 Solution.—To show the concentration of a solution in relation to normality, use the abbreviation "N" and constructions in accordance with the following examples:

> normal   N
>
> twice normal   2N
>
> half normal   0.5N or N/2

Note: A *normal* solution is one having a concentration equivalent to a gram-equivalent of solute per liter. A *molar* solution is one containing 1 gram-molecular weight (mole) in 1 L of solution. The SI style for reporting molar is mol/L (not M); for millimolar, mmol/L (not mM); and for micromolar, μmol/L (not μM).

15.8   Volume.—Use the liter to show volume of liquid or gas. For measurements of a volume of solids, use cubic meters (m^3) or submultiples thereof.

> The gas flow was 3 L/min.

> Each of the polystyrene microspheres had a volume of 0.35×10^{-9} μm^3.

15.9   Fractions vs Decimals.—The decimal form of numbers should be used when a fraction is given with an abbreviated unit of measure (eg, 0.9 L, 5.8 mm) or when a precise measurement is intended. Mixed fractions may be used instead of decimals for less precise measurements (eg, 8½ × 11-in paper, 3⅓ hours, 5¾ years). (These will be almost exclusively with units of measure representing time.)

15.10   Conversion Tables.—Table 4 gives conversions to SI units for hematology and clinical chemistry measurements. Table 5 gives conversions from English to metric measures.

Table 4.—Examples of Conversions to Système International (SI) Units*

System†	Component	Present Reference Intervals (Examples)‡	Present Unit	Conversion Factor	SI Reference Intervals‡	SI Unit Symbols§	Significant Digits‖	Suggested Minimum Increment
		Hematology						
(B) Ercs	Erythrocyte sedimentation rate							
	Female	0-30	mm/hr	1	0-30	mm/h	XX	
	Male	0-20	mm/hr	1	0-20	mm/h	XX	
B	Hematocrit							
	Female	33-43	%	0.01	0.33-0.43	1	0.XX	
	Male	39-49	%	0.01	0.39-0.49	1	0.XX	
B	Hemoglobin Mass concentration							
	Female	12.0-15.0	g/dL	10	120-150	g/L	XXX	
	Male	13.6-17.2	g/dL	10	136-172	g/L	XXX	
	Substance concentration (Hb [Fe])							
	Female	12.0-15.0	g/dL	0.6206	7.45-9.31	mmol/L	XX.XX	
	Male	13.6-17.2	g/dL	0.6206	8.44-10.67	mmol/L	XX.XX	
(B) Ercs	Mean corpuscular hemoglobin Mass concentration	27-33	pg	1	27-33	pg	XX	
	Substance concentration (Hb [Fe])	27-33	pg	0.06206	1.68-2.05	fmol	X.XX	

(B) Ercs	Mean corpuscular hemoglobin concentration						
	Mass concentration	33-37	g/dL	10	330-370	g/L	XX0
	Substance concentration (Hb [Fe])	33-37	g/dL	0.6206	20-23	mmol/L	XX
(B) Ercs	Mean corpuscular volume Erythrocyte volume	76-100	cu μm	1	76-100	fL	XXX
B	Red blood cell count (erythrocytes) Female	3.5-5.0	10^6/cu mm	1	3.5-5.0	10^{12}/L	X.X
	Male	4.3-5.9	10^6/cu mm	1	4.3-5.9	10^{12}/L	X.X
(Sf) Ercs	Red blood cell count	0	/cu mm	1	0	10^6/L	XX
B	Reticulocyte count (adults)	10 000-75 000	/cu mm	0.001	10-75	10^9/L	XX
	Number fraction	1-24	0/00 (No. per 1000 erythrocytes)	1	1-24	10^{-3}	XX
		0.1-2.4	%	10	1-24	10^{-3}	XX
B	Thrombocytes (platelets)	150-450	10^3/cu mm	1	150-450	10^9/L	XXX
(B) Lkcs	White blood cell count	3200-9800	/cu mm	0.001	3.2-9.8	10^9/L	XX.X
	Number fraction (differential)	. . .	%	0.01	. . .	1	0.XX
(Sf) Lkcs	White blood cell count	0-5	/cu mm	1	0-5	10^6/L	XX

Clinical Chemistry

P	Acetaminophen Toxic	>5.0	mg/dL	66.16	>300	μmol/L	XX0	10 μmol/L

Table 4.—Examples of Conversions to Système International (SI) Units* (cont)

System†	Component	Present Reference Intervals (Examples)‡	Present Unit	Conversion Factor	SI Reference Intervals‡	SI Unit Symbol§	Significant Digits‖	Suggested Minimum Increment
S	Acetoacetic acid	0.3-3.0	mg/dL	97.95	30-300	µmol/L	XX0	10 µmol/L
B, S	Acetone	Negative	mg/dL	172.2	Negative	µmol/L	XX0	10 µmol/L
P	Adrenocorticotropin (ACTH): see *Corticotropin*							
S	Alanine aminotransferase (ALT)	0-35 (37°C)	Units/L	1.00	0-35	U/L	XX	1 U/L
			Karmen units/mL	0.482	...	U/L	XX	1 U/L
			Reitmann-Frankel units/mL	0.482	...	U/L	XX	1 U/L
S	Albumin	4.0-6.0	g/dL	10.0	40-60	g/L	XX	1 g/L
S	Aldolase	0-6 (37°C)	Units/L	1.00	0-6	U/L	XX	1 U/L
			Sibley-Lehninger units/mL	0.7440	...	U/L	XX	1 U/L
S	Aldosterone Normal salt diet	8.1-15.5	ng/dL	27.74	220-430	pmol/L	XX0	10 pmol/L
	Restricted salt diet	20.8-44.4	ng/dL	27.74	580-1240	pmol/L	XX0	10 pmol/L
U	Aldosterone, sodium excretion = 25 mmol/24 h	18-85	µg/24 hr	2.774	50-235	nmol/d	XXX	5 nmol/d
	= 75-125 mmol/24 h	5-26	µg/24 hr	2.774	15-70	nmol/d	XXX	5 nmol/d
	= 200 nmol/24 h	1.5-12.5	µg/24 hr	2.774	5-35	nmol/d	XXX	5 nmol/d

S	α₁-Antitrypsin	150-350	mg/dL	0.01	1.5-3.5	g/L	X.X	0.1 g/L
S	α-Fetoprotein, radioimmunoassay	0-20	ng/mL	1.00	0-20	μg/L	XX	1 μg/L
Amf	α-Fetoprotein	Depends on gestation	mg/dL	10	Depends on gestation	mg/L	XX	1 mg/L
S	α₂-Macroglobulin	145-410	mg/dL	0.01	1.5-4.1	g/L	X.X	0.1 g/L
S	Aluminum	0-15	μg/L	37.06	0-560	nmol/L	XX0	10 nmol/L
P	Amino acid fractionation Alanine	2.2-4.5	mg/dL	112.2	245-500	μmol/L	XXX	5 μmol/L
	α-Aminobutyric acid	0.1-0.2	mg/dL	96.97	10-20	μmol/L	XXX	5 μmol/L
	Arginine	0.5-2.5	mg/dL	57.40	30-145	μmol/L	XXX	5 μmol/L
	Asparagine	0.5-0.6	mg/dL	75.69	35-45	μmol/L	XXX	5 μmol/L
	Aspartic acid	0.0-0.3	mg/dL	75.13	0-20	μmol/L	XXX	5 μmol/L
	Citrulline	0.2-1.0	mg/dL	57.08	15-55	μmol/L	XXX	5 μmol/L
	Cystine	0.2-2.2	mg/dL	41.61	10-90	μmol/L	XXX	5 μmol/L
	Glutamic acid	0.2-2.8	mg/dL	67.97	15-190	μmol/L	XXX	5 μmol/L
	Glutamine	6.1-10.2	mg/dL	68.42	420-700	μmol/L	XXX	5 μmol/L
	Glycine	0.9-4.2	mg/dL	133.2	120-560	μmol/L	XXX	5 μmol/L
	Histidine	0.5-1.7	mg/dL	64.45	30-110	μmol/L	XXX	5 μmol/L
	Hydroxyproline	0-trace	mg/dL	76.26	0-trace	μmol/L	XXX	5 μmol/L
	Isoleucine	0.5-1.3	mg/dL	76.24	40-100	μmol/L	XXX	5 μmol/L

Table 4.—Examples of Conversions to Système International (SI) Units* (cont)

System†	Component	Present Reference Intervals (Examples)‡	Present Unit	Conversion Factor	SI Reference Intervals‡	SI Unit Symbol§	Signifi- cant Digits‖	Suggested Minimum Increment
	Amino acid fractionation (cont)							
	Leucine	1.0-2.3	mg/dL	76.24	75-175	μmol/L	XXX	5 μmol/L
	Lysine	1.2-3.5	mg/dL	68.40	80-240	μmol/L	XXX	5 μmol/L
	Methionine	0.1-0.6	mg/dL	67.02	5-40	μmol/L	XXX	5 μmol/L
	Ornithine	0.4-1.4	mg/dL	75.67	30-400	μmol/L	XXX	5 μmol/L
	Phenylalanine	0.6-1.5	mg/dL	60.54	35-90	μmol/L	XXX	5 μmol/L
	Proline	1.2-3.9	mg/dL	86.86	105-340	μmol/L	XXX	5 μmol/L
	Serine	0.8-1.8	mg/dL	95.16	75-170	μmol/L	XXX	5 μmol/L
	Taurine	0.3-2.1	mg/dL	79.91	25-170	μmol/L	XXX	5 μmol/L
	Threonine	0.9-2.5	mg/dL	83.95	75-210	μmol/L	XXX	5 μmol/L
	Tryptophan	0.5-2.5	mg/dL	48.97	25-125	μmol/L	XXX	5 μmol/L
	Tyrosine	0.4-1.6	mg/dL	55.19	20-90	μmol/L	XXX	5 μmol/L
	Valine	1.7-3.7	mg/dL	85.36	145-315	μmol/L	XXX	5 μmol/L
U	Amino acid nitrogen	...	mg/24 hr	0.07139	...	mmol/d	...	...
P	Amino acid nitrogen	...	mg/dL	0.7139	...	mmol/L	...	...
U	δ-Aminolevulinate (as aminolevulinic acid)	1.0-7.0	mg/24 hr	7.626	8-53	μmol/d	XX	1 μmol/d

	Component	Conventional reference interval	Conventional unit	Factor	SI reference interval	SI unit	Significant digits	Suggested minimum increment
P, S	Amitriptyline, therapeutic	50-200	ng/mL	3.605	180-720	nmol/L	XX0	10 nmol/L
V, P	Ammonia							
	As ammonia (NH_3)	10-80	µg/dL	0.5872	5-50	µmol/L	XXX	5 µmol/L
	As ammonium (NH_4^+)	10-85	µg/dL	0.5543	5-50	µmol/L	XXX	5 µmol/L
	As nitrogen (N)	10-65	µg/dL	0.7139	5-50	µmol/L	XXX	5 µmol/L
S	Amylase, enzymatic	0-130 (37°C)	Units/L	1.00	0-130	U/L	XXX	1 U/L
	Roche dye unit	...	Dye units/dL	1.59	...	U/L	...	...
	Somogyi/Caraway	50-150	Somogyi units/dL	1.850	100-300	U/L	XX0	10 U/L
	Street Close	...	Street Close units/dL	5.7	...	U/L	...	...
S	Androstenedione Male >18 y	0.2-3.0	µg/L	3.492	0.5-10.5	nmol/L	XX.X	0.5 nmol/L
	Female >18 y	0.8-3.0	µg/L	3.492	3.0-10.5	nmol/L	XX.X	0.5 nmol/L
S	Angiotensin converting enzyme	<40	nmol/mL/min	16.67	<670	$nmol \cdot L^{-1} \cdot s^{-1}$	XX0	10 $nmol \cdot L^{-1} \cdot s^{-1}$
H	Arsenic (as As)	<1	µg/d (ppm)	13.35	<13	nmol/g	XXX.X	0.5 nmol/g
U	Arsenic As As	0-5	µg/24 hr	13.35	0-67	nmol/d	XX	1 nmol/d
	As As_2O_3	<25	µg/dL	0.0505	<1.3	µmol/L	XX.X	0.1 µmol/L
P	Ascorbate (as ascorbic acid)	>0.5	mg/dL	56.78	>30	µmol/L	X0	10 µmol/L
S	Aspartate aminotransferase (AST)	0-35 (37°C)	Units/L	1.00	0-35	U/L	XX	1 U/L

Table 4.—Examples of Conversions to Système International (SI) Units* (cont)

System†	Component	Present Reference Intervals (Examples)‡	Present Unit	Conversion Factor	SI Reference Intervals‡	SI Unit Symbol§	Significant Digits‖	Suggested Minimum Increment
	Aspartate aminotransferase (AST) (cont)							
			Karmen units/mL	0.482	...	U/L	XX	1 U/L
			Reitmann-Frankel units/mL	0.482	...	U/L	XX	1 U/L
S	Barbiturate, overdose Total expressed as Phenobarbital	Depends on composition of mixture; usually not known	mg/dL	43.06	...	μmol/L	XX	5 μmol/L
	Phenobarbital sodium		mg/dL	39.34	...	μmol/L	XX	5 μmol/L
	Barbitone		mg/dL	54.29	...	μmol/L	XX	5 μmol/L
S	Barbiturate, therapeutic: see Pentobarbital, Phenobarbital, Thiopental							
S	Bile acids Total (as chenodeoxycholic acid)	Trace-3.3	mg/L	2.547	Trace-8.4	μmol/L	X.X	0.2 μmol/L
	Chenodeoxycholic acid	Trace-1.3	mg/L	2.547	Trace-3.4	μmol/L	X.X	0.2 μmol/L
	Cholic acid	Trace-1.0	mg/L	2.448	Trace-2.4	μmol/L	X.X	0.2 μmol/L
	Deoxycholic acid	Trace-1.0	mg/L	2.547	Trace-2.6	μmol/L	X.X	0.2 μmol/L
	Lithocholic acid	Trace	mg/L	2.656	Trace	μmol/L	X.X	0.2 μmol/L

Df	Bile acids (after cholecystokinin stimulation) Total (as chenodeoxycholic acid)	14.0-58.0	mg/mL	2.547	35.0-148.0	mmol/L	XX.X	0.2 mmol/L
	Chenodeoxycholic acid	4.0-24.0	mg/mL	2.547	10.0-61.4	mmol/L	XX.X	0.2 mmol/L
	Cholic acid	2.4-33.0	mg/mL	2.448	6.8-81.0	mmol/L	XX.X	0.2 mmol/L
	Deoxycholic acid	0.8-6.9	mg/mL	2.547	2.0-18.0	mmol/L	XX.X	0.2 mmol/L
	Lithocholic acid	0.3-0.8	mg/mL	2.656	0.8-2.0	mmol/L	XX.X	0.2 mmol/L
S	Bilirubin Total	0.1-1.0	mg/dL	17.10	2-18	μmol/L	XX	2 μmol/L
	Conjugated	0.0-0.2	mg/dL	17.10	0-4	μmol/L	XX	2 μmol/L
S	Bromide, toxic As bromide ion	>120	mg/dL	0.1252	>15	mmol/L	XX	1 mmol/L
	As sodium bromide	>150	mg/dL	0.09719	>15	mmol/L	XX	1 mmol/L
		>15	mEq/L	1.00	>15	mmol/L	XX	1 mmol/L
S	Cadmium	<3	μg/dL	0.08897	<0.3	μmol/L	X.X	0.1 μmol/L
S	Calcitonin	...	pg/mL	1.00	...	ng/L	XXX	10 ng/L
S	Calcium Male	8.8-10.3	mg/dL	0.2495	2.20-2.58	mmol/L	X.XX	0.02 mmol/L
	Female <50 y	8.8-10.0	mg/dL	0.2495	2.20-2.50	mmol/L	X.XX	0.02 mmol/L
	Female ≥50 y	8.8-10.2	mg/dL	0.2495	2.20-2.56	mmol/L	X.XX	0.02 mmol/L
			mEq/L	0.500	...	mmol/L	X.XX	0.02 mmol/L
S	Calcium, ionized	2.00-2.30	mEq/L	0.500	1.00-1.15	mmol/L	X.XX	0.01 mmol/L

Table 4.—Examples of Conversions to Système International (SI) Units* (cont)

System†	Component	Present Reference Intervals (Examples)‡	Present Unit	Conversion Factor	SI Reference Intervals‡	SI Unit Symbol§	Significant Digits‖	Suggested Minimum Increment
U	Calcium, normal diet	<250	mg/24 hr	0.02495	<6.2	mmol/d	X.X	0.1 mmol/d
P	Carbamazepine, therapeutic	4.0-10.0	mg/L	4.233	17-42	µmol/L	XX	1 µmol/L
B, P, S	Carbon dioxide content (bicarbonate + CO_2)	22-28	mEq/L	1.00	22-28	mmol/L	XX	1 mmol/L
B	Carbon monoxide (proportion of Hb that is COHb)	<15	%	0.01	<0.15	1	X.XX	0.01
S	Carotenes, beta	50-250	µg/dL	0.01863	0.9-4.6	µmol/L	X.X	0.1 µmol/L
U	Catecholamines (total, as norepinephrine)	<120	µg/24 hr	5.911	<675	nmol/d	XX0	10 nmol/d
S	Ceruloplasmin	20-35	mg/dL	10.0	200-350	mg/L	XX0	10 mg/L
P	Chlordiazepoxide Therapeutic	0.5-5.0	mg/L	3.336	2-17	µmol/L	XX	1 µmol/L
	Toxic	>10.0	mg/L	3.336	>33	µmol/L	XX	1 µmol/L
S	Chloride	95-105	mEq/L	1.00	95-105	mmol/L	XXX	1 mmol/L
P	Chlorpromazine	50-300	ng/mL	3.136	150-950	nmol/L	XX0	10 nmol/L
P	Chlorpropamide, therapeutic	75-250	mg/L	3.613	270-900	µmol/L	XX0	10 µmol/L
P	Cholestanol, as a fraction of total cholesterol	1-3	%	0.01	0.01-0.03	1	X.XX	0.01

		Conventional	Conventional unit	Factor	SI	SI unit	Sig. digits	Minimum increment
P	Cholesterol ≤29 y	<200	mg/dL	0.02586	<5.20	mmol/L	X.XX	0.05 mmol/L
	30-39 y	<225	mg/dL	0.02586	<5.85	mmol/L	X.XX	0.05 mmol/L
	40-49 y	<245	mg/dL	0.02586	<6.35	mmol/L	X.XX	0.05 mmol/L
	≥50 y	<265	mg/dL	0.02586	<6.85	mmol/L	X.XX	0.05 mmol/L
P	Cholesterol esters, as a fraction of total cholesterol	60-75	%	0.01	0.60-0.75	1	X.XX	0.01
S	Cholinesterase	620-1370 (25°C)	Units/L	1.00	620-1370	U/L	XXX0	10 U/L
P	Chorionic gonadotropin (β-HCG)	Negative if not pregnant	mIU/mL	1.00	Negative if not pregnant	IU/L	XX	1 IU/L
B	Citrate (as citric acid)	1.2-3.0	mg/dL	52.05	60-160	μmol/L	XXX	5 μmol/L
P	Clomipramine (includes desmethyl metabolite)	50-400	ng/mL	3.176	150-1270	nmol/L	XX0	10 nmol/L
S	Complement, C3	70-160	mg/dL	0.01	0.7-1.6	g/L	X.X	0.1 g/L
S	Complement, C4	20-40	mg/dL	0.01	0.2-0.4	g/L	X.X	0.1 g/L
S	Copper	70-140	μg/dL	0.1574	11.0-22.0	μmol/L	XX.X	0.2 μmol/L
U	Copper	<40	μg/24 hr	0.01574	<0.6	μmol/d	X.X	0.2 μmol/d
U	Coproporphyrins	<200	μg/24 hr	1.527	<300	nmol/d	XX0	10 nmol/d
P	Corticotropin (ACTH)	20-100	pg/mL	0.2202	4-22	pmol/L	XX	1 pmol/L
S	Cortisol 8 AM	4-19	μg/dL	27.59	110-520	nmol/L	XX0	10 nmol/L

Table 4.—Examples of Conversions to Système International (SI) Units* (cont)

System†	Component	Present Reference Intervals (Examples)‡	Present Unit	Conversion Factor	SI Reference Intervals‡	SI Unit Symbol§	Significant Digits‖	Suggested Minimum Increment
	Cortisol (cont)							
	4 PM	2-15	μg/dL	27.59	50-410	nmol/L	XX0	10 nmol/L
	Midnight	<5	μg/dL	27.59	<140	nmol/L	XX0	10 nmol/L
U	Cortisol (free)	10-110	μg/24 hr	2.759	30-300	nmol/d	XX0	10 nmol/d
S	Creatine Male	0.17-0.50	mg/dL	76.25	10-40	μmol/L	X0	10 μmol/L
	Female	0.35-0.93	mg/dL	76.25	30-70	μmol/L	X0	10 μmol/L
U	Creatine Male	0-40	mg/24 hr	7.625	0-300	μmol/d	XX0	10 μmol/d
	Female	0-80	mg/24 hr	7.625	0-600	μmol/d	XX0	10 μmol/d
S	Creatine kinase (CK)	0-130 (37°C)	Units/L	1.00	0-130	U/L	XXX	1 U/L
S	Creatine kinase isoenzymes, MB fraction	>5 in myocardial infarction	%	0.01	>0.05	1	X.XX	0.01
S	Creatinine	0.6-1.2	mg/dL	88.40	50-110	μmol/L	XX0	10 μmol/L
U	Creatinine	Variable	g/24 hr	8.840	Variable	mmol/d	XX.X	0.1 mmol/d
S, U	Creatinine clearance‖	75-125	mL/min	0.01667	1.24-2.08	mL/s	X.XX	0.02 mL/s
B	Cyanide, lethal	>0.10	mg/dL	384.3	>40	μmol/L	XXX	5 μmol/L
S	Cyanocobalamin (vitamin B₁₂)	200-1000	pg/mL	0.7378	150-750	pmol/L	XX0	10 pmol/L

		Conventional range	Conventional units	Factor	SI range	SI units		Increment
S	Cyclic adenosine monophosphate	2.6-6.6	µg/L	3.038	8-20	nmol/L	XXX	1 nmol/L
U	Cyclic adenosine monophosphate Total urinary	2.9-5.6	µmole/g of creatinine	113.1	330-630	nmol/mmol of creatinine	XX0	10 nmol/mmol of creatinine
	Renal tubular	<2.5	µmole/g of creatinine	113.1	<280	nmol/mmol of creatinine	XX0	10 nmol/mmol of creatinine
S	Cyclic guanosine monophosphate	0.6-3.5	µg/L	2.897	1.7-10.1	nmol/L	XX.X	0.1 nmol/L
U	Cyclic guanosine monophosphate	0.3-1.8	µmol/g of creatinine	113.1	30-200	nmol/mmol of creatinine	XX0	10 nmol/mmol of creatinine
U	Cystine	10-100	mg/24 hr	4.161	40-420	µmol/d	XX0	10 µmol/d
P, S	Dehydroepiandrosterone (DHEA) 1-4 y	0.2-0.4	µg/L	3.467	0.6-1.4	nmol/L	XX.X	0.2 nmol/L
	4-8 y	0.1-1.9	µg/L	3.467	0.4-6.6	nmol/L	XX.X	0.2 nmol/L
	8-10 y	0.2-2.9	µg/L	3.467	0.6-10.0	nmol/L	XX.X	0.2 nmol/L
	10-12 y	0.5-9.2	µg/L	3.467	1.8-31.8	nmol/L	XX.X	0.2 nmol/L
	12-14 y	0.9-20.0	µg/L	3.467	3.2-69.4	nmol/L	XX.X	0.2 nmol/L
	14-16 y	2.5-20.0	µg/L	3.467	8.6-69.4	nmol/L	XX.X	0.2 nmol/L
	Premenopausal female	2.0-15.0	µg/L	3.467	7.0-52.0	nmol/L	XX.X	0.2 nmol/L
	Male	0.8-10.0	µg/L	3.467	2.8-34.6	nmol/L	XX.X	0.2 nmol/L

15.10 Conversion Tables

Table 4.—Examples of Conversions to Système International (SI) Units* (cont)

System†	Component	Present Reference Intervals (Examples)‡	Present Unit	Conversion Factor	SI Reference Intervals‡	SI Unit Symbol§	Significant Digits‖	Suggested Minimum Increment
U	Dehydroepiandrosterone: see Steroids, ketosteroid fractions							
P, S	Dehydroepiandrosterone sulfate (DHEA-S)							
	Newborn	1670-3640	ng/mL	0.002714	4.5-9.9	µmol/L	XX.X	0.1 µmol/L
	Prepubertal children	100-600	ng/mL	0.002714	0.3-1.6	µmol/L	XX.X	0.1 µmol/L
	Male	2000-3350	ng/mL	0.002714	5.4-9.1	µmol/L	XX.X	0.1 µmol/L
	Female Premenopausal	820-3380	ng/mL	0.002714	2.2-9.2	µmol/L	XX.X	0.1 µmol/L
	Postmenopausal	100-610	ng/mL	0.002714	0.3-1.7	µmol/L	XX.X	0.1 µmol/L
	Pregnancy (term)	230-1170	ng/mL	0.002714	0.6-3.2	µmol/L	XX.X	0.1 µmol/L
S	11-Deoxycortisol	0-2	µg/dL	28.86	0-60	nmol/L	XX0	10 nmol/L
P	Desipramine, therapeutic	50-200	ng/mL	3.754	170-700	nmol/L	XX0	10 nmol/L
P	Diazepam Therapeutic	0.1-0.25	mg/L	3512	350-900	nmol/L	XX0	10 nmol/L
	Toxic	>1.0	mg/L	3512	>3510	nmol/L	XX0	10 nmol/L
P	Dicoumarol, therapeutic	8-30	mg/L	2.974	25-90	µmol/L	XX	5 µmol/L
P	Digoxin Therapeutic	0.5-2.2	ng/mL	1.281	0.6-2.8	nmol/L	X.X	0.1 nmol/L
		0.5-2.2	µg/L	1.281	0.6-2.8	nmol/L	X.X	0.1 nmol/L

	Toxic	>2.5	ng/mL	1.281	>3.2	nmol/L	X.X	0.1 nmol/L
P	Dimethadione, therapeutic	<1.00	g/L	7.745	<7.7	mmol/L	X.X	0.1 mmol/L
P	Diphenylhydantoin: see *Phenytoin*							
P	Disopyramide, therapeutic	2.0-6.0	mg/L	2.946	6-18	µmol/L	XX	1 µmol/L
P	Doxepin, therapeutic	50-200	ng/mL	3.579	180-720	nmol/L	XX0	10 nmol/L
S	Electrophoresis, protein Albumin	60-65	%	0.01	0.60-0.65	1	X.XX	0.01
	Alpha 1	1.7-5.0	%	0.01	0.02-0.05	1	X.XX	0.01
	Alpha 2	6.7-12.5	%	0.01	0.07-0.13	1	X.XX	0.01
	Beta	8.3-16.3	%	0.01	0.08-0.16	1	X.XX	0.01
	Gamma	10.7-20.0	%	0.01	0.11-0.20	1	X.XX	0.01
	Albumin	3.6-5.2	g/dL	10.0	36-52	g/L	XX	1 g/L
	Alpha 1	0.1-0.4	g/dL	10.0	1-4	g/L	XX	1 g/L
	Alpha 2	0.4-1.0	g/dL	10.0	4-10	g/L	XX	1 g/L
	Beta	0.5-1.2	g/dL	10.0	5-12	g/L	XX	1 g/L
	Gamma	0.6-1.6	g/dL	10.0	6-16	g/L	XX	1 g/L
P	Epinephrine (radioenzymatic procedure)	31-95 (at rest for 15 min)	pg/mL	5.458	170-520	pmol/L	XX0	10 pmol/L
U	Epinephrine (fluorimetric procedure)	<10	µg/24 hr	5.458	<55	nmol/d	XX	5 nmol/d
S	Estradiol, male >18 y	15-40	pg/mL	3.671	55-150	pmol/L	XXX	1 pmol/L

Table 4.—Examples of Conversions to Système International (SI) Units* (cont)

System†	Component	Present Reference Intervals (Examples)‡	Present Unit	Conversion Factor	SI Reference Intervals‡	SI Unit Symbol§	Significant Digits‖	Suggested Minimum Increment
U	Estriol (nonpregnant) Onset of menstruation	4-25	µg/24 hr	3.468	15-85	nmol/d	XXX	5 nmol/d
	Ovulation peak	28-99	µg/24 hr	3.468	95-345	nmol/d	XXX	5 nmol/d
	Luteal peak	22-105	µg/24 hr	3.468	75-365	nmol/d	XXX	5 nmol/d
	Menopausal women	1.4-19.6	µg/24 hr	3.468	5-70	nmol/d	XXX	5 nmol/d
	Male	5-18	µg/24 hr	3.468	15-60	nmol/d	XXX	5 nmol/d
S	Estrogens (as estradiol) Female	20-300	pg/mL	3.671	70-1100	pmol/L	XXX0	10 pmol/L
	Peak production	200-800	pg/mL	3.671	750-2900	pmol/L	XXX0	10 pmol/L
	Male	<50	pg/mL	3.671	<180	pmol/L	XX0	10 pmol/L
U	Estrogens, placental (as estriol)	Depends on period of gestation	mg/24 hr	3.468	Depends on period of gestation	µmol/d	XXX	1 µmol/d
T	Estrogen receptors Negative	0-3	fmole of estradiol bound/mg of cytosol protein	1.00	0-3	fmol of estradiol bound/ mg of cytosol protein	XXX	1 fmol/mg of protein

								Minimum increment
	Doubtful	4-10	fmole of estradiol bound/mg of cytosol protein	1.00	4-10	fmol of estradiol bound/mg of cytosol protein	XXX	1 fmol/mg of protein
	Positive	>10	fmole of estradiol bound/mg of cytosol protein	1.00	>10	fmol of estradiol bound/mg of cytosol protein	XXX	1 fmol/mg of protein
P, S	Estrone Female 1-10 Days of cycle	43-180	pg/mL	3.699	160-665	pmol/L	XXX	5 pmol/L
	11-20 Days of cycle	75-196	pg/mL	3.699	275-725	pmol/L	XXX	5 pmol/L
	21-30 Days of cycle	131-201	pg/mL	3.699	485-745	pmol/L	XXX	5 pmol/L
	Male	29-75	pg/mL	3.699	105-275	pmol/L	XXX	5 pmol/L
U	Estrone, female	2-25	µg/24 hr	3.699	5-90	nmol/d	XXX	5 nmol/d
P	Ethchlorvynol, toxic	>40	mg/L	6.915	>280	µmol/L	XX0	10 µmol/L
P	Ethosuximide, therapeutic	40-110	mg/L	7.084	280-780	µmol/L	XX0	10 µmol/L
P	Ethyl alcohol	100	mg/dL	0.2171	17-22	mmol/L	XX	1 mmol/L
P	Ethylene glycol, toxic	>30	mg/dL	0.1611	>5	mmol/L	XX	1 mmol/L
P	Fatty acids, nonesterified	8-20	mg/dL	10.00	80-200	mg/L	XX0	10 mg/L
F	Fecal fat (as stearic acid)	2.0-6.0	g/24 hr	3.515	7-21	mmol/d	XX	1 mmol/d
S	Ferritin	18-300	ng/mL	1.00	18-300	µg/L	XX0	10 µg/L

Table 4.—Examples of Conversions to Système International (SI) Units* (cont)

System†	Component	Present Reference Intervals (Examples)‡	Present Unit	Conversion Factor	SI Reference Intervals‡	SI Unit Symbols§	Significant Digits‖	Suggested Minimum Increment
P	Fibrinogen	200-400	mg/dL	0.01	2.0-4.0	g/L	X.X	0.1 g/L
U	Fluoride	<1.0	mg/24 hr	52.63	<50	μmol/d	XX0	10 μmol/d
Ercs	Folate	140-960	ng/mL	2.266	550-2200	nmol/L	XX0	10 nmol/L
S	Folate (as pteroylglutamic acid)	2-10	ng/ml	2.266	4-22	nmol/L	XX	2 nmol/L
			μg/dL	22.66	...	nmol/L	...	2 nmol/L
P	Follicle-stimulating hormone (FSH)							
	Female							
	Follicular phase	2.0-15.0	mIU/mL	1.00	2-15	IU/L	XX	1 IU/L
	Peak production	20-50	mIU/mL	1.00	20-50	IU/L	XX	1 IU/L
	Male	1.0-10.0	mIU/mL	1.00	1-10	IU/L	XX	1 IU/L
U	Follicle-stimulating hormone (FSH)							
	Follicular phase	2-15	IU/24 hr	1.00	2-15	IU/d	XXX	1 IU/d
	Midcycle	8-40	IU/24 hr	1.00	8-40	IU/d	XXX	1 IU/d
	Luteal phase	2-10	IU/24 hr	1.00	2-10	IU/d	XXX	1 IU/d
	Menopausal women	35-100	IU/24 hr	1.00	35-100	IU/d	XXX	1 IU/d
	Male	2-15	IU/24 hr	1.00	2-15	IU/d	XXX	1 IU/d
P	Fructose	<10	mg/dL	0.05551	<0.6	mmol/L	X.X	0.1 mmol/L

P	Galactose (children)	<20	mg/dL	0.05551	<1.1	mmol/L	X.X	0.1 mmol/L
B	Gases (arterial) Po$_2$	75-105	mm Hg	0.1333	10.0-14.0	kPa	XX.X	0.1 kPa
	Pco$_2$	33-44	mm Hg	0.1333	4.4-5.9	kPa	X.X	0.1 kPa
S	γ-Glutamyltransferase (GGT)	0-30 (30°C)	Units/L	1.00	0-30	U/L	XX	1 U/L
S	Gastrin	0-180	pg/mL	1	0-180	ng/L	XX0	10 ng/L
S	Globulins: see *Immunoglobulins*							
S	Glucagon	50-100	pg/mL	1	50-100	ng/L	XX0	10 ng/L
P	Glucose (fasting)	70-110	mg/dL	0.05551	3.9-6.1	mmol/L	XX.X	0.1 mmol/L
Sf	Glucose	50-80	mg/dL	0.05551	2.8-4.4	mmol/L	XX.X	0.1 mmol/L
P	Glutethimide Therapeutic	<10	mg/L	4.603	<46	μmol/L	XX	1 μmol/L
	Toxic	>20	mg/L	4.603	>92	μmol/L	XX	1 μmol/L
S	Glycerol (free)	<1.5	mg/dL	0.1086	<0.16	mmol/L	X.XX	0.01 mmol/L
S	Gold, therapeutic	300-800	μg/dL	0.05077	15.0-40.0	μmol/L	XX.X	0.1 μmol/L
U	Gold	<500	μg/24 hr	0.005077	<2.5	μmol/d	X.X	0.1 μmol/d
P, S	Growth hormone Male (fasting)	0-5	ng/mL	1.00	0-5	μg/L	XX.X	0.5 μg/L
	Female (fasting)	0-10	ng/mL	1.00	0-10	μg/L	XX.X	0.5 μg/L
S	Haptoglobin	50-220	mg/dL	0.01	0.50-2.20	g/L	X.XX	0.01 g/L
B	Hemoglobin Male	14.0-18.0	g/dL	10.0	140-180	g/L	XXX	1 g/L

Table 4.—Examples of Conversions to Système International (SI) Units* (cont)

System†	Component	Present Reference Intervals (Examples)‡	Present Unit	Conversion Factor	SI Reference Intervals‡	SI Unit Symbol§	Significant Digits‖	Suggested Minimum Increment
	Hemoglobin (cont) Female	11.5-15.5	g/dL	10.0	115-155	g/L	XXX	1 g/L
U	Homogentisate (as homogentistic acid)	Negative	mg/24 hr	5.947	Negative	μmol/d	XX	5 μmol/d
U	Homovanillate (as homovanillic acid)	<8	mg/24 hr	5.489	<45	μmol/d	XX	5 μmol/d
S	β-Hydroxybutyrate (as β-hydroxybutyric acid)	<1.0	mg/dL	96.05	<100	μmol/L	XX0	10 μmol/L
U	5-Hydroxyindoleacetate (as 5-hydroxyindoleacetic acid [5-HIAA])	2-8	mg/24 hr	5.230	10-40	μmol/d	XXX	5 μmol/d
S, P	17-α-Hydroxyprogesterone Children	0.2-1.4	μg/L	3.026	0.5-4.5	nmol/L	XX.X	0.5 nmol/L
	Male	0.5-2.5	μg/L	3.026	1.5-7.5	nmol/L	XX.X	0.5 nmol/L
	Female	0.3-4.2	μg/L	3.026	1.0-13.0	nmol/L	XX.X	0.5 nmol/L
	Female, postmenopausal	0.3-1.7	μg/L	3.026	1.0-5.0	nmol/L	XX.X	0.5 nmol/L
U	Hydroxyproline 1 wk-1 y	55-220	mg/24 hr/sq m	7.626	420-1680	μmol·d^{-1}·m^{-2}	XX0	10 μmol·d^{-1}·m^{-2}

	1-13 y	25-80	mg/24 hr/sq m	7.626	190-610	$\mu mol \cdot d^{-1} \cdot m^{-2}$	XX0	10 $\mu mol \cdot d^{-1} \cdot m^{-2}$
	22-65 y	6-22	mg/24 hr/sq m	7.626	40-170	$\mu mol \cdot d^{-1} \cdot m^{-2}$	XX0	10 $\mu mol \cdot d^{-1} \cdot m^{-2}$
	≥66 y	5-17	mg/24 hr/sq m	7.626	40-130	$\mu mol \cdot d^{-1} \cdot m^{-2}$	XX0	10 $\mu mol \cdot d^{-1} \cdot m^{-2}$
P	Imipramine, therapeutic	50-200	ng/mL	3.566	180-710	nmol/L	XX0	10 nmol/L
S	Immunoglobulins IgG	500-1200	mg/dL	0.01	5.00-12.00	g/L	XX.XX	0.01 g/L
	IgA	50-350	mg/dL	0.01	0.50-3.50	g/L	XX.XX	0.01 g/L
	IgM	30-230	mg/dL	0.01	0.30-2.30	g/L	XX.XX	0.01 g/L
	IgD	<6	mg/dL	10	<60	mg/L	XX0	10 mg/L
	IgE 0-3 y	0.5-1.0	Units/mL	2.4	1-24	$\mu g/L$	XX	1 $\mu g/L$
	3-80 y	5-100	Units/mL	2.4	12-240	$\mu g/L$	XX	1 $\mu g/L$
P, S	Insulin	5-20	$\mu U/mL$	7.175	35-145	pmol/L	XXX	5 pmol/L
		5-20	mU/L	7.175	35-145	pmol/L	XXX	5 pmol/L
		0.20-0.84	$\mu g/L$	172.2	35-145	pmol/L	XXX	5 pmol/L
S	Iron Male	80-180	$\mu g/dL$	0.1791	14-32	$\mu mol/L$	XX	1 $\mu mol/L$
	Female	60-160	$\mu g/dL$	0.1791	11-29	$\mu mol/L$	XX	1 $\mu mol/L$

Table 4.—Examples of Conversions to Système International (SI) Units* (cont)

System†	Component	Present Reference Intervals (Examples)‡	Present Unit	Conversion Factor	SI Reference Intervals‡	SI Unit Symbols§	Significant Digits‖	Suggested Minimum Increment
S	Iron-binding capacity	250-460	µg/dL	0.1791	45-82	µmol/L	XX	1 µmol/L
P	Isoniazid Therapeutic	<2.0	mg/L	7.291	<15	µmol/L	XX	1 µmol/L
	Toxic	>3.0	mg/L	7.291	>22	µmol/L	XX	1 µmol/L
P	Isopropanol	Negative	mg/dL	0.1664	Negative	mmol/L	XX	1 mmol/L
P	Lactate (as lactic acid)	0.5-2.0	mEq/L	1.00	0.5-2.0	mmol/L	X.X	0.1 mmol/L
		5-20	mg/dL	0.1110	0.5-2.0	mmol/L	X.X	0.1 mmol/L
S	Lactate dehydrogenase (L→P)	50-150 (37°C)	Units/L	1.00	50-150	U/L	XXX	1 U/L
			Wroblewski units/mL	0.482	...	U/L	XXX	1 U/L
S	Lactate dehydrogenase isoenzymes LD_1	15-40	%	0.01	0.15-0.40	1	X.XX	0.01
	LD_2	20-45	%	0.01	0.20-0.45	1	X.XX	0.01
	LD_3	15-30	%	0.01	0.15-0.30	1	X.XX	0.01
	LD_4	5-20	%	0.01	0.05-0.20	1	X.XX	0.01
	LD_5	5-20	%	0.01	0.05-0.20	1	X.XX	0.01

	LD$_1$	10-60	Units/L	1	10-60	U/L	XX	1 U/L
	LD$_2$	20-70	Units/L	1	20-70	U/L	XX	1 U/L
	LD$_3$	10-45	Units/L	1	10-45	U/L	XX	1 U/L
	LD$_4$	5-30	Units/L	1	5-30	U/L	XX	1 U/L
	LD$_5$	5-30	Units/L	1	5-30	U/L	XX	1 U/L
B	Lead, toxic	>60	µg/dL	0.04826	>2.90	µmol/L	X.XX	0.05 µmol/L
			mg/dL	48.26	...	µmol/L	X.XX	0.05 µmol/L
U	Lead, toxic	>80	µg/24 hr	0.004826	>0.40	µmol/d	X.XX	0.05 µmol/d
P	Lidocaine (Xylocaine)	1.0-5.0	mg/L	4.267	4.5-21.5	µmol/L	X.X	0.5 mmol/L
S	Lipase	0-160 (30°C)	Units/L	1.00	0-160	U/L	XX0	10 U/L
		<2	Cherry-Crandall (Tietz-Fiereck)	278	<560	U/L	XX0	10 U/L
P	Lipids, total	400-850	mg/dL	0.01	4.0-8.5	g/L	X.X	0.1 g/L
P	Lipoproteins Low-density (LDL), as cholesterol	50-190	mg/dL	0.02586	1.30-4.90	mmol/L	X.XX	0.05 mmol/L
	High-density (HDL), as cholesterol Male	30-70	mg/dL	0.02586	0.80-1.80	mmol/L	X.XX	0.05 mmol/L
	Female	30-90	mg/dL	0.02586	0.80-2.35	mmol/L	X.XX	0.05 mmol/L
S	Lithium ion, therapeutic	0.50-1.50	mEq/L	1.00	0.50-1.50	mmol/L	X.XX	0.05 mmol/L
			µg/dL	0.001441	...	mmol/L	X.XX	0.05 mmol/L
			mg/dL	1.441	...	mmol/L	X.XX	0.05 mmol/L

283

Table 4.—Examples of Conversions to Système International (SI) Units* (cont)

System†	Component	Present Reference Intervals (Examples)‡	Present Unit	Conversion Factor	SI Reference Intervals‡	SI Unit Symbols§	Significant Digits‖	Suggested Minimum Increment
S	Luteinizing hormone Male	3-25	mIU/mL	1.00	3-25	IU/L	XXX	1 IU/L
	Female	2-20	mIU/mL	1.00	2-20	IU/L	XXX	1 IU/L
	Peak production	30-140	mIU/mL	1.00	30-140	IU/L	XXX	1 IU/L
S	Lysozyme (muramidase)	1-15	µg/mL	1.00	1-15	mg/L	XXX	1 mg/L
U	Lysozyme (muramidase)	<2	µg/mL	1.00	<2	mg/L	XX	1 mg/L
S	Magnesium	1.8-3.0	mg/dL	0.4114	0.80-1.20	mmol/L	X.XX	0.02 mmol/L
		1.6-2.4	mEq/L	0.500	0.80-1.20	mmol/L	X.XX	0.02 mmol/L
P	Maprotiline, therapeutic	50-200	ng/mL	3.605	180-720	nmol/L	XX0	10 nmol/L
P	Meprobamate Therapeutic	<20	mg/L	4.582	<90	µmol/L	XX0	10 µmol/L
	Toxic	>40	mg/L	4.582	>180	µmol/L	XX0	10 µmol/L
B	Mercury Normal	<1.0	µg/dL	49.85	<50	nmol/L	XX0	10 nmol/L
	Chronic exposure	>20	µg/dL	0.04985	>1.00	µmol/L	X.XX	0.01 µmol/L
U	Mercury Normal	<30	µg/24 hr	4.985	<150	nmol/d	XX0	10 nmol/d

	Exposure Organic	>45	µg/24 hr	4.985	>220	nmol/d	XXO	10 nmol/d
	Inorganic	>450	µg/24 hr	0.004985	>2.20	µmol/d	X.XX	0.01 µmol/d
U	Metanephrines (as normetanephrine)	0-2.0	mg/24 hr	5.458	0-11.0	µmol/d	XX.X	0.5 µmol/d
P	Methanol	Negative	mg/dL	0.3121	Negative	mmol/L	XX	1 mmol/L
P	Methaqualone Therapeutic	<10	mg/L	3.995	<40	µmol/L	XXO	10 µmol/L
	Toxic	>30	mg/L	3.995	>120	µmol/L	XXO	10 µmol/L
S	Methotrexate, toxic	>2.3	mg/L	2.200	>5.0	µmol/L	X.X	0.1 µmol/L
P	Methsuximide (as desmethyl-suximide), therapeutic	10-40	mg/L	5.285	50-210	µmol/L	XXO	10 µmol/L
P	Methyprylon Therapeutic	<10	mg/L	5.457	<50	µmol/L	XXO	10 µmol/L
	Toxic	>40	mg/L	5.457	>220	µmol/L	XXO	10 µmol/L
S	β_2-Microglobulin (<50 y)	0.80-2.40	mg/L	84.75	68-204	nmol/L	XXX	2 nmol/L
U	β_2-Microglobulin (<50 y)	<140	µg/24 hr	0.08475	<12	nmol/d	XXX	2 nmol/d
P	N-Acetyloprocainamide, therapeutic	4.0-8.0	mg/L	3.606	14-29	µmol/L	XX	1 µmol/L
U	Nitrogen, total	Diet dependent	g/24 hr	71.38	Diet dependent	mmol/d	XXO	10 mmol/d
P	Norepinephrine (radio-enzymatic procedure)	215-475 (at rest for 15 min)	pg/mL	0.005911	1.27-2.81	nmol/L	X.XX	0.01 nmol/L

Table 4.—Examples of Conversions to Système International (SI) Units* (cont)

System†	Component	Present Reference Intervals (Examples)‡	Present Unit	Conversion Factor	SI Reference Intervals‡	SI Unit Symbols§	Significant Digits‖	Suggested Minimum Increment
U	Norepinephrine (fluorimetric procedure)	<100	μg/24 hr	5.911	<590	nmol/d	XX0	10 nmol/d
P	Nortriptyline, therapeutic	25-200	ng/mL	3.797	90-760	nmol/L	XX0	10 nmol/L
P	Osmolality	280-300	mOsm/kg	1.00	280-300	mmol/kg	XXX	1 mmol/kg
U	Osmolality	50-1200	mOsm/kg	1.00	50-1200	mmol/kg	XXX	1 mmol/kg
U	Oxalate (as anhydrous oxalic acid)	10-40	mg/24 hr	11.11	110-440	μmol/d	XX0	10 μmol/d
Amf	Palmitic acid	Depends on gestation	mmol/L	1000	Depends on gestation	μmol/L	XXX	5 μmol/L
P	Pentobarbital	20-40#	mg/L	4.419	90-170	μmol/L	XX	5 μmol/L
P	Phenobarbital, therapeutic	2-5	mg/dL	43.06	85-215	μmol/L	XXX	5 μmol/L
P	Phensuximide	4-8	mg/L	5.285	20-40	μmol/L	XX	5 μmol/L
P	Phenylbutazone, therapeutic	<100	mg/L	3.243	<320	μmol/L	XX0	10 μmol/L
P	Phenytoin Therapeutic	10-20	mg/L	3.964	40-80	μmol/L	XX	5 μmol/L
	Toxic	>30	mg/L	3.964	>120	μmol/L	XX	5 μmol/L
P	Phosphatase, acid (prostatic)	0-3	King-Armstrong units/dL	1.77	0-5.5	U/L	X.X	0.5 U/L

Specimen	Component	Conventional Reference Interval	Conventional Unit	Factor	SI Reference Interval	SI Unit	Significant Digits	Suggested Minimum Increment
S	Phosphatase, alkaline	30-120	Bodansky units/dL	5.37	...	U/L	X.X	0.5 U/L
			Kind-King units/dL	1.77	...	U/L	X.X	0.5 U/L
			Bessey-Lowry-Brock units/dL	16.67	...	U/L	X.X	0.5 U/L
			Units/L	1.00	30-120	U/L	XXX	1 U/L
			Bodansky units/dL	5.37	...	U/L	XXX	1 U/L
			King-Armstrong units/dL	7.1	...	U/L	XXX	1 U/L
			Bessey-Lowry-Brock units/dL	16.67	...	U/L	XXX	1 U/L
S	Phosphate (as phosphorus, inorganic)	2.5-5.0	mg/dL	0.3229	0.80-1.60	mmol/L	X.XX	0.05 mmol/L
U	Phosphate (as phosphorus, inorganic)	Diet dependent	g/24 hr	32.29	Diet dependent	mmol/d	XXX	1 mmol/d
P	Phospholipid phosphorus, total	5-12	mg/dL	0.3229	1.60-3.90	mmol/L	X.XX	0.05 mmol/L
Ercs	Phospholipid phosphorus, total	1.2-12	mg/dL	0.3229	0.40-3.90	mmol/L	X.XX	0.05 mmol/L
P	Phospholipids, substance fraction of total phospholipid							
	Phosphatidyl choline	65-70	% of total	0.01	0.65-0.70	1	X.XX	0.01
	Phosphatidyl ethanolamine	4-5	% of total	0.01	0.04-0.05	1	X.XX	0.01
	Sphingomyelin	15-20	% of total	0.01	0.15-0.20	1	X.XX	0.01
	Lysophosphatidyl choline	3-5	% of total	0.01	0.03-0.05	1	X.XX	0.01

Table 4.—Examples of Conversions to Système International (SI) Units* (cont)

System†	Component	Present Reference Intervals (Examples)‡	Present Unit	Conversion Factor	SI Reference Intervals‡	SI Unit Symbols§	Significant Digits‖	Suggested Minimum Increment
Ercs	Phospholipids, substance fraction of total phospholipid Phosphatidyl choline	28-33	% of total	0.01	0.28-0.33	1	X.XX	0.01
	Phosphatidyl ethanolamine	24-31	% of total	0.01	0.24-0.31	1	X.XX	0.01
	Sphingomyelin	22-29	% of total	0.01	0.22-0.29	1	X.XX	0.01
	Phosphatidyl serine and phosphatidyl inositol	12-20	% of total	0.01	0.12-0.20	1	X.XX	0.01
	Lysophosphatidyl choline	1-2	% of total	0.01	0.01-0.02	1	X.XX	0.01
P	Phytanic acid	Trace-0.3	mg/dL	32.00	<10	μmol/L	XX	5 μmol/L
S	(Human) placental lactogen (HPL)	>4 after 30-wk gestation	mg/L	46.30	>180	nmol/L	XX0	10 nmol/L
U	Porphobilinogen	0-2	mg/24 hr	4.420	0-8.8	μmol/d	X.X	0.5 μmol/d
U	Porphyrins Coproporphyrin	45-180	μg/24 hr	1.527	68-276	nmol/d	XXX	2 nmol/d
Ercs	Protoporphyrin	15-50	μg/dL	0.0177	0.28-0.90	μmol/L	X.XX	0.02 μmol/L
U	Uroporphyrin	5-20	μg/24 hr	1.204	6-24	nmol/d	XX	2 nmol/d
Ercs	Uroporphyrinogen synthetase	22-42	mmole/mL/hr	0.2778	6.0-11.8	mmol·L^{-1}·s^{-1}	X.X	0.2 mmol·L^{-1}·s^{-1}

		Conventional range	Conventional units	Factor	SI range	SI units	Sig.	SI increment
S	Potassium ion	3.5-5.0	mEq/L	1.00	3.5-5.0	mmol/L	X.X	0.1 mmol/L
			mg/dL	0.2558	...	mmol/L	X.X	0.1 mmol/L
U	Potassium ion (diet dependent)	25-100	mEq/24 hr	1.00	25-100	mmol/d	XX	1 mmol/d
U	Pregnanediol Normal	1.0-6.0	mg/24 hr	3.120	3.0-18.5	μmol/d	XX.X	0.5 μmol/d
	Pregnancy	Depends on gestation						
U	Pregnanetriol	0.5-2.0	mg/24 hr	2.972	1.5-6.0	μmol/d	XX.X	0.5 μmol/d
P	Primidone Therapeutic	6-10	mg/L	4.582	25-46	μmol/L	XX	1 μmol/L
	Toxic	>10	mg/L	4.582	>46	μmol/L	XX	1 μmol/L
P	Procainamide Therapeutic	4.0-8.0	mg/L	4.249	17-34	μmol/L	XX	1 μmol/L
	Toxic	>12	mg/L	4.249	>50	μmol/L	XX	1 μmol/L
P	Progesterone Follicular phase	<2	ng/mL	3.180	<6	nmol/L	XX	2 nmol/L
	Luteal phase	2-20	ng/mL	3.180	6-64	nmol/L	XX	2 nmol/L
T	Progesterone receptors Negative	0-3	fmole of progesterone bound/mg of cytosol protein	1.00	0-3	fmol of progesterone bound/mg of cytosol protein	XXX	1 fmol/mg of protein

15.10 Conversion Tables

Table 4.—Examples of Conversions to Système International (SI) Units* (cont)

System†	Component	Present Reference Intervals (Examples)‡	Present Unit	Conversion Factor	SI Reference Intervals‡	SI Unit Symbol§	Significant Digits‖	Suggested Minimum Increment
	Progesterone receptors (cont)							
	Doubtful	4-10	fmole of progesterone bound/mg of cytosol protein	1.00	4-10	fmol of progesterone bound/mg of cytosol protein	XXX	1 fmol/mg of protein
	Positive	>10	fmole of progesterone bound/mg of cytosol protein	1.00	>10	fmol of progesterone bound/mg of cytosol protein	XXX	1 fmol/mg of protein
P	Prolactin	<20	ng/mL	1.00	<20	µg/L	XX	1 µg/L
P	Propoxyphene, toxic	>2.0	mg/L	2.946	>5.9	µmol/L	X.X	0.1 µmol/L
P	Propranolol hydrochloride (Inderal), therapeutic	50-200	ng/mL	3.856	190-770	nmol/L	XX0	10 nmol/L
S	Protein, total	6-8	g/dL	10.0	60-80	g/L	XX	1 g/L
Sf	Protein, total	<40	mg/dL	0.01	<0.40	g/L	X.XX	0.01 g/L
U	Protein, total	<150	mg/24 hr	0.001	<0.15	g/d	X.XX	0.01 g/d

	Analyte	Reference range	Unit	Factor	SI range	SI unit	Sig. digits	Min. increment
P	Protryptyline	100-300	ng/mL	3.797	380-1140	nmol/L	XXO	10 nmol/L
B	Pyruvate (as pyruvic acid)	0.3-0.9	mg/dL	113.6	35-100	μmol/L	XXX	1 μmol/L
P	Quinidine Therapeutic	1.5-3.0	mg/L	3.082	4.6-9.2	μmol/L	X.X	0.1 μmol/L
	Toxic	>6.0	mg/L	3.082	>18.5	μmol/L	X.X	0.1 μmol/L
P	Renin Normal sodium diet	1.1-4.1	ng/mL/hr	0.2778	0.30-1.14	$ng \cdot L^{-1} \cdot s^{-1}$	X.XX	$0.02\ ng \cdot L^{-1} \cdot s^{-1}$
	Restricted sodium diet	6.2-12.4	ng/mL/hr	0.2778	1.72-3.44	$ng \cdot L^{-1} \cdot s^{-1}$	X.XX	$0.02\ ng \cdot L^{-1} \cdot s^{-1}$
S	Salicylate (salicylic acid), toxic	>20	mg/dL	0.07240	>1.45	mmol/L	X.XX	0.05 mmol/L
B	Serotonin (5-hydroxytryptamine)	8-21	μg/dL	0.05675	0.45-1.20	μmol/L	X.XX	0.05 μmol/L
S	Sodium ion	135-147	mEq/L	1.00	135-147	mmol/L	XXX	1 mmol/L
U	Sodium ion	Diet dependent	mEq/24 hr	1.00	Diet dependent	mmol/d	XXX	1 mmol/d
U	Steroids Hydroxycorticosteroids (as cortisol) Female	2-8	mg/24 hr	2.759	5-25	μmol/d	XX	1 μmol/d
	Male	3-10	mg/24 hr	2.759	10-30	μmol/d	XX	1 μmol/d
U	17-Ketogenic steroids (as dehydroepiandrosterone) Female	7-12	mg/24 hr	3.467	25-40	μmol/d	XX	1 μmol/d
	Male	9-17	mg/24 hr	3.467	30-60	μmol/d	XX	1 μmol/d

Table 4.—Examples of Conversions to Système International (SI) Units* (cont)

System†	Component	Present Reference Intervals (Examples)‡	Present Unit	Conversion Factor	SI Reference Intervals‡	SI Unit Symbol§	Significant Digits‖	Suggested Minimum Increment
	Steroids (cont)							
U	17-Ketosteroids (as dehydroepiandrosterone)							
	Female	6-17	mg/24 hr	3.467	20-60	µmol/d	XX	1 µmol/d
	Male	6-20	mg/24 hr	3.467	20-70	µmol/d	XX	1 µmol/d
U	Ketosteroid fractions							
	Androsterone							
	Female	0.5-3.0	mg/24 hr	3.443	1-10	µmol/d	XX	1 µmol/d
	Male	2.0-5.0	mg/24 hr	3.443	7-17	µmol/d	XX	1 µmol/d
	Dehydroepiandrosterone							
	Female	0.2-1.8	mg/24 hr	3.467	1-6	µmol/d	XX	1 µmol/d
	Male	0.2-2.0	mg/24 hr	3.467	1-7	µmol/d	XX	1 µmol/d
	Etiocholanolone							
	Female	0.8-4.0	mg/24 hr	3.443	2-14	µmol/d	XX	1 µmol/d
	Male	1.4-5.0	mg/24 hr	3.443	4-17	µmol/d	XX	1 µmol/d
B	Sulfonamides, as sulfanilamide, therapeutic	10.0-15.0	mg/dL	58.07	580-870	µmol/L	XX0	10 µmol/L
P	Testosterone							
	Female	<0.6	ng/mL	3.467	<2.0	nmol/L	XX.X	0.5 nmol/L
	Male	4.0-8.0	ng/mL	3.467	14.0-28.0	nmol/L	XX.X	0.5 nmol/L

P	Theophylline, therapeutic	10.0-20.0	mg/L	5.550	55-110	µmol/L	XX	1 µmol/L
P	Thiocyanate (nitroprusside toxicity)	≥10	mg/dL	0.1722	≥1.7	mmol/L	X.X	0.1 mmol/L
P	Thiopental	Individual	mg/L	4.126	Individual	µmol/L	XX	5 µmol/L
S	Thyroid tests Thyrotropin (thyroid-stimulating hormone [TSH])	2-11	µU/mL	1.00	2-11	mU/L	XX	1 mU/L
S	Thyroxine (T₄)	4-11	µg/dL	12.87	51-142	nmol/L	XXX	1 nmol/L
S	Thyroxine-binding globulin (TBG), as thyroxine	12-28	µg/dL	12.87	150-360	nmol/L	XX0	10 nmol/L
S	Thyroxine, free	0.8-2.8	ng/dL	12.87	10-36	pmol/L	XX	1 pmol/L
S	Triiodothyronine (T₃)	75-220	ng/dL	0.01536	1.2-3.4	nmol/L	X.X	0.1 nmol/L
S	T₃ uptake	25-35	%	0.01	0.25-0.35	1	X.XX	0.01
P	Tolbutamide, therapeutic	50-120	mg/L	3.699	180-450	µmol/L	XX0	10 µmol/L
S	Transferrin (β₁-siderophilin)	170-370	mg/dL	0.01	1.70-3.70	g/L	X.XX	0.01 g/L
P	Triglycerides (as triolein)	<160	mg/dL	0.01129	<1.80	mmol/L	X.XX	0.02 mmol/L
P	Trimethadione, therapeutic	<50	mg/L	6.986	<350	µmol/L	XX0	10 µmol/L
P	Trimipramine, therapeutic	50-200	ng/mL	3.397	170-680	nmol/L	XX0	10 nmol/L
S	Urate (as uric acid)	2.0-7.0	mg/dL	59.48	120-420	µmol/L	XX0	10 µmol/L
U	Urate (as uric acid)	Diet dependent	g/24 hr	5.948	Diet dependent	mmol/d	XX	1 mmol/d

Table 4.—Examples of Conversions to Système International (SI) Units* (cont)

System†	Component	Present Reference Intervals (Examples)‡	Present Unit	Conversion Factor	SI Reference Intervals‡	SI Unit Symbol§	Signifi-cant Digits‖	Suggested Minimum Increment
S	Urea nitrogen	8-18	mg/dL	0.3570	3.0-6.5	mmol/L of urea	X.X	0.5 mmol/L
U	Urea nitrogen	12-20 (diet dependent)	g/24 hr	35.70	430-700	mmol/d of urea	XX0	10 mmol/d
U	Urobilinogen	0-4.0	mg/24 hr	1.693	0.0-6.8	μmol/d	X.X	0.1 μmol/d
P	Valproic acid, therapeutic	50-100	mg/L	6.934	350-700	μmol/L	XX0	10 μmol/L
U	Vanillylmandelic acid (VMA)**	<6.8	mg/24 hr	5.046	<35	μmol/d	XX	1 μmol/d
P, S	Vitamin A (retinol)	10-50	μg/dL	0.03491	0.35-1.75	μmol/L	X.XX	0.05 μmol/L
U	Vitamin B₁ (thiamine hydro-chloride)	60-500	μg/24 hr	0.002965	0.18-1.48	μmol/d	X.XX	0.01 μmol/d
S	Vitamin B₂ (riboflavin)	2.6-3.7	μg/dL	26.57	70-100	nmol/L	XXX	5 nmol/L
B	Vitamin B₆ (pyridoxal)	20-90	ng/mL	5.982	120-540	nmol/L	XXX	5 nmol/L
P, S	Vitamin B₁₂ (cyanocobalamin)	200-1000	pg/mL	0.7378	150-750	pmol/L	XX0	10 pmol/L
			ng/dL	7.378	...	pmol/L	...	...
B,P,S	Vitamin C: see *Ascorbate*							
P	Vitamin D₃ (cholecalciferol)	24-40	ng/mL	2.599	60-105	nmol/L	XXX	5 nmol/L
	25-OH-cholecalciferol	18-36	ng/mL	2.496	45-90	nmol/L	XXX	5 nmol/L

P, S		Conventional	Conventional unit	Factor	SI	SI unit	Sig. digits	Increment
P, S	Vitamin E (α-tocopherol)	0.78-1.25	mg/dL	23.22	18-29	μmol/L	XX	1 μmol/L
P	Warfarin sodium, therapeutic	1.0-3.0	mg/L	3.243	3.3-9.8	μmol/L	XX.X	0.1 μmol/L
U	Xanthine	5-30	mg/24 hr	6.574	30-200	μmol/d	XX0	10 μmol/d
	Hypoxanthine	...	mg/24 hr	7.347	...	μmol/d	XX0	10 μmol/d
B	D-Xylose (25-g dose)	30-40 (30-60 min)	mg/dL	0.06661	2.0-2.7 (30-60 min)	mmol/L	X.X	0.1 mmol/L
U	D-Xylose excretion (25-g dose)	21-31 (excreted in 5 hr)	%	0.01	0.21-0.31 (excreted in 5 h)	1	X.XX	0.01
S	Zinc	75-120	μg/dL	0.1530	11.5-18.5	μmol/L	XX.X	0.1 μmol/L
U	Zinc	150-1200	μg/24 hr	0.0153	2.3-18.3	μmol/d	XX.X	0.1 μmol/d

*This table is modified from *The SI Manual in Health Care.*

†P represents plasma; B, blood; S, serum; U, urine; Amf, amniotic fluid; T, tissue; Sf, spinal fluid; V, venous; Lkcs, leukocytes; and Ercs, erythrocytes.

‡These reference values are not intended to be definitive since each laboratory determines its own values. They are provided for illustration only.

§An arabic one in this column indicates that this item, formerly expressed in percent, should be expressed as a decimal (or the appropriate part of 1).

‖"Significant digits" refers to the number of digits used to describe the reported results. XX implies that results expressed to the nearest whole number are meaningful; XX0, that results are only meaningful when rounded to the nearest 10, and that results reported to lower numbers or decimal points are beyond the sensitivity of the procedure.

¶Creatinine clearance (corrected for body surface area) = $\dfrac{\mu mol/L \text{ (urine creatinine)}}{\mu mol/L \text{ (serum creatinine)}} \times mL/s \times \dfrac{1.73}{A}$, where A is the body surface area in square meters (m²).

#Aggressive treatment of severe head injury or metabolic coma.

**This is a misnomer, but because of its popularity the name VMA has been retained. In many publications it is being referred to as 4-hydroxy-3-methoxy mandelic acid.

Table 5.—Approximate Conversions to Metric Measures

Symbol	When You Know	Multiply by	To Find	Symbol
Length				
in	inches	2.5*	centimeters	cm
ft	feet	30	centimeters	cm
yd	yards	0.9	meters	m
. . .	miles	1.6	kilometers	km
Area				
sq in	square inches	6.5	square centimeters	cm²
sq ft	square feet	0.09	square meters	m²
sq yd	square yards	0.8	square meters	m²
. . .	square miles	2.6	square kilometers	km²
. . .	acres	0.4	hectares	. . .
Mass (Weight)				
oz	ounces	28	grams	g
lb	pounds	0.45	kilograms	kg
. . .	short tons (2000 lb)	0.9	tonnes	. . .
Volume				
tsp	teaspoons	5	milliliters	mL
tbsp	tablespoons	15	milliliters	mL
fl oz	fluid ounces	30	milliliters	mL
c	cups	0.24	liters	L
pt	US pints	0.47	liters	L
qt	US quarts	0.95	liters	L
gal	US gallons	3.8	liters	L
cu ft	cubic feet	0.03	cubic meters	m³
cu yd	cubic yards	0.76	cubic meters	m³
Temperature (Exact)				
°F	Fahrenheit temperature	5/9 (after subtracting 32)	Celsius temperature	°C

*1 inch = 2.54 cm (exactly).

Adapted from *Metric Conversion Card*. Washington, DC: US Dept of Commerce, National Bureau of Standards; July 1972. NBS Special Publication 365.

16.0 Numbers and Percentages

Any policy on the use of numbers in textual material runs up against the paradox that numbers written as *figures* seem to express a more precise meaning than those spelled out as *words*. Hence the editorial policy of many literary works is to spell out all numbers and that of numerous scientific works is to use figures when a degree of accuracy is intended. Unfortunately, when a publication chooses to use words in some instances and figures in others, it becomes difficult to reconcile apparent inconsistencies. The rules outlined in this section attempt to reduce these inconsistencies perceived by the reader. However, with that goal in mind, common sense and editorial judgment must prevail over hard-and-fast rules.

16.1   **Usage.**—In titles, subtitles, and text, spell out numbers one through nine, and use arabic numerals for all numbers greater than nine, except as specified below. No commas are used in numbers. In numbers of four digits, the digits are set closed up. In numbers of five or more digits, a half-space is used where previously a comma would have appeared. No commas or spaces are used in numbers containing decimal points, even in numbers of five or more digits.

16.1.1   *Beginning a Sentence.*—At the beginning of a sentence, spell out all numbers, even though similar or coordinate numbers are written as numerals elsewhere in the same sentence.

> Three hundred twenty-eight men and 126 women were included in the study.

> Forty-seven patients were hospitalized, 34 were treated as outpatients, and 8 required no further therapy.

Occasionally an exception may be made for the idiom of starting a sentence with a specific year.

> 1985 may be remembered as the year of the artificial heart.

When spelling out numerals, hyphenate 21 through 99 and any compound numerals containing the numbers 21 through 99 (eg, one hundred thirty-two). When compound numbers are spelled out, do not use commas or *and*.

> Twenty-five institutions were participants in this cooperative study.

> Eight thousand one hundred twelve cases of salmonellosis have been confirmed.

When a unit of measure follows a number at the beginning of a sentence, it too must be written out, even though the same unit is abbreviated elsewhere in the same sentence. Because this construction can be cumbersome, it is often preferable to reword the sentence.

> Fifteen milligrams of the drug was administered at 9 PM and 25 mg at 3:30 AM.

> Ten to thirty-six picomoles per liter is the range of reference levels of free thyroxine.

> *Better*: The range of reference levels of free thyroxine is 10 to 36 pmol/L.

16.1.2   *Ordinals*.—Spell out ordinals *first* through *ninth* unless they are part of an array that includes a higher ordinal. Ordinals greater than *ninth* are expressed as numerals (*10th*, etc) except at the beginning of a sentence. Use the following suffixes: 21*st*, 32*nd*, 43*rd*, 54*th*.

> Only the Fifth Battalion responded.

> The 3rd, 9th, and 12th battalions responded the next day.

> Eleventh-grade pupils may leave early.

> (*But:* Fourteenth Amendment)

16.1.3   *Consecutive Numerical Expressions*.—When one numerical expression immediately follows another, spell out the one that can more easily be expressed in words, or reword the sentence.

> She bought eleven 95-cent brushes.

> In the first group of fifteen hundred, 690 were men.

> *Or:* In the first group, 690 of the 1500 patients were men.

16.1.4   *Series, Range, or Span of Years*.—Numbers that constitute a series or range should be written as figures if at least one of them is greater than nine or is a mixed or decimal fraction. For the purposes of this rule, a series is two or more numbers into which a larger group has been broken down. The paragraph is the framework within which this rule holds true, so that, for example, the number 3 (as in *3 of the 12 patients*) would remain a figure throughout the paragraph but not necessarily beyond.

In the first set of subjects, 19 had been treated for hypertension and 7 had a history of angina pectoris.

Of the 300 tumors, between 2 and 11 were adenocarcinomas.

Use arabic numerals whenever numbers are presented as part of a quantitative array (three numbers or more in a series), even if none of the individual numbers exceeds nine.

In March, April, and May, the manager added 9, 7, and 2 employees, respectively.

Do not omit digits when indicating a span of years or page numbers in the text. (See also 2.10.15, References, Page Numbers and Dates, and 6.12.3, Hyphens, Expressing Ranges and Dimensions.)

1973 to 1977 (*not* 1973-77)

pages 1181 to 1189 (*not* 1181-9)

16.1.5 *Enumerations.*—Indicate a short series of enumerated items by run-in numerals or lowercase italic letters enclosed within parentheses.

For long or complex enumerations, indented numbers followed by a period (without parentheses) may be used.

For an enumeration in which items are subdivided, follow a modified outline style.

16.1.6 *Abbreviating Number.*—The word *number* may be abbreviated *No.* in tables, or in the text when used as an adjective. Do not use the number sign (#) in place of the abbreviation.

Heart disease is the No. 1 cause of death in the United States.

16.2   **Forms of Numbers**

16.2.1 *Decimals.*—The decimal form should be used when a fraction is given with an abbreviated unit of measure (eg, 0.5 g, 2.7 mm) or when a precise measurement is intended. Place a zero before the decimal point in numbers less than 1.0, except in instances where the number could never equal 1.0 (as in statistical probability, levels of significance, correlation coefficients, etc). Retain the zero before SD, t, z, F, and χ^2. (See 17.3, Statistics, Significant Digits.)

The patient was receiving 3.5 mg/kg of gentamicin sulfate every 8 hours; her serum level reached a peak of 5.8 mg/L after the first dose.

But: .22-caliber rifle $P<.05$ $r=.86$

16.2.2 *Fractions.*—For less precise measurements, mixed fractions may be used instead of decimals.

He waited 3½ hours.

They ran 6¼ miles.

Spell out common fractions and use a hyphen only when the fraction modifies a noun. The word *quarter* may be used for *fourth*.

half of the cases	a three-fourths–filled jar
two thirds of the diagnoses	two-thirds majority
a half-dozen explanations	one quarter of the page

16.2.3 *Large Numbers.*—Round numbers in millions and billions, tenths of millions, and tenths and hundredths of billions are written as follows:

1 million	$3 billion	2.5 million
4.5 billion	8.33 billion	

16.2.4 *Percentages.*—The term *percent* derives from the Latin *per centum*, meaning by the hundred, or in, to, or for every hundred. *Percentage* is an extension of the term and means "a number or amount stated in percent." *Percentile* is defined as the value on a scale of 100 that indicates the percentage of the distribution that is equal to or below it.

Eight percent of the work remained to be done.

Heart disease was present in a small percentage of the subjects.

Her examination score indicated that she was in the 97th percentile of her class.

Use arabic numerals and the symbol % for percentages. The symbol is set close to the numeral and is repeated with each number in a series or range of percentages. Do not omit the percent symbol with a percentage of zero.

A 5% incidence is common.

The reported incidence varied from 0% to 5%.

At the beginning of a sentence, spell out both numeral and percent, even if the percentage is part of a series or range. Often it is preferable to reword the sentence so that a comparison between percentages is more readily apparent.

Twenty-seven percent to 30% of the patients were expected to survive. (*Better:* The expected survival rate was 27% to 30%.)

Numbers from which a percentage is derived should always be included; this is particularly important when the sample size is less than 100 (see also 17.3, Statistics, Significant Digits). To give primacy to the original data, it is preferable to put the percentage in parentheses.

Of the 26 cases, 73% (19) occurred in infants.

Preferred: Of the 26 cases, 19 (73%) occurred in infants.

Any discrepancy in the sum of percentages in a tabulation (eg, errors in rounding off numbers, missing values, or multiple procedures) should be accounted for.

16.2.5 *Proportions and Rates.*—Use the virgule construction for proportions and rates. A colon is used for ratios. When a proportion, rate, ratio, or percentage is stated *in addition to the numerator and denominator that yielded it*, it is preferable to put the numerator and denominator *outside* parentheses in "*n* of *d*" form. Putting the numerator inside parentheses in "*n/d*" form is the next preferred.

Death occurred in 6 (30%) of the 20 patients.

Death occurred in 30% (6/20) of the patients.

The "*n/d*" form should never be used in running text.

Avoid: Death occurred in 6/20 of the patients.
Better: Death occurred in 6 of the 20 patients.

16.2.6 *Roman Numerals.*—Roman numerals should be marked "roman" for the typesetter. The following table indicates the roman equivalent for arabic numerals 1 through 5000. In general, roman numerals to the right of the greatest numeral are added to that numeral, and numerals to the left are subtracted. A horizontal bar over a roman numeral multiplies its value by 1000.

1	I	20	XX
2	II	30	XXX
3	III	40	XL
4	IV	50	L
5	V	60	LX
6	VI	70	LXX
7	VII	80	LXXX
8	VIII	90	XC
9	IX	100	C
10	X	200	CC
11	XI	300	CCC
12	XII	400	CD
13	XIII	500	D
14	XIV	600	DC
15	XV	700	DCC
16	XVI	800	DCCC
17	XVII	900	CM
18	XVIII	1000	$\overline{M}$
19	XIX	5000	$\overline{V}$

16.2   *Forms of Numbers*

Use roman numerals with proper names. Note that *no* comma is used before the numeral.

Henry Ford III   Friendship VII   Louis XIV

Avoid the use of roman numerals except when part of formally established nomenclature (see 12.0, Nomenclature). Use roman numerals for cancer stages, arabic for cancer grades. In pedigree charts, use roman numerals to indicate generations, arabic numerals to indicate families or individual family members.

In bibliographic material (ie, references, book reviews), do not use roman numerals to indicate volume number, even though roman numerals may have been used in the original. Retain lowercase roman numerals that refer to pages in a foreword, preface, or introduction. (In book reviews, titles of books should follow their original form, including the retention of roman numerals.)

For the use of roman numerals in biblical and classical references, follow the most recent edition of the University of Chicago's *The Chicago Manual of Style*.

16.3   Numerals.—Use arabic numerals for the following, regardless of whether the number is less than or greater than nine.

16.3.1   *Addresses.*—Use numerals for building, house, floor, and room or suite numbers. For numbered streets, spell out ordinals *first* through *ninth*, and use numerals for *10th* and above.

7 Edgewood Ln   1329 E Fifth St   Bldg 1, Suite 82

8 10th Ave   Room 654, Palmolive Bldg

16.3.2   *Ages.*—Use numerals for all ages.

She brought her 3-month-old baby.

The boy was 9 years old, 8 years younger than his sister, aged 17 years.

16.3.3   *Dates.*—Use numerals for months only in tables. Do not use ordinals in dates. Military or European date forms (eg, 29 August 1972) should be converted to conventional form (August 29, 1972).

16.3.4   *Designators.*—Use arabic numerals after designators (see also 8.7, Capitalization, Designators).

day 8   case 4   treatment protocol 5

chapter 3   page 85   line 10

16.3.5 *Figure and Table Numbers.*—Use arabic numerals for figure and table designations.

> Results are shown in Fig 3.
>
> The correlation was not statistically significant (*P*<.05, Table 6).

16.3.6 *Money.*—Use the dollar sign for US and Canadian currency and the pound sign for British currency. Spell out *cents*. Use ciphers (zeros) or periods only when a fraction of a dollar is indicated.

> He paid $8.97 for the groceries and $6 for the medication.
>
> The $1 million budget suffered cutbacks that were sure to affect the $20 000 grants.
>
> What can you buy for 5 cents?
>
> There's no such thing as a 5-cent candy bar.

16.3.7 *Temperature.*—Use the degree sign with Celsius or Fahrenheit measures of temperature.

> Her temperature was 37.8°C (100.0°F).
>
> She had 0.8°C of fever (temperature, 37.8°C).
>
> The plates were cultured at 20°C, 3° lower than usual.

16.3.8 *Time.*—The measures of time *years*, *months*, *weeks*, *days*, *hours*, *minutes*, and *seconds* take arabic numerals.

> The procedure was continued for 3 days.
>
> Readings were taken every 2 seconds.

16.3.9 *Time of Day.*—Use ciphers (zeros) or colon only when a fraction of an hour is intended. AM and PM are set in small capital letters.

> The plane leaves Chicago, Ill, at 11:05 AM and arrives in Providence, RI, at 2 PM.

In some cases, the context may require, or be more suited to, giving the time without AM or PM. In these instances, it is advisable to specify the time of day.

> We had our first meal at 11 o'clock in the morning.
>
> *But:* The needle was inserted at the 4-o'clock position.

With 12 o'clock, simply use *noon* or *midnight* to indicate which is intended.

16.3.10 *Units of Measure.*—All quantities take the arabic form when given with an abbreviated or nonabbreviated unit of measure. (See 11.1, Abbreviations, Units of Measure, and 15.0, Units of Measure.)

> The node was 25 mm in diameter.
>
> He was given 2 g of tetracycline orally.
>
> Thoracentesis yielded 1 L of fluid.
>
> The heat expended during the experiment was 33.6 J.
>
> We run 2 miles every morning.

17.0 Statistics

Authors are responsible for proper study design, data collection, statistical analysis, and reporting of results. Unless the authors are also experienced biostatisticians, the services of a statistician should be enlisted and subsequently acknowledged in the manuscript.

17.1 **Study Design.**—Authors should consult with a statistician early on to ensure an appropriate research design and the correct analysis for their data. The manuscript should include a sufficiently detailed statistical methods section covering the following areas:

- study design selected
- type of pairing (related samples vs unrelated or independent samples)
- randomization procedures
- methods of choosing patients and controls
- matching of patients and controls
- "blinding" of subjects and investigators
- specific hypotheses to be tested
- statements regarding sample size choice based on statistical power calculations
- delineation of dependent and independent variables, covariates, and subgroups of key interest
- steps taken to prevent study biases
- completeness of patient follow-up
- statistical methods used for the analysis of the different variables
- problems of interpreting α-levels for multiple comparisons, interactions, and subgroup analyses
- confidence intervals and their derivation

17.2 **Reporting of Results.**—To illustrate the level of detail required to describe statistical methods and results, a list of commonly used statistical symbols and tests is provided (see 17.5, Commonly Used Statistical Symbols and Tests). Thus, for example, when t tests are used, degrees of freedom and the nature of hypothesis testing (ie, α-levels, one-tailed vs two-tailed significance testing) should be indicated. Models (eg, analysis of variance, covariance, multiple regression, log-linear models) should be described. Details such as covariates used, degrees of freedom, and specific contrasts should be stated. χ^2 and other tests should be described in sufficient detail to inform the reader of what was done. In the presentation of summary statistics, authors must be particularly careful in their use of the notation "$a \pm b$," to ensure that both a and b are specified and used appropriately. For example, if a and b represent mean and standard deviation, respectively, this expression should be written as "$a \pm b$ (SD)" the first time it appears; if b is the standard error of the mean, it should be written as "$a \pm b$ (SEM)" the first time it appears. The notation $\pm$ should be used only if the values so described are symmetric on each side of the number preceding the $\pm$. If the values are asymmetric, the authors should consider other possible measures of central tendency and variability, such as the median and range. If authors insist on presenting the standard deviation, it can be shown in the text as "mean (b, SD)" or in a column labeled "SD" in tables, but without the misleading $\pm$. In general, authors should make certain that, in the report of results,

- the reader can readily determine exactly what significance tests and which comparisons and data transformations were performed
- the appropriate measures of central tendency, eg, mean, mode, median, geometric mean, harmonic mean, are used (*average* is too vague)
- corresponding measures of variability are stated explicitly and used correctly (eg, SEM should not be used indiscriminately to replace SD to make the variation appear smaller; SD should be used for symmetric distributions)
- assumptions underlying the statistical methods are met
- statistical references are provided for methods cited
- computational methods are described (eg, statistical software packages and routines used)
- statistical and clinical significance are carefully distinguished, and expressions such as "highly significant" are avoided
- numbers and percentages are rounded correctly and summary data are reported to the appropriate number of significant digits (see 17.3, Significant Digits, and 17.4, Rounding Off)
- tables and figures agree with the descriptions in the text
- causality is not inferred when only association is reasonable
- the representativeness and generalizability of the results are discussed
- specific statements of statistical power are provided, when appropriate.

For additional information on the design of studies and collection and analysis of data, see 21.2, Resource Bibliography, Additional Readings.

17.3   **Significant Digits.**—The precision with which an observer can measure data is indicated by the number of significant digits used in displaying their measurement. Authors sometimes use more significant digits than their actual observations justify. This error often occurs in converting ratios to percentages.

In general, there should be no more digits in a decimal quotient than there are in the denominator. For example, $7/17 = 0.41$ (41%), not 0.412 (41.2%), but $70/171 = 0.409$ (40.9%). Because percentages *imply* two significant digits ($0.05 = 5\%$), it is acceptable to use two significant digits if the denominator is only a single digit, eg, $1/7 = 14\%$.

$1/7 = 0.14$ (14%)

$10/70 = 0.14$ (14%)

$100/700 = 0.143$ (14.3%)

17.4 **Rounding Off.**—Rounding off may be required to omit other than significant digits, or for easier communication. For example, the author may wish to speak of 250 million Americans rather than 249 987 693 Americans.

The rules for rounding off are simple:

- If the last digit is less than 5, it can simply be dropped; eg, 0.172 can be rounded to 0.17.
- If the last digit is greater than 5, drop the last digit and increase the preceding digit by 1; eg, 0.176 can be rounded to 0.18.
- If the last digit is 5, drop it and increase the preceding digit by 1 if this digit is odd but leave it unchanged if it is even; eg, 0.175 can be rounded up to 0.18 but 0.185 is rounded down to 0.18.

Depending on the appropriate number of digits the author chooses, 0.1428571 may be shown as 0.142857, 0.14286, 0.1429, 0.143, or 0.14.

With the advent of powerful calculators and computers, it is now possible to calculate values to any number of decimal places, but the necessity of demonstrating this prowess is doubtful. A P value of .0312 conveys no more information than $P = .03$ or $P < .05$, in most cases.

A χ^2 value to one decimal place is sufficient: $\chi^2 = 16.3$, not $\chi^2 = 16.31$.

Unless there is a specific reason to denote extremely small P values, it is clearer to simplify: $P = .000013$ should be expressed as $P \ll .01$.

17.5 **Commonly Used Statistical Symbols and Tests.**—The following may be used without expansion (eg, $P < .01$) except where noted by an asterisk. (See also 11.10, Abbreviations, Clinical and Technical Terms.)

Symbol	Description
$\lvert x \rvert$	absolute value (of x)
Σ	sum
$>$	greater than

17.5   Statistical Symbols and Tests

Symbol	Description
$\geq$	greater than or equal to
$<$	less than
$\leq$	less than or equal to
$\wedge$	hat, used to denote an estimate
ANOVA	analysis of variance; model must be specified*
ANCOVA	analysis of covariance; model must be specified*
α	alpha, probability of type I error
$1 - \alpha$	confidence coefficient
β	beta, probability of type II error; or population regression coefficient
$1 - \beta$	power of a statistical test
b	sample regression coefficient
CI	confidence interval; α-level and derivation of confidence interval must be specified*
CV	coefficient of variation $(s/\bar{x}) \cdot 100$*
D	difference
df	degrees of freedom
D^2	Mahalanobis distance, distance between the means of two groups
Δ	delta, change
δ	delta, true sampling error
ϵ	epsilon, true experimental error
e	exponential
$E(x)$	expected value of the variable x
f	frequency; or a function of, usually followed by an expression in parentheses
$F_{1-\alpha}(v_1, v_2)$	F test, ratio of two variances, with $1 - \alpha$ = confidence coefficient and $df = v_1, v_2$ for numerator and denominator, respectively
$G^2(df)$	likelihood ratio χ^2
H_0	null hypothesis
H_1	alternate hypothesis; specify whether one- or two-sided
κ	kappa statistic

Symbol	Description
λ_i	lambda, hazard function for interval i; eigenvalue; or estimate of parameter for log-linear models
Λ	Wilks' lambda
ln	natural logarithm
log	logarithm to base 10
MANOVA	multivariate analysis of variance; specify model*
μ	mu, population mean
n	total sample size
N	total population size
n!	(n) factorial
NS	not significant*
OR	odds ratio*
P	probability
χ_y^2	Yates' corrected χ^2 (1 df)
$\chi_{1-\alpha}^2$ (df)	χ^2 test
r	sample correlation coefficient
R^2	multiple correlation coefficient
RR	relative risk*
ρ	rho, population correlation coefficient
S_D	standard deviation of a difference D
s^2	sample variance
σ^2	sigma squared, population variance
σ	sigma, population standard deviation
SD	standard deviation of a sample
SE or SEM	standard error of the mean
t	Student's t; specify α-level, degrees of freedom, one-tailed vs two-tailed
T^2	Hotelling's T^2 statistic
U	Mann-Whitney U (Wilcoxon) statistic
z	normal distribution or standard z score

*Expand at first mention, with abbreviation following immediately in parentheses.

18.0 Mathematical Composition

Mathematical formulas and other expressions involving special symbols, character positions, and relationships may present difficulties. Helpful to both authors and copy editors are *Mathematics Into Type*, the *Style Manual of the American Institute of Physics*, the *CBE Style Manual*, the University of Chicago's *Chicago Manual of Style*, the *CRC Standard Mathematical Tables*, and *Fundamental Formulas of Physics*.

If a formula is lengthy, it may be necessary to break it before an operation sign (see 18.3.1, Simplifying, Long Formulas). Long formulas may be handled either as copy or as prepared art, depending on the availability of special characters.

18.1   **Copy Preparation.**—Simple formulas may remain in the text of the manuscript if no ambiguity for the layout artist, typesetter, or proofreader will result. Complicated formulas should be placed on a separate page and marked in detail for both alignment and characters.

If there are a large number of equations in a manuscript, they should be numbered consecutively. Numbered equations should each be set on a separate line, centered, with the parenthetical numbers set flush left.

(1) $x = r \cos\,\theta$
(2) $y = r \sin\,\theta$
(3) $z = (x^2 + y^2)$

When an equation is included in the text, it is usually preferable to center it on a separate line. All symbols should be defined and the units in which they are expressed should be stated. Standard abbreviations should be used in expressing units of measure (see 11.11, Abbreviations, Units of Measure). Occasionally it may be preferable to describe an equation in the running text, rather than to set it off as an actual formula:

The serum sodium level before therapy, minus the level after therapy, indicated the effectiveness of the treatment.

18.2   **Copy Marking.**—It is essential to mark carefully each character, letter, and symbol that may be mistaken for an alternate form (eg, x^2, X^2, χ^2, $\times 2$, $2x$, x_2).

311

18.2 Copy Marking

The following are correct markings for elements of equations:

superior	x2
inferior	x2
inferior to superior	x x1
superior to superior	x x2
inferior to inferior	x ri
superior to inferior	x 1 2
inferior with superior and subinferior	x

18.3 **Simplifying.**—Use a virgule (see 6.10.4, Virgule [Solidus], In Equations) to avoid stacking of fractions unless it sacrifices clarity.

$$y = (x_1 + x_2) \ / \ (x_1 - x_2) \text{ instead of } y = \frac{x_1 + x_2}{x_1 - x_2}$$

Whenever a fraction is "unstacked," it is important that proper parentheses be used to avoid ambiguity. The expression

$$a + \frac{b + c}{d} + e$$

if written as $a + b + c/d + e$ is ambiguous and could mean either

$$\frac{a + b + c}{d + e}$$

or

$$a + b + \frac{c}{d} + e$$

or

$$a + b + \frac{c}{d + e}$$

The expression's meaning is unambiguous if set off as follows:

$$a + [(b + c)/d] + e$$

Use of radicals may sometimes be avoided by substituting a fractional exponent.

$$(a^2 - b^2)^{1/2} \text{ instead of } \sqrt{a^2 - b^2}$$

312

A negative exponent may simplify some expressions.

$$\frac{A}{(x+y)^2} = A(x+y)^{-2}$$

Parentheses, brackets, and braces should be used to simplify expressions.

$$E = 1.96\{[P(1-P)]/m\}^{1/2} \text{ instead of } E = 1.96\sqrt{\frac{P(1-P)}{m}}$$

Note: In mathematical formulas, the parentheses are placed *inside* brackets (see 6.9.3, Brackets, In Formulas).

18.3.1 *Long Formulas.*—Long formulas may often be given in two or more lines by breaking them at operation signs outside brackets or parentheses and keeping the indention the same whenever possible (since some formulas may be too long to permit indention).

$$Y = [(a_1 + b_1)/(a_2 - b_2)]$$
$$+ [(\sigma_1 + \sigma_2)/(\sigma_2 - \sigma_1)]$$
$$+ [(s_1 + s_2)/(t_1 + t_2)]$$

However, if a formula loses comprehensibility by being unstacked and broken up, and if it will all fit on one line, it is preferable to leave it stacked.

18.3.2 *Expressing Multiplication and Division.*—The product of two or more units of measure is preferably indicated by a centered dot ($\cdot$) (eg, $7 \text{ kg} \cdot \text{m}^2$). However, in scientific notation the times sign ($\times$) is used (eg, 3×10^{-10} cm) (see 15.1.3, Units of Measure, Multiplication Sign vs Times Dot). A virgule or solidus (/), a horizontal line, or a negative exponent may be used to express division of one unit by another, eg,

$$\text{m/s} \qquad \text{or} \qquad \frac{\text{m}}{\text{s}} \qquad \text{or} \qquad \text{m} \cdot \text{s}^{-1}$$

A negative exponent merely denotes the reciprocal of the expression, ie,

$$x^{-n} = 1/x^n \qquad A^{-1} = 1/A \qquad B^{-2} = 1/B^2$$

The virgule should not be repeated on the same line unless parentheses are used to avoid ambiguity. Negative exponents may also be used to clarify an expression. For example, the expression 2 mL/kg/min is unclear. Instead, use 2 mL/kg per minute or $2 \text{ mL} \cdot \text{kg}^{-1} \cdot \text{min}^{-1}$.

By using only multiplication and negative exponents instead of multiple division signs, the appropriate arithmetic step is uniquely and directly attached to each term of the expression and avoids the potential ambiguity of having virgules between a variable number of terms.

18.3 Simplifying

The following are examples of commonly used expressions.

$> 10^5$ CFUs/mL $\qquad$ 24.5 ± 0.5

$P << .01$ $\qquad$ $T_{1/2} = 10.0$ h

$f(x) = x + \Delta x$ $\qquad$ $y = dx/dt$

$\displaystyle\sum_{i=0}^{n} a_i x_i$ $\qquad$ $\displaystyle\int_{10}^{13} 2x\,dx$

$r!(n-r)!$ $\qquad$ $\dfrac{e^x + e^{-x}}{2}$

$\text{kg} \cdot \text{m} \cdot \text{s}^{-2}$ $\qquad$ $x + \dfrac{x^2}{2} + \dfrac{x^3}{3} + \dfrac{x^4}{4} + \cdots + \dfrac{x^n}{n}$

$L \approx 2 \times 10^{10}$ m $\qquad$ $F \sim \dfrac{m_1 m_2}{r^2}$

Note: The factorial sign (!) is used to show the product of numbers from 1 up to the expression immediately preceding the factorial sign, ie,

$n! = n \times (n - 1) \times (n - 2) \times \ldots \times 1$

$5! = 5 \times 4 \times 3 \times 2 \times 1 = 120$

$1! = 1$

$0! = 1$ (by convention)

18.3.3 Typography and Capitalization.—In general, lines, variables, unknown quantities, and constants (eg, x, y, z, A, B, C) are set in italics, while units of measure (eg, kg, mL, s, m), symbols (including Greek characters [see 14.0, Greek Letters]), and numbers are set roman. Arrays and vectors should be set boldface. Mathematical functions, such as sin, cos, ln, and log, are set roman.

$$\mathbf{V} = a\mathbf{i} + b\mathbf{j} + c\mathbf{k}$$

$$\mathbf{A} = \begin{bmatrix} a_{11} & a_{12} & a_{13} \\ a_{21} & a_{22} & a_{23} \\ a_{31} & a_{32} & a_{33} \end{bmatrix}$$

For equations that are written out, set the words and letters roman and capitalize the equation using the same rules that apply to titles (see 8.4, Capitalization, Titles and Headings).

$$U = \frac{\text{Efficacy}}{\text{Toxicity } - \text{ Risk}} \times \frac{\text{Money Saved by Its Use}}{\text{Cost of Contrast Medium}}$$

Note: Copy editors must specify equation breaks and spacing of numbers and characters for the typesetter. Proofreaders must carefully check that such instructions have been followed. Readers are advised to see section 3.2 in *Mathematics Into Type* (see 21.2, Resource Bibliography, Additional Readings).

5

TECHNICAL
INFORMATION AND
BIBLIOGRAPHY

Chapter 19

19.0 Printing and Production Terms

access—The ability to find a particular location in a body of stored data. Data stored on magnetic tape are subject to only sequential access, whereas data stored on disks permit random access.

align—To place type or illustrations so that they line up horizontally or vertically with related elements.

alphanumeric—Consisting of letters, numbers, and symbols as a code for a computer command.

art repair (rebuilding)—Replacing of arrows, lines, and/or type on line art to produce illustrations with uniform type and size.

artificial intelligence—Computer programming that attempts to mimic the decision-making processes of the human brain.

artwork—Illustrative material (photographs, drawings, etc) intended for reproduction.

ascender—The part of letters such as d, f, h, and k that extends above the midportion of the letter.

ASCII—Abbreviation for American Standard Code for Information Interchange character set, the group of characters recognized by most computers and computer programs.

bad break—In page makeup, any of various unsightly or misleading arrangements of type occurring at the bottom or top of a page or column, eg, a paragraph ending consisting of only a word or two at the top of a page or column (called a *widow*), a subheading falling on the last line of a page or column, or the second part of a hyphenated word starting a page.

basis weight of paper—Determined by the weight in pounds of a ream (500 sheets) of paper cut to a given standard size for that grade. For example, 500 sheets, 25×38 in, of 80-lb coated paper will weigh 80 lb.

binary—The binary system of numbers, which employs only the digits 1 and 0. This is the basis for digital computers.

binding—The process by which printed units are attached to form a book, magazine, or pamphlet. It may include such operations as folding, collating, stitching, and gluing.

bit—In computer terminology, a binary digit, either 0 or 1.

blackprint—A photoprint made from film that has been positioned (stripped) for platemaking. It is used to check relative arrangement of image elements.

19.0   Printing and Production Terms

bleed—A printed image that continues off the page when the edge of the paper has been trimmed in binding. A partial bleed extends above, below, or to the side of the established live area of the page.

blind folio—A page number counted but not printed on the page.

body type—The type used for the text of a work, as distinguished from the display type used for title, chapter headings, subheadings, etc.

broadside—Text or illustrations positioned on the length rather than the width of the page, usually requiring the reader to turn the publication on its side to read it.

bug—In computer terminology, something that causes an error in hardware or software.

bullet—A dot of a given weight (●) used to highlight paragraphs or individual elements in a list. (See also **centered dot**.)

bytes—A sequence of binary digits (bits) (eg, usually eight bits to a byte) that codes for a character, usually an alphanumeric symbol.

caliper—Thickness of paper or film.

camera-ready copy—Artwork, type proofs, typewritten material, etc, ready to be photographed for reproduction without further alteration.

caret—A sign (∧) indicating where to insert a correction or additional material.

cell—A basic subdivision of a computer memory that can hold one unit of a computer's basic operating data unit.

centered dot—A heavy dot (●) used to highlight a paragraph, also called a bullet. A lighter centered dot (·) is used in mathematical composition to signify multiplication and in chemical formulas to indicate hydration.

central processing unit (CPU)—The part of the computer that performs all the chief functions of the system.

character—A letter, numeral, symbol, or punctuation mark.

character count—In copyfitting, a character count is made by computing the number of characters and spaces in an average line of the manuscript and multiplying it by the number of lines in the manuscript.

clear—In computer technology, to erase stored data and to restore circuits to their beginning state.

codes—In computer-assisted composition, combinations of letters, numbers, and symbols representing instructions to the computer, entered through a keyboard.

color separations—Films of the four process colors (cyan, yellow, magenta, and black) that make up all color illustrations. Separations are made by camera or by electronic scanning.

compatible—In computer terminology, ability to use together, as software with hardware.

composition, computer-assisted—A process in which text in digital form is recorded on a magnetic medium (tape or disk) and processed through a computer, where line-ending, hyphenation, justification, and other typographic decisions are carried out. The resulting product is used to drive a photomechanical or cathode-ray tube (CRT) typesetter.

condensed type—Type in which the characters are set narrower than normal, permitting more material to be set in a line of the same width.

continuous tone—An image that has gradations of tone from dark to light, in contrast to an image formed of pure blacks and whites such as a pen-and-ink drawing or a page of type.

copy—Typescript, original artwork, photographs, etc.

copyfitting—The process of estimating the space required to print a given quantity of copy in a desired type size. The number of characters in the manuscript is estimated and divided by the number of characters per pica for the typeface and size to be used; this is divided by the measure of the typeset line, and then by the number of lines of type per page. The result is an estimate of the number of printed pages the manuscript will occupy.

cover—The front and back pages of a publication. The four surfaces making up the covers in a publication are often designated covers 1, 2, 3, and 4.

cover stock—Paper, usually heavier than the paper used for the body of the publication.

cromalin proof—A proof made from color separations that shows all colors as a single composite. This is used by publishers to approve film separations and by printers to match colors at press time.

crop—To reduce the size of an image by removing extraneous areas. Cropping is performed by masking, and crop marks are placed on the sides, top, and bottom of a photograph or drawing as a guide to the camera operator.

CRT composition—A process in which a cathode-ray tube (CRT) typesetter, driven by a computer, generates type images on the surface of a CRT from digital records of the letterforms and transfers the images to photographic paper or film.

cyan—One of the four process colors (cyan, magenta, yellow, and black); a shade of blue.

data bank—Information stored in a computer for later retrieval and use.

data processing—In computer technology, handling stored information so as to produce an end product.

database—In statistical work, the total number of responses on which a percentage is based. In computer terms, a group of facts in storage from which information can be obtained and organized in various forms and formats.

debug—To trace and correct errors in a computer program.

default—In computer programming, the condition or instruction that results if the programmer does not specify some other option.

descender—The part of such letters as *p*, *q*, and *y* that extends below the baseline.

digitize—To describe something, such as the shape of a letter, in terms of binary digits, so that it can be entered in, and retrieved from, computer storage.

disk—A circular plate coated with a magnetic substance and used for the storage and retrieval of data.

diskette—A disk coated with magnetically sensitive material used for permanent storage of information, usually in personal computers.

display type—Type that is larger than the body type used for setting the text of a printed work. Display faces are used for the title pages, headlines in advertising, etc.

dot matrix printer—A device producing hard copy from a series of wires (pins) that strike against an ink source. The dots created form characters. Quality varies; currently manuscripts printed on dot matrix printers cannot be input by most optical scanners for typesetting because the spaces between the dots create an uneven structure.

double spread—Printed matter (text, tables, illustrations) that extends across two pages (left- and right-hand pages).

drive—The hardware, consisting of the motor, read/write heads, and electronics, that is used with a disk.

drop folio—A page number printed at the bottom of the page.

dummy—A layout of a page to represent the size and appearance after typesetting and makeup.

duotone—A two-color halftone reproduction from a black-and-white photograph.

elite type—Typewriter type that equals 12 characters to the inch.

em—The square of the type size; ie, a 6-point em is 6 points wide. Used to specify to the typesetter the amount of space desired for indention.

emulsion side—The side of a photographic film to which a chemical coating is applied and on which the image is developed.

en—Half an em.

expanded type—Type in which the characters are wider than normal.

face—The open side of a publication.

figure—An illustration (eg, photograph, drawing, graph).

file—In computer terminology, any body of related, digitally stored information.

flush—In typesetting, lines aligned vertically along the left (flush left) or the right (flush right).

flush and hang—To set the first line flush left on the measurement and indent the remaining lines.

flyleaf—Any blank page at the front or back of a book.

folio—A page number.

font—A complete assortment of characters in one face and size of type.

foot—The bottom of a page.

form, press form—A group of pages (usually 8, 12, 16, or 32 pages), printed at the same time, that are folded into consecutively numbered pages.

format—The shape, size, style, margins, type, and general appearance of a publication.

function key—On a keyboard, a key that gives an instruction to the machine or computer, as opposed to keys that govern letters, numbers, marks of punctuation, etc.

19.0　Printing and Production Terms

galley proof—A proof of the material set in type before being made into a page.

gatefold—A foldout page.

ghosting—Shadows produced by uneven ink coverage (variations are due to wide contrasts in the colors or tones being printed).

glitch—In computer terminology, something that causes a system to malfunction, such as a mechanical defect or a programming error.

gutter—The two inner margins of facing pages of a publication.

H & J—Hyphenation and justification; division of words into lines of prescribed measurement.

hairline rule—A thin rule, usually measuring one-half point.

halftone—A black-and-white photograph that has shades of gray. (See 2.12, Manuscript Preparation, Illustrations.)

halftone screen—A grid used in the halftone process to break the image into dots. The fineness of the screen is denoted in terms of lines per inch (120, 133, 150).

hard copy—Printed copy, artwork, etc, in contrast to copy recorded on magnetic tape, disks, etc.

hardware—In computer terminology, machinery, circuitry, and other physical entities.

head—The top of a page.

head margin—Top margin of a page.

idiot tape—In computerized typesetting, magnetic tape bearing only the keyboarded text itself—hyphenation, justification, and other instructions are added later by a computer programmed to perform these functions.

imposition—The process of arranging pages of a press form so that the pages will be in sequential order when printed and folded.

impression—The transfer of image by pressure from type, plate, or blanket to paper.

indent—To set a line of type so that it begins or ends inside the normal margin.

inferior—A number or symbol that prints partly below the base line, eg, A_2 (a subscript).

initial—A large letter used to begin a chapter or section. A "sunken" two-line or three-line initial cuts down into the text two or three lines; a "stickup" initial aligns at the bottom with the first line of text but sticks up into the white space above.

ink fountain—Device on the press that supplies the ink to the inking rollers.

ink jet printer—A device by which ink is forced through a series of nozzles; this method of printing is usually used to produce the mailing address or a short message to the subscriber.

input—To enter information, instructions, text, etc, into a computer system. Input devices include the direct-input keyboard, off-line keyboard, and optical character recognition (OCR) reader.

insert—Printed material (usually on different paper than that used in the publication) that is positioned between signatures in the binding process.

interface—In computer terminology, the ability of separate computers to interact; also, the actual hardware that performs the function.

justify—To add or delete space between words or letters to make copy align on both sides.

kerning—To modify spacing between characters, usually to bring letters closer together.

keyline—Tissue or acetate overlay separating or defining elements for line or halftone artwork for color separations or special camera work.

laser printer—A high-quality, moderate-speed printer.

layout—A designer's conception of the finished product; includes sizing and positioning of the elements.

leaders—A row of dots designed to carry the reader's eye across space.

leading—Spacing between lines of type; a carryover term from hot metal composition. For example, 9-point type on an 11-point base allows 2 points of leading below the type.

ligature—Two or more connected letters, such as æ, œ, ff, fi.

line art—Illustration composed of lines and/or lettering (charts, graphs).

line printer—A machine, driven by a computer, that prints out stored data one line at a time.

live area—The area of a page within the margins.

logic—The configuration of computer circuits for data processing; also the circuits themselves.

logo—One or more words or other combinations of letters or designs often used for company names, trademarks, etc.

long page—In makeup, a page that runs longer than the live area of the page.

macro—In computer terminology, a series of keystrokes that, when stored by name, can be invoked by that name to perform repetitive tasks.

magenta—One of the four process colors (cyan, magenta, yellow, and black); a shade of red.

mainframe—In computer terminology, a large central processing unit.

makeready—The portion of the printing process immediately preceding the actual press run, where colors, ink coverage, and register are adjusted to produce the desired quality; may also apply to the binding process.

makeup—The arranging of type lines and illustrations into page form or press designation for printing.

markup—The process of marking manuscript copy with directions of type fonts and sizes, spacing, indention, etc, for typesetting.

master proof—The set of galley or page proofs carrying all corrections and alterations.

measure—The length of the line (width of the column) in which type is set.

memory—In computer terminology, the part of a central processing unit in which digitized information is permanently stored.

menu—In computer usage, a series of options in the software program, usually presented on the computer monitor to the user, from which to choose.

modem—Modulator-demodulator, an electronic telecommunication device that converts computer-generated data (bits) into impulses that can be carried over telephone lines.

moiré—Screen pattern caused by incorrect screen angles (see 2.12, Manuscript Preparation, Illustrations).

monitor—The televisionlike screen, usually connected to a keyboard, that allows the computer user to see the material inserted into the computer.

OCR—Optical character recognition. In computerized typesetting, an OCR input device is capable of scanning a typescript and interpreting the typed characters.

opaque—To paint out on the negative those areas that are not wanted on the plate.

optical character recognition—*see* **OCR**.

orphan—One or two short words at the end of a paragraph.

outline halftone—A portion taken from a halftone that is the shape or modified shape of a subject.

overlay—A hinged flap of paper or transparent plastic that covers a piece of artwork. It may protect the work or specify instructions for the camera operator.

page proof—A proof set in the form of the finished page.

pasteup—The assembling of the various elements of type and illustration as a guide to the printer for makeup.

PC—Personal computer—usually self-contained (keyboard, monitor, printer, central processing unit, and memory devices).

PE—Abbreviation for printer's error, used in correcting proofs.

penalty copy—Copy that is difficult to typeset (heavily corrected, difficult to read, heavy with tabular material, etc) for which the typesetter charges more than the regular rate.

perfect binding—Process in which signatures are collated, the gutter edge is cut and ground, adhesive is applied to the signatures, and the cover is applied.

perforate—To punch lines of small holes or slits in a sheet so that it may be torn off with ease.

photostat—A camera process that duplicates graphic matter; also the graphic matter thus produced.

pica—In printing, a unit of measure. There are 12 points to a pica. Six picas equals approximately 1 in.

pica type—Typewriter type that equals 10 characters to the inch.

PMS (Pantone Matching System) colors—A color identification system, developed by Pantone Inc, for printers and designers to use so that finished products match.

pockets—Sections on the binder in which individual signatures are placed and then selected as required for each copy bound.

point—The printer's basic unit of measurement, 0.0138 in (approximately 1/72nd of an inch).

preprint—Part of a book or journal printed and distributed before publication, usually for promotional or educational purposes.

press form—*see* **form**

press plates—The plates used to print multiple copies on the press.

press run—The total number of copies of journals or books printed.

print order—The number of copies of journals or books ordered by the publisher.

printout—Output of a line printer or other device that produces normal-reading copy from computer-stored data.

process colors—Cyan, magenta, yellow, and black; used to produce color illustrations.

program—A set of data-processing instructions for a computer. To program is to devise and enter such a set of instructions.

progressive proofs—Proofs of process color plates, showing each color individually and progressively combined (one proof with all colors), as the plates will print.

proof—A hard copy of typeset and graphic material used to check accuracy of typesetting and positioning.

ragged right—Set with the right-hand margin unjustified.

RC (resin-coated) paper—Paper used in composition to produce a type proof of the quality needed for photographic reproduction.

recto—A right-hand page.

register—To print an impression on a sheet in correct relationship to other impressions already printed on the same sheet, eg, to superimpose exactly the various color impressions. When such impressions are not exactly aligned, they are said to be out of register.

remake—To alter the makeup of a page or series of pages.

reprint—A reproduction of an original printing.

reproduction proof—A high-quality type proof pulled for use in photoengraving or in offset lithography.

reverse out—An image of type or of a drawing appearing in white surrounded by a solid block of color or black.

right reading—Produced to read as original copy, as in right-reading film.

river—In composition, an undesirable streak of white space running down through several lines of type, breaking up the even appearance of the page.

run in—To merge a paragraph with the preceding one.

runaround—Type set to fit around an illustration or a box.

running foot—A line of copy, usually giving publication name, subject, or chapter title, repeated at the bottom of consecutive pages.

running head—A line of copy, usually giving publication name, subject, or chapter title, repeated at the top of consecutive pages.

runover—Material not fitting in the space allowed.

saddle-stitch-binding—Process by which signatures and covers are assembled by inserting one into another and then attached by inserting staples into the centerfold.

sans serif—*see* **serif**

scribe—Thin strips of nonprinting areas, such as those between figure parts.

score—To crease thick paper or cards slightly so they can be folded exactly at certain points.

selective binding—A method of binding in which contents of each copy produced are determined by instructions transmitted electronically from a computer tape. Signatures are selected to produce a copy for a specific recipient or recipient group.

self-cover—A cover made of the same paper as that used for the text and printed as part of a larger press form.

serif—A short, light line projecting from the top or bottom of a main stroke of a letter; originally, in handwritten letters, a beginning or finishing stroke of the pen. Sans serif faces lack serifs.

short page—In makeup, a page that runs shorter than the established live area.

show through—Unusually heavy inking that can be seen on the opposite side of the paper.

signature—A printed sheet comprising several pages that has been folded, so that the pages are in consecutive order according to pagination.

sink—Starting type below the top line of the live area.

slug—A line or lines of copy inserted to draw the attention of the reader.

software—Computer programs, as opposed to the "hardware" of the computer's physical structure.

solid—[Type] set with no space between lines.

spacing—Lateral spaces between words, sentences, or columns, and paragraph indentions.

spine—The backbone area between covers 1 and 4. The width depends on the number of pages in the publication.

stet—Instruction that marked or crossed-out copy or type is to be retained as it originally appeared.

stipple—A pattern of fine dots, usually applied by hand to art, negatives, positives, or the press plate to approximate small tinted areas.

storing data—To put data in computer storage by recording the data in digital form on a magnetic medium, such as tapes, disks, or drums, either inside or outside the computer.

straight copy—Material that can be set in type with no handwork or special programming (copy that contains no mathematics, tables, etc).

strip—To join film in a unit according to a press imposition prior to platemaking.

style—A publisher's rules of uniformity in matters of punctuation, capitalization, word division, spelling, and other details.

subscript—*see* **inferior**

superior—A number or symbol that prints partly above the base line, eg, A^2 (superscript).

superscript—*see* **superior**

tearsheet—A page cut or torn from a book or periodical.

tints—Various even tone areas of a solid color, usually expressed in percentages.

tipped-in—[A sheet or signature] glued to another signature prior to binding.

transpose—In proofreading and editing, to switch the positions of two words, sentences, paragraphs, etc.

trim—The edges that are cut off three sides (top [head], bottom [foot], and right [face]) of a publication after binding.

trim line—The line where a publication will be cut to even edges.

trim size—The final size of the publication.

typeface—A named type design, such as Baskerville or Helvetica, produced as a complete font.

typescript—A typewritten manuscript.

typesetter—A person, firm, or machine that sets type.

verso—A left-hand page.

video display terminal—In computer technology, an input keyboard with a video screen on which the keyboarded material can be viewed (also known as a CRT [cathode-ray tube], monitor, terminal, or VDT).

web press—A press that prints on a continuous roll (web) of paper.

widow—A short line ending a paragraph and positioned at the top of a page or column.

word processor—A general term for a variety of electronic machines on which text consisting of words and figures can be keyboarded, displayed on a video screen, edited, and recorded in magnetic form.

wrong font—A type of different size or face from that of the context in which it accidentally appears.

20.0 Copy Editing and Proofreading Marks

20.1 **Copy Editing Marks.**—Use the following examples as a guide to copy marking.

bullet	● (indicate point size)
set in italics	published in JAMA
set in boldface	Comment
set in roman	terms such as provision and delivery
delete underlining (italics)	in vivo, in vivo
capitals	National institutes of Health
small capitals	406 BC, 4 PM, PCO₂, Case
italic capitals	usa
lowercase one capital letter	She was President of the committee.
lowercase a capital series	TABLE 5.—FACILITIES AND ORGANIZATIONS OF 47 DIVISIONS OF SURGICAL ONCOLOGY
superscript	Studies by Savrin et al show results similar to those reported by Barrorso.
subscript	H_2O
en dash	basement membrane-like
em dash	CASE 1.
apostrophe	
period	That is all
comma	Groups 1, 2, and 3 all received 10 mL of bacterial suspension.

semicolon	He was generous; he had the fault.
colon	The briefest commandment is this: Don't.
insert parentheses	Her pulse rate was normal (72 beats per minute).
hyphen	symptom=free interval
insert a hyphen	follow-up period
close up	following
plus sign	The correlation coefficient was +.97.
minus sign	The value could not exceed −1.
insert word(s)	A group of volunteers has been assembled.
change word(s)	Doors which that close usually open.
transpose elements	will answer only to his name will only to his name answer
correct a typographic error	the complicated septic ulcer
delete elements	computed axial tomography
delete and close up	computerized tomography
insert space	underway
mark Greek letter	μg/dL
indent 1 em space	Symptoms
indent 2 em spaces	Fever
flush left	Table stub
flush right	Signature
center element	Centerhead
set as two lines, centered	Gross and Microscopic Examination

paragraph	¶ Cholecystectomy is one of the most common elective surgical procedures and a major source of hospitalization.
convert to alternative form	In 10 patients, (seven) of whom (70 (percent)) were in their 20s, dilatation (&) curettage was only (1) of several treatments. [*Note:* if capitalization or hyphenation is involved, it is preferable to *write out* the desired change to avoid ambiguity: 20 patients were seen on *Twenty* August 15. This was 1/3 the amount expected.] *one third*
stet (let marked text stand)	All but one patient completed at least 7 days of the study. *stet*

20.2 **Copy Editing Sample.**—The sample page below has been edited. Note that the copy editor's markings occur *within the text* of the typewritten page, in contrast to the *marginal* markings of the proofreader (see 20.3, Proofreading Marks). (See 20.1 for a list of copy editing marks.)

]REPORT OF A CASE[

¶ Case 1.--A (nineteen)-year old woman was seen for the (1st) time in
M

may of 1982 with complaints of stabbing pain of (one) years duration *downward*

in the posterior aspect of the left calf from the knee downwards, *stet*

throbbing sensations on the dorsum of the left foot and ankle, and

edema of the foot and leg.

Her history revealed that the patient *she had* had "fleshy tumors" of the

left leg since she was 1½ years old. Since then she *had* undergone *mixed fraction*

(nine) or (ten) operations for removal of these tumors, the last (1)

having been performed in 1981. There was no known family

history of congenital vascular malformations. The patient was not

known to have any allergies *and* was taking no medication.

20.3   Proofreading Marks.—The following marks are made in the margins of the proof. See 20.4, Proofreading Sample, for examples of their use.

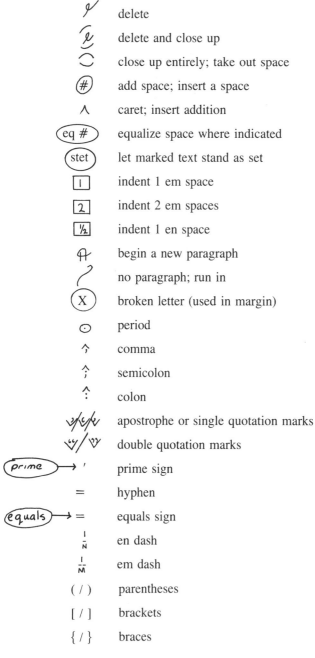

	delete
	delete and close up
	close up entirely; take out space
	add space; insert a space
	caret; insert addition
	equalize space where indicated
	let marked text stand as set
	indent 1 em space
	indent 2 em spaces
	indent 1 en space
	begin a new paragraph
	no paragraph; run in
	broken letter (used in margin)
	period
	comma
	semicolon
	colon
	apostrophe or single quotation marks
	double quotation marks
	prime sign
	hyphen
	equals sign
	en dash
	em dash
	parentheses
	brackets
	braces

(wf)	wrong font
(lc)	lowercase
(c + lc)	lowercase with initial capitals
(c + sc)	small capitals with initial capitals
(caps)	set in large capitals
(sc)	set in small capitals
(roman)	roman or regular type (lightface)
(lf)	set in lightface (not italic or boldface) type
(ital)	set in italic type
(bf)	set in boldface type
(bf ital)	set in boldface italic type
(sc ital)	set in small capital italic type
⋀	subscript or inferior letter or figure
⋁	superscript or superior letter or figure
⊏	move to left
⊐	move to right
⊔	lower
⊓	raise
?	ragged margin
(‖ -])	flush left, with longest line flush right
⊐ ⊏	put in center of line or page
(tr)	transpose; change order the
/	virgule
∽	approximately
=	straighten line
‖	align type up and down
=	align type across
(hair #)	hairline space
(?)	query to author

327

/   used to separate two or more marks and often used as a concluding stroke at the end of an insertion

⟨hanging indent⟩   hanging indention—this style should have all lines after ⌐the⌐ first marked for the desired indention

⌐L   break line here,⌐ not elsewhere

(SWK)   set when known

20.4   Proofreading Sample.—The following example shows how a proof is marked by the proofreader and how those corrections appear in the revised proof.

(circled: Set ALL CAPS BF Center) ⟶ Report of a Case

CASE 1.—A 19-year-old woman was seen for the first time in

May 1982 with complaints of stabbing pain of 1 year's duration in

the posterior aspect of the (right) calf from the knee downward,

throbbing sensations on the dorsum of the left foot and ankle and

edema of the foot and leg.

Her history revealed that she had had "fleshy tumors" of the leg

since she was 1½ years old. Since then, she had undergone 9 (to) 10

operations for removal of these tumors, the last one in 1981. There

was no known family history of congenital vascular malformations.

The patient was not known to have any allergies and was taking no

medication.

Revised Proof

REPORT OF A CASE

CASE 1.—A 19-year-old-woman was seen for the first time in May 1982 with complaints of stabbing pain of 1 year's duration in the posterior aspect of the left calf from the knee downward, throbbing sensations on the dorsum of the left foot and ankle, and edema of the foot and leg.

Her history revealed that she had had "fleshy tumors" of the left leg since she was 1½ years old. Since then, she had undergone 9 or 10 operations for removal of these tumors, the last one in 1981. There was no known family history of congenital vascular malformations. The patient was not known to have any allergies and was taking no medication.

21.0 Resource Bibliography

21.1   **References.**—Many excellent additional sources are available to the style-book user. The following were consulted in the preparation of this manual. Some of these sources now have new editions.

1.0   Types of Articles

Huth EJ. *How to Write and Publish Papers in the Medical Sciences*. Philadelphia, Pa: ISI Press; 1982.

Lundberg GD, Carney MJ. Peer review at *JAMA*—1985. *JAMA*. 1986;255:3286-3292.

Riesenberg DE. Case reports in the medical literature. *JAMA*. 1986;255:2067.

Southgate MT. *Advice to Authors*. Chicago, Ill: American Medical Association; 1964.

2.0   Manuscript Preparation

A Uniform System of Citation. 14th ed. Cambridge, Mass: The Harvard Law Review Association; 1986.

American National Standard for Bibliographic References: ANSI Z39.29-1977. New York, NY: American National Standards Institute; 1977.

The Chicago Manual of Style. 13th ed. Chicago, Ill: University of Chicago Press; 1982.

International Committee of Medical Journal Editors. Uniform requirements for manuscripts submitted to biomedical journals. *Ann Intern Med*. 1982;96:766-771. *Br Med J Clin Res*. 1982;284:1766-1770.

Warriner JE. *Warriner's English Grammar and Composition: Complete Course*. Franklin edition. Orlando, Fla: Harcourt Brace Jovanovich Publishers; 1982.

3.0   Legal and Ethical Considerations

Babbage C. Cited by: Schiedermayer DL, Siegler M. Believing what you read: responsibilities of medical authors and editors. *Arch Intern Med*. 1986;146:2043-2044.

Knox R. The Harvard fraud case: where does the problem lie? *JAMA*. 1983;249:1797-1807.

Radulescu G. Duplicate publication is boring. *AJDC*. 1985;139:119-120.

Relman AS. Lessons from the Darsee affair. *N Engl J Med*. 1983;308:1415-1417.

Some Notes on Plagiarism and How to Avoid It [handout]. Evanston, Ill: Northwestern University.

Sources: Their Use and Acknowledgment. Hanover, NH: Dartmouth College; 1964.

Southgate MT. Conflict of interest and the peer review process. *JAMA.* 1987;258:1375.

Stewart WW, Feder N. The integrity of the scientific literature. *Nature.* 1987;325:207-214.

4.0   Editorial Assessment and Processing

Bailar JC III, Patterson K. Journal peer review: the need for a research agenda. *N Engl J Med.* 1985;312:654-657.

Cole S, Cole JR, Simon GA. Chance and consensus in peer review. *Science.* 1981;214:881.

Harnad S. *Peer Commentary on Peer Review: A Case Study in Scientific Quality Control.* New York, NY: Cambridge University Press; 1983.

Horrobin DF. Peer review: a philosophically faulty concept which is proving disastrous for science. *Behav Brain Sci.* 1982;5:217-218.

Lock S. *A Difficult Balance: Editorial Peer Review in Medicine.* Philadelphia, Pa: ISI Press; 1986. First published by the Nuffield Hospitals Trust, London, England, 1985.

Lundberg GD, Carney MJ. Peer review at *JAMA*—1985. *JAMA.* 1986;255:3286-3292.

Sci Technol Hum Values. 1985;10(3):3-102.

5.0   Grammar

Bernstein TM. *The Careful Writer: A Modern Guide to English Usage.* New York, NY: Atheneum; 1984.

Day RA. *How to Write and Publish a Scientific Paper.* 2nd ed. Philadelphia, Pa: ISI Press; 1983.

Fowler HW; Gowers E, ed. *A Dictionary of Modern English Usage.* 2nd ed. New York, NY: Oxford University Press; 1965.

Warriner JE. *Warriner's English Grammar and Composition: Complete Course.* Franklin edition. New York, NY: Harcourt Brace Jovanovich Publishers; 1982.

8.0   Capitalization

Anastasi A. *Psychological Testing.* 5th ed. New York, NY: Macmillan Publishing Co Inc; 1982.

9.0   Correct and Preferred Usage

American Psychological Association. *Publication Manual of the American Psychological Association.* 3rd ed. Washington, DC: American Psychological Association; 1983:45-49.

Baron D. *Grammar and Gender.* New Haven, Conn: Yale University Press; 1986.

Baron D. *Grammar and Good Taste: Reforming the American Language.* New Haven, Conn: Yale University Press; 1982.

The Chicago Manual of Style. 13th ed. Chicago, Ill: University of Chicago Press; 1982.

CBE Style Manual Committee. *CBE Style Manual: A Guide for Authors, Editors, and Publishers in the Biological Sciences.* 5th ed. Bethesda, Md: Council of Biology Editors Inc; 1983.

Follett W. *Modern American Usage.* New York, NY: Hill & Wang; 1966:358.

Fowler HW; Gowers E, ed. *A Dictionary of Modern English Usage.* 2nd ed. New York, NY: Oxford University Press; 1965.

Huth EJ. *Medical Style & Format: An International Manual for Authors, Editors, and Publishers.* Philadelphia, Pa: ISI Press; 1987.

Miller C, Swift K. *The Handbook of Nonsexist Writing.* New York, NY: Lippincott & Crowell; 1980.

11.0 Abbreviations

The Chicago Manual of Style. 13th ed. Chicago, Ill: University of Chicago Press; 1982:190-192, 376-398.

Delong MF. *Medical Acronyms & Abbreviations.* Oradell, NJ: Medical Economics Books; 1985.

International Committee of Medical Journal Editors. Uniform requirements for manuscripts submitted to biomedical journals. *Ann Intern Med.* 1982;96:766-771. *Br Med J Clin Res.* 1982;284:1766-1770.

Sloane SB. *Medical Abbreviations and Eponyms.* Philadelphia, Pa: WB Saunders Co; 1985.

12.0 Nomenclature

● Introduction

Biggs R, ed. *Human Blood Coagulation, Haemostasis and Thrombosis.* 2nd ed. Oxford, England: Blackwell Scientific Publications; 1976:16.

Paterson PY, Sommers HM. A proposed change in bacterial nomenclature: 'a rose by any other name is not a rose.' *J Infect Dis.* 1981;44:85-86.

Shows TB, Alper CA, Bootsma D, et al. International system for human gene nomenclature (1979)—ISGN 1979. *Cytogenet Cell Genet.* 1979;25:97.

Wildy P. *Classification and Nomenclature of Viruses: First Report of the International Committee on Nomenclature of Viruses.* New York, NY: S Karger AG; 1971;5:7. In: Melnick JL, ed. Monographs in Virology.

● 12.1 Blood Groups

Crookston MC. Written communication. October 8, 1986.

Giblett ER. Erythrocyte antigens and antibodies. In: Williams WJ, Beutler E, Erslev AJ, Lichtman MA. *Hematology.* 3rd ed. New York, NY: McGraw-Hill International Book Co; 1983:1491-1502.

Issit PD, Crookston MC. Blood group terminology: current conventions. *Transfusion.* 1984;24:2-7.

Wintrobe MM, Lee GR, Boggs DR, et al. *Clinical Hematology.* 8th ed. Philadelphia, Pa: Lea & Febiger; 1981:453-469.

● **12.2   Cancer Staging**

Beahrs OH, Henson DE, Hutter RVP, Myers MH (American Joint Committee on Cancer), eds. *Manual for Staging of Cancer.* 3rd ed. Philadelphia, Pa: JB Lippincott Co; 1988.

Brennan MJ, Swanson M. Written communication. April 10, 1987.

Hermanek P, Sobin LH, eds. *TNM Classification of Malignant Tumours.* 4th ed. Geneva, Switzerland: International Union Against Cancer (UICC); 1987.

● **12.3   Cardiology**

12.3.1 *Electrocardiographic Terms*

Castellanos A, Myerburg RJ. The resting electrocardiogram. In: Hurst JW, Logue RB, Rackley CE, et al. *The Heart.* 6th ed. New York, NY: McGraw-Hill International Book Co; 1986:206-215.

Fisch C. Electrocardiography and vectorcardiography. In: Braunwald E, ed. *Heart Disease: A Textbook of Cardiovascular Medicine.* 2nd ed. Philadelphia, Pa: WB Saunders Co; 1984:195-207.

Goldman MJ. *Principles of Clinical Electrocardiography.* 11th ed. Los Altos, Calif: Lange Medical Publications; 1982:1-35.

Lipman BS, Dunn M, Massie E. *Clinical Electrocardiography.* 7th ed. Chicago, Ill: Year Book Medical Publishers; 1984:1-33.

Resnekov L. Written communication. September 16, 1986.

12.3.2 *Heart Sounds and Murmurs*

Braunwald E, ed. *Heart Disease: A Textbook of Cardiovascular Medicine.* 2nd ed. Philadelphia, Pa: WB Saunders Co; 1984:30-32.

Leatham A, Leech GJ, Harvey WP, de Leon AC Jr. Auscultation of the heart. In: Hurst JW, Logue RB, Rackley CE, et al. *The Heart.* 6th ed. New York, NY: McGraw-Hill International Book Co; 1986:157-195.

Resnekov L. Written communication. September 16, 1986.

● **12.4   Clotting Factors**

Biggs R. *Human Blood Coagulation, Haemostasis, and Thrombosis.* 2nd ed. Oxford, England: Blackwell Scientific Publications; 1976:15-16. A third edition of this work came out in 1984.

Kasper C. Written communications. October 15, 1984; November 19, 1984; September 6, 1986.

Triplett DA. *Hemostasis: A Case-Oriented Approach.* New York, NY: Igaku-Shoin Medical Publishers Inc; 1985:3-27.

Williams WJ. Biochemistry of plasma coagulation factors. In: Williams

WJ, Beutler E, Erslev AJ, Lichtman MA. *Hematology*. 3rd ed. New York, NY: McGraw-Hill International Book Co; 1983:1202.

Wintrobe MM, Lee GR, Boggs DR, et al. *Clinical Hematology*. 8th ed. Philadelphia, Pa: Lea & Febiger; 1981:405-406, 391-392.

● **12.5   Diabetes Mellitus**

Ginsberg-Fellner F, Witt ME, Franklin BH, et al. Triad of markers for identifying children at high risk of developing insulin-dependent diabetes mellitus. *JAMA*. 1985;254:1469-1472.

Griffiths MC, Fleeger CA, Miller LC, eds. *USAN and the USP Dictionary of Drug Names*. Rockville, Md: US Pharmacopeial Convention Inc; 1985:171.

National Diabetes Data Group. Classification and diagnosis of diabetes mellitus and other categories of glucose intolerance. *Diabetes*. 1979;28:1039-1057.

National Diabetes Data Group. Report of the expert committee on glycosylated hemoglobin. *Diabetes Care*. 1984;7:602-606.

● **12.6   Drugs**

AMA Division of Drugs. *AMA Drug Evaluations*. 5th ed. Chicago, Ill: American Medical Association; 1983. A sixth edition of this work came out in 1986.

Larsen PR (chairman), Alexander NM, Chopra IJ, et al (Committee on Nomenclature of the American Thyroid Association). Revised nomenclature for tests of thyroid hormones and thyroid-related proteins in serum. *J Clin Endocrinol Metab*. 1987;64:1089-1092.

Fuerst S, Van Laan S, eds. *AMA International Drug Nomenclature Edit Copy*. Chicago, Ill: American Medical Association; 1986.

Gilman AG, Goodman LS, Rall TW, Murad F, eds. *Goodman and Gilman's the Pharmacological Basis of Therapeutics*. 7th ed. New York, NY: Macmillan Publishing Co Inc; 1985.

Griffiths MC, Fleeger CA, Miller LC, eds. *USAN and the USP Dictionary of Drug Names*. Rockville, Md: US Pharmacopeial Convention Inc; 1985:5-12, 383-386.

● **12.7   Endocrinology**

Cryer PE. *Diagnostic Endocrinology*. 2nd ed. New York, NY: Oxford University Press; 1979:8-32.

Griffiths MC, Fleeger CA, Miller LC, eds. *USAN and the USP Dictionary of Drug Names*. Rockville, Md: US Pharmacopeial Convention Inc; 1985.

● **12.9   Genetics**

Instructions to authors. *J Biol Chem*. 1987;262:1-11.

Motulsky AG. Written communication. September 15, 1986.

21.1   References

12.9.1   *DNA, RNA, and Amino Acids*

Lehninger AL. *Principles of Biochemistry*. New York, NY: Worth Publishers; 1982:95-100, 871-885, 897.

Thompson JS, Thompson MW. *Genetics in Medicine*. 4th ed. Philadelphia, Pa: WB Saunders Co; 1986.

12.9.2   *Restriction Enzymes*

Bethesda Research Laboratories Catalogue and Reference Guide. Bethesda, Md: Bethesda Research Laboratories; 1985.

Smith HO, Nathans D. A suggested nomenclature for bacterial host modification and restriction systems and their enzymes. *J Mol Biol*. 1973;81:419-423.

New England BioLabs, Inc, 1986-1987 Catalog. Beverly, Mass: New England BioLabs Inc; 1987.

12.9.3   *Human Gene Nomenclature*

Klinger HP. Progress in nomenclature and symbols for cytogenetics and somatic-cell genetics. *Ann Intern Med*. 1979;91:487-488.

McAlpine PJ, Shows TB, Miller RL, Pakstis AJ. The 1985 catalog of mapped genes and report of the nomenclature committee. *Cytogenet Cell Genet*. 1985;40:8-66.

McAlpine PJ, Van Cong N, Boucheix C, Pakstis AJ, Doute RC, Shows TB. The 1987 catalogue of mapped genes and report of the nomenclature committee. *Cyogenet Cell Genet*. 1987;46:29-101.

McKusick VA. *Mendelian Inheritance in Man: Catalogs of Autosomal Dominant, Autosomal Recessive, and X-linked Phenotypes*. 7th ed. Baltimore, Md: The Johns Hopkins University Press; 1986:x.

Shows TB, Alper CA, Bootsma D, et al. International system for human gene nomenclature (1981)—ISGN 1981. *Cytogenet Cell Genet*. 1982;32:221-245.

Shows TB, McAlpine PJ, Bouchiex C, et al. Guidelines for human gene nomenclature: an international system for human gene nomenclature (ISGN 1987). *Cytogenet Cell Genet*. 1987;46:12-28.

Shows TB, McAlpine PJ, Miller RL. The 1983 catalogue of mapped genetic markers and report of the nomenclature committee. *Cytogenet Cell Genet*. 1984;37:340-393.

Thompson JS, Thompson MW. *Genetics in Medicine*. 4th ed. Philadelphia, Pa: WB Saunders Co; 1986.

12.9.4   *Oncogenes*

Marshall CJ, Rigby PWJ. Viral and cellular genes involved in oncogenesis. *Cancer Surv*. 1984;3:183-214.

Weinberg B. A molecular basis of cancer. *Sci Am*. 1983;249:126-142.

Weiss RA, Marshall CJ. Oncogenes. *Lancet*. 1984;2:1138-1142.

Yunis JJ. The chromosomal basis of human neoplasia. *Science.* 1983;221:227-236.

12.9.5 Chromosomes

Garson OM. Introduction to nomenclature. *Clin Haematol.* 1980;9:3-18.

ISCN (1981). An international system for human cytogenetic nomenclature—high-resolution banding (1981). *Birth Defects.* 1981;17(No. 5). Also in *Cytogenet Cell Genet.* 1981;31:1-23.

Paris conference (1971). Standardization in human cytogenetics. *Birth Defects.* 1972;8(No.7). Also in *Cytogenet Cell Genet.* 1972;11:313-362.

Paris conference (1971) supplement (1975). Standardization in human cytogenetics. *Birth Defects.* 1975;11(No. 9). Also in *Cytogenet Cell Genet.* 1975;15:201-238.

Sandberg AA, Hecht BK-M, Hecht F. Nomenclature: the Philadelphia chromosome or Ph without superscript. *Cancer Genet Cytogenet.* 1985;14:1.

Thompson JS, Thompson MW. *Genetics in Medicine.* 4th ed. Philadelphia, Pa: WB Saunders Co; 1986.

12.9.6 Animal Genetic Terms

CBE Style Manual Committee. *CBE Style Manual: A Guide for Authors, Editors, and Publishers in the Biological Sciences.* 5th ed. Bethesda, Md: Council of Biology Editors Inc; 1983.

Green MC, ed. *Genetic Variants and Strains of the Laboratory Mouse.* New York, NY: Gustav Fischer Verlag; 1981.

Morse HC III. The laboratory mouse—a historical perspective. In: Foster HL, Fox F, eds. *The Mouse in Biomedical Research.* Orlando, Fla: Academic Press Inc; 1981;1:6-10.

Staats J. Standardized nomenclature for inbred strains of mice: eighth listing. *Cancer Res.* 1985;45:945-977.

● 12.11 Hepatitis

Diseases of the Liver and Biliary Tract: Standardization of Nomenclature, Diagnostic Criteria, and Diagnostic Methodology. Washington, DC: US Government Printing Office; 1977. Fogarty International Center Proceedings. No. 22. US Dept of Health, Education, and Welfare publication NIH 77-725.

Iber FL. Written communication. September 1986.

Immunization Practices Advisory Committe (ACIP). Recommendations for protection against viral hepatitis. *MMWR.* 1985;34:313-335.

Schiff L, Schiff ER. *Diseases of the Liver.* 5th ed. Philadelphia, Pa: JB Lippincott; 1982:465-466, 475.

21.1   References

- **12.12   Immunology**

  12.12.1   *Complement*

  Atkinson JP, Frank MM. Complement. In: Parker CW, ed. *Clinical Immunology*. Philadelphia, Pa: WB Saunders Co; 1980;1:219-223.

  Bennington JL, ed. *Saunders Dictionary and Encyclopedia of Laboratory Medicine and Technology*. Philadelphia, Pa: WB Saunders Co; 1984:355-356.

  Cooper NR. The complement system. In: Stites DP, Stobo JD, Fudenberg HH, Wells JV, eds. *Basic and Clinical Immunology*. 5th ed. Los Altos, Calif: Appleton & Lange; 1984:119-131.

  Cooper NR, Cochrane CG. The biochemistry and biologic activities of the complement and contact systems. In: Williams WJ, Beutler E, Erslev AJ, Lichtman MA, eds. *Hematology*. 3rd ed. New York, NY: McGraw-Hill International Book Co; 1983:98-99.

  Lockey RF, Ledford DK. Written communication. September 25, 1986.

  Wintrobe MM, Lee GR, Boggs DR, et al. *Clinical Hematology*. 8th ed. Philadelphia, Pa: Lea & Febiger; 1981:312-313.

  World Health Organization. Nomenclature of complement. *Bull WHO*. 1968;39:935-938.

  12.12.2   *Human Leukocyte (HLA) and Other Histocompatibility Antigens*

  Albert ED, Baur MP, Mayr WR, eds. *Histocompatibility Testing 1984*. New York, NY: Springer-Verlag; 1984:1-11.

  Kostyu DD, Reisner EG. Human leukocyte and platelet antigens and antibodies. In: Williams WJ, Beutler E, Erslev AJ, Lichtman MA. *Hematology*. 3rd ed. New York, NY: McGraw-Hill International Book Co; 1983:1505-1507, 1515.

  Lockey RF, Ledford DK. Written communication. September 25, 1986.

  Parker CW, ed. *Clinical Immunology*. Philadelphia, Pa: WB Saunders Co; 1980:63-69, 85.

  Schwartz BD. The human major histocompatibility HLA complex. In: Stites DP, Stobo JD, Fudenberg HH, Wells JV, eds. *Basic and Clinical Immunology*. 6th ed. Los Altos, Calif: Appleton & Lange; 1987:50-64.

  Schwartz BD. Written communication. March 2, 1987.

  Wintrobe MM, Lee GR, Boggs DR, et al. *Clinical Hematology*. 8th ed. Philadelphia, Pa: Lea & Febiger; 1981:470-478.

  World Health Organization. Nomenclature for factors of the HLA system 1980. *Immunology*. 1982;46:231-234.

  12.12.3   *Immunoglobulins*

  Goodman JW. Immunoglobulins, I: structure and function. In: Stites DP, Stobo JD, Fudenberg HH, Wells JV. *Basic and Clinical Im-*

munology. 5th ed. Los Altos, Calif: Lange Medical Publications; 1984:30-42.

Lockey RF, Ledford DK. Written communication. September 25, 1986.

Ricardo MJ, Tomar RH. Immunoglobulins and paraproteins. In: Henry JB, ed. *Todd, Sanford, Davidsohn Clinical Diagnosis and Management by Laboratory Methods*. Philadelphia, Pa: WB Saunders Co; 1984:860-878.

Richardson B. Immunoglobulin. In: Bennington JL, ed. *Saunders Dictionary and Encyclopedia of Laboratory Medicine and Technology*. Philadelphia, Pa: WB Saunders Co; 1984:790-792.

12.12.4 Lymphocytes and Monoclonal Antibodies

Bernard A, Boumsell L. The clusters of differentiation (CD) defined by the First International Workshop on Human Leucocyte Differentiation Antigens. *Hum Immunol*. 1984;11:1-10.

Ferrone S, Dierich MP. *Handbook of Monoclonal Antibodies: Applications in Biology and Medicine*. Park Ridge, NJ: Noyes Publications; 1985:473-477.

Foon KA, Schroff RW, Gale RP. Surface markers on leukemia and lymphoma cells: recent advances. *Blood*. 1982; 60:1-19.

Lockey RF, Ledford DK. Written communication. September 25, 1986.

McMichael AJ, Beverley PCL, Gilks W, et al, eds. *Leucocyte Typing III: White Cell Differentiation Antigens*. New York, NY: Oxford University Press; 1987. Proceedings of the Third International Workshop and Conference on Human Leucocyte Differentiation Antigens.

Monoclonal Antibody Source Book. Mountain View, Calif: Becton Dickinson Monoclonal Center Inc; 1985.

Stobo JD. Lymphocytes. In: Stites DP, Stobo JD, Fudenberg HH, Wells, JV, eds. *Basic and Clinical Immunology*. Los Altos, Calif: Appleton & Lange; 1984:69-85.

• 12.13   Isotopes

Cahn RS, Dermer OC. *Introduction to Chemical Nomenclature*. 5th ed. Boston, Mass: Butterworths Publishers Inc; 1979:9, 174-176.

Chilton HM, Witcofski RL. *Nuclear Pharmacy: An Introduction to the Clinical Application of Radiopharmaceuticals*. Philadelphia, Pa: Lea & Febiger; 1986.

Griffiths MC, Fleeger CA, Miller LC, eds. *USAN and the USP Dictionary of Drug Names*. Rockville, Md: US Pharmacopeial Convention Inc; 1985:11, 379.

Instructions to authors. *J Biol Chem*. 1987;262:5.

Wolf AP. Letter to the editor (reply). *J Nucl Med*. 1981;22:392-393.

21.1   References

● **12.14   Neurology**

12.14.2   Electroencephalographic (EEG) Terms

Binnie CD, Rowan AJ, Gutter TH. *A Manual of Electroencephalographic Technology.* New York, NY: Cambridge University Press; 1982:131-137, 325-331.

Cooper R, Osselton JW, Shaw JC. *EEG Technology.* London, England: Butterworths; 1980:91-98.

Hughes JR. *EEG in Clinical Practice.* Boston, Mass: Butterworths; 1982.

Jasper HH. Report of the Committee on Methods of Clinical Examination in Electroencephalography. *Electroencephalogr Clin Neurophysiol.* 1958;10:370-375.

Joynt R, Satran R. Written communication. December 30, 1986.

Satran R. Written communication. February 9, 1987.

● **12.15   Obstetric Terms**

Pritchard JA, MacDonald PC. *Williams Obstetrics.* 16th ed. Norwalk, Conn: Appleton-Century-Crofts; 1980:304.

● **12.16   Organisms**

12.16.1   Genus and Species

Berger SA, Edberg SC. Microbial nomenclature: a list of names and origins. *Diagn Microbiol Infect Dis.* 1987;6:343-356.

Brenner DJ. Taxonomy, classification, and nomenclature of bacteria. In: Lennette EH, Balows A, Hausler WJ Jr, Shadomy HJ, eds. *Manual of Clinical Microbiology.* 4th ed. Washington, DC: American Society for Microbiology; 1985:1-7.

12.16.2   Viruses

Case K. Nomenclature: human immunodeficiency virus. *Ann Intern Med.* 1986;105:133.

Coffin J, Haase A, Levy JA, et al. Human immunodeficiency viruses. *Science.* 1986;232:697.

Fraenkel-Conrat H. *The Viruses: Catalogue, Characterization, and Classification.* New York, NY: Plenum Press; 1985.

Kucera LS, Myrvik QN. *Fundamentals of Medical Virology.* 2nd ed. Philadelphia, Pa: Lea & Febiger; 1985:1-15.

Mandell GL, Douglas RG Jr, Bennett JE. *Principles and Practice of Infectious Diseases.* 2nd ed. New York, NY: John Wiley & Sons Inc; 1985:846-861.

Marx JL. AIDS virus has a new name—perhaps. *Science.* 1986;232:699-700.

Matthews REF. Classification and nomenclature of viruses: third report of the International Committee on Taxonomy of Viruses. *Intervirology.* 1979;12:129-296.

Matthews REF. Classification and nomenclature of viruses: fourth report of the International Committee on Taxonomy of Viruses. *Intervirology.* 1982;17:1-199.

Melnick JL. Taxonomy and nomenclature of viruses, 1982. *Prog Med Virol.* 1982;28:208-221.

Roizman B. Written communication. March 1987.

Wildy P. *Classification and Nomenclature of Viruses: First Report of the International Committee on Nomenclature of Viruses.* New York, NY: S Karger AG, 1971;5:1-26. In: Melnick JL, ed. Monographs in Virology.

● **12.17   Pulmonary and Respiratory Terminology**

Cugell DW. Personal communication. September 12, 1986.

Fishman AP. *Assessment of Pulmonary Function.* New York, NY: McGraw-Hill International Book Co; 1980:285-296.

Fishman AP, ed. *Handbook of Physiology: A Critical, Comprehensive Presentation of Physiological Knowledge and Concepts.* Bethesda, Md: American Physiological Society; 1986;2(section 3, pt 1):endpapers.

Macklem PT. Symbols and abbreviations. In: Fishman AP, ed. *Handbook of Physiology: A Critical, Comprehensive Presentation of Physiological Knowledge and Concepts.* Bethesda, Md: American Physiological Society; 1986;2(section 3, pt 1):ix.

West JB. *Respiratory Physiology: The Essentials.* 3rd ed. Baltimore, Md: Williams & Wilkins; 1985:1-183.

13.0   Eponyms

Dirckx JH. *The Language of Medicine: Its Evolution, Structure, and Dynamics.* 2nd ed. New York, NY: Praeger Publishers; 1983.

Huth EJ. *How to Write and Publish Papers in the Medical Sciences.* Philadelphia, Pa: ISI Press; 1982:120-121.

15.0   Units of Measure

Conn RB. Scientific medicine and Système International units. *Arch Pathol Lab Med.* 1987;111:16-19.

Lundberg GD, Iverson C, Radulescu G. Now read this: the SI units are here. *JAMA.* 1986;255:2329-2339.

McQueen MJ. Conversion to SI units: the Canadian experience. *JAMA.* 1986;256:3001-3002.

Metric Commission Canada, Sector 9.10 Health and Welfare. *The SI Manual in Health Care.* 2nd ed. Ottawa, Ontario: Metric Commission Canada; 1982.

Young DS. Implementation of SI units for clinical laboratory data: style specifications and conversion tables. *Ann Intern Med.* 1987;106:114-129.

21.1   *References*

Other Services

For those who require an immediate answer to tough grammar, usage, and language questions, the Humanities Division of Tidewater Community College, Virginia Beach, Va, publishes the *Grammar Hotline Directory*. The pamphlet lists grammar hotlines throughout the United States and Canada. To obtain a copy, send a stamped, self-addressed envelope to Grammar Hotline Directory, Writing Center, Tidewater Community College, 1700 College Crescent, Virginia Beach, VA 23456. The directory is updated annually in January.

21.2   Additional Readings

American Psychological Association. *Publication Manual of the American Psychological Association.* 3rd ed. Washington, DC: American Psychological Association; 1983.

Armitage P. *Statistical Methods in Medical Research.* New York, NY: Halsted Press; 1971.

Baron D. *Grammar and Gender.* New Haven, Conn: Yale University Press; 1986.

Baron D. *Grammar and Good Taste: Reforming the American Language.* New Haven, Conn: Yale University Press; 1982.

Baskette FK, Sissors JC. *The Art of Editing.* New York, NY: Macmillan Publishing Co Inc; 1971.

Bernstein TM. *Dos, Don'ts & Maybes of English Usage.* New York, NY: Times Books; 1977.

Bernstein TM. *Miss Thistlebottom's Hobgoblins: The Careful Writer's Guide to the Taboos, Bugbears and Outmoded Rules of English Usage.* New York, NY: Simon & Schuster; 1971.

Bernstein TM. *The Careful Writer: A Modern Guide to English Usage.* New York, NY: Atheneum; 1984.

Beyer WH, ed. *CRC Standard Mathematical Tables.* 27th ed. Boca Raton, Fla: CRC Press Inc; 1984.

Bishop CT. *How to Edit a Scientific Journal.* Philadelphia, Pa: ISI Press; 1984.

Boston BO, ed. *Stet! Tricks of the Trade for Writers and Editors.* Alexandria, Va: Editorial Experts Inc; 1986.

Brownlee KA. *Statistical Theory and Methodology in Science and Engineering.* 2nd ed. New York, NY: John Wiley & Sons Inc; 1965.

CBE Style Manual Committee. *CBE Style Manual: A Guide for Authors, Editors, and Publishers in the Biological Sciences.* 5th ed. Bethesda, Md: Council of Biology Editors Inc; 1983.

The Chicago Manual of Style. 13th ed. Chicago, Ill: University of Chicago Press; 1982.

Cochran WG. *Sampling Techniques.* 2nd ed. New York, NY: John Wiley & Sons Inc; 1963.

Cochran WG, Cox GM. *Experimental Designs.* 2nd ed. New York, NY: John Wiley & Sons Inc; 1957.

Colton T. *Statistics in Medicine.* Boston, Mass: Little Brown & Co Inc; 1974.

Conover WJ. *Practical Nonparametric Statistics.* New York, NY: John Wiley & Sons Inc; 1980.

Copperud RH. *American Usage and Style: The Consensus.* New York, NY: Van Nostrand Reinhold Co; 1980.

Daniel C, Wood FS, Gorman JW. *Fitting Equations to Data: Computer Analysis of Multifactor Data for Scientists and Engineers.* New York, NY: John Wiley & Sons Inc; 1971.

Day RA. *How to Write and Publish a Scientific Paper.* 3rd ed. Phoenix, Ariz: Oryx Press; 1988.

Delong MF. *Medical Acronyms & Abbreviations.* Oradell, NJ: Medical Economics Books; 1985.

Dodd JS, ed. *The ACS Style Guide: A Manual for Authors and Editors.* Washington, DC: American Chemical Society; 1985.

Feinstein AR. *Clinical Epidemiology: The Architecture of Clinical Research.* Philadelphia, Pa: WB Saunders Co; 1985.

Fishbein M. *Medical Writing: The Technic and the Art.* 4th ed. Springfield, Ill: Charles C Thomas Publisher; 1978.

Fleiss J. *Statistical Methods for Rates and Proportions.* 2nd ed. New York, NY: John Wiley & Sons Inc; 1981.

Follett W; Barzun J, ed. *Modern American Usage: A Guide.* New York, NY: Hill & Wang; 1966.

Fowler HW; Gowers E, ed. *A Dictionary of Modern English Usage.* 2nd ed. New York, NY: Oxford University Press Inc; 1965.

Friedman LM, Furberg CD, DeMets DL. *Fundamentals of Clinical Trials.* Littleton, Mass: PSG Publishing Co Inc; 1981.

Gordon KE. *The Transitive Vampire: A Handbook of Grammar for the Innocent, the Eager, and the Doomed.* New York, NY: Times Books; 1984.

Gordon KE. *The Well-Tempered Sentence: A Punctuation Handbook for the Innocent, the Eager, and the Doomed.* New Haven, Conn: Ticknor & Fields; 1983.

Guide for Wiley Interscience and Ronald Press. 2nd ed. New York, NY: John Wiley & Sons Inc; 1974.

Hamilton B, Guidos B, eds. *MASA: Medical Acronyms, Symbols & Abbreviations.* New York, NY: Neal-Schuman Publishers Inc; 1984.

Hawkins C, Sorgi M, eds. *Research: How to Plan, Speak and Write About It.* Berlin, West Germany: Springer-Verlag; 1985.

Hodges JC, Whitten ME. *Harbrace College Handbook.* 9th ed. New York, NY: Harcourt Brace Jovanovich Inc; 1982.

Holley FS. *Los Angeles Times Stylebook: A Manual for Writers, Editors, Journalists and Students.* New York, NY: Meridian; 1981.

Holum JR. *Fundamentals of General, Organic, and Biological Chemistry.* 3rd ed. New York, NY: John Wiley & Sons Inc; 1986.

Huth EJ. *How to Write and Publish Papers in the Medical Sciences.* Philadelphia, Pa: ISI Press; 1982.

Huth EJ. *Medical Style & Format: An International Manual for Authors, Editors, and Publishers.* Philadelphia, Pa: ISI Press; 1987.

Jordan L, ed. *The New York Times Manual of Style and Usage.* New York, NY: Times Books; 1976.

Kilpatrick JJ. *The Writer's Art.* Kansas City, Mo: Andrews McMeel & Parker Inc; 1984.

King LS. *Why Not Say It Clearly: A Guide to Scientific Writing.* Boston, Mass: Little Brown & Co Inc; 1978.

Krieg NR, Holt JG, eds. *Bergey's Manual of Systematic Bacteriology.* Baltimore, Md: Williams & Wilkins; 1984.

MacMahon B, Pugh TF. *Epidemiology.* Boston, Mass: Little Brown & Co Inc; 1970.

Metric Commission Canada. *SI Manual in Health Care.* 2nd ed. Toronto, Ontario: Metric Commission Canada; 1982.

Miller C, Swift K. *The Handbook of Nonsexist Writing.* New York, NY: Lippincott & Crowell; 1980.

Morris W, Morris M. *Harper Dictionary of Contemporary Usage.* 2nd ed. New York, NY: Harper & Row Publishers Inc; 1985.

Nordic Publication Committee for Medicine; Svartz-Malmberg G, Goldmann R, eds. *Nordic Biomedical Manuscripts: Instructions and Guidelines.* Oslo, Norway: Universitets Forlaget; 1978.

Plotnik A. *The Elements of Editing: A Modern Guide for Editors and Journalists.* New York, NY: Macmillan Publishing Co Inc; 1982.

Safire W. *On Language.* New York, NY: Avon Books; 1981.

Sloane SB. *Medical Abbreviations and Eponyms.* Philadelphia, Pa: WB Saunders Co; 1985.

Snedecor GW, Cochran WG. *Statistical Methods.* 7th ed. Ames, Iowa: Iowa State University Press; 1980.

Strunk W Jr, White EB. *The Elements of Style.* 3rd ed. New York, NY: Macmillan Publishing Co Inc; 1979.

Swanson E. *Mathematics Into Type: Copyediting and Proofreading of Mathematics for Editorial Assistants and Authors.* Rev ed. Providence, RI: American Mathematical Society; 1979.

Warriner JE. *Warriner's English Grammar and Composition: Complete*

Course. Franklin edition. New York, NY: Harcourt Brace Jovanovich Publishers; 1982.

Webb RA. *The Washington Post Deskbook on Style*. New York, NY:
McGraw-Hill International Book Co; 1978.

Williams JM. *Style: Ten Lessons in Clarity and Grace*. 2nd ed. Glenview,
Ill: Scott Foresman & Co; 1985.

Winer BJ. *Statistical Principles in Experimental Design*. 2nd ed. New
York, NY: McGraw-Hill International Book Co; 1971.

World Health Organization. *The SI for the Health Professions*. Geneva,
Switzerland: World Health Organization; 1977.

Wyngaarden JB, Smith LH Jr, eds. *Cecil Textbook of Medicine*. 18th ed.
Philadelphia, Pa: WB Saunders Co; 1988.

Zinsser W. *On Writing Well: An Informal Guide to Writing Nonfiction*.
2nd ed. New York, NY: Harper & Row Publishers Inc; 1980.

21.3   **On-line Resources.**—Biomedicine is especially well represented by a wide
variety of on-line resources that cover the international literature. Speed,
flexibility, and timeliness make these on-line resources particularly attractive to physicians and other health professionals as an aid to answering
a clinical question, compiling a subject bibliography, verifying an elusive
citation, or building a personal reprint file.

21.3.1   *MEDLINE.*—The best known and most widely used of these electronic
retrieval systems in the medical field is MEDLINE, produced by the National Library of Medicine. This family of bibliographic databases provides
access to citations from more than 3000 medical and biomedical journals
worldwide that cover a period from 1966 to the present. Abstracts are
available for 60% of the citations. In addition to journal articles, substantive
editorials, letters, and obituaries are indexed. Approximately 24000 citations are added to the file monthly.

Quality control: To maintain the integrity of the information contained in
its databases, the National Library of Medicine has instituted two policies
to improve the quality of MEDLINE services.

The first policy was the addition in 1984 of the index term *retraction
of publication*, enabling the on-line searcher to locate an article that has
been officially withdrawn from publication either by the editor of the
journal in which it originally appeared or by the authors themselves. What
appears under this heading is the reference to the notice of retraction. The
citation to the original article is appended to the retraction notice as follows:
''Retraction of [author, journal, date].'' The citation to the original article
is then modified with the words ''Retracted by [author or editor, journal,
date].'' This service covers only those articles retracted since 1984.

Second, in 1987 the indexing staff at the National Library of Medicine began to correct errors in articles by amending the citation in MEDLINE. Only those errors that have been formally acknowledged by the editors of the journal or authors of the article will be corrected. A note that a correction has been made will be incorporated in the citation, along with a reference to the published correction as follows: "Published erratum appears in [journal, date]." For those errors occurring in a section of the article not reflected in the on-line citation, ie, tables, diagrams, text, or references, an error statement will appear in the citation, immediately following the title of the article. If the erratum notice is published in time to meet the annual printing deadline, the correction will also appear in *Cumulated Index Medicus.*

Gaining access: There are various methods of gaining access to MEDLINE. Medical librarians acting as search intermediaries can dial directly into the MEDLINE database through several database vendors. In addition to the National Library of Medicine, other vendors to contact for subscription information include AMA/NET, DIALOG Information Services, BRS Information Technologies, and Mead Data Central.

Increasingly, physicians are searching the literature themselves via microcomputers. The National Library of Medicine has produced a user-friendly access to MEDLINE entitled GRATEFUL MED. PaperChase, developed by physicians as an in-house private retrieval system for MEDLINE searching, can also be used without formal training. Equipment necessary for on-line searching includes a computer terminal, a modem, a telephone jack, a printer, and a password that allows the user to enter the system.

Database vendors and producers are making end-user searching simpler by developing easy-to-use software packages. "Front-end" systems acting as a user-friendly intermediary between the database and the physician perform certain steps in the search process automatically, eliminating the need for physicians to learn complicated database commands. A front-end system helps the physician formulate a search strategy off-line, log into the database, and enter the search argument. When the search is completed and the relevant information has been retrieved, the front-end logs off the system and automatically downloads the search results. The retrieved information can then be viewed on the terminal screen, printed off-line at a reduced charge, or saved in a disk file. Front-end systems with postprocessing capabilities enable the searcher to edit and reformat the results or use them in creating a personal reprint file. Front-end software packages for searching the National Library of Medicine databases are available from the Institute for Scientific Information (Sci-Mate), Personal Bibliographic Software Inc (Pro-Search), and SDC Information Services (Searchmaster).

The cost of a search is typically built on a flat search fee for each database inquiry and the number of minutes a user works on-line. Search fees vary, depending on the level of complexity and, like a telephone call, whether the user is working on-line at peak daytime rates or at lower evening rates.

21.3.2 *CD-ROM (Compact Disk–Read Only Memory).*—The optical storage technology that produces audio compact disks can also be used to store large amounts of information. More than 275 000 pages of text can be stored on a single compact disk. Used in conjunction with search software, CD-ROM technology has enormous potential for medical information retrieval. A microcomputer can easily be used to search a CD-ROM database with the addition of a CD player, a controller card, and a cable. Cambridge Scientific Abstracts and other vendors market CD-ROM editions of MED-LINE.

21.3.3 *MEDIS and COLLEAGUE.*—Several database producers have created entire data banks especially for the health professional. These data banks offer access to a number of different medical databases. MEDIS, a product of Mead Data Central, and COLLEAGUE, produced by BRS Information Technologies, are full-text random access systems that not only include access to the MEDLINE family of databases but offer the convenience of allowing the physician to search for any term that appears in the bibliographic citation, abstract, text, tables, diagrams, or references, thus greatly expanding retrieval capabilities. Using either of these systems, the medical professional, with minimal system training, could locate pertinent citations in MEDLINE and then, depending on availability, print out the text of those articles on-line.

21.3.4 *AMA/NET.*—Sponsored by the American Medical Association, AMA/NET provides the clinician with access to more than 20 information products. AMA/NET provides access to MEDLINE through PaperChase and an on-line version of GRATEFUL MED and three levels of access to the EMPIRES clinical literature subset of EXCERPTA MEDICA, exclusively available on AMA/NET. The Social and Economic Aspects of Medicine (SEAM) provides more than 30 000 references to articles and books on the sociology and economics of medicine. AP Medical News Update provides continuously updated access to medical articles from Associated Press. DxPlain is an interactive diagnostic decision support tool available exclusively on AMA/NET. And for convenience and completeness, access is provided to several public information sources, including the Centers for Disease Control and the surgeon general's office.

21.3.5 *Other National Library of Medicine Databases.*—The following databases illustrate the types of biomedical information available via electronic retrieval systems. In addition to MEDLINE, the National Library of Medicine produces the following.

*CATLINE (*CAT*alog On-*LINE*):* This electronic version of the card catalog at the National Library of Medicine includes bibliographic records for more than 600 000 book and serial titles in the fields of medicine, health care, nursing, and dentistry.

*AVLINE (*Audio*V*isual *Catalog On-*LINE*):* This database contains citations to more than 14 000 audiovisual programs, including films and videotapes in medicine, nursing, and dentistry. Records contain a summary of the program, and most are peer reviewed.

CANCERLINE: This is a data bank for the cancer clinician and researcher. CANCERLIT, a bibliographic database, includes citations to journal articles, conference proceedings, books, and government reports from 1963 to the present. CANCERPROJ and CLINPROT are full-text systems. CANCERPROJ contains summaries of research projects registered with the International Cancer Research Data Bank Branch. CLINPROT contains summaries of clinical trials of anticancer agents and therapies. The protocols are from the National Cancer Institute and include location of the study and name of the principal investigator. A user-friendly version of CLINPROT, entitled PHYSICIAN DATA QUERY or PDQ, is available from the National Library of Medicine and other database vendors.

*TOXLINE (*TOX*icology Literature On-*LINE*):* This database is a collection of bibliographic citations in the area of pharmacological, biochemical, and toxicologic effects of drugs and other chemicals. The citations are provided by a variety of subfile producers, including the National Library of Medicine, the Hazardous Materials Technical Center, and the Toxicology Research Projects, to name a few.

*TOXLIT (*TOX*icology* LIT*erature From Special Sources):* This is a separate collection of citations in the area of toxicologic effects of drugs and other chemicals. The citations in this database are provided by subfile producers that require royalty charges and are, therefore, separated from the citations in TOXLINE.

HAZARDOUS SUBSTANCES DATA BANK (HSDB): Part of the TOXNET data bank, this full-text system contains toxicity information on more than 4000 potentially hazardous substances. Records are peer reviewed and include safety and first-aid information, exposure standards, and regulatory requirements. Comparable with this service is the Registry of Toxic Effects of Chemical Substances (RTECS), which contains information regarding more than 80 000 substances. RTECS records do not contain the safety or first-aid information found in HSDB and are not peer reviewed.

*HISTLINE (HISTory of Medicine On-*LINE*):* This database contains more than 65 000 references to the book and journal literature in the history of medicine. Sources for the citations are *Index Medicus, Current Catalog,* and a core list of additional medical history journals. Abstracts are not available.

HEALTH PLANNING AND ADMINISTRATION: Produced in conjunction with the American Hospital Association, this file contains more than 300 000 references covering the nonclinical aspects of health care. The scope of subject matter includes health economics, manpower issues, government regulation, professional liability, and health care provision systems. Coverage is from 1975 to the present. The citations that make up this file are taken from MEDLINE in addition to the journal literature from the areas of health care provision and management.

BIOETHICS: This file comprises citations to journal and newspaper articles, books, court decisions, and public laws pertaining to the ethical and public policy issues involved in the provision of health care. Produced by the Kennedy Institute at Georgetown University in conjunction with the National Library of Medicine, this database contains more than 19 000 citations and covers the period from 1973 to the present.

21.3.6 *Other Databases.*—Databases of interest to the health professional from sources other than the National Library of Medicine include the following.

BIOSIS PREVIEWS: Produced by the Biosciences Information Services, BIOSIS PREVIEWS covers the international literature in the life sciences and includes citations to journals, books, conference proceedings, and reports from 1970 to the present.

CURRENT AWARENESS IN BIOLOGICAL SCIENCES (CABS): Designed for the biologic scientist, this database concentrates on the literature of biochemistry, biology, genetics, immunology, pharmacology, toxicology, and endocrinology. The file covers the period 1983 to the present and is available through Pergamon Press.

PSYCHINFO: Produced by the American Psychological Association, PSYCHINFO contains bibliographic citations to journals, books, and report literature in psychology and related fields. The file covers from 1967 to date.

EXCERPTA MEDICA: This bibliographic retrieval system is comparable with MEDLINE but with emphasis on the European literature. Produced by Elsevier, a Dutch publishing company, EXCERPTA MEDICA indexes 5000 journals from 1980 to the present. Indexing for this database is done by physicians.

21.3   On-line Resources

SCIENCE CITATION INDEX: Rather than using index terms to describe the contents of journal articles, SCIENCE CITATION INDEX uses cited references as index terms. By entering the bibliographic citation to a key article in a particular field, the physician can retrieve a bibliography of articles that have cited that key article. SCIENCE CITATION INDEX covers the fields of science and technology, including medicine and the biomedical sciences. Coverage is from 1974 to the present.

This list is by no means comprehensive. For more detailed information regarding these or other databases, contact a medical librarian.

21.3.7   *Resources*

AMA/NET
  Subscriber Support
  1560 Broadway
  Suite 900
  Denver, CO 80202
  (800) 426-2873

BRS/COLLEAGUE
  1290 Avenue of the Americas
  Suite 2345
  New York, NY 10019
  (212) 765-4840

BRS Information Technologies
  1200 Rte 7
  Latham, NY 12110
  (800) 345-4277

Cambridge Scientific Abstracts
  5161 River Rd
  Bethesda, MD 20816
  (301) 951-1400
  (800) 843-7751

DIALOG Information Services Inc
  3460 Hillview Ave
  Palo Alto, CA 94304
  (415) 858-3785

Institute for Scientific Information
  3501 Market St
  Philadelphia, PA 19104
  (800) 523-4092
  (215) 386-0100

MEDIS
  Mead Data Central
  9393 Springboro Pike
  PO Box 933
  Dayton, OH 45401
  (800) 553-3685

National Library of Medicine
  MEDLARS Management System
  8600 Rockville Pike
  Bethesda, MD 20209
  (301) 496-6193

PaperChase
  Division of Computer Medicine
  Beth Israel Hospital
  330 Brookline Ave
  Boston, MA 02215
  (617) 735-5610

Pergamon Press
  Fairview Park
  Elmsford, NY 10523
  (914) 592-7700

Personal Bibliographic Software Inc
  PO Box 4250
  Ann Arbor, MI 48106
  (313) 996-1580

SDC Information Services
  2500 Colorado Ave
  Santa Monica, CA 90406
  (213) 453-6194

6

Appendix

Virus Names

	Vernacular	Official Name
Family	poxvirus group	*Poxviridae*
Genus	vaccinia subgroup	*Orthopoxvirus*
Family	herpesvirus group	*Herpesviridae*
Subfamily	herpes simplex virus group	*Alphaherpesvirinae*
Genus	human herpesvirus 1 group	. . .
Species	herpes simplex virus type 1 (human [alpha] herpesvirus 1)	. . .
	varicella-zoster (human [alpha] herpesvirus 3)	. . .
Subfamily	cytomegalus group	*Betaherpesvirinae*
Genus	human cytomegalovirus group	. . .
Species	human cytomegalovirus (human [beta] herpesvirus 5)	. . .
Subfamily	lymphoproliferative virus group	*Gammaherpesvirinae*
	Epstein-Barr virus (human [gamma] herpesvirus 4)	. . .
Family	adenovirus family	*Adenoviridae*
Genus	mammalian adenoviruses	*Mastadenovirus*
Species	human adenovirus 2	*Mastadenovirus* h 2
Family	parvoviruses	*Parvoviridae*
Genus	adenoassociated virus (AAV)	*Dependovirus*
Species	adenoassociated virus type 2 (AAV type 2)	. . .
Family	reoviruses	*Reoviridae*
Genus	reovirus subgroup	*Reovirus*
Species	reovirus type 1	. . .
Genus	orbiviruses	*Orbivirus*
Genus	rotaviruses	*Rotavirus*
Species	human rotavirus	. . .
Family	togaviruses	*Togaviridae*
Genus	arbovirus group A	*Alphavirus*
Species	Eastern equine encephalomyelitis virus	. . .

351

Appendix

	Vernacular	Official Name
Genus	arbovirus group B	*Flavivirus*
Species	yellow fever virus	. . .
Genus	rubella virus	*Rubivirus*
Species	rubella virus	. . .
Family	coronavirus group	*Coronaviridae*
Genus	coronavirus	*Coronavirus*
Species	human coronavirus	. . .
Family	paramyxoviruses	*Paramyxoviridae*
Genus	paramyxovirus group	*Paramyxovirus*
Species	mumps virus	. . .
	parainfluenza 1	. . .
Genus	measles-rinderpest distemper (MRD) group	*Morbillivirus*
Species	measles virus	. . .
Genus	respiratory syncytial virus group	*Pneumovirus*
Species	respiratory syncytial virus	. . .
Family	influenza virus group	*Orthomyxoviridae*
Genus	influenza virus	*Influenzavirus*
Species	influenza A, influenza B, influenza C (see also 12.16.2, Nomenclature, Viruses)	. . .
Family	bullet-shaped virus group	*Rhabdoviridae*
Genus	vesicular stomatitis virus group	*Vesiculovirus*
Species	vesicular stomatitis virus	. . .
Genus	rabies virus group	*Lyssavirus*
Species	rabies virus	. . .
Family	arenavirus group	*Arenaviridae*
Genus	LCM virus group	*Arenavirus*
Species	lymphocytic choriomeningitis virus	. . .
Family	RNA tumor viruses (retroviruses)	*Retroviridae*
Subfamily	RNA tumor virus group	*Oncovirinae*
Genus	type C oncovirus group	. . .
Subgenus	mammalian type C oncoviruses	. . .
Species	feline sarcoma and leukemia viruses	. . .
Subfamily	lentiviruses	*Lentivirinae*
Species	human immunodeficiency virus (see also 12.16.2, Nomenclature, Viruses)	. . .
Family	picornavirus group	*Picornaviridae*
Genus	enterovirus	*Enterovirus*
Species	human poliovirus 1, human poliovirus 2, human poliovirus 3	. . .
	coxsackievirus A1, etc	. . .
	echovirus 1, etc	. . .
	enterovirus 69, etc	. . .

352

	Vernacular	Official Name
Genus	EMC virus group	*Cardiovirus*
Species	encephalomyocarditis (EMC) virus	. . .
Genus	common cold virus	*Rhinovirus*
Species	human rhinovirus 1A	. . .
Family	papovavirus group	*Papovaviridae*
Genus	papillomavirus	

INDEX

Abbreviations (*see also* Acronyms; Symbols)
  academic honors, 11.1
  addresses, 11.4
  agency names, 11.8
  all-capital, plural of, 6.11.5
  on axis captions of illustrations, 2.12.6
  at beginning of sentence/title, 15.3.3
  blood groups, 12.1
  business firm names, 11.7
  in bylines, 11.1
  chemical compounds and elements, 11.12
  chromosomes, 12.9.5, 12.9.6
  clinical terms, 11.10
  in compound words, 6.12.1
  days of week, 11.3
  definition, 11.0
  degrees (academic), 11.1
  denoting person, 7.1
  dermatomes, 12.18
  DNA types, 12.9.1
  drugs, 12.6.1
  elements, 11.12
  eras, 11.3
  in figures, 2.11.3
  first mention of, 15.3.4
  genus names, 12.16.1
  government agencies, 11.8
  hepatitis antigens/antibodies, 12.11
  intervertebral spaces, 12.18
  journal names, 2.10.14, 11.9
  mathematical, 18.1
  military services, 11.2.1
  military titles, 11.2.2
  months, 11.3
  mouse strain names, 12.9.6
  names of persons, 11.6
  organization names, 11.8
  in parentheses, 6.8.10
  period use with, 6.4.3, 15.4
  plurals of, 7.1, 15.3.2
  policy on, 11.0
  in reference lists, 11.9
  RNA types, 12.9.1
  SI units, 11.11
  spinal nerves, 12.18
  states, 11.5
  in tables, 2.13.9
  in column headings, 2.13.6
  footnote and, 2.13.6
  technical terms, 11.10
  territories, 11.5
  time units, 15.1.6, 15.3.1
  of titles (personal), 11.6
  in titles (publication), 2.1.5
  units of measure, 11.11, 15.3
  US possessions, 11.5
  vertebrae, 12.18
ABO blood group system, 12.1
Abstract of article
  reference to, 2.10.22
  requirements, 2.5
Academic course names, capitalization, 8.3
Academic degrees (*see* Degrees [academic])
Accent marks in foreign languages, 10.2
Acceptance date in footnote, 2.3.2
Accuracy, responsibility for
  references, 2.10.3
  totals in tables, 2.13.11
Acknowledgments
  assistance with research or report, 2.8.3
  copyrighted material use, 3.3.5
  figures reproduced from other sources, 2.11.7
  financial support, 2.8.1
  National Auxiliary Publications Service (NAPS), 2.8.6
  neglect of (plagiarism), 3.2
  participants in group study, 2.8.5
  position in manuscript, 2.8
  proprietary statement, 2.8.2
  reproduction of figures/tables, 2.8.4, 2.13.6
Acquired immunodeficiency syndrome virus, nomenclature, 12.16.2
Acronyms
  for agencies, 11.8
  articles before, 9.9
  definition, 11.0
  for organizations, 11.8
  plurals, 6.11.5, 7.1
  policy on, 11.0
  in pulmonary function testing, 12.17.2
  for technical terms, 11.10
  words of origin, capitalization, 8.6
Active voice of verb, 5.8.1

Index

Addenda to article, 2.7
Addresses
  abbreviations in, 11.4
  commas in, 6.1.8
  numbers in, 16.3.1
  with proper name, state in parentheses,
    6.8.4
  for reprints, 2.3.7
  parentheses with, 6.8.8
Adjectives
  in compound words, 6.12.1
  description, 5.4
  nonspecific gender and, 9.10.2
  nouns used as, 5.6.2, 5.6.3
Adverbs
  in compound word, 6.12.5
  description, 5.4
Advertisements in journals, 4.6
Affiliations of authors, 2.3.3
AFIP (Armed Forces Institute of
    Pathology) negative number in
    legends, 2.11.6
Age of person
  numbers in, 16.3.2
  reference to, 9.5
Agency names, abbreviations, 11.8
AIDS virus, nomenclature, 12.16.2
Air Force titles, abbreviations, 11.2.2
Alignment of tables, 2.13.6
Alleles, terminology
  animal, 12.9.6
  human, 12.9.3
Alphabetization, surnames with prefixes,
    2.10.9
American Joint Committee on Cancer,
    staging system, 12.2.2
American Society for Information Science
    as repository for auxiliary material
    (see National Auxiliary Publications
    Service)
Amino acids, terminology, 12.9.1
Amount of substance, units of measure for,
    15.1
Ampersand
  in business firm abbreviations, 11.7
  comma omitted before, 6.1.3
Animal genetic terms, 12.9.6
Anonymous material, reference to, 2.10.24
Antibodies (see also Immunoglobulins)
  hepatitis, abbreviations, 12.11
  monoclonal, terminology, 12.12.4
Antigens, terminology
  blood groups, 12.1
  hepatitis, 12.11
  histocompatibility, 12.12.2
  T-lymphocyte, 12.12.4
  transplantation, 12.12.2

Apgar score, 12.15
Apostrophe
  in contractions, 5.8.6
  plural forms and, 6.11.5
  in possessive words
    compound, 6.11.3
    eponyms, 13.1
    indefinite pronouns, 6.11.1
    indicating joint possession, 6.11.4
    money units, 6.11.6
    nouns, 6.11.1
    organization name, 6.11.4
    pronouns, 6.11.2
    time units, 6.11.6
  vs prime, 6.11.7
Apparatus, nomenclature, 12.8
Appeals Court cases, references to,
    2.10.42
Appendixes vs figures/tables, 2.14
Appositives, commas with, 6.1.1
Appreciation for assistance,
    acknowledgment, 2.8.3
Arabic numerals, 16.1, 16.3 (see also
    Numbers)
Area
  multiplication symbol and, 15.1.3
  units of measure, 15.1
Armed Forces Institute of Pathology
    (AFIP) negative number in legends,
    2.11.6
Armed services (see Military services)
Army titles, abbreviations, 11.2.2
Arrays (mathematical), 18.3.3
Arrows/arrowheads in figures, 2.11.3
Articles (journal)
  serialized, references to, 2.10.16
  several-part, 2.7
  types, 1.0
Articles (parts of speech) before *h* and *y*,
    9.9
Artwork (see Illustrations)
Asian names, 2.3.3
Assistance, acknowledgment, 2.8.3
Asterisk
  as footnote symbol, 2.13.6
  multiple reference citations, 2.10.7
Audiotapes, references to, 2.10.38
Authors
  affiliations, 2.3.3
  committee as, reference to, 2.10.24
  copyright and (see Copyright)
  death, designation in footnote, 2.3.4
  duties in duplicate publication, 3.1
  fraudulent research by, 3.2
  multiple
    designation in footnote, 2.3.3
    in references, 2.10.8

356

names
 in bylines, 2.2
 particles in, 2.10.9
 in references, 2.10.8, 2.10.9, 2.10.30
 in running foot/head, 2.4.2
 plagiarism by, 3.2
 responsibility for reference accuracy,
  2.10.3
Average, statistical, 17.2
Award names, capitalization, 8.1.3
Axis captions on illustrations, 2.12.6

B cells (lymphocytes), nomenclature,
 12.12.4
Back-formations, 9.3
Bacteria, genus and species names,
 12.16.1
Bacteriophages, nomenclature, 12.16.2
Bands, chromosome, terminology, 12.9.5
Bar, indicating activated complement,
 12.12.1
Bar charts, legends in, 2.11
Biblical references, 2.10.41
 colon in, 6.3.3
 Roman numerals in, 16.2.6
Bibliographies (*see also* References)
 deposited with NAPS, 2.15
Black-and-white illustrations
 with color illustrations, numbering in
  text, 2.12.7
 specifications, 2.12.1
Block quotations, punctuation with, 6.6.6,
 6.6.12
Blood group terminology, 12.1
 gene symbols, 12.9.3
Blood pressure units, 15.1.9
Body parts, reference to, 9.6
Boldface type
 in mathematical expressions, 18.3.3
 tabular totals set in, 2.13.11
Bonds, chemical, marking for printer, 11.12
Book reviews, 1.6
 Roman numerals in, 16.2.6
Books
 parts of, in reference, 2.10.31
 references to (*see under* References)
Braces in mathematical expressions, 18.3
Brackets
 in formulas, 6.9.3
 in mathematical expressions, 18.3
 within parentheses, 6.9.2
 question mark placement and, 6.4.1
 in quotations, 6.6.1, 6.9.1
Breaks
 in thought, punctuation for (*see* Comma;
  Dash)
 word division, 6.12.4

Bulletins, government, references to,
 2.10.32
Business firm names
 abbreviations, 11.7
 capitalization, 8.3
Bylines, 2.2

Calendar designators (*see* Dates; Time;
 Years)
Calorie, conversion to joule, 15.1.11
Cancer grades, arabic numerals in, 16.2.6
Cancer staging
 Roman numerals in, 16.2.6
 terminology, 12.2
Capitalization
 agency names, 8.3
 award names, 8.1.3
 business firms, 8.3
 changes in, with ellipses, 6.7.7
 after colon, 8.5
 compass directions, 8.1.1
 conference names, 8.3
 degrees (academic), 8.2
 deities, 8.1.8
 designators (Table, Figure), 8.7
 diseases, 8.1.5
 eponyms, 8.1.5, 13.1
 event names, 8.1.3
 figure designator, 8.7
 figure legends, 2.11.2
 foreign-language titles in references,
  2.10.11
 in foreign languages, 10.1.3
 gene names, 12.9.3
 general rules, 8.0
 genus and species names, 12.16.1
 geographic names, 8.1.1
 after Greek letters, 8.4.2, 14.2
 headings, 8.4
 hepatitis abbreviations, 12.11
 holidays, 8.1.8
 in hyphenated compounds, 8.4.2
 institution names, 8.3
 language names, 8.1.2
 legislation, 8.1.3
 mathematical expressions, 18.3.3
 mouse strain names, 12.9.6
 after numbers, 8.4.2
 official names, 8.3
 organisms, 8.1.7
 organization names, 8.3
 political parties, 8.1.2
 populations, 8.1.2
 prefixes and, 8.4.2
 proper nouns, 8.1
 proprietary names, 8.1.6, 12.8
 in quotations, 8.5

Index

Capitalization—*continued*
  race names, 8.1.2
  in references, 8.4.1
  religions, 8.1.2
  seasons, 8.1.8
  small words
    in official names, 8.3
    in titles, 8.4
  sociocultural designations, 8.1.2
  in subtitles, 2.10.12, 8.4, 8.5
  suffixes and, 8.4.2
  table designators, 2.13.6, 8.7
  in tables, 2.13.7
  test names, 8.1.9
  titles (personal), 8.2
  titles (publication), 2.1.6, 8.4
    in references, 2.10.10
  trademarks, 8.1.6, 12.6.3
  virus names, 12.16.2
  words from which acronyms are derived,
    8.6
  words derived from proper nouns, 8.1.4
Capitalized word in compound word,
  6.12.1
Captions (*see* Legends)
Cardiology terminology, 12.3
Case agreement in pronoun use, 5.7.1
Case report, patient identification in,
  2.11.5
CD (clusters of differentiation),
  monoclonal antibodies, 12.12.4
CD-ROM (Compact Disk–Read Only
  Memory), databases on, 21.3.2
Cell markers of lymphocytes, terminology,
  12.12.4
Centered format for tables, 2.13.6
CH₅₀ assay, 12.12.1
Chapter of book in reference, 2.10.31
Chapter:verse, colon use in, 6.3.3
Charts (*see also* Illustrations)
  deposited with NAPS, 2.15
Chemical bonds, marking for printer,
  11.12
Chemical compounds
  abbreviations, 11.12
  hyphenation and, 6.12.5
  terminology, 12.6
  usage, 11.12
Chemical elements
  abbreviations, 11.12
  isotopes, 12.13.1
Chemical formulas, brackets/parentheses
  in, 6.9.3
Chemical names of drugs, 12.6
  nonproprietary name substitution for,
    12.6.1
Chimera in karyotype designation, 12.9.5

Chinese names, surname in, 2.3.3
Chromosome bands, terminology, 12.9.5
Chromosomes
  Philadelphia, abbreviations, 12.9.5
  terminology
    animal, 12.9.6
    human, 12.9.5
    long/short arms, 12.9.5
    rearrangement, 12.9.5, 12.9.6
    stains, 12.9.5
Citations
  legal, references to, 2.10.42
  of references in text, 2.10.7
Clarity
  comma used for, 6.1.1
  hyphen used for, 6.12.2
Classical literature, references to, 2.10.41
  Roman numerals in, 16.2.6
Clauses
  description, 5.4
  joined by conjunctions, comma used
    with, 6.1.5
  relative pronoun use in, 5.7.2
  separation by comma, 6.1.1
Clinical terms, abbreviations, 11.10
Clock position, reference to, 9.7
Clotting factors, terminology, 12.4
Clusters of differentiation (CD),
  monoclonal antibodies, 12.12.4
Coagulation factors, terminology, 12.4
Coast Guard titles, abbreviations, 11.2.2
Code names of drugs, 12.6
  nonproprietary name substitution for,
    12.6.1
Codons, terminology, 12.9.1
Coined words, quotation marks with, 6.6.7
Collective nouns
  plurals of, 7.2
  subject-verb agreement and, 5.9.5
  units of measure as, 15.5
Colloquialisms, 9.4
Colon
  capitalization after, 8.5
  contraindications for use, 6.3.1
  in enumerations, 6.3.2
  in numerical expressions, 6.3.3
  purpose, 6.3
  quotation introduced by, 6.3.2
  quotation mark placement and, 6.6.5
  in ratios, 6.3.3, 16.2.5
  in references, 6.3.4
    biblical, 6.3.3
    with place of publication, 2.10.28
  in subtitles, 2.10.12
  in time expressions, 6.3.3
  between title and subtitle, 6.3.4
  between volume and page, 6.3.4

358

Color illustrations
  with halftones, numbering in text,
    2.12.7
  specifications, 2.12.1
Color terms in compound words, 6.12.1
Column headings in tables, 2.13.6
  capitalization, 2.13.7
Combination drugs, terminology, 12.6.1
Comma
  in addresses, 6.1.8
  with appositives, 6.1.1
  in byline, 2.2.1
  for clarity, 6.1.1
  before clause, 5.7.2
  between clauses joined by conjunctions,
    6.1.5
  in complement name, 12.12.1
  in dates, 6.1.9
  with degrees (academic), 6.1.7
  after dependent clauses, 6.1.1
  with *eg*, 6.1.4
  in genotype terms, 12.9.3
  with *ie*, 6.1.4
  after introductory phrase, 6.i.1
  with nonrestrictive clause, 6.1.1
  between numbers, 6.1.10
  in numbers, 6.1.10, 15.1.2, 16.1
  omission before ampersand, 6.1.3
  omission indicated by, 6.1.13
  in organization names, 6.1.3
  vs parentheses, 6.8.1
  with parenthetical expressions, 6.1.6
  placement, 6.1.12
  purpose, 6.1
  quotation mark placement and, 6.6.5
  in reference citations, 2.10.7
  for separating groups of words, 6.1.1
  in series, 6.1.2
  before subordinate conjunction, 6.1.5
  with titles (personal), 6.1.7, 11.6
  between units of measure, 6.1.11
  with *viz*, 6.1.4
Committee as author, reference to, 2.10.24
Communication, personal/written,
  references to, 2.10.39
Compact Disk–Read Only Memory (CD-
  ROM), databases on, 21.3.2
Company names
  abbreviations, 11.7
  capitalization, 8.3
Comparison
  incomparable words and, 9.2.3
  parallel construction in, 5.5
Compass directions, capitalization, 8.1.1
Compilations, copyright, 3.3.8
Complement, nomenclature, 12.12.1
Complexes, chemical, terminology, 12.6.2

Compound numbers, spelled-out,
  hyphenation, 16.1.1
Compound sentence, semicolon use in,
  6.2.1
Compound subject, subject-verb agreement
  and, 5.9.6
Compound words
  capitalization, 8.4.2
  en dash in, 6.5.2
  hyphen in, 6.12.1, 6.12.2
  plurals of, 7.3
  possessive form, 6.11.3
  titles as, 6.12.6
Compounds, chemical (*see* Chemical
  compounds)
Computer database resources, 21.3
Computer-generated art, 2.12.1
Computer printouts deposited with NAPS,
  2.15
Concentration of solution, units of
  measure, 15.7
Conferences
  discussions at, copyright and, 3.3.6
  names, capitalization, 8.3
Congress names, capitalization, 8.3
Congressional act, reference to, 2.10.37
Congressional hearings, reference to,
  2.10.42
Congressional Record, reference to,
  2.10.36
Conjunctions
  clauses joined by, comma used with,
    6.1.5
  subordinate, clauses introduced by,
    comma used with, 6.1.5
Consent
  for experimental work, 3.4
  for photograph publication, 2.12.8
Constant regions of immunoglobulins,
  terminology, 12.12.3
Constants (mathematical), typography,
  18.3.3
Contractions, 5.8.6
Conversation, references to, 2.10.39
Copy editing
  manuscript, 4.3
  marks for, 20.1
  sample passage, 20.2
Copy marking of mathematical
  expressions, 18.2
Copy preparation of mathematical
  expressions, 18.1
Copying of copyrighted works, 3.3.5,
  3.3.7
Copyright
  assignment form, 3.3.1
  co-owners of, 3.3.1

Index

Copyright—*continued*
  commissioned works, 3.3.3
  compilations of preexisting material,
    3.3.8
  derivative works, 3.3.8
  discussion material, 3.3.6
  duplicate publication and, 3.1
  employer ownership, 3.3.3
  "fair use" and, 3.3.5
  government employees' works, 3.3.2
  infringement, 3.3.5
  international, 3.3.9
  notice of, 3.3.4
  originality required for, 3.3.4
  permission for reproduction of works,
    3.3.5, 3.3.7
  registration, 3.3.4
  reprints and, 3.3.7
  reproduction of works, 3.3.5
  reverting to author, 3.3.1
  revised material, 3.3.8
  statutory revision of 1978, 3.3
  symbol designating, 3.3.4
  transfer to publisher, 3.3.1
  validity, 3.3.4
  "works made for hire," 3.3.3
Corrections to printed article, 4.9
Correspondence, publication of, 1.5
  signatures with, 2.2.2
Corticosteroids, terminology, 12.6.4
Court cases, references to, 2.10.42
Cranial nerves, nomenclature, 12.14.1
Credits (*see* Acknowledgments)
Critiques, 1.3
Currency (*see* Money)
Cut-in heads in tables, 2.13.6

Dagger
  as footnote symbol, 2.13.6
  indicating author death, 2.3.4
Dangling participles, 5.4.2
Dash
  em, 2.6.1, 6.5.1
  2-em, 6.5.3
  3-em, 6.5.4
  en, 6.5.2, 6.12.2
  purpose, 6.5
  types, 6.5
Data analysis (*see* Statistics)
data as false singular, 5.9.2
Databases as resources, 21.3
Dates (*see also* Days; Months; Years)
  acceptance for publication, 2.3.2
  commas in, 6.1.9

  doubtful, question mark in, 6.4.1
  journal references, 2.10.15
  numbers in, 16.3.3
  virgule in, 2.13.8, 6.10.3
Days
  abbreviations for names, 11.3
  arabic numerals for, 16.3.8
Deceased author, indication in footnote,
  2.3.4
Decimal point, table column alignment by,
  2.13.6
Decimals, 16.2.1
  vs fractions, 15.9
  period in, 6.4.3
Degrees (academic)
  abbreviations, 11.1
  in bylines, 2.2.1
  capitalization, 8.2
  comma in, 6.1.7
Degrees (temperature), 16.3.7
Deity names, capitalization, 8.1.8
Density, units of measure, 15.1
Dependent clauses, separation by comma,
  6.1.1
Derivative works, copyright, 3.3.8
Dermatomes, terminology, 12.18
Descriptive articles in journal, 1.2
Design of research, 17.1
Designators
  arabic numbers in, 16.3.4
  for figures/tables, capitalization, 8.7
Deuterium, 12.13.6
Diabetes mellitus, terminology, 12.5
Diacritics in foreign language, 10.2
Diaeresis vs umlaut, 10.2
Diagonal line (*see* Virgule)
Dialogue, punctuation for, 6.6.2
Dimensions, hyphen in, 6.12.3
Disclaimer in footnote, 2.3.6
Discussants
  copyright transfer from, 3.3.6
  reference to, 2.10.25
Discussion, quotation marks omitted from,
  6.6.11
Disease names, capitalization, 8.1.5
Dissertation, reference to, 2.10.34
Division, symbols for, 18.3.2
DNA (deoxyribonucleic acid)
  restriction enzymes cleaving, 12.9.2
  terminology, 12.9.1
Dosage of drugs, units of measure, 15.6
Dot as multiplication symbol, 6.4.3,
  15.1.3
Double dagger as footnote symbol, 2.13.6
Double negatives, 5.8.4
Drawings (*see* Figures; Illustrations)

Drug terminology
  abbreviations, 12.6.1
  administration routes, 9.4
  brand names, 12.6
  capitalization, 8.1.6
  chemical names, 12.6
  code names, 12.6
  combination products, 12.6.1
  complexes, 12.6.2
  dosages, units of measure, 15.6
  endocrine products, 12.6.4
  esters, 12.6.2
  foreign vs US names, 12.6.1
  generic names, 12.6, 12.6.1
  hormones, 12.6.4
  information sources for, 12.4, 12.6,
    12.6.1
  interferons, 12.6.4
  isotopes, 12.13
  new drugs, 12.6.1
  nonproprietary names, 12.6, 12.6.1
  proprietary names, 12.6
  quaternary ammonium salts, 12.6.2
  salts, 12.6.2
  steroids, 12.6.4
  in titles, 2.1.3
  trade names, 12.6
  trademarks, 12.6, 12.6.3
    in titles, 2.1.3
  two-word names, 12.6.2
  vitamins, 12.6.4
Duality
  hyphen used for, 6.12.1
  virgule used for, 6.10.1
Duffy blood group system, 12.1
Duplicate publication, legal/ethical
    considerations, 3.1

ECG (electrocardiography) terminology,
    12.3.1
Edition numbers in book references,
    2.10.29
Editorial interpolation in quotations, 6.6.1
  brackets with, 6.9.1
Editorials, 1.4
  signatures with, 2.2.2
Editors
  in book reference, 2.10.30
  duties
    in copy editing, 4.3
    in duplicate publication, 3.1
    in peer review process, 4.2
    in plagiarism situation, 3.2
    in publication process, 4.0
  letters to, 1.5

signatures with, 2.2.2
Editor's note, em dash after, 6.5.1
EEG (electroencephalography)
    terminology, 12.14.2
Electricity, units of measure, 15.1
Electrocardiography terminology, 12.3.1
Electroencephalography terminology,
    12.14.2
Electron micrographs, legends, 2.11.4
Elements, chemical
  abbreviations, 11.12
  isotopes, 12.13.1
Ellipses
  capitalization change with, 6.7.7
  at end of sentence, 6.7.2
  in incomplete expression, 6.7.4
  at paragraph start, 6.7.6
  between paragraphs, 6.7.6
  purpose, 6.7
  in quotations, 6.7.8
  within sentence, 6.7.1
  between sentences, 6.7.3
  in tables, 2.13.6, 2.13.10, 6.7.9
  in verse, 6.7.5
Elliptical construction, subject-verb
    agreement in, 5.9.7
Em dash, 2.6.1, 6.5.1
2-Em dash, 6.5.3
3-Em dash, 6.5.4
Emphasis, parallel construction in, 5.5
En dash, 6.5.2, 6.12.2
Endocrinology, terminology, 12.6.4, 12.7
Endonucleases, restriction, terminology,
    12.9.2
Energy, units of measure, 15.1, 15.1.11
Enumerations (*see also* Series)
  colon before, 6.3.2
  numbers used in, 16.1.5
  parentheses in, 6.8.5
  period in, 6.4.3
  semicolon in, 6.2.2
Enzyme activity, units, 15.1.9
Enzymes, restriction, terminology, 12.9.2
Eponyms
  capitalization, 8.1.5, 13.1
  vs noneponymous terms, 13.2
  possessive form, 13.1
  use, 13.0
Equations (*see also* Mathematical
    expressions)
  centering on separate line, 18.1
  numbering in text, 18.1
  in running text, 18.1
  virgule in, 6.10.4
Equipment, nomenclature, 12.8
Eras, abbreviations, 11.3

Index

Erratum notice after publication, 21.3.1
Errors in usage
 age referents, 9.5
 articles, 9.9
 back-formations, 9.3
 body parts, 9.6
 clock referents, 9.7
 colloquialisms, 9.4
 conversational words, 9.4
 expendable words, 9.2.2
 incomparable words, 9.2.3
 jargon, 9.4
 laboratory values, 9.8
 redundancy, 9.2.1
 sex referents, 9.5
 sexist language, 6.10.1, 9.10
 transformation of nouns into verbs, 9.3
 vulgarisms, 9.4
 words and phrases, 9.1
Essays, 1.3
Esters, terminology, 12.6.2
Ethical considerations (see Legal and
  ethical considerations)
Event names, capitalization, 8.1.3
Exclamation point, 6.4.2
 with parentheses, 6.8.2
Exclusion, 3-em dash as indicator, 6.5.4
Expendable words, 9.2.2
Experimental articles in journal, 1.1
Explanatory footnotes in parentheses,
  6.8.11
Exponents
 copy marking, 18.2
 negative, 18.3.2
 units of measure, 15.1

Factorial sign (!), 6.4.2, 18.3.2
Factors, clotting, terminology, 12.4
Federal Register, reference to, 2.10.36
Federal regulations, reference to, 2.10.36,
  2.10.42
Fellowship, designation in footnote, 2.3.3
Figures (see also Illustrations)
 abbreviations in, 2.11.3
 vs appendixes, 2.14
 arrows/arrowheads in, 2.11.3
 deposited with NAPS, 2.15
 designation in text, 2.11.1, 8.7
 dual unit reporting in, 15.1.7
 legends (see Legends)
 without legends, 2.11.1
 locations in, 2.11.2
 multipart, 2.11.2, 2.12.4
 in news items, 2.11.1
 numbers for, 16.3.5

reproduction from other sources,
  acknowledgment, 2.8.4, 2.11.7
 symbols in, 2.11.3
 vs tables, 2.13.1
Financial support, acknowledgment, 2.8.1
Flush left format in tables, 2.13.6
Folios (see Page numbers)
Footnotes
 acceptance date in, 2.3.2
 author affiliations in, 2.3.3
 deceased author indication, 2.3.4
 disclaimer, 2.3.6
 explanatory, in parentheses, 6.8.11
 multiple citation of references in, 2.10.7
 order of, 2.3.1
 "read before meeting" note, 2.3.5
 reprint address, 2.3.7
 symbols, 2.13.6
 to tables, 2.13.6
Force, units of measure, 15.1
Foreign countries, copyright in, 3.3.9
Foreign-language journal, simultaneous
  publication in, 3.1
Foreign-language titles in references,
  2.10.11
Foreign-language words
 capitalization in, 10.1.3
 diacritics in, 10.2
 hyphenation and, 6.12.5
 italicization, 10.1.1
 plurals, vs English plurals, 7.4
 punctuation in, 10.1.3
Foreign names of drugs
 trademarks, 12.6.3
 vs US name, 12.6.1
Formulas (see also Equations;
  Mathematical expressions)
 chemical, brackets/parentheses in, 6.9.3
Fractions, 16.2.2
 vs decimals, 15.9
 hyphen in, 6.12.1
 vs percentages, 15.1.5
 simplifying, 18.3
 virgule in, 6.10.4
Fragment of sentence, 5.1
 in quotation, capitalization, 8.5
Fraud in scientific work, 3.2
Frequency
 EEG, 12.14.2
 units of measure, 15.1

Gender, nonspecific, 6.10.1, 9.10
Generic names of drugs, 12.6, 12.6.1
Genes, terminology
 animal, 12.9.6

histocompatibility complex, 12.9.3
human, 12.9.3
Genetics terminology
allele symbols
animal, 12.9.6
human, 12.9.3
amino acids, 12.9.1
animals, 12.9.6
chromosomes
animal, 12.9.6
human, 12.9.5
rearrangement, 12.9.5
DNA, 12.9.1
genes, 12.9.3, 12.9.6
genotypes, 12.1, 12.9.1, 12.9.3
karyotypes, 12.9.5
locus symbols, 12.9.3
mouse strains, 12.9.6
oncogenes, 12.9.4
phenotypes
animal, 12.9.6
human, 12.9.3
proto-oncogenes, 12.9.4
restriction enzymes, 12.9.2
RNA, 12.9.1
Genotypes, terminology, 12.9.3
blood groups, 12.1
HLA, 12.12.2
Genus names, 12.16.1
capitalization, 8.1.7
in references, 2.10.10
in titles, 2.1.4
viruses, 12.16.2
Geographic names
capitalization, 8.1.1
hyphenation and, 6.12.5
Gerunds, nouns modifying, 5.6.2
Globulins, terminology, 12.10
Glycosylated hemoglobin, terminology,
12.5.1
Government employees, copyright and,
3.3.2
Governmental agencies
names
abbreviations, 11.8
capitalization, 8.3
publications, references to, 2.10.32
Grammar, 5.0 (*see also* Punctuation;
specific part of speech, eg, Nouns,
Verbs)
modifiers, 5.4
paragraph structure, 5.2
parallel construction, 5.5
participles, 5.4.2
sentence structure, 5.1, 5.5
subject-verb agreement, 5.9
Grants, acknowledgment, 2.8.1

Graphs (*see* Illustrations)
Greek letters
capitalization after, 8.4.2, 14.2
code numbers for, 14.0
in globulin names, 12.10
hyphen after, 6.12.7
in immunoglobulin names, 12.12.3
marking copy for, 14.0
vs spelled-out words, 14.1
uses, 14.0
Greek plurals vs English plurals, 7.4
Group (collective) nouns, subject-verb
agreement and, 5.9.5
Group study participants
as author, reference to, 2.10.24
designation in footnote, 2.3.3
listing, 2.8.5

Halftones
with color illustrations, numbering in
text, 2.12.7
description, 2.12
specifications, 2.12.1
Haplotypes in HLA terminology, 12.12.2
Headings (tables)
column, 2.13.6
capitalization, 2.13.7
cut-in, 2.13.6
Headings (text)
capitalization, 8.4
em dash in, 6.5.1
levels, 2.6.1
number of, 2.6.2
pattern of organization, 2.6
Hearings, congressional, references to,
2.10.42
Heart murmurs/sounds, terminology,
12.3.2
Heavy chains, terminology, 12.12.3
Heavy water, 12.13.6
Helper-suppressor ratio, 12.12.4
Hemoglobin, glycosylated, terminology,
12.5.1
Hepatitis terminology, 12.11
Histocompatibility antigens, terminology,
12.12.1, 12.12.2
Histocompatibility complex genes, 12.9.3
Historical event names, capitalization,
8.1.3
HIV (human immunodeficiency virus),
nomenclature, 12.16.2
HLA (human leukocyte antigen),
nomenclature, 12.12.2
Holiday names, capitalization, 8.1.8
Honorary designations in bylines, 2.2.1

Index

Honors, academic, abbreviations, 11.1
Horizontal alignment in tables, 2.13.6
Hormones, terminology, 12.6.4
  hypothalamic, 12.7.1
  pituitary, 12.7.2
Hour:minute, colon use in, 6.3.3
Hours, numbers in, 16.3.8, 16.3.9
HTLV (human T-cell lymphotropic virus),
  nomenclature, 12.16.2
Human immunodeficiency virus (HIV),
  nomenclature, 12.16.2
Human leukocyte antigen (HLA),
  terminology, 12.12.1
Human T-cell lymphotropic virus (HTLV),
  nomenclature, 12.16.2
Hydrogen isotopes, nomenclature, 12.13.6
Hypervariable regions of immunoglobulins,
  terminology, 12.12.3
Hyphen
  in B-cell as adjective, 12.12.4
  in compound words
    for clarity, 6.12.2
    official titles, 6.12.6
    temporary, 6.12.1
  contraindications for use, 6.12.5
  in dimensions, 6.12.3
  in disease names, 6.12.5
  with en dash, 6.12.2
  in fractions, 16.2.2
  in hepatitis abbreviations, 12.11
  in HLA terminology, 12.9.3, 12.12.2
  between number and unit of measure,
    15.4.2
  orthographic, 6.12
  purpose, 6.12
  in range of numbers, 2.13.8, 6.12.3
  in reference citations, 2.10.7
  in species names, 12.16.1
  in spelled-out numbers, 16.1.1
  in T-cell as adjective, 12.12.4
  in technical terms, 6.12.7
  in titles (official), 6.12.6
  in word division at end of line, 6.12.4
Hyphenated compounds (see Compound
  words)
Hypothalamic hormones, terminology,
  12.7.1

Ig (immunoglobulin), terminology, 12.12.3
Illustrations
  axis captions, 2.12.6
  black-and-white, 2.12.1, 2.12.7
  citing in text, 2.12
  computer-generated, 2.12.1
  consent of subjects, 2.12.8

costs of, 2.12.1
four-color, 2.12.1, 2.12.7
grouping, 2.12.4
halftones, 2.12.1
insets, 2.12.5
legends, 2.12 (see also Legends)
lettering on, 2.12.2
mixed color and black-and-white,
  numbering in text, 2.12.7
numbering, 2.12.7
scale indication, 2.12.3
symbols on, 2.12.2
technical specifications, 2.12.1
transparencies, 2.12.1
types, 2.12
Immunoglobulins, terminology, 12.12.3
Immunology terminology
  cell markers, 12.12.4
  complement, 12.12.1
  constant regions, 12.12.3
  heavy chains, 12.12.3
  histocompatibility antigens, 12.12.2
  hypervariable regions, 12.12.3
  immunoglobulins, 12.12.3 (see also
    Antibodies)
  light chains, 12.12.3
  lymphocytes, 12.12.4
  monoclonal antibodies, 12.12.4
  variable regions, 12.12.3
Imperative mood of verb, 5.8.2
Incomparable words, 9.2.3
Incomplete expression, ellipsis in, 6.7.4
Indefinite pronouns (see also Sexist
  language)
  possessive form, apostrophe in, 6.11.1
  subject-verb agreement and, 5.9.12
Indention of tables, 2.13.6
Independent clauses, separation by
  semicolon, 6.2.1
Index to publications, 4.10
Indian names, surname in, 2.3.3
Indicative mood of verb, 5.8.2
Indirect discourse, quotation marks omitted
  from, 6.6.11
Infants, Apgar score assessment, 12.15
Infinitives, 5.8.5
Influenza virus, terminology, 12.16.2
Information resources, 21.0 (see also
  specific topic)
Informed consent in experiments, 3.4
Initialism, 11.0
Initials (see also Acronyms)
  of persons, 11.6
Insets on illustrations, 2.12.5
Institution names
  abbreviations, 11.8
  capitalization, 8.3

location with, parentheses with, 6.8.4
Institutions, author affiliations with, in
    footnotes, 2.3.3
Insulin terminology, 12.5.2
Interferons, terminology, 12.6.4
Internal Revenue Code, references to,
    2.10.42
International copyright, 3.3.9
International System of Units (*see* SI units)
International Union Against Cancer,
    staging system, 12.2.2
International units for enzyme activity,
    15.1.9
Interview, quotation marks omitted from,
    6.6.11
Introductory clauses, separation by comma,
    6.1.1
Introductory expressions
    em dash after, 6.5.1
    period after, 6.4.3
Irony, quotation marks indicating, 6.6.7
Isotopes, terminology
    in abstract, 2.5
    adopted names, 12.13.2
    elements, 12.13.1
    hydrogen, 12.13.6
    information sources, 12.13
    metastable, 12.13.7
    nonproprietary names, 12.13
    numbers, 12.13, 12.13.1
    symbols, 12.13.1
    trademarks, 12.13.4
    uniform labeling, 12.13.5
    without approved names, 12.13.3
Issue number of journal, reference to,
    2.10.19
Italics
    foreign words, 10.1.1
    HLA genotype, 12.12.2
    journal names, 2.10.14
    mathematical expressions, 18.3.3
    species and genus names, 12.16.1
    titles in references, 2.10.10
    virus names, 12.16.2

Japanese names, surname in, 2.3.3
Jargon, 9.4
Joint possession, apostrophe in, 6.11.4
Joule, conversion from calorie, 15.1.11
Journals
    issue in two or more parts, reference to,
        2.10.18
    names
        abbreviations, 2.10.14, 11.9
        italics, 2.10.14

in running foot, 2.4.1
references to (*see under* References)
special departments, reference to,
    2.10.23
special issue, reference to, 2.10.20
supplements, reference to, 2.10.21
Junior (Jr)
    abbreviation, 11.6
    comma before, 6.1.7
    in references, 2.10.8

Karyotypes, terminology, 12.9.5
Katal, 15.1.9
Kell blood group system, 12.1
Kelvin, 15.1.9
Key words in article, 2.9
Keys in legends, 2.11
Kidd blood group system, 12.1

Labeling of isotope, 12.13.5
Laboratory values, reference to, 9.8
Language names, capitalization, 8.1.2
Latin expressions
    hyphenation and, 6.12.5
    plurals vs English plurals, 7.4
Laws, references to, 2.10.42
Layout of printed article, 4.4
Legal and ethical considerations
    copyright (*see* Copyright)
    data manipulation, 3.2
    duplicate publication, 3.1
    forged data, 3.2
    fraud, 3.2
    informed consent of subjects, 3.4
    parallel publication, 3.1
    peer review
        conflict of interest in, 3.2, 4.2
        procedure, 4.2
    plagiarism, 3.2
Legal references, 2.10.42
    quotations from, 6.6.1
Legends
    abbreviation explanation in, 2.11.3
    capitalization, 2.11.2
    consistency in, 2.11
    em dash in, 6.5.1
    figure designation, 2.11.1
    figures reproduced from other sources,
        2.11.7
    illustrations, 2.12
    indicating location in figure, 2.11.2
    keys in, 2.11
    length limitations, 2.11

Legends—*continued*
multipart figures, 2.11.2
negative number (AFIP) in, 2.11.6
parentheses in, 6.8.7
patient identification in, 2.11.5
photomicrographs, 2.11.4
purpose, 2.11
symbol explanation in, 2.11.3
Legislation, capitalization, 8.1.3
Length, units of measure, 15.1
Lettering on figures, specifications, 2.12.2
Letters
designating multipart figures, 2.11.2
in enumerations, parentheses with, 6.8.3
plurals of, 6.11.5
Letters to editor, 1.5
signatures with, 2.2.2
Leu series of monoclonal antibodies,
12.12.4
Levels of headings, 2.6.1
Lewis blood group system, 12.1
Library special collections, reference to,
2.10.35
Light chains, terminology, 12.12.3
Light intensity, units of measure, 15.1
Lines (rules) in tables, 2.13.6
Local addresses, abbreviations, 11.4
Location with proper name, parentheses
with, 6.8.4
Locus symbols, 12.9.3
major histocompatibility complex,
12.12.2
Looseleaf legal service publications,
references to, 2.10.42
Lower extremity, reference to, 9.6
Lutheran blood group system, 12.1
Lymphocytes, nomenclature, 12.12.4
Lyt series of monoclonal antibodies,
12.12.4

Magnification in microscopy
in legend, 2.11.4
multiplication symbol and, 15.1.3
in parentheses, 6.8.7
Major histocompatibility complex
genes, 12.9.3
terminology, 12.12.2
Manuscript preparation
abstract, 2.5
acknowledgments, 2.8
addenda, 2.7
appendixes, 2.14
bylines, 2.2
footnotes, 2.3

guidelines, 2.0
headings, 2.6
illustrations, 2.12
key words, 2.9
legends (*see* Legends)
National Auxiliary Publications Service
(NAPS) repository, 2.15
references (*see* References)
running foot, 2.4
side headings, 2.6
subheadings, 2.6
subtitles, 2.1
synopsis, 2.5
tables (*see* Tables)
titles, 2.1
Manuscript processing, 4.0
Marine Corps titles, abbreviations, 11.2.2
Mass, units of measure, 15.1
Mathematical derivations deposited with
NAPS, 2.15
Mathematical expressions (*see also*
Equations)
braces in, 18.3
brackets in, 6.9.3, 18.3
breaking into two or more lines, 18.3.1
capitalization, 18.3.3
constants, 18.3.3
copy editing, 18.3.3
copy marking, 18.2
copy preparation, 18.1
division notation, 18.3.2
exclamation point in, 6.4.2
exponents, 18.3
factorial sign (!), 18.3.2
information sources, 18.0
long, 18.0, 18.3.1
multiplication notation, 18.3.2
negative exponent, 18.3
parentheses in, 6.9.3, 18.3
radicals, 18.3
reciprocals, 18.3.2
simplifying, 18.3
typography, 18.3.3
units of measure, 18.3.3
unknown quantities, 18.3.3
variables, 18.3.3
written out in text, 18.3.3
Mathematical functions (sin/cos),
typography, 18.3.3
Matrix, multiplication symbol and, 15.1.3
Mean (statistical), 17.2
Measures (*see* Units of measure)
MEDLINE database, 21.3.1
Meetings
discussions at, copyright and, 3.3.6
paper read before, indication in footnote,
2.3.5

Metastable isotopes, nomenclature, 12.13.7
Metric system (*see* SI units)
MHC (major histocompatibility complex), terminology, 12.12.2
Microorganisms
  genus and species names, 12.16.1
  plurals of, 7.5
Military service names, abbreviations, 11.2.1
Military titles
  abbreviations, 11.2.2
  in bylines, 2.2.1
Minutes, numbers in, 16.3.8, 16.3.9
Misplaced modifiers, 5.4.1
Misspelling in quotations, *sic* used in, 6.6.1
MNSs blood group system, 12.1
Models, statistical, 17.2
Modifiers, 5.4
  dangling participles as, 5.4.2
  misplaced, 5.4.1
  nouns as, 5.6.1
  only as, 5.4.1
  types, 5.4
Molar concentration of solution, 15.7
Money
  numbers in, 16.3.6
  units of, possessive form, 5.6.3, 6.11.6
Monoclonal antibodies, terminology, 12.12.4
Monograph in series, reference to, 2.10.33
Months
  abbreviations, 11.3
  numbers in, 16.3.8
Mood of verb, 5.8.2
Mosaic in karyotype designation, 12.9.5
Mouse strains, terminology, 12.9.6
Multiauthor work, reference to, 2.3.3, 2.10.8
Multiplication, symbols for, 6.4.3, 15.1.3, 18.3.2
Murmurs, cardiac, 12.3.2

Names (*see also* Authors, names; Journals, names; Proper names/nouns)
  drug (*see* Drug terminology)
  genus (*see* Genus names)
  isotopes (*see* Isotopes, terminology)
  mouse strain, 12.9.6
  publication, 6.8.4
  publisher, 2.10.27
  species (*see* Species names)
National Auxiliary Publications Service (NAPS)
  acknowledgment of, 2.8.6, 2.15.3

  address, 2.15
  material deposited with, 2.13.2, 2.15.2
  supplementary material deposited with, 2.15
National Library of Medicine databases, 21.3.1, 21.3.5
Navy titles, abbreviations, 11.2.2
Negative number (photographic) in legends, 2.11.6
Negatives, double, 5.8.4
Neurology, terminology
  cranial nerves, 12.14.1
  dermatomes, 12.18
  electroencephalography, 12.14.2
  spinal nerves, 12.18
Newborn, Apgar score assessment, 12.15
Nomenclature
  amino acids, 12.9.1
  blood groups, 12.1
  cancer staging, 12.2
  cardiology, 12.3
  chromosomes
    animal, 12.9.6
    human, 12.9.5
  clotting factors, 12.4
  complement, 12.12.1
  cranial nerves, 12.14.1
  dermatomes, 12.18
  diabetes mellitus, 12.5
  drugs, 12.6
  electroencephalography, 12.14.2
  endocrinology, 12.6.4, 12.7
  equipment, 12.8
  genes
    animal, 12.9.6
    human, 12.9.3
  genetics, 12.9
  genus, 12.16.1
  globulins, 12.10
  hepatitis types, 12.11
  histocompatibility antigens, 12.12.2
  immunoglobulins, 12.12.3
  immunology, 12.12
  insulin, 12.5.2
  interferons, 12.6.4
  isotopes, 12.13
  lymphocytes, 12.12.4
  monoclonal antibodies, 12.12.4
  mouse strains, 12.9.6
  neurology, 12.14, 12.18
  nucleic acids, 12.9.1
  obstetrics, 12.15
  oncogenes, 12.9.4
  policy, 12.0
  pulmonary function, 12.17
  reagents, 12.8
  respiratory function, 12.17

Nomenclature—*continued*
  restriction enzymes, 12.9.2
  species, 12.16.1
  spinal nerves, 12.18
  steroids, 12.6.4
  vertebrae, 12.18
  viruses, 12.16.2, Appendix
  vitamins, 12.6.4
Nonproprietary names of drugs, 12.6,
    12.6.1
Nonrestrictive clauses, relative pronoun use
    in, 5.7.2
Normal concentration of solution, 15.7
Notes (*see also* Footnotes)
  editor's, 6.5.1
Nouns, 5.6
  agreement with verbs (*see* Subject-verb
    agreement)
  capitalization in foreign-language titles,
    2.10.11
  collective
    plurals of, 7.2
    subject-verb agreement and, 5.9.5
  compound, plurals of, 7.3
  false plural, subject-verb agreement and,
    5.9.3
  false singular, subject-verb agreement
    and, 5.9.2
  as modifiers, 5.6.1
    for gerunds, 5.6.2
    involving money, 5.6.3
    involving time, 5.6.3
  nonspecific gender and, 9.10.2
  plural
    after *one of those*, 5.9.10
    with parenthetical *s*, 5.9.4, 6.8.12
  possessive form, apostrophe in, 6.11.1
  proper (*see* Proper names/nouns)
  singular, 5.9.9
    units of measure as, 15.5
  transformation into verbs, 9.3
Nucleic acids, terminology, 12.9.1
Number sign as footnote symbol, 2.13.6
Numbering
  illustrations in text, mixed halftone and
    color, 2.12.7
  references, 2.10.6
  tables, 2.13.4
Numbers (*see also specific type, eg,* Page
    numbers)
  abbreviation (No.), 16.1.6
  in addresses, 16.3.1
  for age, 16.3.2
  arabic, 16.1, 16.3
  capitalization after, 8.4.2
  chromosomes, 12.9.5
  colon use in, 6.3.3

  commas between, 6.1.10
  commas in, 6.1.10, 15.1.2, 16.1
  in compound words, 6.12.1
  consecutive, 16.1.3
  in dates, 16.3.3
  decimals, 16.1, 16.2.1
  after designators, 16.3.4
  in enumerations, 16.1.5
    parentheses with, 6.8.3
  for figures, 16.3.5
  five or more digits, 16.1
  four-digit, 16.1
  fractions, 16.2.2
    vs decimals, 15.9
  hyphen in, 6.12.1
  large, 16.2.3
  for money, 16.3.6
  one-digit, spelled-out, 16.1
  ordinal, 16.1.2
  in percentages, 16.2.4
  plurals of, 6.11.5
  proportions, 16.2.5
  range of, 16.1.4
  rates, 16.2.5
  Roman numerals, 16.2.6
  rounding off, 15.1.8, 16.2.3, 17.4
  at sentence beginning, 16.1.1
  series, 16.1.4
  significant digits, 15.1.8, 17.3
  spaces in, 16.1
  span of years, 16.1.4
  spelled-out
    in consecutive numerical expressions,
      16.1.3
    vs figures, 16.0, 16.1
    at sentence beginning, 16.1.1
    in subtitles, 16.1
    in tables, abbreviated vs spelled-out,
      2.13.9
  for tables, 16.3.5
  temperature, 16.3.7
  in text, 16.1
  time, 16.3.8, 16.3.9
  in titles, 2.1.2, 16.1
  with units of measure, 15.1.4, 16.3.10
  usage, 16.0, 16.1

Obstetric terms, 12.15
Official titles, hyphen in, 6.12.6
OK series of monoclonal antibodies,
    12.12.4
Omission (*see also* Ellipses; Elliptical
    construction)
  comma indicating, 6.1.13
  of expendable words, 9.2.2

3-em dash as indicator, 6.5.4
in quotations, 6.6.1
On-line resources, 21.3
Oncogenes, terminology, 12.9.4
Ordinal numbers, 16.1.2
Organism names
capitalization, 8.1.7
genus and species names, 12.16.1
Organization names
abbreviations, 11.8
capitalization, 8.3
commas in, 6.1.3
location with, parentheses with, 6.8.4
possessive form, 6.11.4
Orthographic hyphen, 6.12

P blood group system, 12.1
Page numbers
book references, 2.10.29
journal references, 2.10.15
supplement issues, 2.10.21
Roman numerals as, 16.2.6
span of, 16.1.4
Page proofs, 4.5
Paragraph
ellipses at start, 6.7.6
ellipses between, 6.7.6
structure, 5.2
Paragraph symbol as footnote symbol,
2.13.6
Parallel construction in sentence, 5.5
Parallel lines as footnote symbol, 2.13.6
Parallel publication, 3.1
Parentheses
abbreviations and, 6.8.10
with brackets, 6.8.11
brackets within, 6.9.2
vs comma, 6.8.1
in enumerations, 6.8.5
with explanatory footnotes, 6.8.11
in figure legends, 6.8.7
in HLA terminology, 12.12.2
with identifying number/letter, 6.8.3
in legends, 6.8.7
for location insertion in proper name,
6.8.4
in mathematical expressions, 18.3
with plurals, 6.8.12
punctuation with, 6.8.2
question mark placement and, 6.4.1
for references in text, 2.10.2, 6.8.6
in reprint address, 6.8.8
in supplementary expressions, 6.8.1
table column alignment by, 2.13.6
with trademark, 6.8.9

Parenthetical expressions, comma used
with, 6.1.6
Parenthetical plurals, subject-verb
agreement and, 5.9.4
Participles, 5.4.2
Particles in author names, 2.10.9
Pascal, 15.1.9
Passive voice of verb, 5.8.1
Patient identification in legends, 2.11.5
Pedigree chart, roman numerals in, 16.2.6
Peer review
conflict of interest and, 3.2
procedure, 4.2
per, virgule for, 6.10.2
Percentages, 16.2.4
vs fraction of one, 15.1.5
sample size with, 16.2.4
significant digits in, 17.3
in table, accuracy of total, 16.2.4
Period
after abbreviations, 6.4.3, 15.4
in decimals, 6.4.3
at end of sentence, 6.4.3
in enumerations, 6.4.3
in figure designation, 2.11.1
after initials, 11.6
after introductory expression, 6.4.3
with parentheses, 6.8.2
placement, 6.4.3
quotation mark placement and, 6.6.5
after side heading, 2.6.1
Personal communication, references to,
2.10.39
Personal names (*see* Proper names/nouns)
Personal pronouns, 5.7.1
in sexist language, 9.10.1
pH, 15.1.9
Phages, nomenclature, 12.16.2
Phenotypes, terminology
animal, 12.9.6
blood groups, 12.1
HLA, 12.12.2
human, 12.9.3
Philadelphia chromosomes, abbreviations,
12.9.5
Phonetics, virgule in, 6.10.5
Photographic negative number in legends,
2.11.6
Photographs
consent of subjects, 2.12.8
grouping, 2.12.4
insets, 2.12.5
specifications, 2.12.1
Photomicrographs
legends, 2.11.4
stain/magnification for, in parentheses,
6.8.7

Index

Phrases
  description, 5.4
  intervening, subject-verb agreement,
    5.9.1
  separation by comma, 6.1.1
Pituitary hormones, terminology, 12.7.2
Place names, capitalization, 8.1.1
Place of publication, 6.8.4
Plagiarism, 3.2
Platelet factors, terminology, 12.4
Plurals (see also Subject-verb agreement)
  of abbreviations, 7.1, 15.3.2
  apostrophe and, 6.11.5
  false, subject-verb agreement and, 5.9.3
  Greek vs English, 7.4
  Latin vs English, 7.4
  of local addresses, abbreviations avoided
    in, 11.4
  of microorganisms, 7.5
  of nouns
    collective, 7.2
    compound, 7.3
  parenthetical, 6.8.12
    subject-verb agreement and, 5.9.4
  of species and genus names, 12.16.1
  in subject-predicate nominative
    difference in number, 5.9.8
Poetry
  ellipses in, 6.7.5
  virgule in, 6.10.5
Political parties, capitalization, 8.1.2
Population names, capitalization, 8.1.2
Position, reference to, 9.7
Possessive words
  apostrophe in (see under Apostrophe)
  in compound words, 6.12.1
  eponyms as, 13.1
  nouns as adjectives, 5.6.2, 5.6.3
Postal code abbreviations, 11.5
Posthumous publication, indication in
    footnote, 2.3.4
Predicate nominative, subject-verb
    agreement and, 5.9.8
Prefixes
  author names, 2.10.9
  in compound words, 6.12.1
  hyphen with, 6.12.2, 6.12.5
  units of measure, 15.1
Pregnancy, terminology, 12.15
Prepositions
  in compound words, 6.12.1
  pronoun use after, 5.7.1
Pressure, units, 15.1, 15.1.9
Prime vs apostrophe, 6.11.7
Printing terms, glossary, 19.0
Production terms, glossary, 19.0
Pronouns

agreement with antecedent, 5.7
  case agreement, 5.7.1
  em dash before, 6.5.1
  indefinite
    possessive form, apostrophe in, 6.11.1
    subject-verb agreement and, 5.9.12
  nonspecific gender and, 9.10.1
  personal, 5.7.1
  after prepositions, 5.7.1
  relative, 5.7.2
Proofreading manuscript, 4.5
Proofreading marks, 20.3
Proper names/nouns
  abbreviations, 11.6-11.8
  with Asian surnames, 2.3.3
  capitalization, 8.1 (see also
    Capitalization)
  in compound words, 6.12.1
  diacritics in, 10.2
  hyphenation, 6.12.5, 12.16.1
  location with, parentheses with, 6.8.4
  of organizations (see Organization
    names)
  possessive form, 6.11.4
  Roman numerals after, 16.2.6
  words derived from, capitalization, 8.1.4
Proportions, virgule in, 16.2.5
Proprietary names, capitalization, 8.1.6,
    12.8
  drugs, 12.6
Proprietary statement, 2.8.2
Proto-oncogenes, terminology, 12.9.4
Publication
  duplicate, legal/ethical considerations,
    3.1
  parallel, 3.1
  process of, 4.0
Publication name, location with,
    parentheses with, 6.8.4
Publication place in book reference,
    2.10.28
Publisher name in book reference, 2.10.27
Pulmonary terminology, 12.17.1, 12.17.2
Punctuation (see also specific mark, eg,
    Comma; Period; Quotation marks)
  abbreviations, 6.4.3, 6.8.10
    period omitted after, 15.4
  addresses, 6.1.8
  business firm abbreviations, 11.7
  chemical formulas, 6.9.3
  coined words, 6.6.7
  compound words, 6.5.2, 6.12.1, 6.12.2
  dates, 6.1.9, 6.10.3
    doubtful, 6.4.1
  decimals, 6.4.3
  degrees and titles, 6.1.7
  dialogue, 6.6.2

dimensions, 6.12.3
duality expressed by, 6.10.1
for emphasis, dashes in, 6.5
at end of sentence, 6.4
English definition following foreign
    word, 6.6.9
enumerations, 6.2.2, 6.3.2, 6.8.5
equations, 6.10.4
figure legends, 2.11.1-2, 6.8.7
footnote symbol, 2.13.6
footnotes, 6.8.11
in foreign languages, 10.1.3
formulas, 6.9.3
fractions, 6.10
incorrect, confusion from, 5.3
indirect discourse, 6.6.11
interruption indicated by, 6.5.1
introductory expressions, 6.4.3, 6.5.1
ironic expression, 6.6.7
legends of figures, 6.8.7
mathematical formulas, 6.9.3
money units, 6.11.6
as multiplication indicator, 6.4.3
numbers, 6.1.10, 6.3.3, 6.4.3
    identification, 6.8.3
    ranges of, 6.12.3
omitted material indicated by, 6.1.13,
    6.5.4 (*see also* Ellipses)
organization names, 6.1.3
with parentheses, 6.8.2
parenthetical expressions, 6.1.6
parenthetical plurals, 6.8.12
phonetics, virgule in, 6.10.5
plurals formed by, 6.11.5
possession shown by, 6.11.1-4
possessive adjectives, 6.11.6
purpose, 6.0
questions, 6.4.1
quotation insertions, 6.9.1
quotations, 6.3.2, 6.6.1, 6.6.12
ranges of numbers, 6.12.3
reference citations, 2.10.7
references, 6.3.4
    in text, 6.8.6
reprint address, 6.8.8
running foot, 6.5.1
separation of clauses joined by
    conjunctions, 6.1.5
separation of independent clause, 6.2.1
separation of independent statements,
    6.5.3
series, 6.1.2
setting off words, 6.1.4
slang, 6.6.7
supplementary expressions, 6.8.1
after symbols, 6.4.3
in tables, 2.13.5, 2.13.8

time units as possessive, 6.11.6
titles (official), 6.12.6
titles (publication), 1.13.5, 6.6.3, 6.6.10
trademarks, 6.8.9
units of measure, 6.1.11
word separation by, 6.1

Quantities, arabic numerals for, 15.2
Quaternary ammonium salts, terminology,
    12.6.2
Question mark
    within declarative sentence, 6.4.1
    with parentheses, 6.8.2
    placement, 6.4.1
    purpose, 6.4.1
Quotation marks
    apologetic, 6.6.7
    in block quotations, 6.6.6, 6.6.12
    with coined words, 6.6.7
    with common words used in technical
        sense, 6.6.8
    in dialogue, 6.6.2
    in discussion format, 6.6.11
    exclamation point placement and, 6.4.2
    with foreign words, 6.6.9
    in indirect discourse, 6.6.11
    in interview format, 6.6.11
    irony indicated by, 6.6.7
    in legal material, 6.6.1
    in long passages, 6.6.6, 6.6.12
    omission of opening or closing, 6.6.6
    placement, 6.6.5
    purpose, 6.6
    question mark placement and, 6.4.1
    in quotations, 6.6.1
    single, 6.6.4
    with slang, 6.6.7
    in titles, 2.1.1, 6.6.3, 6.6.10
Quotations
    brackets in, 6.9.1
    from copyrighted material, 3.3.5
    diacritics in, 10.2
    editorial interpolation in, 6.6.1
    ellipses omission in, 6.7.8
    first-word capitalization, 8.5
    introduced by colon, 6.3.2
    from legal material, 6.6.1
    omissions in, 6.6.1
    punctuation in, 6.6.1
    within quotations, 6.6.4, 6.6.12
    references to, 2.10.40
    verification, 6.6.1

Race names, capitalization, 8.1.2
Radioisotopes (*see* Isotopes)

Index

Radiology units, 15.1.10
Range of numbers, 16.1.4
  hyphen in, 2.13.8
Ranges, hyphen in, 6.12.3
Rates, virgule in, 16.2.5
Ratio, colon in, 6.3.3, 16.2.5
"Read before meeting" indication in
  footnote, 2.3.5
Reagents, nomenclature, 12.8
Redundancy, 9.2.1
Reference intervals, conversion tables,
  15.10
References
  abbreviations in, 11.9
  to abstracts, 2.10.22
  to anonymous material, 2.10.24
  to audiotapes, 2.10.38
  author listing in, 2.10.8, 2.10.9
  without authors, 2.10.24
  biblical, 2.10.41
  book
    complete data for, 2.10.26
    edition number, 2.10.29
    editors, 2.10.30
    page numbers, 2.10.29
    parts of books, 2.10.31
    place of publication, 2.10.28
    publisher name, 2.10.27
    translators, 2.10.30
    volume number, 2.10.29
  capitalization in, 2.10.10, 2.10.11, 8.4.1
  cited in tables, footnote for, 2.13.6
  cited in text, 2.10.7
  to classical literature, 2.10.41
  colon use in, 6.3.3, 6.3.4
  to communications, unpublished,
    2.10.39
  complete data for
    books, 2.10.26
    journals, 2.10.13
  to Congressional Record, 2.10.36
  to court cases, 2.10.42
  dates in, 2.10.15
  discussants in, 2.10.25
  to dissertations, 2.10.34
  edition number in, 2.10.29
  editors in, 2.10.30
  to federal administrative regulations,
    2.10.42
  to Federal Register, 2.10.36
  to figures reproduced from other
    sources, 2.11.7
  to government publications, 2.10.32,
    2.10.36
  issue number of journal in, 2.10.19
  journal
    to abstracts, 2.10.22

  without authors, 2.10.24
  complete data for, 2.10.13
  dates, 2.10.15
  discussants, 2.10.25
  issue number, 2.10.19
  journal names, 2.10.14
  page numbers, 2.10.15
  parts of issue, 2.10.18
  serialized article, 2.10.16
  special department, 2.10.23
  special issue, 2.10.20
  supplements, 2.10.21
  without volume numbers, 2.10.17
  journal names in, 2.10.14
  to legal citations, 2.10.42
  to library collections, 2.10.35
  listing, 2.10.1
  to looseleaf legal service publications,
    2.10.42
  minimum acceptable data, 2.10.4
  number permitted, 2.10.5
  numbering, 2.10.6
  page numbers in
    books, 2.10.29
    journals, 2.10.15
  page numbers in citations, 2.10.7
  to parts of books, 2.10.31
  to parts of journal issue, 2.10.18
  to personal communication, 2.10.1,
    2.10.39
  place of publication in, 2.10.28
  publisher name in, 2.10.27
  purposes, 2.10.5
  to quotations, 2.10.40
  to regulations, 2.10.36, 2.10.42
  responsibility for accuracy, 2.10.3
  Roman numerals in, 16.2.6
  to secondary citations, 2.10.40
  to serial publications, 2.10.33
  to serialized article, 2.10.16
  to special collections in library, 2.10.35
  to special department of journal, 2.10.23
  to special issue of journal, 2.10.20
  to statutory publications, 2.10.37
  to statutes, 2.10.42
  style for, 2.10
  subtitles in, 2.10.12
  to supplements to journal, 2.10.21
  in text, parentheses indicating, 2.10.2,
    6.8.6
  to theses, 2.10.34
  titles in, 2.10.10
    foreign-language, 2.10.11
  translators in, 2.10.30
  unacceptable types, 2.10.1
  to unpublished material, 2.10.39
  to videotapes, 2.10.38

volume number in, 2.10.29
without volume numbers, 2.10.17
Regulations, references to, 2.10.36,
    2.10.42
Relative pronouns, 5.7.2
Religious terms, capitalization, 8.1.2
"Report of cases" section, format, 2.6.1
Reprints
    address for
        in footnote, 2.3.7
        parentheses with, 6.8.8
    availability, 4.8
    copyright and, 3.3.5, 3.3.7
Reproduction
    copyrighted works, 3.3.5, 3.3.7
    figures/tables, acknowledgment, 2.8.4,
        2.11.7
Research design, statistics in, 17.1
Resources for information, 21.0 (*see also*
    specific topic)
Respiratory terminology, 12.17.1, 12.17.2
Restriction enzymes, terminology, 12.9.2
Restrictive clauses, relative pronoun use in,
    5.7.2
Result reporting, statistical methods for,
    17.2
Review articles, 1.3
Review of manuscripts (*see* Editors; Peer
    review)
Rh blood group system, 12.1
RNA (ribonucleic acid), terminology,
    12.9.1
Roman numerals, 16.2.6
Rounding off numbers, 15.1.8, 17.4
    million/billion, 16.2.3
Rules (lines) in tables, 2.13.6
Running foot, 2.4
    em dash in, 6.5.1
Running head, 2.4

Salts, terminology, 12.6.2
Sample size with percentage, 16.2.4
Scale of illustration, 2.12.3
Scientific notation, times sign in, 15.1.3,
    18.3.2
Season names, capitalization, 8.1.8
Secondary citations, references to, 2.10.40
Seconds, numbers in, 16.3.8
Secretor blood group system, 12.1
Section mark as footnote symbol, 2.13.6
Semicolon
    in byline, 2.2.1
    genotype terms, 12.9.3
    independent clauses separated by, 6.2.1
    in journal references, 2.10.15
    in lengthy enumerations, 6.2.2
    purpose, 6.2

quotation mark placement and, 6.6.5
Senior (Sr)
    abbreviation, 11.6
    comma before, 6.1.7
    in references, 2.10.8
Sentence
    abbreviation at beginning, 15.3.3
    components, 5.1
    ellipsis at end, 6.7.2
    ellipsis between, 6.7.3
    ellipsis within, 6.7.1
    fragment, 5.1
    in quotation, capitalization, 8.5
    number at beginning, 16.1.1
    parallel construction in, 5.5
    parentheses at end, 6.8.2
    percent at beginning, 16.2.4
    punctuation at end, 6.4, 6.7.2, 6.8.2
    question mark within, 6.4.1
Serial publications, reference to, 2.10.33
Series (*see also* Enumerations)
    commas in, 6.1.2
    of numbers, 16.1.4
    parallel construction in, 5.5
    semicolon in, 6.2.2
Sex, reference to, 9.5
Sexist language, 6.10.1, 9.10
SI units (Système International d'Unités)
    abbreviations of, 11.11
    commas in numbers, 15.1.2
    conversion, one-to-one, 15.1.7
    conversion table, 15.10
    derived units, 15.1
    for energy, 15.1.11
    exponents in, 15.1.1
    fraction vs percentage, 15.1.5
    fundamental units, 15.1
    katal, 15.1.9
    kelvin, 15.1.9
    multiplication sign, 15.1.3
    pascal, 15.1.9
    percentage vs fraction, 15.1.5
    pH, 15.1.9
    for radiology, 15.1.10
    significant digits in, 15.1.8
    space between numeral and unit of
        measure symbol, 15.1.4
    in tables, 2.13.6
    for time, 15.1.6
sic, 6.6.1, 6.9.1
Side headings, 2.6
Signatures instead of byline, 2.2.2
Significant digits, 15.1.8, 17.3
Singulars (*see also* Subject-verb agreement)
    false, subject-verb agreement and, 5.9.2
    in subject-predicate nominative
        difference in number, 5.9.8

Index

Slang, quotation marks with, 6.6.7
Slash (*see* Virgule)
Social titles, abbreviations, 11.6
Sociocultural designations, capitalization, 8.1.2
Solidus (*see* Virgule)
Solution concentration, units of measure, 15.7
Sounds, cardiac, terminology, 12.3.2
Special collections in library, reference to, 2.10.35
Special departments of journals, reference to, 2.10.23
Special issue of journal, reference to, 2.10.20
Species names, 12.16.1
  in references, 2.10.10
  in titles, 2.1.4
Spinal nerves, terminology, 12.18
Split infinitives, 5.8.5
Staging of cancer
  Roman numerals in, 16.2.6
  terminology for, 12.2
Stains for microscopy
  in legend, 2.11.4
  in parentheses, 6.8.7
Standard deviation, 17.2
State court cases, references to, 2.10.42
Statements
  first-word capitalization, 8.5
  separation by 2-em dash, 6.5.3
States
  abbreviations, 11.5
  with proper name, parentheses with, 6.8.4
Statistics
  author responsibility for, 17.0
  result reporting, 17.2
  rounding off, 17.4
  significant digits, 17.3
  study design, 17.1
  symbols, 17.5
  tests used in, 17.5
Statutes, references to, 2.10.42
Statutory publications, references to, 2.10.37
Steroids, terminology, 12.6.4
Streets, abbreviations, 11.4
Stubs, table (*see* Table stubs)
Study design, statistics in, 17.1
Subheadings, 2.6
Subject-verb agreement
  collective nouns, 5.9.5
  compound subject, 5.9.6
  elliptical construction problems, 5.9.7
  every/many a, 5.9.9
  false plurals, 5.9.3

false singulars, 5.9.2
indefinite pronouns, 5.9.12
intervening phrase and, 5.9.1
number/number of, 5.9.11
one of those, 5.9.10
parenthetical plurals, 5.9.4, 6.8.12
predicate nominative differing from subject, 5.9.8
total/total of, 5.9.11
units of measure, 15.5
Subjunctive mood of verb, 5.8.2
Subordinate clauses
  comma used with, 6.1.5
  separation by comma, 6.1.1
Subscript
  blood group terminology, 12.1
  copy marking, 18.2
  EEG electrodes, 12.14.2
  electrocardiographic terms, 12.3.1
  heart sound symbols, 12.3.2
  pulmonary physiology terms, 12.17.1
  vitamin names, 12.6.4
Subtitles (*see also* Titles)
  abbreviations in, 2.1.5
  capitalization in, 2.1.6, 8.5
  drug names in, 2.1.3
  genus names in, 2.1.4
  guidelines, 2.1
  numbers in, 2.1.2
  quotation marks in, 2.1.1
  in references, 2.10.12
  species names in, 2.1.4
Suffixes
  in compound words, 6.12.1
  hyphen not used with, 6.12.5
  indicating diseases, 12.16.1
  for ordinals, 16.1.2
Superlative form, words not needing, 9.2.3
Superscript
  allele designations, 12.9.6
  blood group terminology, 12.1
  copy marking, 18.2
  footnote symbols as, 2.13.6
  isotopes, 12.13.1-3
Supplementary expressions, parentheses with, 6.8.1
Supplementary information, deposited with NAPS, 2.13.2, 2.15, 2.15.2
Supplements to journals, reference to, 2.10.21
Supreme Court cases, references to, 2.10.42
Surface antigens, T-lymphocyte, 12.12.4
Surnames of authors (*see* Authors, names)
Syllables, hyphen between, 6.12.4
Symbols (*see also* Abbreviations)
  alleles, 12.9.3

374

amino acids, 12.9.1
blood group genes, 12.9.3
chemical elements, 11.12
copy marking, 18.2
copyright, 3.3.4
electrocardiography, 12.3.1
in figures, 2.11.3, 2.12.2
footnotes, 2.13.6
gene, 12.9.3
genotypes, 12.9.3
heart murmurs/sounds, 12.3.2
HLA genes, 12.9.3
immunoglobulins and components,
    12.12.3
locus, 12.9.3
mathematical, 18.1
mixed with spelled-out names, 15.3.5
period omitted with, 6.4.3
phenotypes, 12.9.3
plurals of, 6.11.5
pulmonary physiology, 12.17.1
statistical, 17.5
TNM cancer staging system, 12.2-4
Symposium discussions, copyright transfer
    from, 3.3.6
Synopsis, 2.5
Système International d'Unités (*see* SI
    units)

T cells (lymphocytes), nomenclature,
    12.12.4
T$_3$/T$_4$ (thyroid hormones), terminology,
    12.6.4
Table stubs, 2.13.6
dual-unit reporting in, 15.1.7
Total as, 2.13.11
Tables
abbreviations in, 2.13.6, 2.13.9
alignment, 2.13.6
vs appendixes, 2.14
capitalization in, 2.13.7
centered format, 2.13.6
column heads, 2.13.6
    capitalization, 2.13.7
comparisons in, 2.13.6
continued to next page, 2.13.5
cut-in heads, 2.13.6
deposited with NAPS, 2.15
designators for, 8.7
dual-unit reporting in, 15.1.7
elements, 2.13.6
ellipses in, 6.7.9
vs figures, 2.13.1
flush left format, 2.13.6
footnotes, 2.13.6
vs graphs, 2.13.1

horizontal alignment, 2.13.6
indentions, 2.13.6
legends, em dash in, 6.5.1
none indications, 2.13.10
numbering in text, 2.13.4
numbers for, 16.3.5
numbers in, 2.13.9
punctuation in, 2.13.5, 2.13.8
purpose, 2.13
reformatting, 2.13.6
reproduction, acknowledgment, 2.8.4
rules (lines), 2.13.6
runovers in, 2.13.6
setup, 2.13.6
SI units in, 2.13.6
space saving in, 2.13.6
specifications, 2.13
supplementary information in, 2.13.2
table stubs, 2.13.6, 2.13.11
vs tabulations, 2.13.3
titles, 2.13.5, 2.13.6
    capitalization, 2.13.7
totals in, 2.13.11
units of measure in, 2.13.6
vertical alignment, 2.13.6
zero vs ellipses for *none*, 2.13.10
Tabulations vs tables, 2.13.3
Technical terms
abbreviations, 11.10
hyphen in, 6.12.7
Technical use of common words, quotation
    marks with, 6.6.8
Temperature
numbers in, 16.3.7
units, 15.1, 15.1.9
Temporary compound words, 6.12.1
Tense of verb, 5.8.3
Territories, abbreviations, 11.5
Test names
capitalization, 8.1.5, 8.1.9
statistical, 17.5
Text references, parentheses indicating,
    2.10.2, 6.8.6
Thesis, reference to, 2.10.34
Thyroid hormones, terminology, 12.6.4
Time (*see also* Dates; Months; Years)
abbreviations, 15.3.1
colon use in, 6.3.3
numbers in, 16.3.8, 16.3.9
units, 15.1, 15.1.6
    possessive form, 5.6.3, 6.11.6
Times dot, 6.4.3, 18.3.2
Titles (academic), capitalization, 8.2
Titles (personal)
abbreviations, 11.6
comma in, 6.1.7
military, 2.2.1

Index

Titles (personal)—*continued*
  official, hyphen in, 6.12.6
  social, 11.6
Titles (publication) (*see also* Subtitles)
  abbreviated unit of measure beginning,
    15.3.3
  abbreviations within, 2.1.5
  capitalization, 2.1.6, 8.4, 14.2
  chapter, in reference, 2.10.31
  colon use in, 6.3.4
  drug names in, 2.1.3
  in foreign languages
    reference to, 2.10.11
    translation, 10.1.2
  genus and species names, 2.1.4, 12.16.1
  guidelines, 2.1
  length, 2.1
  numbers in, 2.1.2
  quotation marks and, 2.1.1, 6.6.2
  in references, 2.10.10, 2.10.11, 2.10.31
    foreign-language, 2.10.11
  in running foot/head, 2.4.2
  section, in reference, 2.10.31
  species names, 2.1.4
  tables, 2.13.5, 2.13.6
  trademarks in, 2.1.3, 12.6.3
  volume number in, in references,
    2.10.30
TNM cancer staging system, 12.2.2-4
Totals in tables, accuracy, 2.13.11
TPAL terminology, 12.15
Trade names of drugs, 12.6
Trademarks
  in abstract, 2.5
  capitalization, 8.1.6, 12.6.3
  drugs, 12.6, 12.6.3
    in titles, 2.1.3
  parentheses with, 6.8.9
  radioisotopes, 12.13.4
Translation from foreign-language
    titles, 2.10.11, 10.1.2
  words of reference, 2.10.11
Translators in book references, 2.10.30
Transparencies, specifications, 2.12.1
Transplantation antigens, 12.12.2
Tritium, 12.13.6
Typesetting manuscript, 4.5
Typography, mathematical expressions,
    18.3.3

Units of measure (*see also* SI units)
  abbreviations, 11.11, 15.3
  at beginning of sentence/title,
    abbreviations, 15.3.3
  commas omitted in, 6.1.11

consistency in, with names and symbols,
    15.3.5
  conversion tables, 15.10
  decimals vs fractions, 15.9
  drug dosage, 15.6
  fractions vs decimals, 15.9
  hyphen in, 6.12.3
  in mathematical expressions,
    typography, 18.3.3
  money, 5.6.3, 6.11.6
  numbers with, 16.3.10
    at beginning of sentence, 16.1.1
    space between, 15.1.4
  plurals of, 7.2
    abbreviations, 15.3.2
  policy, 15.0
  possessive form, 5.6.3, 6.11.6
  punctuation, 15.4
  quantities, arabic numerals in, 15.2
  solution concentrations, 15.7
  subject-verb agreement and, 15.5
  time, 5.6.3, 6.11.6
    abbreviations, 15.3.1
  virgule in, 6.10.2
  volume, 15.8
Universal Copyright Convention, 3.3.9
Unnecessary words, 9.2.2
Unpublished material, references to,
    2.10.39
Upper extremity, reference to, 9.6
US Code, references to, 2.10.42
US military services (*see* Military services)
US possessions, abbreviations, 11.5
Usage, errors in (*see* Errors in usage)

Variable regions of immunoglobulins,
    terminology, 12.12.3
Variables (mathematical), typography,
    18.3.3
Vectors (mathematical), 18.3.3
Verbs, 5.8
  agreement with subject (*see* Subject-verb
    agreement)
  contractions, 5.8.6
  double negatives, 5.8.4
  with false plural nouns, 5.9.3
  with false singular nouns, 5.9.2
  mood, 5.8.2
  omitted, 5.9.7
  plural, 5.9.11
  singular, 5.9.11
  split infinitives, 5.8.5
  tense, 5.8.3
  transformation from nouns, 9.3
  two-letter, capitalization, 8.4
  voice of, 5.8.1

Verse
  ellipses in, 6.7.5
  virgule in, 6.10.5
Vertebrae, terminology, 12.18
Vertical alignment in tables, 2.13.6
Videotapes, references to, 2.10.38
Virgule
  in dates, 2.13.8, 6.10.3
  duality expressed by, 6.10.1
  in equations, 6.10.4
  in genotype terms, 12.9.3
  in hepatitis abbreviations, 12.11
  in influenza virus subtype names,
    12.16.2
  in karyotype, 12.9.5
  in mathematical expressions, 18.3,
    18.3.2
  in mouse strain names, 12.9.6
  per expressed by, 6.10.2
  in phonetics, 6.10.5
  in proportion, 16.2.5
  purpose, 6.10
  in rate, 16.2.5
  in tables, 2.13.8
  in units of measure, 15.4.1
  in verse, 6.10.5
Viruses, nomenclature, 12.16.2, Appendix
Vitamins, nomenclature, 12.6.4
Voice of verb, 5.8.1
Volume numbers
  in book references, 2.10.29
  in book titles, 2.10.30
  colon use with page reference, 6.3.4
  journals without, 2.10.17

Volume (unit of measure), 15.1, 15.8
  multiplication sign with, 15.1.3
von Willebrand factor, terminology, 12.4
Vowels, adjacent, hyphen used with,
    6.12.2
Vulgarisms, 9.4

Weeks, numbers in, 16.3.8
Word division, hyphen in, 6.12.4
Work, units of measure, 15.1
"Works made for hire" concept, copyright
    and, 3.3.3
Written communication, references to,
    2.10.39

Years
  at beginning of sentence, 16.1.1
  comma with, 6.1.9
  numbers in, 16.3.8
  span of, 16.1.4

Zero
  before decimal point, 16.2.1
  in tables, indicating *none*, 2.13.10
ZIP code
  abbreviations with, 11.5
  comma omitted before, 6.1.8